# TRUTH, LIBERTY, RELIGION

Main Entrance and Eastern Chapel Window

# TRUTH, LIBERTY, RELIGION

## Essays celebrating Two Hundred Years of Manchester College

edited by

BARBARA SMITH
*Librarian*
*Manchester College*
*1974–1985*

MANCHESTER COLLEGE OXFORD
1986

*First published in 1986 by*
*Manchester College, Mansfield Road*
*Oxford OX1 3TD*



*British Library Cataloguing in Publication Data*
*Manchester College*
*Truth, liberty, religion : essays celebrating*
*two hundred years of Manchester College.*
*1. Manchester College—History*
*I. Title II. Smith, Barbara*
*207'.42574 LF741.M21*

*ISBN 0–9508715–1–6*

*Copies of this book may be obtained in the UK direct from the publisher, Manchester College, Mansfield Road, Oxford OX1 3TD*

*Copies of this book may be obtained in the USA and Canada from UUA Sales Distribution Center, 25 Beacon Street, Boston, Massachusetts 02108*

*Printed in Great Britain by Biddles Limited, Guildford, Surrey*

# Preface

This collection of essays marks the beginning of the third century in the history of Manchester College. The legatee of a succession of dissenting academies from 1670 onwards, the College was founded in Manchester in 1786. It is now one of those few institutions which can trace a direct and unbroken descent from the influential dissenting academies of the eighteenth century.

The volume arose from the research of twelve readers who visited the College during the decade 1974–84 to use the resources of the Library including archives and manuscripts. The aim of this collection of essays is not only celebratory—it is to demonstrate the depth and diversity of those resources. The general theme is the contribution of Manchester College to developments in education, philosophy, pure and applied sciences and social reform in nineteenth-century Britain. Since these essays were written separately, there is some overlap of information, but this we hope serves to reinforce the theme rather than irritate the reader. We are profoundly grateful to the twelve authors for their time-consuming work and the generosity of their contribution.

The College wishes to thank particularly Lord Briggs, Provost of Worcester College, for the Introduction, as well as for his continuing advice and interest.

The College Council acknowledges especially with grateful thanks the constant support, counsels and endeavours of Gillian Carey (Senior Tutor and English Tutor) and Michael Hill (Vice-Principal and Director of Music) in forwarding the production of this volume from the inception of the project in 1983.

Thanks are due to all College staff for their co-operation, notably to the Rev. Bruce Findlow (Principal 1974–85), Frances Walsh (History Tutor), Joanna Parker (Librarian) and Elizabeth Judge (Bursar).

Timely and generous financial support from the trustees of the Hibbert Trust and the Dr. Daniel Jones Fund is warmly and gratefully acknowledged.

Tony Cross
Principal
Manchester College Oxford

# Contents

# List of Illustrations



ACKNOWLEDGEMENTS

The Publisher would like to thank the following for permission to reproduce the illustrations listed below:

Frontispiece: Catherine T. Herford and Betty Johnston

Plates I, and II, Nos 1–7, 9; Plate IV Nos 1,2. Manchester College Oxford

Plate II, No 8, from F. M. Brown, Mural 12, Manchester Town Hall, (Courtesy of the Corporation of the City of Manchester) Plate III The Rev. Derek J. Baker, and Dr. D. Williams's Library

Plate II, No 10, is taken from the drawing by A. J. Young, 7.12.1904. 'I will not cease from mental fight'.

The Publisher would also like to thank Nancy Richards for her assistance and advice in the selection of illustrations.

# INTRODUCTION

ASA BRIGGS
*Provost*
*Worcester College*
*Oxford*

On 11 October 1889, a year remembered by historians largely for different reasons, there was a brief announcement in the official *Oxford Gazette* that Manchester College had moved to Oxford and that its Principal, the Reverend James Drummond, would be delivering his opening address a fortnight later. 'The College', it stated, 'adheres to its original purpose of freely imparting theological knowledge without insisting on the adoption of particular religious doctrines.' All or any of its classes might be attended by members of the University of Oxford and by the public on payment of the regular fee. Any questions should be addressed to the Principal at 90 High Street. The announcement was signed not by the Principal or by any Oxford dignitaries but by R. D. Darbishire and the Rev. H. Enfield Dowson. The address of the former was given as 26 George Street, Manchester, and of the latter as Gee Cross, near Manchester.

Three years earlier Mansfield College, a Congregational College, had opened its doors in Oxford, but it was the newly arrived Manchester College which was the really old dissenting institution. It was the successor of the famous eighteenth-century Warrington Academy—in direct line; and words used by its first Divinity Tutor, Dr. Thomas Barnes, in his opening address in 1786—'To Truth, to Liberty, to Religion'—were to be placed over the entrance to its first new buildings in Oxford, completed in 1893, almost a century before they were to be employed again in the title of this volume of bicentennial essays. The declaration of intent in 1786 was that 'an ACADEMY should be established in MANCHESTER, on a plan affording a full and systematic course of education for DIVINES and preparatory instruction for the OTHER LEARNED PROFESSIONS as well as for CIVIL and COMMERCIAL life. The institution will be open to young men of every religious denomination, for whom no test, or confession of faith will be required'.

The bicentennial essays in this volume deal mainly with the history of the College before it reached Oxford. Fortunately, however, R. K. Webb, in a sensitive and wide-ranging study of Unitarian history spans the broadest spectra, beginning long before 1786 in 1660, undoubtedly the right place to begin, and ending with a footnote on the BBC, possibly the right institution with which to end; while A. Long in his essay on J. Estlin Carpenter, Principal from 1906 to 1915 and President from 1920 to 1925, is concerned not with what have come to be thought of as 'traditional' Unitarian debates but with the new intellectual currents in the late-nineteenth and twentieth centuries. Carpenter was given two honorary doctorates by Oxford—in Literature in 1903 and, twenty years later, in Divinity. The latter honour was a sign of how much Oxford had changed since 1889—institutionally even more than intellectually. When for the first time the principle of having a specific degree in theology had been accepted in 1868, three years before religious tests for entrants to the University were abolished, the Congregation of the University by its own decree decided to exercise no control over it. By a majority of 116 votes to 61 votes a clerical majority was built into the constitution of the new Board. Religion mattered more than Liberty.

When Manchester College moved to Oxford it was, in fact, the fourth move that it had made over the years; and for this reason alone the chronology included in this volume is a necessary element along with the geography behind it. The first move in 1803 had been to York, another ecclesiastical stronghold, but a centre too of the forces of dissent: the name Academy was now changed to College. The second move was back to Manchester in 1840, when the name Manchester New College was used for the first time, a very different Manchester, now thought of as the shock city of the age. The third move was to London in 1853, when the same name was retained. London at that time seemed the obvious place for the College, for the idea of a link with the new Owens College in Manchester, which had opened its doors in 1851, had failed.

Manchester had appealed in 1786 because it contained 'one of the best public libraries in the kingdom', had a 'well regulated police' and was inhabited by townsfolk who 'seriously attended to the duties of public worship'. London appealed in 1853 not because it was the national capital but because London University was an open place and its examinations set the right standards.

There were no religious tests in the University, which is celebrating its 150th anniversary this year, yet it was possible to teach theology in close relationship with it, for University Hall in Gordon Square, opened in 1849 to commemorate the passing of the Dissenters' Chapels Act five years earlier and situated near University College, had been deliberately designed to provide 'instruction in theology, mental and moral philosophy and other branches of knowledge not at all or not fully taught at "godless" University College'. It seemed the right home for Manchester New College. As the Principal, John James Tayler, put it in his inaugural address, the College in its new setting would serve as a 'school of Theology and Religious Philosophy in direct touch with 'a national seat of secular learning'.

The Dissenters' Chapels Act itself had been as much of a landmark in national history as the abolition of religious tests in Oxford was to be: 'the first legislative recognition of the great principle of unlimited religious liberty and of the right of private judgement is paramount to the profession of any peculiar theological tenets'. An even more important landmark as far as the sponsors of Manchester New College were concerned had been the passing of the Trinity Act in 1813 which legalised Unitarian thought by repealing some of the disabling clauses of seventeenth-century Acts of Parliament.

Unitarians were prominent, as R. K. Webb shows, both in local and in national life in the first decades of the nineteenth century: they were a cultural elite. Yet despite the attractions of London, many of them still felt, because they were a cultural elite, that Oxford—or possibly Cambridge—would be the right centre. It was Tayler, indeed, who in 1864 wrote to James Martineau, the subject of one of the essays in this book, declaring that it was 'nearly inevitable in the course of future events that our dear old College, with its accumulated remains of Warrington, York, Manchester and London, will become ultimately an independent foundation in one of our ancient seats of learning'.

Tayler, son of a dissenting minister and a former student at York, was an ecclesiastical historian who had been very happy in Manchester. He had been a Unitarian minister there for a thirty-three years, and was less excited by the thought of any possible Bloomsbury circle than by the presence of the Manchester circle which revolved around Cross Street Chapel, which had been founded as long ago as 1694. One of his students at Manchester had been another Taylor, spelt differently, who, like his father before him, was to edit the *Manchester Guardian*; and it was significant that the central offices of that great liberal newspaper were in Cross Street also. The history of Manchester would have been very different had Cross Street Chapel not exerted such a powerful influence on it, for it was the Cross Street circle which had fostered its intellectual and social life since Manchester began to grow in the eighteenth century. Indeed, the decision to set up the Manchester Academy in 1786 had been taken in the Cross Street Chapel Room, and the College's Jubilee celebrations were held there—and not at York—in 1836.

It is not surprising, therefore, that the two signatories of the Manchester College notice in the *Oxford Gazette* in 1889 gave Manchester addresses. Darbishire, the secretary of the College for 37 years, was to lay the foundation stone of the new building in Oxford; he, too, was an old student, and his father had been secretary before him from 1821 to 1836 and from 1840 to 1852 and served as President from 1863 to 1867. Dowson, a student when the College was in London, was secretary from 1880 to 1903 and was to serve as President from 1917 to 1920. His second name was Enfield, the name of one of the Warrington Academy tutors and grandfather of one of the Manchester College students at York.

For all the moves of the College therefore—moves in place and in time—there are extraordinarily impressive continuities in the story unfolded in this volume, continuities which will be of general interest to historians concerned with relating intellectual to social history. Great cities, often thought to be impersonal, had strong personal networks, and there was a national network also affecting economic as well as cultural life. There are, of course, contrasts in the story also, the sharpest of them that between Manchester and Oxford as places, and not surprisingly when the College moved to Oxford in 1889 it dropped the adjective 'new'. The two places presented very different images in the nineteenth century—smoky chimneys and dreaming spires; a society in movement, internationally orientated, and a traditional society large parts of which were closed to the world; the dissidence of dissent and the confident influence of an Establishment.

Yet as so often in English intellectual and social history the contrasts were attenuated. In 1888, one year before the move to Oxford the great Unitarian theologian, James Martineau, who had opposed the move, had been awarded an Oxford doctorate.

He figures prominently in this bicentennial volume of essays, for his contribution to the development both of Manchester College and of Unitarian thought was substantial. There were other links too between Manchester College and Oxford earlier in the century. Francis Newman, brother of the Cardinal and Professor of Classical Literature at Manchester New College from 1840 to 1846, was a graduate of my own College emerging in 1826 with a double first and moving to Balliol. The most sensitive essay on him was written by Basil Willey, neither an Anglican nor a Unitarian, but a Methodist. 'In the history of nineteenth century English thought', he began, 'there is no story more striking, or more full of moral significance, than that of the divergent courses of the brothers Newman. It is as if two rivers, taking their rise in the same dividing range, should yet be deflected, so that one pours its waters into the Mediterranean, the other into the German Ocean.'

The metaphor of the watershed has appealed to historians of Victorian England. By the time Manchester College moved to Oxford the watershed had already been crossed as far as the University was concerned. Moreover, it was not a coincidence that it was in the city of Manchester that a crowded public meeting had been held in the Free Trade Hall in 1866 to demand the abolition of the religious tests which kept nonconformists out of Oxford. Indeed, it was at that meeting that the liberal Goldwin Smith, Regius Professor of History in Oxford, proclaimed optimistically that 'our alliance with Manchester . . . made our cause that of a party in the nation'.

There may have been slender evidence at that time that nonconformists wanted to go to Oxford—as Walter Bagehot, son of a Unitarian, had put it succinctly in 1852—'What do the people in Wigan care for the dons in Oxford?'—but when the long battle to abolish tests was won at last—with little to spare—in 1871, it seemed right to many Unitarians, at least, that a move to Oxford was desirable. In 1875 the idea of a move there won substantial support, and four years later it was Darbishire who proposed an amendment to a Special Committee resolution declaring that 'the establishment of the College at Oxford or Cambridge, as one of the great seats of national University life, would eminently conduce to the more effective education of Ministers from Free Churches in this country'. In fact, Cambridge was never seriously in the reckoning. Nor was a return to Manchester which always had some support. The centenary celebrations in 1886 included a memorial service in Cross Street Chapel, but when the question of moving to Oxford was raised again in 1888—after a further Sub-Committee report—the resolution was carried by 42 votes to 36. Martineau voted against, but he and his supporters were defeated again when at their request the question was put to a poll and 138 of the Trustees declared themselves in favour of the move to Oxford and 109 against. (Nine were neutral).

These were exciting times. Nor did the excitement end when the College moved to Oxford—with the opponents of the move reconciled and with one of them, Frederick Nettlefold (associated with Birmingham, not Manchester) presenting the great window in the College Chapel after the new building had been completed, in 1893. Some of the further problems are described in V. D. Davis's *History of the Manchester College*, published in 1932. Yet, as Principal Drummond put it in his address at the opening of the new building, 'the future must reveal its secrets. Meanwhile, we are here, restored by the providence of God, to the inspiring associations of a noble inheritance'.

The noble inheritance was to be enriched by the presence of Manchester

College in an age when masses were to count for more than elites. In 1914 Estlin Carpenter, Drummond's successor, was to be appointed Wilde Lecturer in Comparative Religion, in the University: there was no one else in the University with the same talents and interests, and under his guidance the study of comparative religion flourished at Manchester College: Rabindranath Tagore had already visited the College a year earlier and was to preach in the Chapel on a second visit in 1930. Carpenter's successor, L. P. Jacks, with very different talents and interests, became one of the best known Oxford personalities. He arrived in Oxford via Birmingham (and its famous Church of the Messiah) not via Manchester, and he has been described not unfairly as 'the last of the Victorian prophets in the line of Carlyle whom he greatly venerated'. One of his best known works—and he wrote profusely—was *The Education of the Whole Man* (1931), and one of his sons became Director of Oxford University's Department of Education in 1938. The dynasties, so important in the history of Unitarianism, included a renewed link with London University, when in 1967 students accepted by the College were again admitted to read for London External Degrees. The openness of London was still an advantage, and it was not until 1974 that details relating to the College appeared in the pages of the official *Oxford University Handbook*.

The future must, as always, reveal its secrets. Yet it is plain from the essays in this book that the history of Manchester College is not peripheral to the study of English intellectual and social history between 1786 and 1986 but central. Reverting to ancient metaphors, the history reveals all the eddies of one major current, sometimes a counter-current, in the national mainstream and the idea of a mainstream was never absent. Moreover, the history raises important questions not only about Manchester and Oxford or the relationship between intellectual and social history, but about science and religion on the one hand and 'secularism' on the other, and, not least, the purposes of education in a changing culture and society. Many old questions raised in these pages became stale: far more old questions still remain alive. In its bicentenary year, Manchester College has been trying to address them.

# Manchester College Oxford
# Chronology of Antecedents and Development 1786–1986

## Antecedents: Religious Dissent and Education in England 1660–1786

**1661** Corporation Act requires all members of Borough Corporations to attend rites of Church of England.

**1662** The Act of Uniformity renewed. Effective exclusion of Dissenters from Oxford and Cambridge. Resignation of upwards of 2,000 rectors and vicars, many of whom begin teaching. Many small academies set up, centred on individual tutors, often forced to move.

**1664** The Conventicle Act forbids meetings for worship of more than five people, except in accordance with rites of Church of England.

**1665** Five Mile Act forbids non-conforming clergy to come within five miles of any Borough, especially places where they formerly ministered.

**1669** Richard Frankland, graduate of Cambridge, ejected from a cure near Durham, establishes Rathmel Academy, near Settle, Yorkshire. Moves five or six times in next twenty-seven years.

**1673** The 1st Test Act imposes sacramental tests on Dissenters for positions in armed forces.

**1687** Isaac Newton's *Philosophiae Naturalis Principia Mathematica.*

**1689** Act of Toleration permitting freedom of worship under licence to Protestants dissenting from Church of England; however, Arians/Socinians/Unitarians† as well as Roman Catholics excluded.

† It may assist readers to have broad definitions of the following three terms all of which are difficult to define with any real precision. All undergo shifts in meaning to a greater or lesser degree—the latter term: 'Unitarianism' in particular needs to be understood in historical context.

*Unitarianism*—a term, possibly of Magyar origin, which came into use in the sixteenth century to indicate anti-Trinitarian Christianity. In the eighteenth and early nineteenth centuries, it indicated those who affirmed the 'full' humanity of Christ, as opposed to Arians. Later it came to mean belief in the 'unipersonality' of God.

*Socinianism*—often used simply as an opprobrious term to indicate actual or

**1689–92** John Locke's *Letter Concerning Toleration* Nos. 1, 2, 3.

**1690** John Locke's *Essay Concerning Human Understanding* published.

**1698** Death of Richard Frankland without successor at Rathmel.

**1699** John Charlton, pupil of Frankland, conducts Academy at Manchester until 1713.

**1708** Thomas Dixon, pupil of Charlton, conducts Academy in Whitehaven, afterwards in Bolton, until his death in 1729.

**1733** Caleb Rotherham, pupil of Dixon conducts Academy in Kendal until 1753.

**1757** John Seddon, alumnus of Kendal, is prime mover in the establishment of Warrington Academy, where John Taylor, a contemporary of Caleb Rotherham at Dixon's Academy is a colleague.

## WARRINGTON ACADEMY

**1757–86** A more formal academy, financed by subscribers, controlled by trustees, with teachers (at least three in number) formally appointed by the governing body and with prescribed conditions of service (see histories by William Turner, H. A. Bright and H. McLachlan). Joseph Priestley and other tutors maintain links with French philosophers, many of them prominent in politics and with revolutionary tendencies.

**1786** Warrington Academy, in decline since the death of the Divinity Tutor, John Aikin the elder, in 1780, closes largely because of the reputation of the students for indiscipline.

## HISTORY OF MANCHESTER COLLEGE

### MANCHESTER ACADEMY

**1786** Manchester Academy founded to take the place of Warrington Academy at a meeting held in Manchester on 22nd February 1786.

**1789–98** Divinity Tutor (i.e. Principal): Thomas Barnes.
Warrington Academy library transferred to Manchester Academy. 'Elegant pile' of buildings erected in Dawson (now Mosley) Street, later to prove a financial burden. Wide curriculum includes Classics, Hebrew, Logic, Ethics, the Works and Laws of Nature, History, Geography, Languages, elements of Jurisprudence. Tutors include John Dalton 1793–1800.

---

suspected anti-Trinitarianism. Strictly—anti-Trinitarian Christianity as developed by Laelius and Faustus Socinus and set forth classically in the Racovian Catechism (1605) of which Faustus was the chief inspirer.

*Arianism* — a fourth-century term revived in the eighteenth century to indicated an interpretation of the person of Christ which ranks him below the Father in divine status but still distinct and higher in nature than all other created beings. A half-way house to late eighteenth-century Unitarianism.

**1789** French Revolution.

**1793–1815** Anglo-French Wars. Severence of links between British Rationalists and French Philosophers.

**1798–1803** Divinity Tutor (Principal): George Walker.

**1803** Closure of Manchester Academy precipitated by financial problems following reduction in numbers of lay students, difficulty in recruiting tutors and indiscipline of students.

### MANCHESTER COLLEGE, YORK

**1803** Manchester College, York opens under Charles Wellbeloved with more permanent funding.

**1803–40** Divinity Tutor (i.e. Principal): Charles Wellbeloved.

**1807** Abolition of the Slave Trade.

**1810** John Kenrick tutor in classical languages. William Turner (Junior) an alumnus and graduate of Glasgow appointed tutor in mathematics.

**1811** New College buildings house twelve divinity students and ten lay students.

**1813** The Trinity Act legalises Unitarian thought by repealing some of the disabling clauses of the 17th century Acts of Parliament.

**1819** John Kenrick's sabbatical leave in Germany brings to Manchester College German influence in scholastic method, particularly in Biblical Studies.

**1822** James Martineau opts for ministry and enters College. Wellbeloved's defence of Unitarianism in answer to Archdeacon Wrangham. Missionary activities of students in surrounding countryside.

**1825** Unitarian Societies amalgamate to form British and Foreign Unitarian Association—later the General Assembly of Unitarian and Free Christian Churches [Manchester College predating the Association and neither financed nor controlled by it, continues to be an independent foundation in close association with the General Assembly and recognised for the training of Unitarian ministers].

**1828–29** Repeal of the Test and Corporation Acts.

**1828** Foundation of London University.

**1831** British Association for the Advancement of Science holds its first meeting, at York.

**1830–33** Charles Lyell's *Principles of Geology* published.

**1832** 1st Parliamentary Reform Bill.

**1833** John Keble's sermon on 'National Apostasy' initiates Tractarian Movement.

**1833** Abolition of Slavery.

**1836** Royal Charter gives University of London the right to grant degrees in medicine, arts and law, without doctrinal subscription.

**1839** Proposals to remove Manchester College to London to take advantage of proximity of University College. An alternative proposal for a return to Manchester deemed more advantageous for students preparing for ministry because of strength of local dissent.

**1840** Royal Warrant confers on Manchester New College the right to enter students for London University degree examinations.

### MANCHESTER NEW COLLEGE, MANCHESTER

**1840–53** Manchester New College, Manchester, founded with greatly enlarged staff of eight professors including John Kenrick, James Martineau, Francis Newman (brother of Cardinal Newman) later Professor of Latin in University of London. William Gaskell (Minister at Cross Street Chapel Manchester and husband of Elizabeth Gaskell the novelist) and John James Tayler. Students live in nearby lodgings; financial difficulties soon apparent.

**1840–46** Principal: Robert Wallace.

**1844** The Dissenters Chapels Act celebrated by . . .
Foundation of University Hall in Gordon Square near University College London. (Hall now occupied by Dr Williams's Library.)

**1846–50** Principal: John Kenrick.

**1847** Diocese of Manchester created (pop. 405,831).
Foundation of Trust by Robert Hibbert.

**1848** Elizabeth Gaskell's first novel, *Mary Barton*, published.

**1850–53** Principal: George Vance Smith.

**1851** Owens College founded in Manchester free of all religious test and without a faculty of theology, later to develop into Manchester University.

**1851** Religious Census. Unitarian churches in England, Wales and Scotland 334. Total Attendances 31,909.

**1852** Proposal to remain in Manchester connected with Owens College defeated. Decision to move to London solely as a theological college, with literary and scientific teaching to be provided by University College, London.

### MANCHESTER NEW COLLEGE, LONDON

**1853** Move to London with two professors and Martineau as lecturer in philosophy.

**1853–69** Principal: John James Tayler.

**1854** Unitarian Home Missionary Board establishes a College in Manchester (now The Unitarian College, Manchester).

**1857** Controversy over Martineau's appointment as Professor. Resolution affirms that it would be a violation of fundamental principle of College to attempt to secure the representation of the views of any particular school of religious thought.

**1859** Darwin's *Origin of Species* published.

**1860** First admission of ministerial student from Hungary.

**1869–85** Principal: James Martineau.

**1871** Abolition of theological subscription at Oxford and Cambridge except in Faculties of Theology.

**1872** First discussions of a move to Oxford or Cambridge. College takes over maintenance and administration of University Hall, London.

**1878** Hibbert Lectures instituted.
University of London opens degrees to women and admits women students.

**1885** Retirement of Martineau from Principalship—President of College 1885–1887.

**1885–1906** Principal: James Drummond.

### MANCHESTER COLLEGE OXFORD

**1889** Decision to move to Oxford as Free School of Theology for graduate students. Temporary accommodation in High Street.

**1893** Completion of main buildings (architect Thomas Worthington) on land bought from Merton College in Mansfield Road. Accommodation for staff and students provided by purchase of Nos. 24–30 Holywell Street.

**1894** Appointment of Lucy Toulmin Smith as librarian, the first woman in charge of a public library.

**1896** Admission of first Indian student.

**1901–05** College recognised as a Permanent Private Hall of Oxford University.

**1901** First woman admitted for full training for the Ministry.
First student from Japan admitted.

**1902** Hibbert Journal published.

**1906–15** Principal: Joseph Estlin Carpenter.

**1914–18** First World War.

**1915–31** Principal: Lawrence Pearsall Jacks.

**1919** Arlosh Hall built.
Abolition of theological tests in Oxford Faculty of Theology.

**1921–31** Lectures by R. H. Tawney introduces education as an academic study for lay students, mainly recruited from the Workers' Educational Association.

**1931–38** Principal: John Henry Weatherall.

**1938–49** Principal: Robert Nicol Cross.

**1939–45** Second World War. College buildings taken over by Government Departments including Admiralty mapping. Rare books (16–18C) housed by Bodleian Library.

**1951–56** Principal: Sidney Spencer.

**1956–65** Principal: Lancelot Austin Garrard.

**1957** Revision of Trust Deeds.

**1965–74** Principal: Harry Lismer Short

**1965** Manchester College granted status of 'Society or Institution for Higher Study' by Oxford University (Statute XXI 26 2a). Definition of right of ministerial students to matriculate for Oxford degrees in Theology or Theology and Philosophy.

**1965–6** American lay undergraduates admitted for one year courses in English, History, Theology; these courses later expanded to include Music, Philosophy and Social Studies.

**1967** Manchester College authorised to enter names on the Register of Diploma Students of Oxford University. Students admitted for Diploma in Economics and Special Diploma in Social Administration.

**1967** Students admitted to read for London (External) General Degree.

**1969** Sir Alister Hardy (President of Manchester College) establishes the 'Religious Experience Research Unit' in premises within the College.

**1971** Students admitted to read for London (External) Honours Degrees in English, and subsequently for Music, Philosophy, History.

**1971** Additional accommodation provided by building new block of eight rooms (Vaughan House).

**1974–85** Principal: Bruce Findlow.

**1985–** Principal: Anthony John Cross.

# 1
# THE UNITARIAN BACKGROUND

R. K. WEBB
*Professor of History*
*University of Maryland*
*Baltimore County, USA*

The restoration of King Charles II in 1660 put an end to the formal unity of the English church. Nearly seven hundred ministers were deprived when the priests whom they had replaced in the Interregnum were returned to their livings. In 1662, over nine hundred more followed their consciences out of the Church when the Act of Uniformity of that year demanded unreserved assent to the prayerbook and required that those who had entered the ministry in the preceding twenty years be reordained. Together with schoolmasters and fellows of colleges, these ministers made up the roughly two thousand 'ejected' of Dissenting legend. Dissent did not soon find its footing as a distinct, organized alternative, however. Some, particularly among the Presbyterians whose hopes had been raised by Charles II's promises of accommodation of reformed ideas about the Church, continued to cling to the ideal of comprehension—the building of a truly national church agreed on fundamentals of doctrine and governance while allowing for differences in liturgy and other practices. Others, particularly those whose forefathers had followed their reforming zeal into the isolation of the gathered churches, hoped for a measure of toleration of their separateness, such as they had known under Oliver Cromwell. But Parliament, representing the determination of the great part of the country that the turmoil of the Interregnum should not recur, gave short shrift to the king's promises (whether serious or politic) and moved not to conciliate but to destroy nonconformity.

A statute of 1661, the Corporation Act, eroded the political base of nonconforming laymen by requiring that members of the corporations that governed the country's towns take communion in the Established Church. The Conventicle Act of 1664, re-enacted six years later, forbade more than five people from coming together for religious worship except in a parish church, while an act of 1665 prevented deprived ministers who would not swear an oath to refrain from attempting to alter church or state from coming within five miles of any parish where they had served or of any incorporated town or parliamentary borough. On the authority of these and other statutes and alarmed by the literally disturbing activities of the more radical sects, local authorities turned persecutors. The worst sufferers were the Quakers, who continued to bear witness to their beliefs with astonishing boldness, but all Dissenters lived with the threat of harassment or imprisonment, a threat that often became a reality, in some ways worse for its arbitrariness.

In 1672 the crypto-Catholic king issued a Declaration of Indulgence suspending the laws against nonconformity; until he was forced to withdraw it the next year, some Dissenters took advantage of the leniency to form congregations, as they did under a new Declaration of Indulgence of the openly Catholic James II in 1687. When the country's urgent, and latterly hysterical, anti-Catholicism swamped even the newfound enthusiasm for the divine right of kings, the result was the Glorious Revolution of 1688, of which the Dissenters were major beneficiaries. The

Toleration Act of 1689 allowed the practice of non-Anglican religions, subject to oaths to protect the kingdom from subversion and to registration of places of worship. Toleration did not, however, extend to those who denied the Trinity: reflecting concern over the Unitarian controversy that had agitated the Church over the past couple of decades, this ban would have struck few Dissenters as anything but salutary.

The impulse to persecute was neutralized but not extinguished. When the passions of Whigs and Tories were inflamed in the later years of Queen Anne's reign (1702–1714), rioters attacked meeting houses, and a Tory-dominated parliament made two significant efforts to counter Dissenting gains. Some Dissenters had managed to hold office by technically observing the Corporation Act and taking communion once a year in the parish church; this practice was forbidden by the Occasional Conformity Act of 1710. Even more threatening, the Schism Act of 1714 sought to prevent Dissenters from teaching in schools or academies and so to cut off the supply of ministers and zealous laymen. Anne's death prevented the Schism Act from coming into force, and both prejudicial acts were repealed in 1719. Disinclined to bring any issue to a head, the victorious Whigs who dominated the political life of England under the first two Hanoverian kings repealed neither the Corporation Act nor the anti-Catholic Test Acts of the 1670s, but Dissenters with less than the straitest consciences were able to skirt the prohibitions—in addition to occasional conformity they were helped by indemnity acts passed from time to time by parliament—and to establish themselves in some towns as a political force. More important, the generation between 1690 and 1720 saw the beginning of the continuous history of many congregations. Gone was the hole-and-corner existence, and gradually, as security and prosperity grew in tandem, congregations no longer needed to tuck their places of worship away behind other buildings or build them to resemble farmhouses. True to their Puritan heritage, the Dissenters built in a distinctively simple style, typically oriented to a pulpit against a long wall rather than to a chancel in the east end. The large plain-glass windows of the new chapels symbolize a clarity and openness that became an increasingly evident, and to some troubling, characteristic of eighteenth-century Dissent.

From the 1570s, some Puritans, known as Presbyterians, argued that bishops lacked biblical warrant and that governance of the Church should be confided to a hierarchy of mixed lay and clerical bodies rising from the congregational to the national level, a plan similar to that established in Scotland by John Knox and his allies. By contrast, Independents (later known as Congregationalists) insisted that congregations were answerable to no higher authority; their views of governance were shared by the Baptists, who were, however, set apart by their contention that the rite of baptism should be administered only to believing adults. Committed to the ideal of a national church, the Presbyterians were more severely shaken than were the gathered churches by the exclusion and persecution after 1662. Although by the end of the century Presbyterians too had become congregational in structure, they were never entirely assimilated to the gathered churches. While Presbyterians drew worshippers from all parts of society, their congregational organization tended to be hierarchical, and they drew a larger proportion of adherents than the other denominations from wealthier and more elevated levels of society. Another difference affected theological development: Independent and Baptist insistence on religious experience as the test of membership and the tight discipline they imposed on their members meant that those congregations were, typically, more closely knit than the Presbyterians and less open to new currents of thought. These divergences caused the failure of the so-called 'Happy Union' of 1691, when in the heady circumstances of the newly granted Toleration, Presbyterians and Independents had come together as the United Brethren to administer a Common Fund, established a year earlier for the education of ministerial students and for the support of the Dissenting faith. But profound disagreement soon arose over the issue of antinomianism—the belief that a truly saved Christian was not bound by law—and over the evangelistic activities of Richard Davis, a powerful Northampton preacher. By 1695 a separate Congregational Fund had come into existence. The old Common Fund, known in time as the Presbyterian Fund, seems to have been administered with characteristic openness: at any rate in 1714 the trustees did not scruple over a grant to the secretary of the Congregational Fund![1]

So long as explicit theological controversy was avoided, Dissenters could agree in matters of mutual concern. At the national level, this cooperation was most clearly evinced in the Dissenting Deputies, a London-based organization that by the 1730s was defending, though they were less successful in advancing, the civil position of Dissent. At the local level, a town might have but one Dissenting congregation, in which believers of all theological and emotional inclinations worshipped together and listened to sermons of fairly firm orthodoxy and serious moral intent. When Job Orton returned to his native Shrewsbury as minister in 1741, the small Independent congregation merged with the High Street congregation; Orton later wrote that the distinction between Presbyterian and Independent was 'idle & insignificant everywhere. But where there are two meetings in some towns these names are kept up for distinction's sake; & if they mean anything independent with the vulgar signifies calvinistical.'[2] Isaac Watts and Philip Doddridge were Independents in whom the Calvinist inheritance had been profoundly modified; they were admired in nearly all parts of the Dissenting spectrum (and by many in the Church as well), and their famous hymns were sung by all, without regard to labels.

What was the strength of Dissent in the country? Dr. Michael Watts has recently subjected such treacherous statistical measures as have survived to a helpful analysis. He calculates that of the approximately 1,600 ministers licensed following the Declaration of Indulgence of 1672, nearly sixty per cent were Presbyterian, something more than a quarter Independent, and about thirteen per cent Baptist. A survey of 1715 suggests that 637 congregations were Presbyterian, 203 Independent, 206 Particular Baptist, 122 General Baptist, and 672 Quaker. Watts calculates the total numbers of Dissenters as 338,210 in the early eighteenth century, a bit over six per cent of the English population, just under six per cent of the Welsh population. In England the Presbyterians could claim a little over three per cent of the population, the Independents just over one per cent, and the other denominations just under that proportion; though in some areas—Lancashire and Cheshire, Devon, Northumberland—the Presbyterian proportion was considerably higher, as much as eight per cent in Lancashire, while Congregationalists showed their most impressive strength in North Wales, the Home Counties, and East Anglia.[3]

In 1730 a young English Dissenter, Strickland Gough, touched off a debate about the decline of the Dissenting interest, arguing that Dissenters were ignorant of their distinguishing principles and that the Dissenting message was not conveyed in a sufficiently elevated and gentlemanly fashion, while other writers insisted on neglect of godliness as the cause of the falling off. Historians since have taken up the language of decline, generally siding with those critics of eighteenth-century religion who deplore its abandonment of serious evangelical piety for fashionable intellectual enthusiasms that could not speak to ordinary men and women. That there was a gentle declension in numbers and influence seems incontestable: one authoritative local study, of Exeter, shows that the Dissenters in that nonconformist stronghold fell from perhaps a third or a quarter of the population in 1715 to something under a fifth in 1744. But it also seems true that all parts of the religious spectrum were fading, the Church as well as Dissent: in an age that lacked zealousness and distrusted enthusiasm, there are neither simple patterns nor simple explanations.[4] The decline was strikingly reversed after the middle of the century by the success of Methodism and the missionary labours of John Wesley, George Whitefield, and Howell Harris; with the rise of Evangelicalism in the Church of England; and as Dissent took on new life. Dissenting distinctions gained meaning. Those who prospered most were Congregationalists and Baptists, and among the latter the Particular Baptists and the New Connexion of the General Baptists, who split in 1770. By early in the nineteenth century, English Presbyterianism had ceased to exist; its congregations had failed, divided, or turned Unitarian; the remains of the Old Connexion of the General Baptists became Unitarian as well.[5]

Unitarians have tended to see their history as that of a saving remnant; non-Unitarians have usually resorted to the language of blame and condemnation; while others, less committed, have sometimes set Unitarianism in an inapposite tradition leading from Deism to secularism. None of these contentions catches historical reality. An intensely religious movement, Unitarianism must be seen as emerging from long trends in the history of English and European intellect and as the beneficiary of a new degree of specialization that came with a far more complex society. The religious revolution of the late eighteenth century did not give the victory to Unitarians—though many of them thought that in time they would conquer all. But if they remained a tiny minority, for more than a century that minority had an extraordinary impact on the country.

In the first half of the seventeenth century, rationalism was the preserve of small coteries such as the free thinkers around Lord Falkland at Great Tew in the 1630s or the Cambridge Platonists at mid-century. After the Restoration, with the founding of the Royal Society and the importation of Cartesian ideas from France, rationalism became far more widely diffused and in time dominant. By the end of the century, the most influential works from which eighteenth-century thinkers drew their principal ideas and inspiration had been written—Sir Isaac Newton's *Principia* and *Opticks* and John Locke's *Essay concerning Human Understanding*. In 1696, Locke's embarrassing disciple, John Toland, launched the Deistic controversy with his *Christianity not Mysterious*, and for nearly forty years Deists argued with impressive seriousness that God had started the world going and left it with natural religion as an all-sufficient guide to science and morality; while distressed Churchmen bombarded their booksellers with defenses of Christianity so contradictory as to leave the orthodox forces in considerable disarray.

Significant rationalist inroads on Dissent came late and through different channels. In the first place, Dissenters were distinguished from Churchmen and the Catholic tradition by their insistence on the sufficiency of the Bible: they entirely agreed with the famous dictum of the Caroline churchman, William Chillingworth (a member of the Falkland circle), that the Bible was the religion of Protestants; and while biblicism could lead to the most literal-minded fundamentalism, it could also be attuned to rationalist criticism of contradictions in the Bible and of its inconsistencies with churchly tradition. Precisely that kind of criticism was brought to bear on the concept of the Trinity by Dr. Samuel Clarke in 1712: *The Scripture-Doctrine of the Trinity* collated all the biblical texts touching on the Trinity and formulated what came to be known, in allusion to the famous fourth-century controversy, as Arianism—that the Godhead was not made up of three coequal and eternal Persons but that God the Father was supreme and Jesus, though pre-existent and divine, was subordinate. Clarke drew many followers as well as opponents in the latitudinarian world of eighteenth-century Anglicanism and was instrumental in convincing many Dissenters as well. Clarke's immediate impact on Dissent, however, came through the enthusiasm of a small group of students at the academy in Exeter, who had been persuaded by his arguments. Local suspicion of heterodoxy at the academy called into question the doctrinal reliability of two of the three ministers in the town, and when the threatened schism could not be resolved within Exeter or by advice from ministers in the locality, the question was referred (as was the custom) to the London ministers, who met for three sessions of intense discussion of the issues at Salters' Hall in 1719. In a crucial division on the question of appending a declaration of belief in the Trinity to advices sent to the Exeter congregations, the opponents, later known as Non-Subscribers, won by a small majority. The vote was not about the Trinity (had it been the result might have differed) but about the admissibility of human formulations: as one distinguished observer reported crisply, 'The Bible carried it by four.'[6]

After the crisis of Salters' Hall, Dissent returned to its uneasily accommodating ways, but the leaven of Arianism continued to work. At Mill Hill, Leeds, where ministers and congregations readily moved between that Presbyterian chapel and its Congregationalist neighbor Call Lane, the strictly Calvinist and Trinitarian William Pendlebury, son of an ejected minister, was succeeded in 1729 by Joseph Cappe, who held more relaxed views and whose son became a prominent Unitarian; in 1748, the openly heretical Thomas Walker assumed the pulpit. Joseph Ryder, a master clothier who attended Call Lane but was accustomed from time to time to go to Mill Hill, recorded his distress. One of Walker's sermons in 1751 led Ryder to say that 'to hear the doctrines which our pious forefathers suffered for, but not only so, such doctrines as the Scriptures, in my apprehension of things, appear clearly to hold forth—in a manner confuted—it gives me great concern.' In 1755, when William Graham of Halifax, preaching at Mill Hill, recommended charity to those who differed in opinion, Ryder wondered how all things could be right, and one young man boldly told Graham that he had taken the crown from the head of King Jesus and put it on his own. Ryder was soon deciding on the claims of some of Walker's unhappy hearers for admission to Call Lane but even there disputes arose about the imputed righteousness of Christ and about the Trinity, and when Ryder was rebuked for not speaking up, he confessed to his diary that, lacking convincing arguments, he felt silence the better course.[7]

The inroads of rationalism on eighteenth-century Dissent were reflected in the history of the most famous extra-congregational Dissenting institutions, the Dissenting academies. To matriculate at Oxford or to take a degree at Cambridge, undergraduates had to subscribe the Thirty-nine Articles, an act to which few Dissenters could bring themselves. A fourteenth-century statute, arising out of a short-lived attempt to found a new university at Stamford, forbade university graduates to teach at any university-level institution other than the two ancient universities. Nevertheless, among the ejected ministers were some university men who, at considerable risk, chose to teach Dissenting boys who would otherwise have had no training beyond school. Small, migratory, and usually dependent on the labors of a single tutor, the early academies have proved difficult to trace with confidence; but it has been estimated that around twenty-four were founded in the period prior to 1689, perhaps eighteen in the next thirty years. Most of them took both lay and divinity students, with lay students not infrequently predominating. As in other aspects of Dissent, denominational labels bespoke neither an exclusive clientele nor a particular theological position: the fine Unitarian historian Alexander Gordon in the early part of this century argued that the Independent academies were in fact more adventurous. But adventuresomeness was not a characteristic of the early academies. With one exception, teaching was done in Latin; divinity, metaphysics, and ethics were emphasized; mathematics was at a discount—forbidden in one, indeed, as dangerous to faith—but science played an increasing role as proof of the natural religion so convincing to a rational piety.

Though their managers could withdraw support when the drift of an institution displeased them, the existence of denominational funds lent a new stability to the eighteenth-century academies, and indeed new funds, like the Coward Trustees or the King's Head Society, came into existence to support academies, often limited to divinity students, that might be kept free from heterodoxy. By mid-century a few academies had begun to develop their own autonomous governing boards and to cast their financial nets more broadly; but while modern institutional forms could ensure a larger, more specialized and learned staff than was possible with only a devoted tutor and his one or two assistants, the very size of the newer institutions encouraged openness to new ideas and contributed to a laxness of discipline that in time proved the undoing of several. But before the winds of doctrine reached hurricane force in the 1780s, some of the academies were notable for educational experimentation. Pride of place in the first half of the century must go to the academy conducted at Northampton by Philip Doddridge from 1729 to his death in 1751. Doddridge taught entirely in English, a practice (anticipated by Samuel Morton at Newington Green outside London in the 1670s) that led to a weakening of language study but that also facilitated reading and discussion of modern works on all subjects. The most striking characteristic of Doddridge's academy was his insistence on exposing students to all sides of all issues: they read competing authorities and were trained to make up their own minds, in the classroom and in the world outside, an openness found in other academies as well. Moreover, some of the best students went on to a year or two at one of the Scottish universities—the Presbyterian Fund sent thirty-four students to Glasgow and twenty elsewhere between 1690 and 1753, Dr. Williams's Trust sent thirty-eight to Glasgow between 1734 and 1780. At Glasgow, as in the other Scottish universities, the course culminated in the study of moral philosophy. The chair in that subject was held in succession by four of the most distinguished moral philosophers of the century—Francis Hutcheson, Adam Smith, Thomas Reid, and Dugald Stewart—and in that cradle of enlightenment, the new science of political economy was being born.[8]

*

Doddridge's academy re-opened in Daventry in 1752 under the superintendence of Caleb Ashworth. The first student to enrol was Joseph Priestley, a nineteen-year-old Yorkshireman who had rebelled against his family's strictly Calvinistic faith, partly from his sunnily optimistic nature, partly from the influence of neighboring ministers with whom he studied or whom he met in the society that gathered in the house of the aunt who raised him. At Daventry, he recalled, the divinity classes ranged over liberty and necessity, the sleep of the soul, and every current issue of controversy, with Ashworth taking the orthodox side, his subtutor, Samuel Gray, the heterodox side. Leaving Daventry in 1755 a confirmed Arian, Priestley spent a short, unhappy pastorate at Needham Market, in Suffolk, where his heterodoxy soon became known (though he did not preach it), causing him to be shunned by neighboring ministers, impoverished by the withdrawal of a grant from the Independent Fund, and rejected by his congregation. Transplanted to more congenial surroundings at Nantwich in 1758, he took up teaching, reluctantly but with notable success, and in 1761 became tutor in languages and belles lettres at the academy that had opened four years earlier in Warrington, lecturing on such innovative subjects as theory of language, oratory and criticism, the history and constitution of England, and history and general policy. Although it was works written to support his teaching, particularly a chart of biography, that won him election as a Fellow of the Royal Society, Priestley had also begun research on electricity, moving on to crucial experiments on the composition of air during his pastorate at Mill Hill, Leeds, from 1767 to 1772. From 1772 until his removal to Birmingham in 1781, he was literary companion and librarian to the Earl of Shelburne at Bowood, a period in which, in rapid succession, he published five major treatises (as well as many lesser works) that gave him his crucial position in the evolution of English Unitarianism: *Institutes of Natural and Revealed Religion* (1772–1773); *An Examination of Dr Reid's Inquiry into the Human Mind . . .* (1774), a scathing attack on the principles of the Scottish 'common sense' school; *Disquisitions relating to Matter and Spirit* (1777); *The Doctrine of Philosophical Necessity, Illustrated* (1777); *A Free Discussion of the Doctrines of Materialism and Philosophical Necessity* (1778), a celebrated exchange with his Arian friend Richard Price; and the *Letters to a Philosophical Unbeliever* (1780), to note only the major works.

Priestley was one of those rare thinkers—Jeremy Bentham and Karl Marx are greater, more influential instances—who drew together many strands in the thought of their time to produce a synthesis of signal creative power; but what Priestley did in the metaphysical and theological realm has been overshadowed, even eclipsed, by his contributions to radical political theory and by the astonishing scientific work that places him at the origin of the modern science of chemistry. But at least down to the middle of the nineteenth century in England, the Priestleyan philosophy carried conviction to many advanced intellects strategically poised in a rapidly changing society.

The most original part of Priestley's philosophy was his materialism. By rejecting the impenetrability of matter—his hypothesis that matter is a result of attraction and repulsion has a strikingly modern sound—he resolved to his own satisfaction the ancient problem of the interaction of mind and body. By positing a material origin of consciousness, he could turn his denial of the autonomy and pre-existence of the soul into a powerful weapon against the Arian belief in the pre-existence of Christ. And Priestley made it abundantly clear that the burden of all his metaphysical works was to undermine the Arianism he had come increasingly to doubt until reading Nathaniel Lardner's *Letter on the Logos* (1730) in 1767 finally convinced him of the Unitarian position that God the Father alone is divine and Jesus no more than human. Priestley's many works of biblical exegesis and criticism—of which his *History of the Corruptions of Christianity* (1782) is the most famous—as well as his enthusiastic and at times dubious excursions into the history of the first centuries of the Church were directed to proving that in its origins Christianity was Unitarian and that it was the malign influence of Greek thought that had started Christianity on its unhappy descent into mystery and obfuscation. At least from the time of Locke and certainly well into the Victorian age, it seemed self-evident that clearing away mystery (the Trinity being the murkiest case) would lead irresistibly to the Christianization of the world.

While not all Unitarians followed Priestley in his materialism—he himself did not consider it essential—many found his 'necessarian' hypothesis utterly convincing. Here, with wonderful modesty, Priestley saw himself not as an originator but as the transmitter and popularizer of the arguments that the physician and psychologist David Hartley put forward in his *Observations on Man* in 1748. Hartley had proposed an ingenious theory of nerve vibrations as the mechanism by which sense impressions were conveyed to the brain and converted there into perception, a hypothesis Priestley accepted but omitted from his abridgement of the *Observations*. Far more important was Hartley's theory of association—that the repeated conjunction of simple ideas in the brain led to complex ideas, so intermixed that the triggering of one component by the senses could bring the whole of a complex idea into consciousness. Three consequences follow. One is an explanation of behavior, physical and moral, in terms of motives and responses, a causal relationship that fitted neatly with the then fashionable, and long influential, psychology based on a calculus of pleasure and pain. A second, practical consequence was the key role that the system ascribed to education, for control of sense impressions—of input into the mental process—could make it possible to control completely the outcome: the mind, as plastic as Locke had assumed, did not work through (or suffer the limitations of) innate faculties such as the moral sense, a doctrine that led to Priestley's scornful dismissal of the Scottish philosophers, though they proved more appealing to some of Priestley's disciples a generation or two later.

The third consequence, overarching and controversial, rose from individual psychology to a complete metaphysic. If the mind worked in obedience to motives, then so long as motives remained unchanged, the same ideas and behavior would follow. Moral choice was not, therefore, an exercise of free will but an illusion, for every action was determined by previous experience and the motives that arose from it. On the metaphysical level, this individual determinism merged with the providence and foreknowledge of a benevolent God. Mere mortals could never perceive the totality of God's plan, although more and more of it was being revealed by the discoveries of the laws that governed the natural world, individual well-being, and the social state. What in our foreshortened view appears as evil must be seen as a part of the divine scheme to bring all mankind, through the sovereign effects of pleasure and pain, to ultimate perfection—in this life or the next. Detractors saw Priestley's determinism as a fatalism that would make men mere pawns unable to control their fate or anyone else's: had he not, they asked, simply provided a pretext for antinomianism or epicureanism? Priestley and his followers replied—and demonstrated—that theirs was an active faith. Error (others might say sin) came from flouting divine law, and God, working always through the agency of human beings, decreed that suffering must follow. Experiencing evil directly or witnessing its effects altered the volitional circumstances; new motives led to different, more enlightened action, to improve one's self or others. As Priestley put it, 'we are satisfied that all evil is ultimately subservient to good, and that it is the intention of Providence finally to exterminate all evil; in this most delightful employment we may, and ought, as his own children, to act like God, exerting ourselves, by every means in our power, to remove the distresses of our fellow creatures.' His most prominent immediate disciple summed it up in a trenchant metaphor: 'The farmer who believes that God knows, and has ordained that the next harvest shall be plentiful, or otherwise, does not for that reason neglect to cultivate and to sow the ground.'[9]

Certainly this strenuous effort at improvement was, in their view, morally superior to a salvation that was bought of a jealous God by the crucifixion of His son. But if free will, Christ's divinity, and the Atonement were rejected, and if the soul was merely a consequence of a physical process in a body that disintegrated at death, what possible claim did Priestleyan Unitarians have to be Christians? The Priestleyans had two answers. One was that, far from depreciating the role of Jesus, their insistence on His full humanity enhanced it: a man who had learned to be perfect was far more telling, as teacher and as example, than a god who had temporarily taken on human form for a morally loathsome sacrifice. The other answer followed from the old Puritan insistence on the centrality of the Bible. Priestleyans held confidently to two key Christian ideas—one, resurrection and a life after death, where the moral destiny of individuals and humanity would be worked out; the other the miracles attested to by the Bible as proof to a rude age of the divinity of Christ's mission. For all their efforts at criticizing and purging the text of the Bible, Unitarians remained firmly wedded to Revelation, sanitized perhaps but Revelation still. And in his *Letters to a Philosophical Unbeliever*, Priestley attacked the arch-skeptic David Hume with a vengeance: 'Compared with Dr. Hartley, I consider Mr. Hume as not even a child.'[10]

Among exact contemporaries who shared his Unitarian convictions,

Priestley's sweeping metaphysical views made somewhat uncertain progress. Joshua Toulmin, one of the most admired of Unitarian preachers, noted simply that Priestley had said everything that needed saying on the subject of necessity and that, as a result, he found it unnecessary to give the matter further thought. The physician and writer John Aikin, son of the principal at Warrington, noted that the doctrine of necessity gave deep satisfaction to Priestley's own religious and moral yearnings and that a number of his followers also found it 'compatible with all the best principles of human conduct'; yet he himself saw moral discipline in terms of Stoic resignation rather than of heroic activism. The minor writer Mary Hays, friend of Godwin and Mary Wollstonecraft, published an exposition of materialism and necessity in 1793 but ultimately confessed that her own disappointments in life and the depressing state of the world had led her into frank epicureanism.[11]

A younger generation saw things differently. After six years of agonizing thought, Thomas Belsham, head of Daventry Academy, announced his conversion to Unitarianism in 1789, resigning to become head of the new academy at Hackney. In his new, ponderously sunny phase, Belsham turned on the Arians as idolators and was, as teacher and preacher, a major force in consolidating and transmitting the necessarian philosophy. Belsham's rejection of Calvinism had a powerful impact in the academies, where in the eighties Priestley's ideas swept through the students, young men who shared the characteristic that John Kenrick saw in the older minister John Kentish—a demand for clear and definite ideas about everything.[12] It is easy to understand Priestley's appeal: he was a brilliant, incessant controversialist—sometimes superficial, almost always generous—who commanded attention and could readily compel assent among prepared minds; he offered an active, reforming faith in a period of movement; he weighted his philosophical arguments with his awesome reputation as a scientist and spoke to enthusiasts for modernity; yet in insisting on the supreme importance of the pursuit of truth, he was prepared for that pursuit to lead where it might and did not require that all Unitarians share every conclusion in every area that his protean mind encompassed: he was, in short, a dogmatist without dogmatism.

In the 1790s, under the impact of the French Revolution and the fear it engendered in England, the hopes of the eighties began to sour, and Priestley added a new dimension to his persuasiveness—martyrdom. In July 1791 a church-and-king mob burned Priestley's house and laboratory in Birmingham, the two Unitarian chapels—New Meeting, where Priestley had been minister since 1781, and Old Meeting—and the houses of a number of prominent Unitarian residents. After issuing a dignified appeal to his fellow citizens, and rejecting the urgings of some scientific admirers that he leave controversial theology aside, Priestley withdrew from Birmingham and became minister of the Gravel-pit Chapel in Hackney; in 1794 he emigrated to the United States, where he settled in Northumberland, Pennsylvania. He was joined, temporarily or permanently, in the emigration by a number of Unitarians who despaired of a country sunk in repression, and many more contemplated fleeing to a land that seemed to embody the promise that had been dashed at home. The last decade of Priestley's life (he died in 1804) was not marked by the originality that had characterized his years at Leeds, Bowood, and Birmingham, but he did take his final theological step, to full acceptance of the doctrine of universal restoration, the conviction that all mankind would ultimately be saved.[13]

Unitarianism remained illegal under the Toleration Act until 1813, but the first avowedly Unitarian chapel was opened in 1774 in Essex Street, off the Strand in London, by Theophilus Lindsey, the son-in-law of Archdeacon Francis Blackburne around whom had grown up a circle of liberal-minded Anglicans dedicated to removing the requirement of subscription to the Thirty-nine Articles. As a result of Parliament's rejection of the so-called Feathers Tavern Petition in 1772, Lindsey left the Church, to become a close collaborator and friend of Priestley. The growth of a Unitarian commitment in established Presbyterian and General Baptist chapels was less dramatically proclaimed; the evolution depended on the age and theological position of ministers and on the strength of lay leaders, who frequently forced the transition. Nearly everywhere conservatively inclined members of newly Unitarian congregations withdrew to the more sympathetic surroundings of Congregationalist chapels. The falling-off in numbers—and in some, if not all congregations of prosperity—and the ever-present threat of isolation and persecution were profoundly discouraging; so were the extremism into which some young Unitarians fell—rejection of public prayer or advocacy of revolutionary politics—and the sad decision of the trustees to close Hackney College, which had become a hotbed of radical enthusiasm. But sermons and private correspondence alike testify to the force of Priestley's prescriptions in hard times: the resolute pursuit of truth and the frank insistence on Unitarian principles would in the end triumph; by the workings of providence, evil would produce good, in the religious and public life of the nation.[14]

Manchester Academy was founded in a time of great optimism and survived the gloom and discouragement of the nineties. Moving to York in 1803, as the clouds were breaking and when glorious prospects seemed confirmed by reality as well as theory, the college became the principal forcing ground of Priestleyanism. It was seconded in this role by schools like those of Dr. Morell in Brighton and the Rev. Lant Carpenter in Bristol, by the growing complex of provincial cultural institutions in which wealthy and established Unitarians played a major part, and by intense discussions in households and social circles revolving around chapels. The attractive society of liberal and Unitarian Norwich has been described, and the endless discussions of philosophical and political questions among the Martineau family and their friends are remarkably documented. We know much, too, about the patrician merchant aristocracy of Liverpool, centered on Renshaw Street Chapel, with its luminaries among the Roscoes and Rathbones and the Manchester Gregs.

The diary of Thomas Asline Ward and the voluminous papers of Joseph Hunter—minister at Bath from 1809 to 1833, celebrated antiquary, and deputy keeper of the Public Records—reveal the impressive interests of the circle around Upper Chapel in Sheffield. The political and mercantile leaders of Nottingham met frequently with the minister of High Pavement Chapel in the early 1820s to read and discuss, at a remarkable level of sophistication and concern, serious works of theology. The freemasonry of established and liberal Dissent carried its members, in meetings, family visits, and marriage, throughout the country—into the liberal Unitarian society of Newcastle, Derby, Leicester, and Bristol; and evidence is beginning to come to light of similar constellations in smaller towns like Bridport or Stockton.[15]

By the 1830s, younger members of these prosperous and educated families were making their way not only in the provinces but in London as well—in the professions, and in business, as intellectuals and writers, as politicians and administrators. One instance may serve. In 1816 appeared a book called *Illustrations of the Divine Government, tending to show, that Every Thing is under the Direction of Infinite Wisdom and Goodness, and will Terminate in the Production of Universal Purity and Happiness*. It was written by Thomas Southwood Smith, a Baptist convert to Unitarianism who had studied medicine at Edinburgh and who practised both as physician and minister in Yeovil. Like everything he wrote, Southwood Smith's book is a thoroughgoing enforcement of necessarianism. In 1821, having married (for a time) into one of the great London Unitarian families, Smith moved to the metropolis to pursue a distinguished medical career. With his less intellectually impressive but no less influential friend John Bowring (from Exeter), Smith carried Unitarian ideas into the circle of intimates around Jeremy Bentham. The *Westminster Review* and the University of London (now University College), those famous 'Benthamite' foundations of the mid-1820s were as much Unitarian in inspiration and support as they were Benthamite, and when Southwood Smith began his important governmental career—with Edwin Chadwick he was the chief mover in the public health activity of the thirties and forties—by joining the factory commission in 1833, Harriet Martineau, who thought his appointment was her doing, boasted that she had put a Unitarian philosopher into government. In parliament—thirteen of fourteen Dissenting members in the mid-thirties were said to be Unitarian—in the burgeoning civil service, in the formation of opinion, as mayors and members of the new town councils after 1835, Unitarians had an influence on English life in the early Victorian period out of all proportion to their numbers.[16]

Economic and social changes long in gestation—population growth, the expansion of the empire, the many wars with France, the beginnings of agricultural and industrial revolutions and the emergence of a consumer society—were having evident, ambiguous effects on English society of the late eighteenth and early nineteenth centuries. Some old-established centers—Norwich is a good example—fell into decline before discovering new ways to wealth later in Victoria's reign; other towns grew at an astonishing pace, with all the problems that came with uncontrolled growth, lagging technology, and inadequate institutions. Many individuals found their livelihood endangered and their standard of life falling as they had to cope with new disciplines, economic fluctuations that defied understanding, and a state whose old protective legislation was falling into disuse or irrelevance and whose new legislation, like the revised poor law of 1834, could be harsh. But the long-term trends were upward, reflected in the gradual bettering of conditions of life, a spreading optimism and confidence, and impressive efforts to understand the new dispensation and to devise institutions and methods to deal with its consequences.

In such a situation, opportunity offered itself in a thousand guises, and many Unitarians were strategically placed to grasp it. Though some old Dissenting families retained a connection with land as well as trade in the eighteenth century—the Bayleys of Manchester, the Phillipses of Whitefield, for example—Dissent derived much of its special character from the comfortable, proud, independent citizens sketched so well by Daniel Defoe. 'Though they stood behind their counter,' wrote one of Manchester College's greatest scholars and teachers John Kenrick, his eighteenth-century forbears 'had a quiet, gentlemanly dignity of bearing, very different from the brisk obsequiousness of their modern representatives.' But Kenrick also observed that this social group was declining in the nineteenth century, 'where its place is not supplied by manufacturing prosperity,' a decline mirrored in the falling away of Presbyterian and Unitarian chapels in, say, the old commercial and industrial centers in the southwest.[17] But in other parts of the country manufacturing prosperity more than made up the difference.

As the raising of capital was still often done on a local and personal basis, the Unitarian network allowed likeminded men to pool resources; singly or in combination, Unitarian firms played a major role in the industrialization of England. In several Essex villages, the Courtauld brothers (their father had left a small declining business as a throwster in the 1780s to pursue his radical bent as a farmer on the American frontier) founded a silk business that grew rapidly to an immense scale, as happened in other branches of the textile trade—the Strutts in Belper, Hollinses in Mansfield, McConnels and Kennedys in Manchester, Gregs in Styal, Fieldens in Todmorden, Ashtons in Hyde. The Midland metal-working trades counted their Kenricks, Martineaus, Chamberlains, and Nettlefolds; and Unitarian fortunes were amassed in pottery, paper and glass making, chemicals, sugar refining, and the grocery trade. Unitarian brewers included Flowers and Carters, and Martineaus were partners in Whitbreads; William Teacher, the distiller, was a member of the St. Vincent Street congregation in Glasgow. Lewis Loyd left the Unitarian ministry in 1792 to become a banker, and his son, the first Lord Overstone, dominated the world of banking in the time of Sir Robert Peel. A port city like Liverpool numbered not only Unitarian merchants like the Rathbones but rich shipowners like the Holts and Booths and insurers like the Bowrings. There were a number of Unitarian legal practices; a medical profession refounding itself on a new scientific basis also contributed leading members to congregations; both daily and periodical journalism drew on the ministry and the educated and confident Unitarian laity for recruits; while that newly emerging segment of society that Noël Annan has called the intellectual aristocracy contained a remarkable number of Unitarian names.

The prominence of Unitarian economic success has to some extent skewed perception of the denomination. To be sure, some of the old congregations were so dominated by wealthy, forceful members that the poorer people who had once attended would have felt increasingly ill at ease among them: the great mid-Victorian philanthropist William Rathbone VI liked to say that the minister at Renshaw Street Liverpool should preach periodically on the text 'Howl, ye rich!' But Unitarianism was not exhausted by the prosperous upper middle class. The General Baptist congregations in the southeast drew almost exclusively on the tradesmen and artisans of rural and small-town society, and they tried, with less and less success, to maintain their old traditions of an unpaid (or little paid) ministry and the imposition of congregational discipline. Congregations like that at Taunton long continued to draw on the wide social range of an ancient market town. In the hills north of Manchester several self-educated men of humble background launched the Methodist Unitarian movement that brought half a dozen new chapels into existence in the first decade of the nineteenth century, chapels that remained distinctly working-class in composition down until recent times. A very significant missionary movement launched at about that time by the Rev. Richard Wright and contributed to by many others—including students at Manchester College, York in the 1820s—led to the founding of a number of small, unpretentious—and sometimes evanescent—congregations. The stormy passage of the ex-Chartist and Methodist Joseph Barker through Unitarianism in the mid-forties left a handful of chapels behind. And benevolent Unitarian employers (who tended to be more enlightened than their brethren of other faiths) regularly built chapels for their workpeople. The Gregs founded both Methodist and Unitarian chapels at Styal; Samuel Courtauld was much concerned to get a minister who could speak meaningfully to the workpeople in his chapels at Halstead and High Garrett; unseen, the Strutts could enter their private pew at the top of an ingeniously designed chapel at Belper and overlook their workers in the pews below and the children on the forms opposite; the growth of towns like Crewe or Swindon led to the founding of Unitarian congregations; the Fieldens constructed a magnificent Gothic church at Todmorden, as did the railway manufacturing Peacocks in Gorton; in 1872 the Ashtons, who were members of the old Presbyterian but now Unitarian congregation at Gee Cross, built the imposing Unitarian Church at Flowery Field right across from the factory, for their community. As one studies the minute books and finances of congregations, it is evident throughout the nineteenth century that Unitarianism drew on no homogeneous social grouping but on a continuum of social station, wealth, and prestige, from almost the humblest to the grandest.[18]

What Unitarianism was not was emotional or revivalistic. But even conceding the intellectualism of the denomination, there was steady concern to make the message acceptable to working people who had been emancipated from a Calvinist or fundamentalist upbringing that was increasingly at odds with scientific and ethical developments in the nineteenth century. The Baptist converts who flocked into Unitarianism early in the nineteenth century were in the forefront of this proselytizing work, preaching the liberating doctrine of universal restoration: Robert Aspland took the lead in organizing the denomination's propaganda efforts, Richard Wright was its principal missionary, W. J. Fox (once a ploughboy) was its most spell-binding preacher, though he left (or was driven out because of domestic irregularities) in the mid-thirties to found the congregation that became the South Place Ethical Society. And John Relly Beard, a Unitarian of modest General Baptist origins, who was active in missionary work at Manchester College and who preached to two poor congregations in Salford, founded in 1854 the Unitarian Home Missionary Board, with the express intent of training for the ministry men of poorer background and more constricted educational opportunity than the students who went to Manchester College; they would also, it was assumed, better serve in pulpits that ministered to working-class and lower middle-class audiences.

In the religious census of 1851, Unitarian chapels in England and Wales could count 68,554 seats and an attendance of 28,483 in the morning, 8,881 in the afternoon, and 12,697 in the evening, for a total of 50,061. (Evening congregations were far more likely to draw curious hearers from other denominations, as sermon-shopping was a form of popular entertainment for the devoutly inclined.) The number of chapels reached 250 in mid-century, with a handful of congregations in Scotland and around thirty in Wales, many concentrated in a part of Cardiganshire known by the Methodists as *Y'Smotyn Du*, 'the black spot.' More and more closely associated were the forty-odd congregations of the Non-subscribing Presbyterian churches in Ireland (mostly in Ulster), which had emerged from a schism over rationalism in 1828, though the Irish ministers of that time remained Arian and never experienced the stimulus of Priestleyanism that so galvanized their English brethren. The numbers of congregations remained fairly constant until the Second World War, but earlier in the twentieth century, the numbers attending began to plummet.[19] This denominational history must, however, be seen against a background of doctrinal revolution within Unitarianism.

*

More clearly than other movements of which it has been said, Priestleyanism carried within it the seeds of its own destruction. They lay in the very biblicism that had been the source of earlier Dissenting strength and the ground of the Unitarian claim to Christianity. In Britain and on the Continent, and particularly in Germany, the early nineteenth century saw a stunning reorientation of biblical studies: the Bible became another document to be analyzed by the canons of historical criticism, philology, and, in time, anthropology and comparative religion; soon, notions of divine inspiration and infallibility could be held confidently only by those who asked no questions. The enormous strides made by science in the new century raised fatal doubts about the exceptions to law represented by miracles and made arguments from design and the religion of nature less compelling. Moreover, a revolutionary shift in sensibility—the advent of romanticism—outmoded eighteenth-century style on every front. The balanced, lapidary rhetoric of those many sermons on the pursuit of truth, the beneficence of Providence, the testimony of nature, and the moral consequences of God's law had carried its own impressive conviction and still, if one reads it aright, retains the capacity to move; but while the sermons of Victorian Unitarians were no less intellectual, their language assaults the emotions more directly and is harder for us to analyze, sometimes even to comprehend. Ministers and members of congregations began to worry about the formality of chapel life, the old Puritan reticence between members and toward strangers. And the old meeting-house style gave way to Gothic: now that Unitarians were no longer discriminated against, it was argued, there was no need for a distinctive architecture and new chapels (usually called churches) could be built in 'the true Christian style.'[20]

Responses from Unitarians to these broad cultural shifts were extraordinarily varied. Some held firmly to the Priestleyan inheritance right to the end of their lives: Southwood Smith was one such writer who, though he felt the need for some updating of his works with regard to biblical criticism (which he had not the time to carry out), found the substance of his arguments about divine governance as convincing as ever. Others held fast to the materialist and necessarian philosophy but abandoned Unitarianism for free thought or positivism; the most famous of these was Harriet Martineau, while George Eliot, brought out of her evangelical phase in a Unitarian circle in Coventry, was able to make the transition to positivism while bypassing Unitarianism completely. Some found their way into the Church of England—Frederick Denison Maurice, the son of a Unitarian minister, followed Coleridge into a position of towering if idiosyncratic influence on Anglican theology and practice—and a few ended as Roman Catholics. Many joined Lucy Aikin in turning away from the necessarianism that had been intellectually but not emotionally convincing, to seek a 'higher,' view than the cold, heartless, 'earthbound' philosophy of rationalism. Joseph Hunter, who had come out of Manchester College, York in 1809 a committed Priestleyan, had grown disenchanted with Unitarianism by the 1830s, partly from the lack of success that attended his ministry in Bath, more from his patrician resentment of the ascendancy of fervently Unitarian ministers from inferior social backgrounds; by the mid-thirties he was querying materialism; in the early forties following his wife's death he rejected the Priestleyan explanation of evil. Within a few years, and after much soul-searching, he came to doubt the value of the resolute pursuit of truth: science had destroyed natural religion, criticism had wrecked revealed religion, and untrammeled inquiry seems to lead only to doubt and atheism, but, through faith, he could cling to 'the sweeter pleasures of Safety, Hope, Joy, which the religious man has, though he may not be able to prove his title to them.'[21]

It is against this background of doctrinal and emotional changes that we must see the reorientation of Unitarian thought that took place over thirty years from the early 1830s. James Martineau, dealt with elsewhere in this volume, was the most important contributor, but he was ably seconded by his friends John James Tayler, John Hamilton Thom, and Charles Wicksteed. External evidences, Tayler wrote to Thom, cannot work 'till the inner man is previously touched and already won by a deep feeling of spiritual want. Yet I hardly ever met with an Unitarian of the old school who did not regard such a statement as mystical and almost incomprehensible, while to my mind it flashes with all the conclusiveness of the clearest light.' Thom insisted that a scientific religion simply was not a Christian religion: it was the religion of a lawgiver, not of God the Father; the religion of a moral and intellectual creature, not of 'a conscious and spiritual *child*.' The Priestleyan confidence that truth would finally prevail was without warrant, for 'the only light which God makes victorious is the light that warms, the light of life and sacrifice.'[22] The demeanor of the 'new school' in controversy was troubling. Condescending and dismissive toward the Priestleyans—in James Martineau's case often devious, deliberately shocking, and cruel—they made bitter enemies. The Priestleyans, led by Martineau's old York contemporaries, fought a dogged rear-guard action in press, pulpit, and private correspondence. In 1865, Samuel Bache of the Church of the Messiah in Birmingham—the name of this successor to Priestley's New Meeting affirmed Locke's insistence that accepting Jesus as the Messiah was the central tenet of Christianity—failed in an effort to force a definition of the Unitarian faith in terms of the old scriptural verities of miracles and resurrection. An attempt to impose a quasi-creed sat ill with a denomination that had prided itself on freedom from human formularies.[23]

Martineau and his friends spoke meaningfully to many of the young men entering the ministry, especially from Manchester College, which he and Tayler dominated from the 1850s; and congregations tended increasingly to share that conviction. While not all Unitarians were intellectuals or even theologically literate, private correspondence and congregational records testify to the shift in sensibility. Soon after J. H. Thom became minister at Renshaw Street in Liverpool, he fell out with his congregation, unaccustomed to his style of preaching; the encounter was won by the young Irishman in a startling confrontation with great Liverpool merchant princes whose children and successors came to adore him. A few years earlier, in Leicester, the congregation of Great Meeting gave a piece of plate worth a hundred pounds to their recessive, scholarly minister Charles Berry, in gratitude for twelve doctrinal lectures he had given to a packed chapel. When Berry died in 1877, Alfred Paget, whose father had made the presentation half a century earlier, referred in a resolution of condolence to Berry's 'earnestness in maintaining what he held as vital truths in Christian doctrine,' truths that no longer had much vitality in them. But, for historical irony, it would be hard to match the history of the congregation at Bury in Lancashire. There in the mid-1830s the congregation decided to replace its 'quaint' chapel dating from 1719 with a new chapel, larger but still in the old meeting-house style. But, wrote a chronicler, the new chapel proved to be ill-built and unpleasing, and within a decade it was found to be positively unsafe. 'The resolution was soon taken to remove altogether an edifice which had been the subject of such great disappointment, and to rear, in all the beauty of Gothic architecture, a church that should be solid and enduring.' In 1837 the opening preacher was Charles Madge, minister at Essex Street and a Priestleyan luminary; in 1851 Charles Wicksteed preached the opening sermon, followed the next Sunday by James Martineau and John James Tayler.[24]

A parallel struggle, to last much longer, was waged over the question of the Unitarian name. In the late 1830s James Martineau began to insist that the term Unitarian was appropriate only to an individual theological position, and that a denomination which encompassed a wide variety of views should not be defined by one, possibly transient doctrine. His call to resume the historic term Presbyterian encountered two difficulties. The orthodox Presbyterianism recently re-established in England under Scottish auspices had already taken title to the name. More important, the proselytizing of the earlier part of the century had been done under the Unitarian banner. Martineau seemed to be asking those who had come into Unitarianism from orthodox Dissent to deny the very instrument of their liberation and the most likely rallying cry for other newly liberated men and women; and it was among these ministers that some of the most exciting preachers and certainly the best organizers had been found —Robert Aspland, Richard Wright, W. J. Fox, George Harris.

In 1859 James Martineau returned to the attack in an open letter called 'Church-Life? or Sect-Life?' in which he appealed to the old ideal of comprehension that had come down from the Presbyterians of the Restoration. In the wake of the quarrel with Bache and his allies, Martineau and his friends founded the short-lived Free Christian Union in the mid-sixties, another tack in nomenclature with a persisting appeal. In the latter years of his long life, Martineau was so widely and genuinely admired that it was difficult or embarrassing to reject him but, despite superficial concessions, he continued to be strongly opposed—by ministers, like Robert Spears in London, whose interests lay in missionary work and in the less socially impressive reaches of the denomination; in newspapers and periodicals, notably the *Unitarian Herald* (1861–1889) and

*Christian Life* (1876–1929), which resisted the largely pro-Martineau enthusiasm of *The Inquirer*; in the work of the Unitarian Home Missionary Board (Unitarian College after 1889, the year Manchester College moved to Oxford); and in denominational affairs. In 1886, the British and Foreign Unitarian Society, pieced together in 1827 from a number of regional propaganda and tract societies, moved into its new headquarters in Essex Hall, the site of Lindsey's chapel. Martineau, who with his allies had already got membership in the 'dogmatic' BFUA limited to individuals, had already tried his hand at a rival organization more to his taste in the comprehensively named National Conference of Unitarian, Liberal Christian, Free Christian, Presbyterian, and other Non-Subscribing or Kindred Congregations, which for fifty years met triennially alongside the BFUA, but in 1887, he proposed a wholesale reform looking to a national church that would culminate in a General Assembly, which would help to support poor ministers and smaller congregations. One congregation after another solemnly met and voted down the plan.[25]

Martineau's denominational ambitions long outlasted his death in 1900. Some of his followers, looking back to the middle way of the great seventeenth-century divine Richard Baxter, revived the notion of a Catholic tradition, and the resulting Free Catholic movement of the early twentieth century had a powerful impact on a few chapels and rippled outward into greater concern about the solemnity of worship and the use of liturgy, a divisive issue ever since Theophilus Lindsey had carried over a revised liturgy from his Anglican past.[26] In 1928 the British and Foreign Unitarian Association (which continued in existence as a trustee for denominational funds and records) and the National Conference were merged into the General Assembly of Unitarian and Free Christian Churches. Though every word in the name but one would have been acceptable to Martineau, some who still bore his impress could not go along with the new-found unity. L. P. Jacks kept Manchester College from joining until 1943, and the refusal of J. M. Lloyd Thomas, minister of Old Meeting, Birmingham, to have anything to do with the national organization ended up in the late forties in the law courts—but well before that Lloyd Thomas had declared himself a Trinitarian and his dwindling congregation had been made homeless by a German bomb.

Despite their differences, 'old school' and 'new school' were united in admiration for the great American Unitarian divine, William Ellery Channing, who early in the nineteenth century had led a sizeable part of New England Congregationalism into Unitarianism. American Unitarians, like the Presbyterians in Scotland and Ireland, had been scarcely touched by Priestley's philosophy, owing much more to Frances Hutcheson, the Scottish moral philosopher. Channing's bold stand against slavery in the 1830s spoke with a moral immediacy that Englishmen of all stripes could admire, while his sermons, widely reprinted and read, touched the new sensibility throughout and beyond Unitarianism. Another ground of agreement was the new institution of the domestic mission. Here, indirectly, another Scottish influence made itself felt—that of Thomas Chalmers, who, prior to his disruption of the Scottish Church in 1843, had gained a notable reputation as a social reformer by making his slum churches in Glasgow and Edinburgh the focus for an exercise in the moral regeneration of a community. Inspired by Chalmers, Channing's friend Joseph Tuckerman had become 'minister of the poor' in Boston, dedicating himself to a kind of social work that has led to his being hailed as a pioneer of the case-work method. In 1834, following considerable publicity in the English Unitarian press, Tuckerman visited England to encourage the founding of domestic missions. Working from premises—some of which in time became regular churches—in the most squalid parts of the burgeoning industrial towns, specially appointed domestic missionaries visited, relieved, and comforted the poor, with very little if any proselytizing intent. The most famous of these missionaries was John Johns, who served in Liverpool from the founding of the mission in 1836 until his death from cholera in 1848; a poet and a dedicated minister from Exeter, Johns was atypical of his fellows, who tended to be of humbler origin, recruited from graduates of the Unitarian Home Missionary Board or from recent converts (frequently Methodists) who were thought to be suited to the demanding work and able to communicate with the poor.[27]

James Martineau said that the Priestleyans saw God's rule over the world as 'Educational Development, for the sake of happiness'; Channing, on the other hand, held out the prospect of 'a Moral Probation, for the sake of holiness.' Martineau was guilty of serious distortion in saying that Priestleyans ruled out all moral qualities and beings to concentrate on the effect of a sovereign God on the merely sentient, thus 'missing whatever is august and holy in life'; but there is a striking contrast in the ethical approach of the two schools. The typical charity of the Priestleyan era was unquestionably educational—schools, universities, mechanics' institutions, libraries; and Southwood Smith saw even his public-health work as at bottom an educational enterprise. Because necessarians thought in terms of providence, cause, and law, they thought in global proportions—searching out discoverable law to apply it to large groups or to society through reformed or newly designed institutions. Their ethic was—to borrow a term then rapidly changing from a static to a dynamic connotation—administrative. Thom, Johns, and their associates saw things differently. Not for them the coercion of law or the creation of institutions dealing with multitudes, nor were they interested in preaching abstract theology or scientific truth. Rather, they were voluntaryists, dealing with individuals by 'heart acting on heart, conscience on conscience, soul on soul, man on man.'[28]

By the sixties the ethical base had begun to shift again, this time to politics. With the Unitarians in the lead, Dissenters had played a crucial part in the reformed municipal governments after 1835; by the sixties they were ready to move in force on to the national stage, most dramatically in the person of Joseph Chamberlain, a member of the Church of the

Messiah in Birmingham. But late Victorian politics were carried on in a far different context from the unreformed boroughs in which William Shepherd, the radical Unitarian minister at Gateacre early in the century, had proved such a sage observer and clever wirepuller. With the advent of the Liberal party in 1859, with the later broadening of the electorate and the consequent need to mobilize opinion, and with the towering figure of William Ewart Gladstone, who saw every political issue in compelling moral and religious terms, the stage was set for a new breed of political preacher—H. W. Crosskey, Bache's successor in Birmingham; Richard Acland Armstrong in Nottingham; John Page Hopps in Leicester; or (later) H. Enfield Dowson at Gee Cross, Hyde—and for Liberal politicians like the Leeds ironmaster and locomotive manufacturer James Kitson. In time some ministers were drawn by strongly felt moral imperatives into socialism and labor politics, often calling forth strongly expressed dislike among established congregational leaders. Martineau was aware that he had been passed by. Unable to attend the ceremonies when the Liverpool Domestic Mission they had helped to found moved into a new building in 1892, Martineau and Thom sent with their regrets a reaffirmation of their faith in 'the moral & religious development of character through personal influence of the higher on the lower.' He was not, Martineau said, blind to the need for external reforms, but he found an excessive and illusory dependence on even the most acceptable of efforts at social reconstruction, a search for secular salvation that led 'to a host of ill-considered & mischievous proposals, the very discussion of which is a waste of opportunities.'[29]

Unitarian leadership in the new political dispensation was less evident than it had been in the first half of the century. The theological differences that had hampered interdenominational cooperation in Dissent had become an unbridgeable gulf as the orthodox churches grew in their theological certainty and in worldly prosperity. Two celebrated lawsuits —the Wolverhampton case and Lady Hewley's case—challenged the Unitarians' right to chapels and endowments that had descended from donors who were orthodox in their opinions, casting a cloud on the Unitarians' right of possession for more than two decades until a final decision by the House of Lords in 1842 affirmed the challengers' contentions. By that time Unitarians had already withdrawn from the Dissenting Deputies, but their standing in the larger political world helped to secure the Dissenters' Chapels Act in 1844, which allowed twenty-five years' possession to assure a valid title. The 'natural leadership' of Dissent which the Unitarians had come into from their Presbyterian base, was decisively, indeed aggressively, rejected, and the future political leadership of Dissent was drawn with greater realism from those denominations which claimed large numbers of adherents and not merely social status. By a curious reversal, however, some Unitarians can be seen at the very same time adopting more specifically characteristic Dissenting attitudes. Unitarians were badly split on the question of supporting the education clauses of Sir James Graham's factory bill of 1843—they could not agree on whether a practicable scheme for mass education outweighed the dangers of the privileged position the proposals gave to ministers of the Established Church—and over the later agitation for disestablishment of the Church of England. Perhaps most striking of all was the growth in commitment to temperance and teetotalism by mid-century. Timothy Davis, minister at Evesham, confided to his diary in the early thirties his puzzlement that his nightly glass of gin and water might in fact be a sin; a little over a decade later, in Bridgwater, the Rev. Russell Lant Carpenter refused that portion of his salary that came from property on which beerhouses sat, and negotiations for a move to Bath broke down over the refusal of the trustees of Trim Street Chapel to give up the income from leasing the wine vaults that their forerunners had cannily built into the ground level of the new Gothic chapel in 1795.[30]

Herbert Spencer, the pioneer sociologist, maintained that institutions proceeded by social law from homogeneous to heterogeneous. The denominational history of Unitarianism seems to reverse that trend. The private chapels that wealthy Unitarian merchants and bankers had maintained early in the century were gone—the little chapel supported in Norton, Derbyshire, by the Shores, bankers in Sheffield, failed in 1842 when their bank failed. Chapels that had been adjuncts of factories were turned over to congregations. The firm hand of local oligarchs on the running of chapel business gave way to at least a semblance of democracy. While there were rich congregations and poor congregations throughout the nineteenth century, in structure one congregation came to seem much like another, and by the twentieth century, the rich chapels—even in the presence of endowments—became an endangered species. In some congregations the old Presbyterian ideal of the learned minister continued, somewhat attenuated, but the studious, retiring or even aloof minister whose obligations were pretty much fulfilled by preaching and teaching was proving an increasing liability. When Robert Brook Aspland (son of Robert Aspland) went to Bristol as an assistant in 1834, he found prosperity in Lewins Mead but a patchy situation elsewhere in the area: Bath and Bridgwater had improved lately, as had Plymouth, but the two ministers at Taunton had fallen into 'internal discord and most un-christian strife,' while at Exeter, the congregation was stagnating, the minister Henry Acton being 'highly popular *in* the pulpit, but indolent and inaccessible out of it.'[31] Ministers had to be not only good preachers but good fellows; they were expected to socialize widely, to take an active part in congregational business, to serve the broader community, and to organize and run a whole host of new activities—youth clubs, temperance societies, ladies' auxiliaries, bazaars and teaparties—that were enforced as much by financial need as by the cult of popularity. A ministry that had been a refuge for young men with scholarly inclinations now gave few opportunities for the true life of learning. While the great economist and Dante scholar Philip Henry Wicksteed maintained a succession of pulpits into the early twentieth century, Unitarian scholars were more likely to find their careers in the colleges in Manchester or Oxford or outside the ministry entirely, in the new universities or in private scholarship and writing.

James Martineau's reform scheme of 1887 had proposed to require a university degree for the ministry, to stem what in his patrician way he saw as an alarming decline in the quality of the ministry—a view Joseph Hunter had expressed more brutally in deploring the rise to influence of lower-class preachers and the disproportionate numbers of Welsh and Irish who found their way into English Unitarian pulpits. Martineau's recommendation was soundly rejected, but his purpose was partially accomplished by the admission of Dissenters to Oxford and Cambridge, by the growth of provincial universities, and by the close association of Unitarian College with the University of Manchester. The growth of universities testified to the new importance assumed in English society at large by learning more oriented to the professions (including the academic profession) than to the more narrowly based but inclusive classical and liberal education of the early nineteenth-century universities and, at a distance, the Dissenting academies. Authority was increasingly sought in the secular not the religious world. In 1912 Philip Henry Wicksteed told the churches that were confronting the social questions of the day without guides that the answers to their cries for help would come only from sociology.[32] A hundred, or even fifty, years earlier, such easy acceptance of the bankruptcy of Christian revelation or natural religion would have been unthinkable.

With sad resignation, James Martineau wrote to a friend in 1885 that the future of English religion did not lie with the Unitarians. 'Whatever aspects of truth we may have saved from neglect, whatever spiritual resources we may have rendered more accessible, pass into other keeping and need another administration before they lay hold of the minds and hearts of men. It is the power of Faith that shall prevail. We have it not, except as a feeble residuum from the power of criticism.'[33] He was both prophetic and too severe. His theological revolution was scarcely victorious before it fell victim to another diffuse and continuing revolution. The austere criticism of the American Unitarian Theodore Parker, with its simple theism, helped to push Unitarian ministers and laymen beyond the metaphysical and ethical complexities (or evasions) in which Martineau had come to rest; the course of science and secular learning pushed them yet further. As it lost theological content, Unitarian thinking seemed to splinter into competing enthusiasms—a fascination with non-Christian religions, social service, socialism, the peace movement, temperance, vegetarianism, even spiritualism. Even religious liberalism became less of an exclusive Unitarian preserve as liberal attitudes began to permeate other denominations, the Quakers most dramatically from the 1870s, the Congregationalists with the emergence of R. J. Campbell's New Theology early in the twentieth century, a development that, following Campbell's conversion to Anglicanism, left a major legacy to Unitarianism in the Pioneer Preacher movement that Campbell had founded and in a generation of ministers who came out of it and who have only just now passed away.[34]

Unitarianism continued to draw ministers and laymen from other denominations, but there was a larger movement, or drift, away, despite palliatives like the Postal Mission founded in 1886 (on an American model) to cater to isolated Unitarians or the touching Van Mission that wended its slow way through the country in the years after 1906. To some extent, the lament of the eighteenth-century Unitarian poet Mrs. Barbauld—that the carriages of the third generation swept Dissenters away into the Established Church—remained true, but Anglicans should have taken as little comfort as the Unitarians in conversions that probably owed more to convenience, opportunity, or esthetic appeal than to genuine religious conviction. Far more threatening was a growing skepticism or indifference, reinforced in the general culture by more satisfying intellectual explanations and by the competition offered by the multiplication of ways of spending time and engaging enthusiasm, even on Sunday.[35]

It is tempting to echo the eighteenth-century complaint that Dissenters had no grasp of their distinguishing principles and to see the attenuation and fragmentation of Unitarian doctrine from the late nineteenth century as a cause of the precipitous decline that accompanied it. But it is probably more convincing to point to the breakup of the Unitarian community. Unitarian schools, for whatever class, gradually disappeared; the colleges were confined to training ministers—Carmarthen being the last to abandon its arts course in 1896; the once-impressive chapel libraries fell into disuse. The old laments that younger members of Unitarian families no longer came, that congregations were being depleted by deaths and removals, became more disheartening as the twentieth century wore on. The close ties and the likemindedness that had characterized Unitarian life fell victims to mobility, the breaching of social barriers, intermarriage, an educational system beholden to other gods, and a culture that has swamped older, thoughtfully Christian religions. In the eighteenth century, with as much pride as defensiveness, Priestley proclaimed the Unitarians 'a sect everywhere spoken against.' Now, almost two hundred years later, they are scarcely known. The misunderstandings that persist owe more to ignorance than to zeal.[36]

## NOTES

1. This episode is recounted in Alexander Gordon, *Freedom after Ejection, 1690–92* (1917).
2. Walter Wilson Biographical Collection, Dr. William's Library.
3. Michael R. Watts, *The Dissenters*, i: *From the Reformation to the French Revolution* (1978), pp. 267–289, with valuable accompanying maps.
4. Allan Brockett, *Nonconformity in Exeter, 1650–1875* (1962), pp. 71–73, 114–117. F. J. Powicke, 'An Apology for the Arians of the 18th Century,' *Transactions of the*

*Congregational Historical Society* (1916–1918), pp. 110–124. For a good example of generalizing about 'decline,' A. D. Gilbert, *Religion and Industrial Society in England: Church, Chapel and Social Change, 1740–1914* (1976), pp. 14–15, 23–41.

5. The narrative account of the revival of Dissent in chapter 5 of Watts, *Dissenters*, is heavily concerned with Methodists, but he touches on the effects on the Church and, in pp. 450–464, on the revival of Old Dissent. Some statistics are given in Gilbert, pp. 36–39, with some interesting graphs, but his figures and his rhetoric must be taken with caution.

6. The Exeter side of the story is told in Brockett, *Nonconformity in Exeter*, and the events in London are best analyzed in Roger Thomas, 'The Non-Subscription Controversy amongst Dissenters in 1719: The Salters' Hall Debate,' *Journal of Ecclesiastical History*, iv, 162–186 (1953).

7. For extracts from Ryder's voluminous diary, Herbert McLachlan, *Essays and Addresses* (1950), pp. 20–39. On Leeds, W. L. Schroeder, *Mill Hill Chapel, Leeds, 1674–1924* (1924), p. 31, and a letter from E. Basil Lupton, March 13, 1922, Nottingham Univ. Library Hi W 46. On the gradual precipitation of denominational distinctions, Jeremy Goring, 'The Break-up of the Old Dissent,' in C. G. Bolam *et al.*, *The English Presbyterians* (1968), pp. 175–218.

8. The most extensive information on the academies is to be found in Herbert McLachlan, *English Education under the Test Acts* (1931). Figures on students going to Glasgow are taken from Olive M. Griffiths, *Religion and Learning: A Study in English Presbyterian Thought from 1662 to the Foundation of the Unitarian Movement* (1935), Appendixes II and III. Alexander Gordon's assessment is in 'Early Nonconformity and Education,' in his *Addresses Biographical and Historical* (1922).

9. Priestley, *A Sermon on the Subject of the Slave Trade* (1788), pp. v–vi; Thomas Belsham, *Elements of the Human Mind* (1802), p. 296.

10. *Works* (ed., J. T. Rutt, 1825), iv, 368.

11. Joshua Toulmin to the Rev. John Sturch, February 14, 1784, Dr. Williams's Library MS 12.45; John Aikin, *Memoirs*, i, 380, 212; Mary Hays to Crabb Robinson, February 27, 1802, September 10, 1804, February 14, 1806, Dr. Williams's Library.

12. John Kenrick, *Memoir of the Rev. John Kentish* (1854), pp. 46–47.

13. The best account of the Birmingham Riots is by R. B. Rose, 'The Priestley Riots of 1791,' *Past and Present*, November 1960, pp. 66–88.

14. Thus John Kentish to Timothy Kenrick, April 11, 1793 (Unitarian College MSS, c.2.2., John Rylands Library): 'There is comfort in the reflection that error is momentary, truth eternal, and I wish that I may have sufficient comprehension and fortitude of mind to act from a conviction of this truth.' Lay opinion on the same line can be found in William Roscoe to William Rathbone IV, December 28, 1794, Rathbone Papers, University of Liverpool, II.1.146, and in many letters to Rathbone from Mrs. Greg in the same box.

15. On Norwich, R. K. Webb, *Harriet Martineau, a Radical Victorian* (1960), ch. 2 and the Martineau family letters from the early twenties in the possession of Dr. R. S. Speck, San Francisco. The Liverpool circle is extensively displayed in the Rathbone Papers, University of Liverpool, the Sheffield circle in the diary of Thomas Asline Ward, excerpted in Alexander B. Bell, ed., *Peeps into the Past* (1909) and in the voluminous papers of Joseph Hunter in the British Library. The very full minute book of the Nottingham discussion group is in Nottingham University Library. On Bridport, Basil Short, *A Respectable Society: Bridport, 1593–1835* (1976), and on Stockton, the letters of the Clephan family in the Northumberland Record Office.

16. The Unitarian predominance in the House of Commons is asserted by John Bowring, *Autobiographical Recollections* (1877), p. 387. Harriet Martineau's boast is in a note to Lord Brougham, April 1833, University College London.

17. Kenrick, *Memoir of Kentish*, p. 10.

18. Rathbone is quoted in L. P. Jacks, *Confessions of an Octogenarian* (1942), pp. 140–141; the text is taken, more or less, from James v:1. H. McLachlan, *The Methodist Unitarian Movement* (1919). *A Review of the Missionary Life and Labours of Richard Wright. Written by Himself* (1824). The radical and Unitarian background of the Courtaulds is well summarized in D. C. Coleman, *Courtaulds: An Economic and Social History*, i (1969) and can be followed in detail in the *Courtauld Family Letters* (8 vols., 1909) and in S. L. Courtauld, ed., *The Huguenot Family of Courtauld*, ii (1966). On the provision of chapels for factory-related congregations, what is said here rests on work in the congregational records and on accounts in the Unitarian press.

19. The most convenient compendium of statistics can be found in Robert Currie, Alan Gilbert, and Lee Horsley, *Churches and Churchgoers: Patterns of Church Growth in the British Isles since 1700* (1977), but the unsatisfactory quality of Unitarian statistics and the historical obscurity and misunderstanding that have surrounded Unitarianism make this book less useful for it than for other denominations.

20. The Mill Hill records contain a packet of materials on the rebuilding of the chapel; this quotation is taken from an argument by the architect that proved persuasive to the committee. See the interesting discussion in Leonard Smith, 'Unitarians and the Gothic Revival: Church Building, 1837–1899,' *Transactions of the Unitarian Historical Society*, xvii, 81–87 (July 1980).

21. Southwood Smith to Charles Wellbeloved, November 29, 1845, Dr. Williams's Library, MS 24.81. Lucy Aikin to William Ellery Channing, June 1, 1830 and October 23, 1831 in A. L. LeBreton, ed., *The Correspondence of William Ellery Channing D.D. and Lucy Aikin, 1826 to 1842* (1874), pp. 44–47, 92–96. Joseph Hunter's disenchantment is documented in his Thought Books, British Library Add. MSS, 39818–839, 39820 and his correspondence in Add. MSS, 35761–35 162.

22. R. K. Webb, 'John Hamilton Thom: Intellect and Conscience in Liverpool,' in P. T. Phillips, ed., *The View from the Pulpit: Victorian Ministers and Society* (1978), pp. 210–243.

23. This long and bitter quarrel is amply documented in *The Inquirer* over the first quarter-century of its existence and, above all, in the letters written by all the leading combatants to the Rev. John Gordon, Unitarian College MSS, John Rylands Library. Another captain on the Priestleyan side was the Rev. Edward Tagart, minister at Little Portland Street and secretary of the British and Foreign Unitarian Society; the Martineau MSS belonging to Dr. R. S. Speck in San Francisco make clear the shrill, snobbish opposition of James Martineau to Tagart's marriage to the widow of Martineau's elder brother Thomas in the 1820s. Bache was Martineau's brother-in-law. To round out the picture of family tensions, the Harriet Martineau MSS in the University of Birmingham Library show Harriet Martineau—long estranged on personal and philosophical grounds from the brother she had once worshipped—helping the philosopher James Bain to organize the opposition to Martineau's candidacy for the chair of philosophy at University College, London in the mid-sixties.

24. On the Liverpool confrontation, Webb, 'Thom,' pp. 217–219. The two incidents involving Berry are taken from the records of Great Meeting, and the fate of the chapel at Bury is traced in an article, presumably by J. H. Warren, in the Warren Papers, Hi W 46, Nottingham University Library.

25. Martineau's important letter—which as H. L. Short points out anticipated the famous church-sect distinction of Ernst Troeltsch by fifty years—is in *Essays, Reviews, and Addresses* (1891), ii, 381–420. Short's account of these disputes in

'Presbyterians under a New Name,' in Bolam *et al.*, *The English Presbyterians*, is admirable for its efficiency and objectivity.

26. On the liturgical question, A. E. Peaston, *The Prayer Book Tradition of the Free Churches* (1964).

27. Johns' reports are remarkable documents of both concern and style. On the Liverpool mission, Anne Holt, *A Ministry to the Poor, being the History of the Liverpool Domestic Mission Society, 1836–1936* (1936). See also Daniel T. McColgan, *Joseph Tuckerman, Pioneer in American Social Work* (1940).

28. Martineau, 'Memoirs and Papers of Dr. Channing,' *Essays, Reviews, and Addresses*, i, 115; 'Personal Influences on Present Theology,' i, 255. Thom, *Religion, the Church and the People* (1849), p. 28.

29. J. H. Thom to L. P. Jacks, October 10, 1892; James Martineau to Jacks, October 9, 1892, in the Ullet Road records, 288 ULL 3/22/11, 3/22/5, Liverpool Record Office. E. P. Hennock, *Fit and Proper Persons: Ideal and Reality in Nineteenth-Century Urban Government* (1973), pp. 221–222, notes the sharp decline by the late nineteenth century of Unitarian councillors in Leeds; Stephen Koss, *Nonconformity in Modern British Politics* (1975), shows a similar falling off in the number of Unitarian M.P.s in the twentieth century.

30. Timothy Davis Diary, June 27, 1831, National Library of Wales. Carpenter's principled difficulties are set out in the records of the Bridgwater and Bath congregations; his brother Philip, minister at Stand (Whitefield), Warrington and later in Montreal, was a leading temperance advocate.

31. On Norton, C. J. Street, 'The Old Nonconformity at Norton, Derbyshire,' *TUHS*, i (1916), 148–149. Aspland to Richard Astley, May 7, 1834, Astley Papers, Shrewsbury Public Library.

32. 'The Churches and Industrial Unrest,' *Inquirer*, September 7, 1912.

33. To R. L. Carpenter, April 25, 1885, Manchester College, Oxford.

34. On the rapid advent of liberalism among the Quakers, Elizabeth Isichei, *Victorian Quakers* (1970), pp. 24–33. Campbell and the Pioneer Preachers still await their historians. The most recent effort to wrestle with a Unitarian theology is *A Free Religious Faith* (1945), the work of a commission of the General Assembly.

35. Mrs. Barbauld's comment is reported by John Bowring, *Autobiographical Recollections*, p. 388.

36. Priestley used the phrase in his farewell sermon to the congregation at the Gravel-pit, Hackney, on March 30, 1794. The last clamorous speaking against was the obsession of Lord Hugh Cecil in the 1930s, when he tried to get the bishop of Liverpool reprimanded for having invited the minister of Ullet Road church to preach in Liverpool Cathedral; Cecil also tried to prevent the Unitarian Prime Minister, Neville Chamberlain, from acting on ecclesiastical appointments as his doing so would be 'unseemly and technically scandalous.' (*Inquirer*, January 6, February 3, June 16 and 23, 1934 and February 12, 1938.) But note should also be taken of the long struggle of Unitarians to gain access to the BBC's religious broadcasting, not resolved until the advent of Sir William Haley as director-general in the 1950s, a curious instance of stonewalling amply illustrated in the frustration of *The Inquirer* over more than twenty years and in Asa Briggs, *A History of Broadcasting in the United Kingdom*, ii (1965), 236, 240 and iv (1979), 497, 499, vol. 4, 778–779. A caution must be advanced, however, against a too simple advocacy of 'secularization' as an explanation. Religious concern is not equatable with attendance at church, and religious organizations continued to touch the lives of people who rarely or never went to church; see Jeffrey Cox, *The English Churches in a Secular Society: Lambeth, 1870–1930* (1982).

# 2
# SONS AND SUBSCRIBERS: LAY SUPPORT AND THE COLLEGE[1]

DAVID L. WYKES
*University of Leicester*

As centres of learning nonconformist academies have long been the subject of scholarly interest and praise, particularly in terms of their advanced curricula and superior educational standards.[2] And since the leading academies provided lay as well as ministerial instruction, historians have generally accepted that in the eighteenth and early nineteenth centuries these institutions offered the best education available for those intending to follow a professional or business career.[3] But in contrast to the work on the institutions themselves, their curricula or standards of education, there has been little detailed consideration of the students they instructed or of the benefits which were supposedly gained. Yet any assessment of the contribution nonconformist academies made to lay education will have to go beyond the surveys of educational methods, subjects taught or the scholarship of individual tutors—important though such themes are in assessing the significance of particular institutions—to consider the students themselves. In the final analysis the contribution of any educational establishment will be judged by those whom it taught. Moreover, the academies which made the greatest contribution to the development of education and society as a whole are generally acknowledged to have been those that taught lay as well as divinity students.

This essay is therefore concerned with the first Manchester (1786–1803) and the York (1803–40) periods of the College history: the years before university reform which so radically altered the role of the College in educating laymen. Most eighteenth-century nonconformist academies had only a short life, and of those that lasted longer only a couple survive today as independent institutions. Of that number none can claim a greater role than Manchester College in educating lay as well as ministerial students. Thus the celebration of the bicentenary of the College provides an opportunity to assess not only the contribution of the College in educating laymen during the first fifty years or so of its existence, but also some consideration of the reasons for its survival and long history. As an independent college relying almost entirely upon private benefactions and support, the survival, let alone success, of the institution depended upon its ability to attract both students and subscribers, particularly during the difficult and crucial early years.

This essay therefore centres on the subscribers and students of the College, their identity and social background, and the reasons for their attendance or support. Considering the importance of the subject, college finances have received little of the attention they deserve. There is almost nothing concerning the financial encouragement which the laity gave, or the sources and methods used to fund particular institutions. Yet the collapse of other academies, such as Warrington and Hackney, make the consequences of the withdrawal or lack of lay support only too clear. It is also important to be certain about the type of education nonconformist academies offered laymen, the benefits which would have accrued as well as the expectations and objectives of parents who sent their sons there. And since a range of educational alternatives was available, the question needs to be considered not only from the perspective of the College itself, the courses offered and the standards upheld, but also in terms of the demand for a particular type or level of education and the social and economic factors behind that demand.

## I

Early interest in the role of the nonconformist academy in educating laymen can be traced to the wider debate amongst economic historians concerning the contribution religious dissenters made to economic growth and industrialisation. Nonconformist academies have been seen to provide lay dissenters with a superior education, and thus the means to explain, in part at least, the supposed advantages they had as businessmen over their Anglican counterparts. With this interpretation still persists the old view that the Test Acts closed Oxford and Cambridge to nonconformists leaving the academies as the only alternative open to dissenters seeking a higher education, and one which was to prove vastly superior to anything the English universities could offer.[4]

Unfortunately, historians have in the past made little effort to examine very closely the possible contribution of the nonconformist academy, or indeed of education generally, to economic growth. While it is not the intention to consider here the practical advantages to be derived from a superior education, it should be noted that a number of recent studies have seriously questioned existing assumptions. Despite the widespread evidence for a considerable interest in science amongst manufacturers, professionals and the middle-classes generally during the late eighteenth and early nineteenth centuries,[5] historians have searched in vain 'for precise examples of a technical innovation's being derived consciously from pre-existent theoretical knowledge of a non-trivial character'.[6] Moreover, historians now recognise that the technical improvements of the Industrial Revolution were not the result of 'large-scale technological breakthroughs' but 'the product of numerous small gains by a community of rival artisans' possessing practical skills but very little formal schooling. 'Even the new machinery in the textile industry involved no principles that an intelligent merchant could not grasp.'[7]

Rather than emphasising its 'industrial utility' a recent trend has been to depict science as having a 'cultural value' attractive to certain social groups, notably dissenters, manufacturers and the medical professions.[8] Likewise, recent studies on the impact of education upon economic growth have cast doubt over traditional assumptions about the direct contribution of literacy, or even of education generally. Indeed, the prevailing view suggests that during the Industrial Revolution innovators were 'practical men' and innovation owed little to formal education.[9] Furthermore, at a purely quantitative level it is clear that the direct contribution of nonconformist academies to business life was very limited. Although about half the 72 academies active between 1663 and 1820 (for which particulars survive) were open to lay students, including most of the leading establishments,[10] the overall numbers they educated can only have been a very insignificant proportion of the total engaged in trade and manufacturing; particularly as many lay students followed careers in law and medicine, not business.

It should be emphasised, however, that it is not intended to deny the importance of science and technology during the Industrial Revolution, nor even the role of nonconformist academies in developing a wider interest in science, but rather to question assumptions that the value of the lay education nonconformist academies provided should necessarily be assessed in utilitarian terms. As the author of the most recent survey of the education of the period has commented: 'the industrial revolution in England did not thrive because all the education supporting it was ample and valuable'.[11]

Educational demand was closely linked to wealth and social background. Parents of modest means could only afford a limited schooling, while the ambitions of the wealthy merchant might extend to a varied and expensive education covering many years. The commonest method of entering business, certainly before the nineteenth century, was by some form of apprenticeship or practical instruction. Prior to this term of service a son would have received his schooling, but the time available was limited by the age at which apprenticeship began, often before the age of 13. While for most businessmen training restricted the period of schooling, for the wealthiest the situation was effectively reversed, with the time devoted to education determining the age at which apprenticeship began. Thus merchants generally served shorter apprenticeships and started at a later age, often not until they were 16 or 17.

It is as important in considering the education of businessmen to be aware of their needs and expectations as of the type of instruction the different institutions offered. Although it is true that lectures on commercial subjects together with more specialised private tuition were available at Warrington Academy and during the first period of Manchester College, the provision of a business education was hardly central to either institution. Parents seeking practical instruction for their sons would have found one of the many commercial academies or private schools, available locally, much more suited to their needs and their pockets. All too often the educational benefits have been evaluated by historians in terms of the wrong criteria.[12] Most historians have assumed that any increase in the level of education will prove advantageous,[13] but a closer examination suggests this assumption is misleading for most businessmen: indeed, that any additional time and money spent in further study could well damage future career prospects for all but the wealthiest.

In part the problem was a practical one, for it is clear that because training followed on from school any extension in formal education merely served to delay the start of a career, perhaps irreparably, since it was a crucial period for developing and acquiring those contacts, attitudes and skills essential to business. When discussing the future of Richard Witts, who had entered Warrington at the age of 17, it was admitted that if he was to join a merchant-house, he was 'too old to be put Apprentice', 'tho' his age requires him now to be soon fixt somewhere.' Witts, however, was exceptional, since as a wealthy young man he could afford to delay his entry into business.[14] The problem was not merely one of timing or cost. With the emphasis on the classics, much of the knowledge acquired from further study was felt by most parents to be of little practical value to everyday business.[15] Moreover, the social values and habits acquired with this additional knowledge, or from the particular institutional environment, were often inimical to successful economic activity. The social ethos of Oxford and Cambridge and the public schools, together with the extravagance, dissipation and indolence associated with them, were considered fatal 'to future success and reputation in any line of life and above all, in business'.[16]

All the evidence suggests that for most businessmen formal schooling was short. Prof. Erickson in her study of Nottingham hosiers discovered that during the first half of the nineteenth century most parents sought schools which provided instruction in commercial subjects, and she could find no evidence to suggest that even the wealthiest families considered a classical education for sons intended for the hosiery trade. She also noted that the period of formal school education was very short: the Unitarian Samuel Hollins, the son of a highly successful manufacturer, was apparently the only businessman active in the Nottingham hosiery trade during the 1840s whose schooling continued until the age of 14. Most left school at ten, and though some had received less than three years formal education it was sufficient to allow them to acquire the basic skills necessary to write letters, draw up accounts and conduct a business.[17] In late eighteenth-century Leicester, William Gardiner (1770–1853), the son of a prominent manufacturer and member of the Presbyterian Great Meeting, was sent to a dame school at the age of two. When he was seven he entered the Silver Street Academy, a day school where he learnt 'little more than writing and the first rules of arithmetic'; by the time he was 16 he had joined his father's firm and was already undertaking independent commissions. He was taught languages by a private tutor, giving up Latin for French, but the rest of his knowledge was acquired from his father's friends or from acquaintances.[18] Thus it has been suggested, the impression is of an education 'not so much regularly acquired as picked up, in a milieu which offered various opportunities'[19], an idea which finds support in the recent work of historians who have studied provincial science and culture.[20]

Studies of other business communities in the late eighteenth and early nineteenth centuries also make it clear that most parents of sons who were destined for business were only interested in an elementary education. But a classical education at a grammar school or university was important to some groups, in particular those intending a career in one of the learned professions.[21] But education was never a matter of vocational training only, it had a social function as well. The wealthiest merchants lived as gentlemen and therefore sought an education for their sons commensurate with the position in life they held.

Eighteenth-century business life provided the wealthy merchant and manufacturer with many opportunities to pursue a variety of interests besides business, for which a liberal education was valuable as a means of usefully employing that time as well as giving a taste for literature, science and other modern subjects. Samuel Galton, the Birmingham gun manufacturer, had been educated at Warrington Academy, and his daughter was to recall that during her childhood her father generally attended his business each day for a few hours, 'but from about one o'clock, when he usually returned, he was chiefly engaged at home in intellectual pursuits; and of these he had an endless variety'. Similarly, at Leeds in the mid-eighteenth century, it had been noted that 'many of the Merchants divided the week between their Pleasures and their Business'.[22] But a liberal education also usefully engaged a youth's time in the interval between school and the age at which business began, as well as providing the means to ensure that a wealthy merchant or manufacturer made good use of the leisure he was later to enjoy. According to the Rev. Ralph Harrison in his opening sermon to the supporters of Manchester College, such accomplishments

> 'give dignity to the possession of wealth, lessen the snares and dangers with which it is surrounded, provide a constant source of rational and innocent enjoyments, and qualify for honourable and important services to their fellow citizens'.[23]

From the mid-eighteenth century onwards it became increasingly common for the leading merchants and manufacturers to seek a much more extensive education for their sons.[24] But it is clear, that even then the proportion of businessmen who attended either a nonconformist academy or university was very small: only the very wealthy could afford such an education and they alone would have found it of value.

## II

In contrast to the attention given by historians studying the nonconformist academy to educational methods, scholarly standards or the curriculum (though from the perspective of the students themselves such studies are undeniably weak), the problem of college finances has been ignored. Yet recurrent financial difficulties not only threatened the very existence of Manchester College on a number of occasions, particularly during the first 17 years, but were responsible for restricting, often severely, the educational activities of the institution for much of the remaining period under consideration. Lay patronage proved vital: their benefactions established the College in 1786, while the importance of continued lay support through annual subscriptions is highlighted by the collapse of Warrington and Hackney. Who, then, supported the new College at Manchester, and why were they willing to become subscribers and benefactors?

Two major influences dominated the setting up and funding of the new College, the former academy at Warrington and Cross Street Chapel, Manchester. The new College's connections with Cross Street were close and intimate: the first two tutors, Barnes and Harrison, were joint ministers of the congregation; the chairman, officers and committee were all members, likewise the majority of the original benefactors. Similarly, 17 of the 54 trustees who voted to dissolve Warrington Academy were among those who signed the address sent to Barnes and Harrison in 1786, and 12 of the 17 became members of the first committee of the new College; moreover, the three leading promoters, Barnes, Harrison and Percival, were all former students of Warrington.[25] The new institution also received the Warrington Academy library and the promise of half the proceeds from the sale of the building, though in reality the financial benefits turned out very meagre indeed.

The strength and importance of these connections in explaining the financial support the College received are even clearer when the original subscription lists are examined: of the 125 annual subscribers and benefactors in 1786, 25 had been students at Warrington (including seven ministers), and a further 15 were parents or other close relatives (mainly brothers and sisters) of former students. About a third of the original supporters of Manchester College therefore had direct links with the earlier academy. Unfortunately, no subscription lists are available for the later years at Warrington. Even so, for something like two-fifths of the individuals who in 1786 promised subscriptions and benefactions to Manchester College, previous links can be traced with Warrington. Another 24 supporters of the College were either trustees or became trustees of Cross Street Chapel, and the importance of the congregation is even clearer when the regional basis of support for the new College is considered.[26]

Manchester alone provided 70 per cent. of the benefactions and 45 per cent. of the subscriptions promised in 1786, and if the rest of the support from Lancashire is included the amount rises to four-fifths and two-fifths of the total respectively. Cheshire, the next largest area of support, accounted for no more than ten per cent. of the subscriptions and nine per cent. of the benefactions. Contributions from Derbyshire and Yorkshire (including the manufacturing towns of the West Riding) were even smaller. The significant feature is not merely the dominance of the Manchester area, but the almost complete absence of support from outside the north of England. London, the greatest concentration of both wealth and dissent, provided only two subscriptions of four guineas and three benefactions totalling 23 guineas. There were only single subscriptions from Leicester and such major centres of dissent as Bristol,

Birmingham and Norwich, and none from Exeter, Leeds, Nottingham or Newcastle.[27] Most of these individual contributions can be explained in terms of family and other links: James Esdaile of London had married a member of the Hadfield family (closely connected with Cross Street Chapel)[28]; Edward Rigby of Norwich, an alumnus of Warrington and grandson of Dr John Taylor, was closely related to the prominent Manchester family of Rigby, and thus by marriage to the treasurer of the College, James Touchet[29]; and the Rev. J. P. Estlin of Bristol was also an alumnus of Warrington.[30]

While the geographical pattern of financial support for the College in 1786 identifies the significance of Manchester (and indirectly Cross Street Chapel), more importantly, it is evidence of how limited that support was and of the strength of competition from the College at Hackney, also founded with many of the same ideals following the collapse of Warrington. An examination of the pattern of support for Hackney College reveals two main features: the dominance of London and the far greater level of patronage than for the institution at Manchester. The published subscription list for Hackney, dated June 1788[31], reveals that the College had received promises of £9,259 in benefactions, more than ten times the figure for Manchester, and £748 5s 6d in subscriptions, over three times the Manchester total. It is obvious that Hackney was much the better supported of the two institutions, indeed the amount promised in annual subscriptions was not far short of the total benefactions for Manchester College. London alone accounted for nearly three-fifths of all Hackney benefactions and just under half the subscriptions. London had also provided the largest body of subscriptions at Warrington Academy. In addition, virtually all the Warrington benefactions were from the south of England[32], illustrating the seriousness for Manchester College of the competition from Hackney in terms of the loss of potential support from London. In fact the impact of Hackney was even more serious since it drew nearly £1,800 (19.4 per cent.) of its benefactions from the north and the Midlands, more than twice the total sum promised to Manchester. Nottingham, for example, failed to make any benefactions or subscriptions to Manchester College, compared with a benefaction of £50 and the 26 subscriptions totalling nearly £55 promised to Hackney.[33] Even when individuals did support both institutions it is clear they were much more generous to Hackney.[34]

If the benefactors and subscribers of Manchester College are examined, then it is obvious that the basis of support was even narrower than the regional pattern suggests. The close connection with Cross Street Chapel has already been identified. Its dominance should not cause much surprise. All the leading promoters of the College were influential members of the congregation, and with the two ministers, Barnes and Harrison, named as tutors, they were well placed to draw financial contributions from a group of individuals likely to be already sympathetic to their objectives. Moreover, it has long been recognised that the congregation was one of the largest, wealthiest and most influential in the country and that its members included many of the leading families in the town. When the list of benefactors is examined closely, it is clear that the support promised by members of Cross Street Chapel was mainly from this group of leading families. They included such prominent merchants and manufacturers as Josiah Birch; William Rigby; Samuel Hardman; the Robinson brothers, Thomas and Robert; James Touchet; Samuel Mather; James Bayley; Jonathan and Thomas Hatfield; and the brothers John, James, Richard, Thomas and Benjamin Potter. In addition, the Hon. Mrs. Sempill and her sister, Mrs. Ann Bayley, daughters and coheiresses of Thomas Butterworth Esq. belonged to one of the leading Manchester families. While Thomas Percival M.D., the principal promoter and first chairman of the College, like his professional colleagues, Charles White F.R.S. and Thomas Henry F.R.S., was prominent in the radical, intellectual and social leadership of the town.

Outside Manchester, the same factors, individual wealth and support for rational dissent, also explain the pattern of support for the College. At Gorton, the Rev. John Atchinson headed a list of five members of his congregation, including four from the same family. They promised a 20 guineas benefaction and six subscriptions totalling 12 guineas. A similar level of support was promised by the much larger town of Liverpool. There was a benefaction of 20 guineas from the banker and former Warrington student Richard Heywood, who also supported Hackney, and subscriptions from six individuals including the Rev. John Yates (a Hackney subscriber and benefactor) and James Currie M.D., both active Liverpool reformers, and the Jamaica merchant James France: all were members of the Paradise Street Chapel, of which Yates was minister and France the chief promoter.[35] At Stockport the College supporters included two early factory owners, Samuel Oldknow, the celebrated muslin manufacturer, and Henry Marsland, a leading cotton spinner. Elsewhere, particularly outside Lancashire and Cheshire, support for the College was much weaker. Whereas at Manchester, Gorton, Liverpool and Stockport, it was in general ministers and the leading members of their congregations who promised support, outside these centres contributions depended upon individual families, including some of the outstanding leaders of eighteenth-century dissent who possessed an almost hereditary attachment to liberal causes. For example, Richard Slater Milnes of Fryston Hall, M.P. for York (1784–1802), who promised 10 guineas (the largest single annual subscription); his first cousin twice removed, James Milnes of Wakefield, one of the leading West Riding merchants, and a subscriber for 4 guineas, together with his son James Milnes (Junior) of Thorne House, later M.P. for Bletchingley (1802–05). All three were leading liberals and prominent reformers during the 1780s and '90s. Another subscriber, Mrs. Rodes of Houghton Hall, was the aunt of R. S. Milnes and the stepsister of Rebecca Crompton, a benefactor, whose nephew Samuel Crompton, a former student of Warrington and a 'very eminent banker of Derby and York' was also a subscriber.[36] Other subscribers to the College, distinguished by their reforming interests and great commercial wealth included, besides Yates and Currie mentioned earlier, the Hull banker Joseph Robinson Pease, a contemporary at Warrington of Barnes and a brother of the Manchester Robinsons, who gave a benefaction of £30 in 1788[37]; William Shore, a member of the prominent Sheffield banking family; the celebrated potter, Josiah Wedgwood; Priestley's friend and patron, William Russell, the Birmingham manufacturer and reformer; and the former Warrington student Ralph Eddowes of Chester, an 'intrepid friend to liberty and independence'.[38] Significantly, the last four together with Yates were among the few who supported both institutions. Such support was an expression of their reforming zeal. In addition, the prominent Whig politician, Lord George Cavendish, gave a benefaction of 10 guineas in 1788.[39]

Financial support for the College, therefore, was determined by the support which existed for rational dissent and the liberal, reformist principles it upheld. Even the benefaction from Cavendish can be defined within these terms, since it was made at a time when the agitation for the repeal of the Test and Corporation Acts was approaching its height, and when it was valuable for a Whig politician to be seen making common cause with his dissenting allies. Dr. Ditchfield has shown how the political and religious values of the College and its promoters helped to encourage and attract support for the institution, and that this support was part of a commitment to liberal causes generally.[40] Since rational dissent lacked any formal denominational or institutional framework, these liberal interests and connections provided the main source of public support, in turn the College was important in acting as a focus and giving material form to those principles and values.

But support for the College was not merely restricted by being limited to rational dissenters and their supporters. While it is of little surprise to discover that the leading benefactors of the College, like the Hon. Mrs. Sempill, Josiah Birch, William Rigby, Isaac Wilkinson, and Mrs. Ann Bayley, were amongst the wealthiest and most important members of their respective communities, individuals who could afford to be generous in their contributions to the causes they favoured, it is clear the majority of subscribers were also individuals of wealth and local standing, even if of a rather different class from the great benefactor. It may be supposed that a greater range of people could have subscribed one or two guineas a year to the College. But Dr. Howe has pointed out in his study of Lancashire cotton masters that philanthropy was predominantly the activity of those individuals controlling medium to large firms, since few owners of smaller firms would have had available even small surplus sums.[41] It is the possession of wealth which predisposes individuals to charitable giving; yet a willingness to contribute to a particular cause is never decided by financial considerations alone. The publication of a subscription list and the sums promised was a recognised method of drawing public attention to a particular cause, but it also helps to suggest the motivation behind such support: an individual's desire for public recognition and confirmation of his or her standing in the community.

Not surprisingly, therefore, promoters often found it difficult to gain support for national causes. The wealthier members of any society or institution were expected to subscribe generously and to head any subscription list, leaving others to contribute lesser sums and the poorer members not at all. No doubt the size of each individual's contribution depended upon the amount promised by others and in particular the level of generosity set by the leading benefactors.

Support for the College was limited to a small minority of wealthy individuals who were distinguished, not only by their wealth, but by a wider than average concern with national interests and causes; a concern not shared by the majority of dissenters. However, consideration of the motivation underlying the voluntary support for the College helps not merely to understand the reasons for that support, but also just how limited an interest it represented.

The promoters of the new institution were only successful in appealing to certain groups—limited in size and often by circumstances. The extensive network of dissenting contacts provided most of the financial support the College received, but due to the competition from Hackney that support was virtually confined to the north of England. Even the contacts Warrington supplied were largely determined within that framework. Because Manchester College survived and Hackney did not, it is easy to forget that a greater number of Warrington trustees, including the former President, John Carill Worsley of Platt near Manchester, favoured London as the location for the new academy, or that Hackney 'experienced an unprecedented degree of patronage' and succeeded in gaining more than ten times the level of benefactions and more than three times the annual subscriptions promised to Manchester College. A single benefactor apparently contributed £1,500 to Hackney, more than the total amount of benefactions and annual subscriptions promised to Manchester College.[42] Despite the wealth which supposedly existed in rational dissent, only 14 individuals out of a total of 364 chose to support both institutions.

Manchester College, as a successor to Warrington, had much the same objectives and design as its rival at Hackney, but it is clear with only a fraction of the necessary financial backing. That such a large part of the necessary funds came from the neighbourhood of Manchester was a considerable achievement, but until it was possible to extend the area of support after the collapse of Hackney in 1796, by appealing to the country as a whole, the body of wealthy individuals sympathetic enough to respond to the call for financial support was extremely limited. The promoters of the College were well aware that 'a plan of this nature cannot be carried into execution without a warm and zealous patronage, nor without considerable activity, exertion and expense'. But despite their initial optimism over the level of support, which appears to have encouraged an over-ambitious building programme, it is clear that during the years at Manchester the College was persistently harassed by severe financial difficulties due to the original incumbrance.[43] Ironically, Hackney suffered similar embarrassment, despite a much greater level of initial support, because of its extravagant expenditure on the college buildings.[44]

III

Without a comprehensive set of accounts it is difficult to unravel the College finances, but there is no denying the seriousness of the overall financial situation during the first Manchester period. From the outset the level of benefactions and subscriptions promised was inadequate to carry out the ambitious plan adopted by the trustees. The erection of an extensive range of College buildings[45] exhausted the funds within the first year and left a serious deficit, though the size of this deficit cannot now be determined. The committee had expected to receive half the proceeds arising from the sale of Warrington Academy[46], but other than the library which Manchester College received, and the philosophical apparatus which went to Hackney, little of material value was saved from the wreck of Warrington Academy. It is clear, that as a consequence, the College was forced to undergo a period of severe retrenchment, which seriously impaired its ability to carry out its other responsibilities. Moreover, the subscription income, which until the early nineteenth century never exceeded £300, and at times fell below £200, was insufficient to pay even the tutors' salaries.[47]

Evidence of the College's financial difficulties can be found in the minutes as early as 1789.[48] As the difficulties increased a crisis was reached with the resignation of Barnes as divinity tutor in December 1792. On considering the situation the trustees were forced to acknowledge that 'their funds are unequal to the support of the professors as originally intended'. Barnes, however, was persuaded to continue as divinity tutor and accept, as a result of the reorganisation, the additional responsibility for the general management of the College, including the domestic arrangements.[49] But his resignation at Midsummer 1797 again precipitated a crisis and the realisation that the funds of the College were inadequate for the original design. The importance of gaining new support was recognised if a delay over the appointment of a successor was to be avoided, and it was subsequently agreed no invitations would be issued until the new subscriptions reached 80 guineas. The initial response to this appeal appears to have been good, and by September, before the major centres of dissent had been canvassed, £80 had already been raised in new subscriptions.[50] Unfortunately, the results of this wider appeal are unknown, but it is interesting to note that the committee decided to include London, Bristol and Norwich, as well as Liverpool, Leeds, Sheffield, Newcastle and a number of smaller towns in the north of England, whereas earlier, in October 1796, just after Hackney had closed, the committee only applied to congregations in Lancashire, Cheshire and Yorkshire for support.[51]

The difficulty the committee had in finding a successor to Barnes as divinity tutor is an indication of the uncertainty surrounding the College during this period. The first five ministers approached all refused, and it appears that George Walker accepted largely because he was persuaded the survival of the institution depended upon his acceptance.[52] Unfortunately, the problem of student discipline became increasingly serious under Walker, and in 1800 both assistant tutors resigned following a particularly outrageous episode of insubordination.[53] Again the critical financial condition of the College forced the committee to leave the vacancies unfilled and to accept that 'the plan of the institution must for the present be suspended on its original scale'.[54] Under the new arrangement Walker was no longer paid a fixed salary, receiving instead an allowance of £20 for each divinity student. To enable him to replace his income, he was 'at liberty to take such a number of lay pupils as shall not interfere with his plans of instruction for the Divinity student'.[55] In March 1801, Pipe-Wolferstan, who was then considering whether to send his son to the College, after talking with Walker came to the conclusion that 'the funds and the existence of the College are quite dubious'. Though subsequently, as a result of his investigation, Pipe-Wolferstan was sufficiently re-assured as to the immediate prospects, as well as impressed by the education offered, to entrust his son to Walker's care. He also had sufficient confidence to pay the necessary fees in advance.[56] The new arrangements were without doubt far less favourable to Walker. With the loss of his tutor's salary he was entirely dependent upon student numbers for his remuneration. In addition Walker was now responsible for all the teaching as well as the general management of the College.

The seriousness of the overall financial position of Manchester College cannot be disputed. On at least two occasions (1797 and 1803) the College very nearly closed as a result. It is clear the financial weakness was long term and severe, and stemmed from the debt originally incurred on the College buildings. The promoters had intended that the benefactions should cover the main capital costs, but for reasons largely beyond their control, the level of contributions was lower than required and the expected sums from the sale of Warrington Academy never materialised. As a result a large part of the annual subscriptions had to be directed towards servicing the College debt rather than carrying out the activities originally intended. The existence of financial difficulties from the earliest years together with the major crises of 1792, 1797 and 1800 were symptomatic of the College's persistent and underlying financial weakness. The response of the committee to these emergencies—the decision to suspend the original plan of the institution, not to replace tutors, and to pay Walker an allowance rather than a fixed salary—points to the inadequate level of funding for the scale of activity desired. The lack of reserves made the College especially vulnerable to any fluctuation in its finances. Though the institution might one year have a favourable balance, adverse conditions in the next, leading to a decline in subscription income or a rise in expenditure, could precipitate a crisis. Faced with this situation the committee had two main alternatives: to appeal for additional support, or failing that, to conduct an extensive retrenchment of expenditure. The evidence from the minutes reveals that they generally adopted the latter approach, though additional support was sought. The appeal for additional funds in 1797, though it apparently enjoyed some initial success, was insufficient by 1800.

Why was the public support required not forthcoming, particularly as there were 'so many rich men who support it'? Wellbeloved, who made this comment, was surprised that no subscription had been raised for a permanent fund, while Walker specifically accused the committee and trustees of making little effort to gain additional support. There is some evidence to support the claim. Touchet resigned as treasurer in July 1797, because of 'the great Trouble with which it has been attended, & his own poor opinion of the Friends & future Subscriptions'.[57]

Though contemporary evidence suggests that greater efforts could have been made on behalf of the College,[58] the situation in the 1790s was far from favourable. It was a period of great economic difficulty, even hardship, particularly serious for the kind of businessman who provided the main financial support. In turn, wartime conditions also increased the problems of the College. Because of inflation, the committee was forced to increase the allowances paid to divinity students[59], while the uncertainty over the College's future did little to encourage additional subscriptions. Timothy Kenrick, who opened a rival academy at Exeter in 1799, noted the difficulties involved in gaining public support during this period:

> 'Our people do not enter into these schemes with all the zeal I could wish, but they do perhaps as much as could be expected, considering the hardness of the times, & how much this town in particular has suffered by the War.'[60]

The 1790s were also an extremely difficult, even hazardous time for Unitarians and radicals. The enthusiasm with which they had welcomed the French Revolution had given way to defeat, isolation and a deep sense of hopelessness. Many former supporters rejected their previous radicalism while the confidence of others in the future of rational dissent and its institutions had been broken.[61] Hackney College, like Warrington before it, was caught up in the radical excitement of the period with disastrous results. Burdened by debt and the reputation of its students for riotous and subversive behaviour the College was dissolved in 1796 having lost the sympathy of most of its former supporters.[62] No wonder that at Manchester in 1797 'there are many who think very despairingly of the future situation of the College—partly, perhaps, in consequence of the general Fate which similar institutions have generally met with'.[63]

In view of the very real financial difficulties which existed, what effect did they and the periodic crises have upon the work of the College? Without denying the seriousness of the situation it would be wrong necessarily to suppose that the educational standards and achievements of the College were low or undistinguished as a result. Dr. Ditchfield has pointed out that the tutors throughout the period were a formidably well-qualified and able group of scholars, even if they did not all equal Dalton and Walker in intellect. Moreover, the College maintained an excellent and comprehensive curriculum, even after 1800 when Walker was alone. Yet inevitably the failure to replace tutors who resigned must have had an impact on standards, particularly when the whole burden of instruction became the responsibility of a single individual. Exhaustion alone would suggest that Walker's teaching must have suffered. In addition to the difficulties he experienced in preparing and teaching a whole range of subjects, they included many with which he was unfamiliar. Despite this, Pipe-Wolferstan's diary records his satisfaction with his son's education and instruction, though he did express some doubts about the level of progress achieved. Walker was forced to conduct all his teaching in a single class and therefore, inevitably, the standard was limited to the general ability of the whole group rather than the particular needs of the better students.[64] But alongside Pipe-Wolferstan's evident satisfaction with the standard of instruction was his concern with the problem of discipline, and it was this concern which eventually caused him to withdraw his son from the College. It proved impossible for a single tutor, preoccupied with his other responsibilities, to provide proper supervision of the students. It is perhaps significant that the worst outbreak of disorder occurred while Walker was away in London. The financial difficulties of the College, which exaggerated the importance of student fees, may also have led to standards being compromised with respect to admissions, and thus further contributing to the disciplinary problems.[65]

Although the College may have managed to maintain a very creditable standard of scholarship, despite the difficulties involved, the evidence relating to the education and support of ministerial students suggests that the financial weakness of the College did adversely affect its ability to carry out one of the principal objects of the institution. It was widely recognised that most divinity students could not support themselves during a lengthy course of study and would therefore need assisting financially. Past lay generosity had led to the establishment of a number of special funds for this very purpose, of which the Lady Hewley Trust, the Presbyterian Fund and the Coward Trust were among the most important. One of the objects of the promoters of Manchester College had been to achieve a sufficient level of annual subscriptions to enable the trustees to offer exhibitions to divinity students and also to pay the tutors' salaries. Despite such intentions the practical results were modest. During the first 12 years only 20 students out of a total of 135 (about 1 in 7) followed the divinity course, of whom four subsequently entered the established church while a number of others preferred lay careers.[66] The proportion of ministers educated at Warrington was very similar, where because of the financial crisis no students were admitted on the foundation after 1776.[67] Burdened by debt, the Manchester committee was forced to seek outside financial support for the maintenance of its ministerial students. Over the three years 1794 to 1796 the trustees paid

£40 towards the board of divinity students 'above amount of exhibitions received', a sum which was only equal to a year's interest on the College debt of £800.[68] During the year 1799–1800, the payments made to ministerial students almost exactly matched the exhibitions received on their behalf.[69] The trustees were not therefore supporting any students on their own foundation.

Since ministerial students were few in number, and only formed a small proportion of the total admissions recorded during the early Manchester period, it must be concluded that the College's financial difficulties did materially affect its ability to educate divinity students. While there were no direct ties with any of the funds for training ministers, denominational or otherwise, without their support the College would probably not have admitted any divinity students who required financial assistance.[70] This was certainly contrary to the intended objects of the institution.

Thus the success in maintaining the educational standards of the College under such adverse conditions are more a tribute to the efforts and dedication of a few tutors than the excellence of the original design. With better financial support the College might well have achieved more, particularly in relation to the divinity students. Greater resources would no doubt have had a beneficial effect upon the general educational standards as well. The College's greatest achievement was its survival and continued educational performance, but while this takes account of the loyalty and dedication of the tutors, officers and subscribers who supported and continued to support the institution, the success of the College can only really be ascertained by examining the students themselves.

## IV

During the period for which evidence survives on admissions at Manchester College (1786–1797), 68 out of a total of 115 lay students (nearly three-fifths) were from Lancashire, with 42 (over a third) from Manchester alone (*v.* Table 1). Lancashire had also been an important source of students for Warrington, providing just over a quarter (26.5 per cent.) of the total. Such a proportion, given the location of the academy, is hardly surprising, but it is clear that Warrington was nothing like as dependent upon a single area of students as Manchester College. Moreover, the location of Warrington, although a factor in explaining the pattern of student origins, was by no means the dominant one. While more than half the lay students who attended Warrington were from the north of England and the Midlands, it should be noted that Manchester, Liverpool, Warrington, Birmingham, Bristol and London accounted for nearly two-fifths of all the students. In contrast over four-fifths of all the students who attended Manchester College came from the north and the Midlands. The fact that only five students came from the south of

TABLE 1
Geographical origins of students attending Manchester College, 1786–97

| | 1786–90 | | 1791–95 | | 1796–97 | | STUDENT TOTALS MNC 1786–97 | | STUDENT TOTALS MCY 1803–37 | |
|---|---|---|---|---|---|---|---|---|---|---|
| | L | D | L | D | L | D | L | D | L | D |
| Lancs. | 21 | 3 | 32 | 3 | 15 | – | 68 | 6 | 29 | 20 |
| W. Riding | 2 | – | – | – | – | – | 2 | – | 9 | 15 |
| N. Riding | – | – | – | – | – | – | – | – | 1 | 6 |
| E. Riding | – | – | – | – | 2 | – | 2 | – | 2 | 1 |
| Derbys. | – | – | – | 1 | – | – | – | 1 | 6 | 3 |
| Ches. | 2 | – | 4 | – | – | 1 | 6 | 1 | 6 | 3 |
| Staffs. | 1 | – | – | – | 1 | – | 2 | – | 1 | – |
| Cumbld. | 2 | 1 | 1 | 1 | – | – | 3 | 2 | 1 | – |
| Westmld. | 5 | – | 2 | – | – | – | 7 | – | 1 | 1 |
| Nthbld. | 1 | 1 | – | – | – | – | 1 | 1 | 3 | 3 |
| Durham | – | – | – | – | – | – | – | – | – | 1 |
| Lincs. | – | – | – | – | – | – | – | – | – | 2 |
| Notts. | 2 | – | 2 | 2 | – | – | 4 | 2 | 5 | 2 |
| Leics. | – | – | – | 1 | – | 1 | – | 2 | 6 | 2 |
| Warws. | – | – | – | – | – | – | – | – | 4 | 7 |
| Worcs. | – | – | – | – | – | – | – | – | 2 | 5 |
| NORTH & MIDLANDS | 36 | 5 | 41 | 8 | 18 | 2 | 95 | 15 | 76 | 71 |
| Glos. | 1 | – | – | – | – | – | 1 | – | 1 | 6 |
| Somerset | – | – | – | 1 | 1 | – | 1 | 1 | 5 | 4 |
| Devon | – | – | – | – | – | – | – | – | 1 | 8 |
| Herts. | – | – | 1 | – | – | – | 1 | – | 2 | 1 |
| Berks. | – | 1 | – | – | – | – | – | 1 | – | – |
| Hants. | 2 | – | – | – | – | – | 2 | – | 2 | 1 |
| Sussex | – | – | – | – | – | – | – | – | 1 | – |
| Kent | – | – | – | – | – | – | – | – | – | 1 |
| Norfolk | – | – | – | – | – | – | – | – | 1 | 4 |
| London | – | – | – | – | – | – | – | – | 18 | 6 |
| S. Wales | 1 | 1 | – | 1 | – | – | 1 | 2 | – | 7 |
| Scotland | – | – | 3 | – | – | – | 3 | – | 4 | – |
| Ireland | – | – | – | – | 2 | – | 2 | – | 1 | 7 |
| W. Indies | 1 | – | 2 | – | – | – | 3 | – | – | – |
| Europe | 4 | – | 1 | – | 1 | – | 6 | – | – | – |
| Madras | – | – | – | – | – | – | – | – | – | 1 |
| ? | – | – | – | – | – | 1 | – | 1 | – | 3 |
| TOTAL | 45 | 7 | 48 | 10 | 22 | 3 | 115 | 20 | 112 | 120 |

Key: L – Number of Lay students
D – Number of Divinity students
? – Unknown
MNC – The first period of Manchester College
MCY – Manchester College, York

[Source: *Roll of Students Entered at Manchester Academy 1786–1803; Manchester College, York 1803–1840* (Manchester, 1868)]

England and none from London indicates the strength of competition from Hackney College before its dissolution in 1796.

Unfortunately it is impossible to test directly the effect of the collapse of Hackney upon student admissions at Manchester College because of the gap in the list of enrolments between 1797 and 1803. At Daventry, however, admissions more than doubled following the closure of Warrington; between 1783 and 1788 lay enrolments alone were over three times higher than the average for the previous 30 years.[71] Moreover, there is evidence to suggest a number of lay students who entered Manchester College after 1796 would earlier probably have attended Hackney. Pipe-Wolferstan is known to have attended a committee meeting of Hackney College in 1794.[72] George Nicholson of London, the senior lay student when the College opened at York in 1803, also had strong connections with metropolitan dissent; indeed he had attended the school in Hackney conducted by the Rev. Joseph Pickbourne, a member of the New Gravel Pit Meeting.[73] By the early nineteenth century, when at York, the College could address prospective parents and justify general appeals for support on the basis of being the only institution open for the education of ministers and lay students on liberal principles.

The largest number of students from Manchester—over a third of the total—is little surprise. The original address had spoken of 'the great populousness of this vicinage, the opulence of the inhabitants, the number and respectability of the Dissenters', which would ensure 'both adequate support and a constant succession of pupils'.[74] On both points the promoters proved over-optimistic, but the dependence of the College upon Manchester and its neighbourhood is clear enough. Also significant was the number of students (over a fifth of the total) who were sons of the original subscribers. In addition a number of parents who patronised Manchester College had previously sent sons to Warrington.[75] Following the collapse of Warrington the north of England seemed likely to be without an academy of its own conducted on liberal principles for the first time since the early eighteenth century. The need therefore for somewhere to educate their sons was probably a major factor behind the support and encouragement parents gave the new institution as subscribers and benefactors. The promoters of Manchester College had spoken of the advantages, 'even necessity', of establishing an academy 'in this part of England'.[76]

Links with existing or former students were also important: 51 of the students (44.4 per cent.) were brothers or near relatives of other students. Family, friends and denominational contacts were an important source of advice and information. Business sources provided another important set of contacts. Manchester's position as 'one of the commercial capitals of Europe' together with its economic dominance of the surrounding region, explains the presence at the College of a number of overseas students, mainly from Europe and the West Indies, as well as the strength and support from the north-west. Hector Mortier's father, a merchant of

Lyon, 'being desirous that his son should acquire an insight into the English methods of manufacturing and of doing business, sent him over to Manchester'. And while in Manchester, Mortier spent three months at the College during the 1788 session.[77] Although not at first obvious, existing family links almost certainly account for the presence at the College of Lord Clive's grandson, William Robinson of Denston Hall, Suffolk.[78] Clive was related to the Bayley family and had spent some of his childhood in Manchester with his uncle Daniel Bayley. Bayley's second wife and widow was a benefactor of the College together with her sister, the widow (and third wife) of the Hon. George Sempill, a colonel in the East India Company, whose second wife had been a sister of Clive as well as Sempill's first cousin.[79] Two of Bayley's grandsons were students at the College between 1790 and 1792, one of whom had been named Edward Clive Bayley in honour of his famous relative.[80]

Some families, however, had no previous links with either Manchester or the College, but first heard of the institution through their connections with dissent. Pipe-Wolferstan's introduction came as a result of his membership of Essex Street Church. In addition he had heard both Barnes and Walker preach, and it is clear he particularly admired Walker's writings on parliamentary reform and slavery. But it was the excellent report of the College his Anglican friends obtained from their contacts in Manchester which finally persuaded Pipe-Wolferstan to send his son there. The prominent Liverpool merchant, William Rathbone, heard of the College in a similar manner from a subscriber. In the end, after much deliberation, Rathbone sent his son to Belsham's school at Hackney, on the basis of his personal acquaintance with Belsham and the advice of a close friend.[81] The dependence of Manchester College upon a network of existing contacts for so many of its students illustrates one of the greatest problems for any new institution—that of establishing a reputation. It is clear the College relied upon much the same connections within dissent for most of the financial support it received.

Identification of the previous links with Manchester or the College may suggest how parents came to hear of the institution, but it does little to explain why the College was chosen in preference to any of the alternatives. The only direct evidence on the factors which helped determine parental choice is provided by Pipe-Wolferstan's diary. His search was prompted by concern over the standard of his son's existing education. His approval of the curriculum offered by the College, his praise of Walker and his subsequent questioning of his son to discover his progress, is evidence of this concern. But there were other factors which helped establish the College in his estimation, some of which only became evident later when they surfaced in his diary; in particular his anxiety over discipline. Dr. Ditchfield has made it clear that Pipe-Wolferstan greatly admired the intellectual and radical ethos which the College possessed under Walker. He was 'consciously supporting a Dissenting enterprise of which he approved'.[82] But if the College's religious ethos, which under Walker was clearly radical, was a factor which attracted Pipe-Wolferstan then it almost certainly proved as powerful in alienating other parents, some of whom might previously have patronised the institution.

Earlier, Warrington's reputation for scholarship combined with its undenominational outlook had found favour with many Anglicans: they were said to form at least a third of the students during the last period of the Academy.[83] Manchester College followed Warrington in declaring the same open principles, but the political and religious situation had changed. The campaign for the repeal of the Test and Corporation Acts, together with the outbreak of the French Revolution and the loyalist reaction which followed, had served to radicalise dissent and to extend and deepen the divisions between rational dissenters and churchmen, or indeed with the rest of dissent. In February 1794 Dalton could still write that the students were 'of all religious persuasions', and up to Barnes' resignation in 1797 the College continued to educate churchmen as well as dissenters. But there is evidence to suggest that after this date it was no longer true. Pipe-Wolferstan was told by his friends in 1801 that most of the students were dissenters, and he himself noted that William Robinson was 'the only churchman at present in the College'.[84] Four of the College's 20 divinity students between 1786 and 1797 were intended for the church, and there were in addition two brothers following lay courses who subsequently took holy orders, but none of them entered the College after 1792, and two of the divinity students had had brothers or close relatives at the College previously. Considering the unfavourable times and Walker's reputation as a radical, the increasing isolation of the College is hardly surprising, and it must be a factor in explaining why Walker had only 13 students in 1801.[85]

In sending his son Stanley to Manchester College, Pipe-Wolferstan was seeking a broad liberal education which would help prepare Stanley for his future station in life. Unfortunately little is known about the factors which influenced other parents. Whereas some undoubtedly shared Pipe-Wolferstan's aims, the pattern of attendance suggests that for many students the College served a rather different purpose. Only eight of the 97 lay students, for whom evidence survives, completed the full three year course the College provided for laymen (*v.* Table 2). It is also apparent that the length of time spent at the College was related to a student's future career. Individuals proposing to enter commerce or manufacturing generally attended for a shorter period than those whose future was in one of the professions.[86] More than two-fifths of all lay students intending business careers were at the College for a year or less while none of those with professional careers in mind attended for less than a year. The rapid turnover of students and the fact that so few stayed the full course is another factor explaining the weakness of the College finances.

The actual pattern of student attendance at Manchester was clearly very different from the ideal that the set curriculum alone would suggest. This raises the crucial question as to what benefit the students gained, or indeed hoped to gain, from their period of study. Since the education received was often limited in scope and time, particularly for students seeking a career in business, it is difficult to believe they could have acquired any great core of detailed knowledge, however good the standard or content of the instruction provided. A youth of 14 or 15 hearing part of a course of lectures on logic, natural philosophy or English was not likely to emerge with a trained mind in those subjects. Nor was the education offered of practical use to business. In contrast, students preparing for the professions not only attended the College on average far longer, but the education they received could be of advantage to a professional career. For example, as a student at Warrington, Thomas Percival showed little interest in the sciences, though intended for a medical career, favouring instead classics, ethics and moral philosophy. At the age of 21 he entered Edinburgh University, and 'having hitherto cultivated with success those branches of knowledge on which a liberal profession is most advantageously grafted, he now bent his labours to the object of his future destination'. While his grandson, the banker Benjamin Heywood, since he was not destined for a profession, during his two years at Glasgow University gave little time to the classics.[87]

This is far from suggesting that a good general education could not prove valuable in developing the mind of the successful merchant or manufacturer, rather, that if assessed only in direct economic or utilitarian terms the contribution the College made appears modest. But if the reasons future businessmen attended the College were to gain an introduction to a variety of modern subjects and to acquire a feel for the latest ideas rather than any detailed sphere of knowledge, then their behaviour is much more easily explained. The shortness of the period involved, as well as the ages on entry, suggest that the College was seen to offer a brief opportunity, during the interval between school and a lifetime of business, to acquire a feeling for the latest religious and intellectual ideas. Almost any period of attendance would leave at least

TABLE 2
Length of attendance by students at Manchester College, 1786–1796

| 1786–96 | Period of attendance in years | | | | | | | | | | | | | | |
|---|---|---|---|---|---|---|---|---|---|---|---|---|---|---|---|
| | ? | $\frac{1}{4}$ | $\frac{1}{2}$ | $\frac{3}{4}$ | 1 | $1\frac{1}{4}$ | $1\frac{1}{2}$ | $1\frac{3}{4}$ | 2 | $2\frac{1}{4}$ | $2\frac{1}{2}$ | 3 | 4 | 5 | 6 |
| Commerce | 3 | 2 | 9 | 1 | 21 | 1 | 12* | 7 | 18 | | 1 | 3 | | | |
| Medicine | 1 | | | | 2 | 1 | | 1 | 4* | | 1 | 1 | | | |
| Law | 2 | | | | 2 | | 1 | | 3* | 1 | | 3 | | | |
| Liberal Professions, Etc. | 2 | | | | 1 | | | | | | | 1 | | | |
| Divinity | 3 | 1 | 1 | | 1 | | | | 1 | | | 2 | 3 | 1 | 1 |
| Church of England | 1 | | | | 1 | | | | 2 | | | | | | |

Key: ? – uncertain
* – median

[Source: *Roll of Students Entered at Manchester Academy, 1786–1803 . . .* (Manchester, 1868)]

some impression of the general intellectual and liberal ethos of the institution, whereas the acquisition of a comprehensive understanding of a particular subject was hardly feasible except as a result of a lengthy and systematic course of instruction. There seems little evidence to support Musson and Robinson's contention of the College's 'early significance as a training ground for industry and trade'.[88]

This distinctive pattern was not peculiar to Manchester College. Apart from a few exceptions where a degree was still important to a career, graduation virtually ceased at the Scottish universities after the early eighteenth century. An open class system enabled students to attend the lectures they wished on payment of the appropriate fee. Expenditure remained very largely what a student cared to make it, though costs were low and could be limited to match individual means. In complete contrast to Oxford and Cambridge, businessmen formed a significant proportion of the students attending Scottish universities, especially Glasgow. But then Glasgow was at the centre of the largest industrial region in Scotland. Manchester College was very similarly placed. Indeed, the parallels between the College and Glasgow University are striking.[89] The modest expenses involved may have contributed to this trend (though there were indirect costs like delayed earnings to consider), but the flexibility of the class system, particularly for those with only a short time in which to further their education, is likely to have been much more significant. Thus time and opportunity appear to have been major factors in helping to explain the attendance of businessmen at the College. The interval between school and work provided a period from a few months to a year or two which could be directed to a variety of interests without seriously interfering with a future career. But attendance at Manchester College or Glasgow offered intellectual benefits as well.

Recent work on the late eighteenth century has stressed the middle-class commitment to science and many historians have also noted the growing middle-class interest in education generally during this period, largely it is suggested, as a result of their rising wealth and expectations.[90] Though science has received the most attention it was by no means the only form of useful knowledge or activity patronised by the middle-classes. Depending upon the size of the town, late eighteenth-century urban society increasingly provided a range of clubs and societies. Besides the much studied literary and philosophical societies, there were political and debating clubs, music, literary and antiquarian societies, as well as a whole host of informal associations and meetings.[91] 'Middle-class scientific self-education was a strong late-Georgian fashion. The attending of lectures, reading of papers, formation of clubs and libraries among doctors, businessmen, middle-class radicals and manufacturers became a socially integrating activity.'[92] But it is not necessary to adopt a concept of 'the social legitimisation of marginal men'[93] to explain this widespread interest in science and other cultural forms. The late eighteenth-century manufacturer or professional was a man of increasing wealth and leisure for whom the acquisition of a liberal conversation and polite knowledge 'would afford a grateful recess from the bustle and attention of business' and 'provide a constant source of rational and innocent enjoyments' that 'will, in every stage and condition of life, render [him] more amiable, more useful, more happy'.[94] And those liberals attracted by Unitarian beliefs were the very group searching for the progressive values offered by Manchester College.

The only comprehensive body of evidence on the students who attended Manchester College consists of the descriptions given on enrolment which are available for the first 12 years. Though less valuable with respect to individual careers, the evidence does at least relate to the courses followed by the students and may therefore offer some clues as to the reasons why they attended the College. Over three-quarters of the laymen gave 'commerce' as their intended career, which with the declarations of another fifth, almost equally divided between law and medicine, account for virtually all the students (*v.* Table 3). Direct comparisons with Warrington are unfortunately impossible, not merely due to the differences in the type of evidence, but because for more than two-fifths of the Warrington students there are no career details whatsoever. But the evidence which is available on individual students, even if it cannot be used for comparative purposes, does suggest that many of those who

TABLE 3

Occupational destinations given by students on enrolment at Manchester College, 1786–1797

| | M | L | C | A | LP | ? | TOTAL Lay | TOTAL Divinity |
|---|---|---|---|---|---|---|---|---|
| 1786 | 3 | 1 | 2 | | | | 6 | 2a |
| 1787 | 2 | 2 | 11 | | | | 15 | 2a |
| 1788 | | 1 | 6 | | | | 7 | – |
| 1789 | 3 | 2 | 4 | | | | 10 | 3 |
| 1790 | | | 7 | | | | 7 | – |
| 1791 | | 1 | 9 | | | | 10 | 4a |
| 1792 | 1 | 1 | 7 | 2 | 1 | | 12 | 2a |
| 1793 | | 1 | 7 | | | | 8 | 2 |
| 1794 | 1 | 1 | 12 | | | | 14 | 1 |
| 1795 | | | 4 | | | | 4 | 1 |
| 1796 | 1 | 1 | 10* | | | 1 | 13 | 2 |
| 1797 | | | 10 | | | | 10 | 1 |
| | 11 | 12 | 89 | 2 | 1 | 1 | 116 | 20 |

Key: M – medicine
L – law
C – commerce/manufacturing
A – agriculture
LP – liberal professions
? – uncertain
a – includes divinity student who took Anglican orders
* – Benjamin Gaskell, though not recorded on the College roll, was a student during 1796 and part of 1797

[Source: *Roll of Students Entered at Manchester Academy, 1786–1803* . . . (Manchester, 1868)]

attended the earlier academy were drawn from a rather different and socially superior background.

The Warrington alumni included a dozen or so individuals who either possessed titles or were of landed gentry status, notably two peers, and sons of three MPs, the brother of an Irish Chancellor of the Exchequer, three baronets and three knights, while those who followed business careers included some of the leading merchants and manufacturers of the period, particularly in provincial banking and overseas trade.[95] One of the earliest students at the academy was Robert Denison (1758) of Nottingham later a leading merchant and factory owner.[96] From Manchester came Daniel Gaskell (1761), father of the MP Benjamin Gaskell; Thomas Potter (1761); Thomas and Robert Robinson (1771 & 1772); Gilbert Kennedy (1773); William Rigby (1779); and the West Indies merchants Robert and Samuel Hibbert (1764): all, incidentally, supporters of Manchester College. The Liverpool students included Samuel Aspinwall (1761), the early patron and partner of Roscoe. There were also representatives of the great Leeds merchant families: Sir James Ibbertson (1763), baronet, and his brother-in-law James Fenton (1769), Milnes Rayner (1765) and Fenton's cousin, the merchant and extensive coalowner William Fenton (1769),[97] and from nearby Wakefield, John Milnes (1764) who, like his father before him, was one of the greatest of the West Riding merchants.[98] Other prominent merchant families included the Cooksons of Newcastle-upon-Tyne; the Brailsfords, Garlicks and Sedgleys of Bristol; and the Luards, Smalleys and Vaughans of London. But it was in banking in particular that students from Warrington became so prominent. The Heywood dynasty, the brothers Richard (1765), Benjamin (1765) and Arthur (1768) and their first cousins, Benjamin Arthur (1769) and Nathaniel (1774), controlled a banking empire which covered Liverpool, Manchester and Wakefield. In addition a brother from each family, Samuel ('Serjeant') Heywood (1768) and his cousin John Pemberton Heywood (1772) were to have highly successful careers as barristers.[99] The other bankers were Joseph Robinson (1764), a brother of the Manchester merchants Thomas and Robert Robinson, who moved to Hull and took the name of Pease; Samuel Crompton (1765) of Derby and York; John Rhodes (1772) of Halifax; Samuel Shore (1778) of Sheffield; John Bright (1769) of Bristol; Nathaniel Brassey (1768) of London; and John Wedgwood (1782), eldest son of the eminent potter. Warrington students were also to distinguish themselves in the leading professions, especially medicine and the law, and some of the most outstanding ministers of the next generation were among the few divinity students educated at the Academy.[100]

The students educated at Manchester College during the first period, while not lacking men who subsequently distinguished themselves, were an altogether more modest and anonymous group of individuals. There were no sons of peers, no knights or baronets, and those landed families whose sons did attend the College were distinguished by their links with dissent rather than by their political or family connections.[101] Provincial bankers and overseas merchants, so prominent at Warrington, were almost entirely absent. Nor were any of the great leaders of industry, found patronising the College during the York period, represented. The few leading businessmen who did send their sons to the College were prominent in the commercial life of Manchester: the various branches of the Bayley and Potter families;[102] Benjamin (1796) the son of Daniel Gaskell; the two sons (1796 & 1797) of the Manchester merchant Samuel Hibbert;[103] John Touchet (1787) whose father was College Treasurer; and John Ashton Yates (1795), the son of the minister of Paradise Street Chapel, Liverpool. Gaskell and Yates both became MPs, representing Maldon (1806–7 & 1812–26) and Carlow County (1837–41) respectively.[104] But even these figures cannot compare with the great merchants and manufacturers educated at Warrington.

The alumni of Manchester College were to gain their distinction in the field of medicine and science rather than in business or law. Historians have noted the close connections between the College, Cross Street Chapel and the Manchester Literary & Philosophical Society.[105] The tutors, Barnes, Harrison, Dalton, Johns and Walker, all played prominent roles in founding the Literary & Philosophical Society or in its subsequent progress, and among the students later active as members were Edward Holme (1787), the last student to graduate MD (1793) from Leyden, and John Moore (1791), both of whom were President (and likewise Presidents of the Manchester Natural History Society), and the celebrated chemist William Henry (1787). While Samuel Hibbert (1796), later Hibbert-Ware, gained fame as a geologist and antiquarian, and the radical Dr. John Thomson (?1799), a divinity student at the College, subsequently studied medicine at Edinburgh University, where during the session of 1806–7 he was President of the student Royal Medical Society.[106] None of the ministers educated at the College were to become outstanding figures in the ministry, though Edward Higginson (1795) is remembered as Martineau's father-in-law. Charles Wellbeloved, William Shepherd, Jeremiah Joyce, William Hincks sen., John Corrie and John Kentish were all students at Hackney.[107] The one outstanding divinity student at Manchester—Lewis Loyd (1789)—distinguished himself in business not the ministry, and he was a student at the College for only 15 weeks, though the marriage which proved so crucial to his career was a result of the contacts he developed while serving as classics tutor (1790–92).[108]

For the majority of students no additional information has been discovered beyond that provided on enrolment. This suggests not only that they failed to distinguish themselves in their subsequent careers, but that they came from more modest backgrounds than the students for whom further details are available; though in the absence of any evidence such deductions need to be treated with caution. Students who came to the College from a distance were probably from families of substance; the cost of travel, board and lodgings alone are likely to have ensured that. But it may not have been the case for students drawn from the neighbourhood of Manchester. The cost of accommodation and board, always the largest expense, was avoided by those who lived at home. It has generally been accepted by historians that cost largely limited student attendance, although those who could not afford the fees for a three-year lay course were unlikely to have been interested in such an extensive course of education anyway.[109] The annual fees were advertised in 1786 at three guineas per lecture course, with languages, writing and commercial subjects extra. No figure was given for board and accommodation, though in October 1795 it was advanced to 30 guineas.[110] Room and board were clearly the main expense, the cost and system of course fees being very similar to those at Glasgow University.[111] Compared with the two English universities, or even Hackney, these sums were modest. In 1788, charges for Hackney were advertised at 60 guineas inclusive of apartment, board and tuition, while at Oxford and Cambridge the costs after 1800 were often more than £200.[112] More recently it has been pointed out that the expense of an education at Manchester College, because of the extras, could considerably exceed the advertised figures. Pipe-Wolferstan paid Walker £137 13s. 4d. for the academic year 1801–2. This sum included the cash and extras for which Pipe-Wolferstan strongly objected having to pay, but the figure of £72 19s. 6d. for tuition, board, accommodation, library and chapel pew rent was little different from the terms advertised in 1800.[113] Even so this was clearly beyond the means of all except the wealthiest parents. What does not appear to have been realised, the costs for out-students (which did not include board or lodging) could be quite modest. In February 1794 Dalton mentioned a figure of 40 guineas for students living in College but only 12 guineas for those residing out.[114] Costs would have been even lower if only part of a lecture course or session was attended. These sums compare very favourably with Glasgow and Edinburgh, particularly as they exclude the expense of travelling to Scotland.[115]

It was therefore possible for poorer students to attend the College. Unfortunately, what is less clear is how many in fact did so. But the intentions of the College are clear enough. Barnes, in his opening address, spoke of the 'great importance to the cause' that a number of academies should exist at the same time in different parts of England so that they might bring a liberal education 'within the reach of many, by whom such advantages could not otherwise have been enjoyed', and the committee declared in September 1799 that 'it is one general object of this establishment to afford the benefits of a liberal education on such easy terms, as to bring them within the reach of those who possess only moderate fortunes'.[116] In contrast, Hugh Worthington jun. in a sermon to the supporters of the institution declared that Hackney was designed 'for those persons among the laity . . . who by their patrimony, or their prospects, are raised far above the lower walks of life'.[117] The situation at Manchester, however, rapidly changed because of the continued deterioration of the College's finances. In May 1800, following the resignation of Johns and Dalton, the committee allowed Walker to make his own private arrangements for lay students as long as they did not interfere with his official duties as theological tutor.[118] Stanley Pipe-Wolferstan and presumably William Robinson and the others, attended the College in effect as Walker's private pupils. With the exception of the rent for Stanley's room, Pipe-Wolferstan paid Walker, not the trustees.[119]

The promoters of Manchester College, in seeking to provide a replacement for Warrington, adopted the same principles and design as the earlier institution. Despite these intentions and the intimacy of the connections with the former academy, competition from Hackney, the hardening of the existing religious and political divisions, together with the location of the new institution at Manchester ensured that the development and character of the College was in many ways radically different from its predecessor. If Warrington can be compared with Oxford and Cambridge in student background, educational objectives and even discipline, then in many ways the analogy for the first period of Manchester College is with Glasgow University. In respect of fees, opportunities and access, the high proportion of future businessmen, the localism of student origins and the level of industrialisation of the region, both institutions exhibit striking similarities. In contrast, Hackney was much closer to the Warrington pattern, setting out to provide an education for the sons of leading dissenting families, and the fees and financial support the College received were in line with that objective. Despite the wealth within rational dissent it is evident there were insufficient resources and interest to support two establishments on the same ambitious plan as Warrington. Fortunately, Manchester College was uniquely placed to educate the sons of middle-class businessmen. The town as the focus of a great industrial region had a considerable locational advantage over Warrington, while the College, from the flexibility of its fees and courses, was much better placed to educate students of only modest means than Hackney. But with the closure of Hackney and the move to York, away from the centre of a great industrial region, the character of the College was to change and become much closer to the traditional Warrington pattern in student background and the type of education provided.

## V

During the years the college was at York (1803–40), Lancashire was still the largest single source of lay students, but only accounting for just over a quarter of all admissions compared with three-fifths during the first Manchester period (*v.* Table 4). Over two-thirds of all lay students were still from the North and the Midlands, though their share had fallen from four-fifths. The wider geographical coverage the College enjoyed while at York only serves to confirm the seriousness of the competition from Hackney College before its demise in 1796. London, having sent no students to Manchester, was the second largest source for the period after 1803, providing just under a sixth of all lay admissions. Altogether more than a quarter of the lay admissions at York came from London and the South.[120]

Despite the wider geographical coverage and the absence of any serious competition from rival nonconformist institutions, the number of lay students was low, only 112 in 37 years, under a third of the annual level of admissions at Manchester and less than a quarter of the average for Warrington.[121] The majority came from the great manufacturing and commercial centres of the country—London, the district around Manchester, the industrial Midlands and the West Riding of Yorkshire—which formed the main strongholds of nineteenth-century Unitarianism. The importance of such connections becomes even clearer if the older centres of dissent are examined. Exeter and Norwich each sent only a single lay student. Both cities were experiencing severe economic difficulties, in particular Norwich where, significantly, the only lay student came from a professional not a manufacturing background. In addition, there were few lay students from outside England; only four from Scotland, one from Ireland and none from Wales. The only student not from the British Isles attended a divinity course in the mid-1830s.[122] The virtual absence of overseas students contrasts markedly with the earlier periods at Manchester and Warrington. Divinity students, however, both socially and geographically, came from a much more diverse background than their lay contemporaries, partly as for much of the period the College was the only institution available for the training of Unitarian ministers, but also because the exhibitions available to ministerial candidates removed the financial obstacles poorer students otherwise faced. Although Lancashire and the West Riding provided over a quarter of the divinity students, Ireland and Wales, both comparatively poor areas, each sent seven students. Few Welshmen, other than candidates for the ministry, had the opportunity to attend a college, and the same was almost certainly true of Ireland.[123]

The great majority of the students who had attended the College during the first 12 years at Manchester were laymen, despite attempts by the trustees to encourage ministerial candidates. In contrast, at York there were slightly more divinity than lay students—123 out of a total of 235. The balance had altered in part because divinity admissions had doubled, but also because of the decline in lay admissions to only a third of the previous level. These changes are explained by a variety of factors. The appointment of Wellbeloved as theological tutor together with the move to York had led to a major change in emphasis. Wellbeloved saw the preparation of students for the ministry as the main function of the College. The plan of studies, therefore, consisted of a five-year divinity course of which the first three years were intended also to offer a comprehensive liberal education to the sons of wealthy laymen.[124] But an expensive liberal education only appealed to a limited number of parents. In addition, other changes which resulted from the move to York also meant the College no longer met the needs of those families of only modest fortunes, who had provided so many of the lay students at

TABLE 4

Geographical origins of students attending Manchester College, York 1803–37

| | 1803–7 | | 1808–12 | | 1813–17 | | 1818–22 | | 1823–27 | | 1828–32 | | 1833–37 | | STUDENT TOTALS MCY 1803–37 | | MNC 1786–97 | |
|---|---|---|---|---|---|---|---|---|---|---|---|---|---|---|---|---|---|---|
| | L | D | L | D | L | D | L | D | L | D | L | D | L | D | L | D | L | D |
| Lancs. | 5 | 1 | 4 | 4 | 8 | 5 | 4 | 1 | 3 | 3 | 3 | 4 | 2 | 2 | 29 | 20 | 68 | 6 |
| W. Riding | – | 3 | – | 2 | 2 | 2 | 3 | 1 | 1 | 2 | 2 | 2 | 1 | 3 | 9 | 15 | 2 | – |
| N. Riding | – | – | 1 | – | – | 1 | – | – | – | 1 | – | 2 | – | 2 | 1 | 6 | – | – |
| E. Riding | – | – | 2 | – | – | – | – | 1 | – | – | – | – | – | – | 2 | 1 | 2 | – |
| Derbys. | 1 | 1 | 2 | – | 2 | – | – | – | – | 1 | – | 1 | 1 | – | 6 | 3 | – | 1 |
| Ches. | – | – | 2 | 1 | – | 1 | – | – | 4 | 1 | – | – | – | – | 6 | 3 | 6 | 1 |
| Staffs. | – | – | – | – | 1 | – | – | – | – | – | – | – | – | – | 1 | – | 2 | – |
| Cumbld. | – | – | – | – | 1 | – | – | – | – | – | – | – | – | – | 1 | – | 3 | 2 |
| Westmld. | – | – | – | – | – | – | – | – | – | 1 | 1 | – | – | – | 1 | 1 | 7 | – |
| Nthbld. | – | 1 | 1 | 1 | 2 | – | – | 1 | – | – | – | – | – | – | 3 | 3 | 1 | 1 |
| Durham | – | – | – | – | – | – | – | 1 | – | – | – | – | – | – | – | 1 | – | – |
| Lincs. | – | – | – | 1 | – | 1 | – | – | – | – | – | – | – | – | – | 2 | – | – |
| Notts. | – | – | – | – | 2 | 1 | 1 | – | 1 | – | 1 | 1 | – | – | 5 | 2 | 4 | 2 |
| Leics. | – | – | – | – | – | – | – | 1 | 5 | – | 1 | 1 | – | – | 6 | 2 | – | 2 |
| Warws. | 1 | – | 1 | – | 1 | – | 1 | 4 | – | 1 | – | 2 | – | – | 4 | 7 | – | – |
| Worcs. | 1 | – | – | 1 | – | 1 | 1 | – | – | 2 | – | – | – | 1 | 2 | 5 | – | – |

Geographical origins of students attending Manchester College, York 1803–37 (continued)

| | | | | | | | | | | | | | | | | | | |
|---|---|---|---|---|---|---|---|---|---|---|---|---|---|---|---|---|---|---|
| NORTH & MIDLANDS | 8 | 6 | 13 | 10 | 19 | 12 | 10 | 10 | 14 | 12 | 8 | 13 | 4 | 8 | 76 | 71 | 95 | 15 |
| Glos. | – | – | – | – | – | – | – | 1 | 1 | 3 | – | – | – | 2 | 1 | 6 | 1 | – |
| Somerset | 1 | – | 1 | – | 2 | 1 | – | 2 | – | 1 | – | – | 1 | – | 5 | 4 | 1 | 1 |
| Devon | – | 1 | – | 2 | – | 2 | 1 | 1 | – | – | – | 1 | – | 1 | 1 | 8 | – | – |
| Herts. | – | – | – | – | 1 | – | 1 | – | – | 1 | – | – | – | – | 2 | 1 | 1 | – |
| Berks. | – | – | – | – | – | – | – | – | – | – | – | – | – | – | – | – | – | 1 |
| Hants. | – | – | 1 | – | – | – | 1 | 1 | – | – | – | – | – | – | 2 | 1 | 2 | – |
| Sussex | 1 | – | – | – | – | – | – | – | – | – | – | – | – | – | 1 | – | – | – |
| Kent | – | – | – | – | – | – | – | – | – | – | – | – | – | 1 | – | 1 | – | – |
| Norfolk | – | 1 | – | – | 1 | 1 | – | 2 | – | – | – | – | – | – | 1 | 4 | – | – |
| London | 1 | – | 1 | 1 | 5 | – | 5 | 2 | 5 | 2 | 1 | – | – | 1 | 18 | 6 | – | – |
| S. Wales | – | 4 | – | 1 | – | 1 | – | 1 | – | – | – | – | – | – | – | 7 | 1 | 2 |
| Scotland | – | – | 3 | – | 1 | – | – | – | – | – | – | – | – | – | 4 | – | 3 | – |
| Ireland | – | – | – | 2 | – | – | 1 | – | – | 1 | – | 3 | – | 1 | 1 | 7 | 2 | – |
| W. Indies | – | – | – | – | – | – | – | – | – | – | – | – | – | – | – | – | 3 | – |
| Europe | – | – | – | – | – | – | – | – | – | – | – | – | – | – | – | – | 6 | – |
| Madras | – | – | – | – | – | – | – | – | – | – | – | – | – | 1 | – | 1 | – | – |
| ? | – | 2 | – | – | – | – | – | – | – | 1 | – | – | – | – | – | 3 | – | 1 |
| TOTAL | 11 | 14 | 19 | 16 | 29 | 17 | 19 | 20 | 20 | 21 | 9 | 17 | 5 | 15 | 112 | 120 | 115 | 20 |

Key: L – number of lay students; D – number of divinity students; ? – unknown; MNC – the first period of Manchester College; MCY – Manchester College, York.
The three divinity students who entered the College in 1838 are not included in this table.

[Source: *Roll of Students Entered at Manchester Academy 1786–1803; Manchester College, York 1803–1840* . . . (Manchester, 1868)]

Manchester. It was no longer possible to obtain a relatively inexpensive education at the College. Moreover, parents now had to meet the costs of travel as well as board and lodging. Nor was it possible for lay students to attend a part of a session or only those lectures of particular interest, since the course of instruction offered at York was intended to be comprehensive and complete, and one that required constant effort and attendance over the whole year.[125] Naturally, these changes in the character and purpose of the institution were reflected in the background and type of student who attended the College.

The lay students educated at York were a much more socially exclusive group than their predecessors at Manchester. This exclusiveness is important in explaining the small number of laymen educated during the later period. In many respects the College after 1803 represents a return to the tradition of Warrington in providing a comprehensive liberal education for the sons of wealthy dissenters, in contrast to the more general educational opportunities available during most of the first Manchester period. There were, however, important contrasts with Warrington. The earlier institution largely succeeded in living up to its claim of being undenominational and the students it educated were distinguished by the high proportion from wealthy merchant or landed backgrounds. In contrast, the lay students at York were almost exclusively Unitarian and from prominent industrial and professional families. In many respects these differences in student background represent the changing character and isolation of rational dissent from mainstream orthodoxy, as well as the new industrial wealth to be found within Unitarianism.

Historians have previously noted that the list of those educated at York included the names of prominent Unitarian families who were amongst the great industrial leaders of the period.[126] This is an impression confirmed by a detailed examination of the evidence. The Strutt, Marsland, Houldsworth and McConnel families alone represented four of the largest cotton-spinning firms of the early nineteenth century, to whom should be added Samuel Ashton of Stockport, whose son was a divinity student on his own foundation, and the son of the radical factory owner John Fielden of Todmorden. Manchester merchants and manufacturers, though no longer so dominant, were still well represented. James Darbishire, John and Robert Philips and John's brother-in-law, Thomas Robinson, together with Thomas Potter, Jeremiah Withington and G. W. Wood, all had sons at York. Some of Liverpool's leading merchant families—the Boltons, Fletchers and Lightbodys—also patronised the institution. Parents from other branches of the textile industry included Thomas Benyon, one time partner of the great Leeds flax-spinner John Marshall, and the Paget brothers, John and William, hosiery manufacturers of Loughborough and their eldest brother Thomas, the Leicester surgeon.[127] The other major growth sector in the nineteenth century, the iron industry, was also well represented. Joseph Dawson of Royds Hall near Bradford, the grandson of the original proprietor of the celebrated Low Moor Ironworks, was a lay student, together with Archibald

Kenrick, son of the Birmingham ironfounder, and William Needham, whose father, the Nottingham ironmaster, was the brother-in-law of Robert Philips. Henry Houldsworth, the leading early nineteenth-century cotton spinner, gradually gave up his interests in spinning to concentrate on the more promising iron industry. In 1839 he opened a large ironworks at Coltness where his eldest son, educated at York, became manager. In addition, James Milnes Stansfeld of Flockton near Bradford, who was a student at the College in the early 1830s, belonged to the prominent West Riding coal and landowning family. Parents active in trade and commerce included the bankers Francis Hart of Nottingham and Samuel Shore of Sheffield, the drysalter and active London Unitarian, John Christie, together with Joshua Godman of Chichester and John Martineau of London, partners in Whitbread's brewery.

While historians have been quick to recognise that the College educated the sons of some of the leading industrialists of the period, the high proportion of students who chose a professional career has been largely ignored. It is clear the pattern had shifted significantly since the Manchester years and that slightly more students followed a professional than a business career. Over three-quarters of the lay students at Manchester gave commerce as their intended calling, compared with just under two-fifths at York (see Tables 3 and 5). The growth in professional careers was largely the result of the higher numbers entering the law. More than a quarter of the lay students compared with only a tenth at Manchester. A number clearly came from prominent legal families. Thomas Lee, the Birmingham attorney, sent three sons; likewise Henry Enfield, the Town Clerk of Nottingham, and the barrister John Pemberton Heywood of Wakefield. Heywood's second son and namesake entered the family bank, but the other two sons became barristers. But many of those educated at York who entered the law came from families engaged in manufacturing or trade. While industrialists were prominent as parents, it is clear that a higher proportion of students entered the professions, and they included the sons of many industrialists and businessmen. William Smith, the radical Unitarian MP, had made his fortune in the wholesale grocery trade, but his son Samuel, educated at York, entered the bar, though probably because his father was by then in serious financial difficulties. John Marshall was the son of a member of Lloyds. The Carter family of Portsmouth had acquired their wealth from brewing and distilling. The father of John Woodhouse Crompton had been a partner with John and William Parkes of Warwick in one of the earliest and most important worsted spinning mills in the Midlands. A number of lay students were to gain a considerable reputation at the bar, of whom undoubtedly the most distinguished was James Carter of Portsmouth, Wellbeloved's son-in-law, who became Chief Justice of New Brunswick (1851–65) and received a knighthood in 1859. George Thomas Nicholson of Waverley Abbey, the senior student in 1803, was High Sheriff for Surrey in 1832, and subsequently Chairman of the Quarter Sessions and Vice-Lieutenant for the County.

TABLE 5
Careers followed by lay students educated at Manchester College, York, 1803–1840

| | M | L | C | LD | Ag | P | ? | TOTAL Lay | TOTAL Divinity |
|---|---|---|---|---|---|---|---|---|---|
| 1803 | | 1 | 2 | | | a | | 4 | 4 |
| 1804 | | | | 1 | | | | 1 | – |
| 1805 | | 2 | 1 | | | | | 3 | 6 |
| 1806 | | | 1 | | | | | 1 | 4 |
| 1807 | | | 2 | | | | | 2 | – |
| 1808 | 1 | 1 | | | | A | | 3 | 1 |
| 1809 | | | 3 | | | a | | 4 | 6 |
| 1810 | | 1 | 1 | | 1 | A | | 4 | 5 |
| 1811 | | 1 | 4 | | | | | 5 | 1 |
| 1812 | | | 1 | | 1 | J | | 3 | 3 |
| 1813 | | | 2 | | | | d | 3 | 1 |
| 1814 | | 1 | 1 | | | | | 2 | 3 |
| 1815 | | 2 | 6 | | 1 | | | 9 | 3 |
| 1816 | 3 | 2 | 3 | | | a | | 9 | 7 |
| 1817 | 1 | 4 | 1 | | | | | 6 | 3 |
| 1818 | | | 1 | 1 | | | | 2 | 2 |
| 1819 | | 2 | 3 | | | A | | 6 | 1 |
| 1820 | | 2 | | | | | 1 | 3 | 4 |
| 1821 | | 1 | 2 | | | | | 3 | 8 |
| 1822 | 1 | 3 | 1 | | | | | 5 | 5 |
| 1823 | | 2 | 1 | | 1 | S | 1 | 6 | 5 |
| 1824 | | | 1 | | | M(2) | 1 | 4 | 3 |
| 1825 | | 3 | 1 | | | | d | 5 | 2 |
| 1826 | | | 1 | | 2 | C | | 4 | 6 |
| 1827 | | 1 | | | | | | 1 | 5 |
| 1828 | | | | | | | | – | 5 |
| 1829 | | | 1 | | | | | 1 | 3 |
| 1830 | | | 1 | | | | 1 | 2 | 1 |
| 1831 | | 1 | 2 | | | | | 3 | 4 |
| 1832 | | 1 | 2 | | | | 1 | 3 | 4 |
| 1833 | | 1 | | | | | | 2 | 6 |
| 1834 | | | 1 | | | | | 1 | 3 |
| 1835 | | | | | | E | | 1 | 2 |
| 1836 | | | | | | | 1 | 1 | 2 |
| 1837 | | | | | | | | – | 2 |
| 1838 | | | | | | | | – | 3 |
| 1839 | | | | | | | | – | – |
| | 6 | 32 | 46 | 2 | 6 | 12 | 8 | 112 | 123 |

Key:
- M – Medicine
- L – Law
- C – Commerce/manufacturing
- LD – Landed
- Ag – Agriculture
- P – Miscellaneous professions
- ? – Uncertain
- d – Died young
- a – subsequently took holy orders
- A – entered the Army
- J – Journalist
- C – Civil Servant
- M(2) – Mining engineer (two)
- E – Engineer
- S – Schoolmaster

The three students who changed from the lay to the divinity course have been included in the divinity total.

[Source: *Roll of Students Entered at Manchester Academy 1786–1803; Manchester College, York, 1803–1840 . . . (Manchester, 1868)*]

The reasons for the movement away from careers in business in favour of the professions are interesting. It is clear that the legal profession had become an increasingly attractive proposition to many wealthy parents patronising the College. Law not only represented the greatest and most prestigious of the professions, and therefore offered a suitable career to young men of wealth and ambition, but it also provided openings for younger sons who could not be accommodated within the family firm. Reasons of prestige may also explain why law was preferred to medicine; the numbers entering the latter were very small by comparison. But the difficult and uncertain economic conditions experienced by business in the decades following the Napoleonic War undoubtedly made the professions generally a more attractive proposition to parents.

## VI

An assessment of the College's contribution at York to the education of laymen is far from easy. The achievements of its alumni in later life were certainly impressive. Former students continued to figure prominently in the industrial leadership of the period, others enjoyed highly successful legal careers, while a number were to distinguish themselves in politics. The York alumni included three MPs, of whom Edward Strutt, after a notable political career, was created Baron Belper in 1856; the father of another was offered a baronetcy (which was declined); and a further three students received knighthoods. In addition, as a result of their wealth and standing in local society, many former students were to play an active part in social and political reform and to take their place amongst the Victorian elite as deputy lieutenants, high sheriffs, and justices of the peace. In terms of individual careers, York alumni enjoyed particular success at law, with a host of Queen's Counsels and two colonial Chief Justices. Mrs Watts in her study has shown that the College at York, by providing lay students with an education which was intended to be especially relevant to future involvement in public life, aimed at producing enlightened, progressive and liberal young men capable of supplying the next generation's leadership. The tutors therefore saw the encouragement of public speaking and the teaching of particular subjects, such as science, mathematics and political economy, as especially important.[128] Certainly it is clear the College did not offer a business education. Even the first Manchester period, which was probably closest to the historian's ideal of the nonconformist academy educating businessmen, taught a broadly based curriculum. At the very least the College at York gave the sons of prominent Unitarian families an education suited to their wealth and social position, but it is also evident that in many cases the College played a more positive role in developing the mind, intellect and tastes of individual students.[129]

It is not possible, however, to claim a direct link between the education the College offered to lay students and their subsequent achievements.

Success in life is strongly linked to wealth, family background and personal ability, and the lay students who attended York clearly had many of the advantages of birth which favour economic and political distinction. More reliable evidence of the value of a York education is available, at least for a professional career. A significant proportion of the divinity students failed to enter the ministry and followed secular careers instead, and since, with one or two exceptions, they possessed none of the advantages of birth or education their lay contemporaries enjoyed, the College can be held responsible for a greater part of their learning and improvement. A number of those who turned to the law were particularly successful. Thomas Baker served a year as minister at Sidmouth before settling at Manchester in 1835, where he practised as a solicitor. He was subsequently Mayor of Manchester (1880–82) receiving a knighthood in 1883. But the most successful was undoubtedly John Smale who, like Sir James Carter, had an outstanding career in the colonial legal service. He was attorney-general (1861–66), later Chief Justice (1866–81) of Hong Kong, receiving a knighthood in 1874.[130] Other divinity students successfully followed more traditional alternatives to the ministry in medicine and teaching. During the first period of the College at Manchester, where a higher proportion of the lay students were from relatively modest backgrounds, it may also be reasonable to conclude that the notable achievements of the alumni in the scientific world reflects the scholarship of their former tutors in that field. But some students could make a success of neither the ministry nor a secular occupation, and they provide a reminder that a successful career in any field depends upon individual ability.

Any attempt to assess the contribution and influence of the College at York must take account of the small number of students involved. In nearly four decades the College only educated 112 laymen. The type of education the College offered was only of interest to wealthy parents who, because of the religious divisions of the period, were nearly all Unitarians. When it is appreciated how restricted the potential source of lay students had become, it is little surprise that the numbers attending the College were so low. Since the parents who could afford to send their sons to York were not bound by financial considerations, why did they choose the College in preference to one of the many alternatives available? Value for money and the excellence of the education offered were clearly important considerations. Existing ties with the College, not least denominational ones, were also significant. It is noticeable how many lay students had earlier attended private schools conducted by Unitarian ministers, undoubtedly an important source of recommendations to the College.[131] In addition, over a third of the lay students educated at York were brothers, and another fifth were cousins. Altogether at least 57 lay students, half the total, were related to other students or to one of the tutors. Though this indicates the closeness of the family ties within the Unitarian movement, it also illustrates the major problem for the College—just how few families sent their sons to York.

The failure of the College to find sufficient numbers of lay students must call into question the appropriateness of the type of education it provided. The highest number of students (lay and divinity) in any one year was 31 in 1816–17, yet the new College buildings were purchased in 1812 with the intention of providing accommodation for up to 40.[132] Moreover, it is clear that student numbers had peaked before the mid-1820s. Half the laymen educated at York had entered by 1817 and more than three-quarters by 1824. The virtual disappearance of lay students in the late 1830s was a major factor in the decision of the College to return to Manchester in 1840. The College was hardly more successful in attracting support for its comprehensive plan of education. It could not persuade those lay students who did attend to follow the full three-year course: over half the students only attended for two years, and under a quarter completed the full three-year course as planned. Similar questions must also be asked about the education of ministerial candidates—the main function of the College. The high standards of scholarship at York and the attempt to provide as comprehensive a course of study as possible are widely recognised, but the question arises as to whether the education actually produced the type of minister most needed, or made the best use of the available resources. Not all the students who entered the College had the ability or basic education to benefit from the demanding level of instruction provided.[133] More seriously, while the solid learning imparted in the five-year divinity course at York answered the demands of wealthy urban congregations for a scholarly ministry, it took little account of the emergence of a newer form of Unitarianism which sought to address a poorer and socially more isolated audience through popular preaching. For such congregations a highly educated minister was entirely inappropriate, besides being quite beyond their means to support. Even the leading congregations experienced increasing difficulties in finding the salary a well educated minister might reasonably expect in view of his qualifications and talents. Except for the brief period covered by Aspland's Unitarian College at Hackney, the needs of the poorer congregations went largely unmet until the Unitarian Home Missionary Board opened in 1854.[134] Of course it is true that the College officers and leading supporters belonged to the group most anxious to provide a broad liberal education for ministers and the sons of wealthy laymen.

However questionable the educational objectives of the College at York might seem in the light of wider denominational needs, there is little doubt that the greatest contribution the College made to lay education was in sustaining the tradition of an educated ministry to meet the demands of the most influential section within the Unitarian movement, and in providing a lay education for wealthy Unitarian parents unwilling to expose their sons to dangers of the English universities or the risks of travelling abroad to Scotland and the continent. Dr. Seed has pointed out the serious dilemma that many wealthy Unitarians faced in deciding how to educate their sons without endangering the family's religious attachment.[135] After the closure of Hackney, Manchester College was alone in the type of education it offered. Whereas the College at Manchester had educated, by inclination as well as by force of circumstances, a broader social range of lay students including individuals of quite modest origins, the lay students at York were quite unrepresentative of Unitarianism or indeed of dissent generally: therein lies the significance of the College during the latter period. Despite the small numbers involved, the College educated many of those who were later to provide the main leadership, both ministerial and lay, within Unitarianism, and in that respect the College fulfilled the aspirations of its tutors and officers.

## VII

The support the College achieved in 1786 can be seen as part of a general commitment to liberal causes, but by the early nineteenth century, largely as a result of the growing divisions within dissent, a clearer identification with Unitarianism is evident. If liberal interests and connections are a central factor explaining the public support for the institution, then in turn the College acted as a focus for these ideals and principles since both rational dissent and Unitarianism lacked any formal denominational organisation of their own. It is clear the College gave individuals a rare opportunity to identify with, and, by means of a subscription, to give material expression to their support for the liberal and rational ideals the College embodied. By the early nineteenth century no other institution provided such an opportunity, hence the bewilderment, even anger, of many potential supporters when the College at York, in its desire to uphold the broader tradition which characterised rational dissent, denied a clear identification with Unitarianism.

But a study of Manchester College is also of wider value to the historian. The absence of any formal denominational organisation makes a general study of rational dissent very difficult. Analysis of student enrolments and the subscription lists of the College can reveal much concerning the strengths and weaknesses of rational dissent and about the development of early nineteenth-century Unitarianism. While it is true that rational dissent could claim individuals and families of great wealth and substance, who were generous in their support and patronage of the College, a more realistic assessment also notes the small numbers involved. The limitations are most apparent during those periods when rival institutions were competing for support. After the collapse of Hackney, Manchester College was able to widen its appeal to the country as a whole on the basis of being the only institution available for the education of ministers and lay students on liberal principles. Yet it is clear the officers still had great difficulty in raising the sums they needed. Despite improving the level of subscriptions nearly five-fold during the first two decades at York, the treasurer never succeeded in increasing the total much beyond £700 a year. Once subscriptions had reached a realistic figure the main concern was with maintaining that level. Local collectors frequently wrote of the difficulties they faced in finding new subscribers and each year the committee was disappointed that so few congregations made a collection on behalf of the institution.[136] Similarly the number of families with the resources sympathetic to the educational aims and ethos of the College was very small. Early nineteenth-century Unitarianism benefited from a very real increase in industrial wealth, but in the aftermath of the French Revolution there had been a significant loss of support. Since rational dissent and Unitarianism provided most of the finance for the College, the surviving subscription lists can be used to identify their main centres as well as the names of individual supporters. A study of the lay support for the College therefore shows the growing dependence of nineteenth-century Unitarianism upon the industrial towns of the Midlands and the north at the expense of earlier centres of rational dissent like Norwich, Exeter and Bristol, as well as the continued significance of London, the greatest concentration of wealth and dissent in the country.

There can be no doubt of the College's dependence throughout its history upon lay support for its existence and survival. Lay benefactors were responsible for establishing the original institution at Manchester in 1786, and for the later benefactions at York, Manchester, London and Oxford. The collapse of Warrington and Hackney make clear the consequences of a withdrawal of support. A series of financial crises very nearly closed the early College at Manchester on a number of occasions, and the problems remained unresolved at York until a successful appeal for additional lay support brought a 'considerable vigour and animation to an almost forlorn and expiring hope'.[137] It was the interest and involvement of a small group of families, the same families who provided much of the support for early nineteenth-century Unitarianism, that saved the College from impending collapse and helped to place the institution on a more secure footing after 1812. It was their benefactions that helped to establish a permanent fund, so essential to the financial stability of the College, and which enabled the trustees to appoint a third tutor in 1810 and to purchase the York buildings. The same group of families provided most of the College officers and committee and many of the lay students who later distinguished themselves in public life. It is clear that without their support the College could not have survived. But the College also depended upon annual subscriptions, and to a lesser extent on congregational collections, to provide the exhibitions for divinity students, the tutors' salaries, and to meet the ordinary expenditure of the College. No independent educational institution, unless exceptionally endowed by past (lay) generosity, can survive without outside financial support, any more than it can exist without students.

## NOTES

1. I am most grateful to the staff of Manchester College for all their hospitality and help, in particular to Mrs. Barbara Smith and her assistants in the Library. Two of my fellow contributors, Dr. Grayson Ditchfield and Mrs. Ruth Watts, have been good enough to read this essay at various stages and to give me the benefit of their knowledge of other aspects of the College's history. I wish also to thank Mr. Rupert Evans and Dr. Aubrey Newman, both of Leicester University, for their interest and encouragement.

2. Irene Parker, *Dissenting Academies in England: Their Rise and Progress among the Educational Systems of the Country* (Cambridge, 1914); H. McLachlan, *English Education Under the Test Act: Being the History of the Nonconformist Academies 1662–1820* (Manchester, 1931); J. W. Ashley Smith, *The Birth of Modern Education, the Contribution of the Dissenting Academies, 1600–1800* (London, 1954); B. Simon, *Studies in the History of Education, 1780–1870* (London, 1960), pp. 26ff; S. Pollard, *The Genesis of Modern Management: A Study of the Industrial Revolution in Great Britain* (London, 1965), pp. 113–4, 116–8. The uniqueness of the nonconformist contribution compared to other institutions has been challenged, initially by N. Hans, *New Trends in Education in the Eighteenth Century* (London, 1951).

3. For a review of the subject see R. M. Hartwell, 'Two Services: Education and the Law' in Hartwell, *The Industrial Revolution and Economic Growth* (London, 1971), pp. 232–3.

4. T. S. Ashton, *The Industrial Revolution, 1760–1830* (Oxford, 1948), pp. 17–21; C. Wilson, *England's Apprenticeship 1603–1763* (London, 1965), pp. 341–2; P. Mathias, *The First Industrial Nation* (London, 1969), pp. 158–9. For a review of the literature see Hartwell, 'Two Services', pp. 229–36.

5. A. E. Musson & E. Robinson, *Science and Technology in the Industrial Revolution* (Manchester, 1969), especially chapter 3.

6. A. R. Hall, 'What Did the Industrial Revolution in Britain Owe to Science?' in N. McKendrick, ed., *Historical Perspectives: Studies in English Thought and Society in Honour of J. H. Plumb* (London, 1974), pp. 129, 143–6. See also C. Gillispie, 'The Natural History of Industry', *Isis*, XLVIII (1957), p. 399; A. Thackray, 'Natural Knowledge in Cultural Context: The Manchester Model', *American Historical Review*, LXXIX (1974), pp. 676–7; P. Mathias, 'Who Unbound Prometheus? Science and Technical Change, 1600–1800' in Mathias, *The Transformation of England* (London, 1979), pp. 81–2.

7. M. Berg, P. Hudson & M. Sonenscher, eds., *Manufacture in Town and Country Before the Factory* (Cambridge, 1983), p. 10; C. Wilson, 'Technology and Industrial Organisation' in C. Singer *et al.*, eds., *A History of Technology: The Late Nineteenth Century, c. 1850 to c. 1900* (Oxford, 1958), p. 799. See also S. D. Chapman, 'Enterprise and Innovation in the British Hosiery Industry, 1750–1850', *Textile History*, V (1974), pp. 20, 25; P. Mathias, 'Skills and Diffusion of Innovation from Britain in the Eighteenth Century' in *Transformation of England*, p. 38.

8. R. S. Potter, 'Science, Provincial Culture and Public Opinion in Enlightenment England', *British Journal for Eighteenth-Century Studies*, III (1980), pp. 20–46; I. Inkster, 'Introduction: Aspects of the History of Science Culture in Britain, 1780–1850 and Beyond' in I. Inkster & J. Morrell, eds., *Metropolis and Province: Science in British Culture 1780–1850* (London, 1983), pp. 11–54; Thackray, 'Natural Knowledge', p. 693.

9. See above, and P. Lundgreen, 'Educational Expansion and Economic Growth in Nineteenth-Century Germany: A Quantitative Survey' in L. Stone, ed., *Schooling and Society: Studies in the History of Education* (Baltimore & London, 1976), p. 47; C. A. Anderson & M. J. Bowman, 'Education and Economic Modernization

in Historical Perspective', *ibid.*, p. 4; A. R. Hall, *Inaugural Lecture, Imperial College: Historical Relations of Science and Technology* (London, 1963), p. 128, cited in Mathias, 'Who Unbound Prometheus?', p. 46; D. C. Coleman, 'Gentlemen and Players', *Economic History Review*, 2nd ser. XXVI (1973), pp. 103–4.

10. McLachlan, *English Education*, pp. 6–15.

11. M. Sanderson, *Studies in Economic and Social History: Education, Economic Change and Society in England, 1780–1870* (London, 1983), p. 31.

12. W. E. Minchinton, 'The Merchant in England in the Eighteenth Century' in *The Entrepreneur: Papers Presented at the Annual Conference of the Economic History Society* (1957), p. 25.

13. See Hartwell, 'Two Services', pp. 228–9.

14. Manchester College, Seddon Correspondence, letter no. 35, Cheney Hart, Salop, to John Seddon, Warrington, 29 Jan. 1762.

15. Josiah Wedgwood, Etruria, to Thomas Bentley, 8 Nov. 1779 in [Lady K. E. Farrar], ed., *Letters of Josiah Wedgwood, 1771 to 1780* (1903, Didsbury [1979]), II, pp. 542–3, letter no. E. 18936–26).

16. Thomas Barnes, 'A Plan for the Improvement and Extension of Liberal Education in Manchester', *Manchester Literary & Philosophical Memoirs*, II (1785), p. 20; P. Mathias, *The Brewing Industry in England, 1700–1830* (Cambridge, 1959), pp. 290, 308–9, where see Samuel Whitbread II; Mathias, *First Industrial Nation*, pp. 159, 164; Coleman, 'Gentlemen and Players', *passim*; *Letters of Josiah Wedgwood*, II, p. 550; see Doddridge's advice to a student intended for trade, cited in Smith, *Birth of Modern Education*, p. 133.

17. C. Erickson, *British Industrialists: Steel and Hosiery, 1850–1950* (Cambridge, 1950), p. 111. See also D. Wardle, *Education and Society in Nineteenth-Century Nottingham* (Cambridge, 1971), chapter VII.

18. William Gardiner, *Music and Friends; or Pleasant Recollections of a Dilettante* (London, 1838; 1853), I, p. 129, & III, pp. 1–3, 14–15, 81–2; Z. Cook & B. Simon, 'Private Schools in Leicester and the County, 1780–1840' in B. Simon, ed., *Education in Leicestershire, 1540–1940: A Regional Study* (Leicester, 1968), pp. 107–8.

19. Cook & Simon, 'Private Schools', p. 108. See also G. Jackson, *Hull in the Eighteenth Century: A Study in Economic and Social History* (London, 1972), p. 279.

20. I. Inkster, 'Scientific Culture and Scientific Education in Liverpool prior to 1812—A Case Study in the Social History of Education' in M. D. Stephens & G. W. Roderick, eds., *Scientific and Technical Education in Early Industrial Britain: Nottingham Studies in the History of Adult Education* (Nottingham, 1981), pp. 30–7; Sanderson, *Education*, pp. 24–6.

21. R. G. Wilson, *Gentlemen Merchants: The Merchant Community in Leeds, 1700–1830* (Manchester, 1971), pp. 209, 244.

22. C. C. Hankin, ed., *Life of Mary Anne Schimmelpennick* (London, 2nd edn., 1858), p. 214; Wilson, *Gentlemen Merchants*, p. 232.

23. Ralph Harrison, *A Sermon Preached at the Dissenting Chapel in Cross Street, Manchester, March xxvi, MDCCLXXXVI, on occasion of the Establishment of an Academy in that Town* (Warrington [1786]), p. 10. See also Barnes, 'A Plan', pp. 17–8, 25–7. Similar views were expressed earlier by the supporters of Warrington Academy, see Manchester College, tract collection, no. 271, Philip Holland, *The Importance of Learning. A Sermon preached before an Assembly of Ministers at Manchester, May 21, 1760* (Warrington, 1760), p. xxv.

24. Wilson, *Gentlemen Merchants*, p. 210; Jackson, *Hull*, pp. 274–6; N. Rogers, 'Money, Land and Lineage: The Big Bourgeoisie of Hanoverian London', *Social History* IV (1979) pp. 446–8.

25. V. D. Davis, *A History of Manchester College* (London, 1932) p. 54.

26. The sources used in this analysis are: 'A List of Benefactions and Annual Subscriptions', printed as an appendix to Harrison, *A Sermon Preached; V[igilii] F[ilius], [pseu* William Turner (1761–1859)], 'Historical Account of Students educated in Warrington Academy', *Monthly Repository* IX (1814), pp. 201ff, reprinted in William Turner, *The Warrington Academy*, ed., G. A. Carter (Warrington, 1957), pp. 51ff; Sir Thomas Baker, 'Biographical Notices' of 'Trustees of the Chapel, 1693–1854' in Baker, *Memorials of a Dissenting Chapel* (London & Manchester, 1884).

27. Analysis of 'A List of Benefactions &c.'. Subscriptions promised totalled £243 12s. and benefactions £881 12s. (not £801 12s. as in Davis, 59 n. 1).

28. Joseph Hunter, 'Familiae Minorum Gentium', ed. J. W. Clay, *Harleian Society*, XXXVII–XL (1894–96), p. 1123; Baker, pp. 40, 92.

29. Carter, *Warrington Academy*, p. 50; Hunter, 'Familiae', pp. 1106, 168.

30. Carter, pp. 59–60.

31. 'List of Subscribers to the New Academical Institution Established in the Neighbourhood of London in 1786' printed as an appendix to Abraham Rees, *The Advantages of Knowledge Illustrated and Recommended in a Sermon . . . to the Supporters of a New Academical Institution among Protestant Dissenters* (London, 1788).

32. Manchester promised £115 9s. 6d. in subscriptions, compared with £120 15s. from London. Lancashire as a whole accounted for two-fifths of the subscriptions but none of the benefactions, see Manchester College, Warrington Academy Register, ff $71^r$–$85^r$.

33. In contrast there is evidence that the Hackney committee made a special application to Nottingham, see Dr. Williams's Library, MS 38.14 'Hackney College Minutes, 1785–1791' [hereafter Hackney Minutes], p. 31 (5 May 1786).

34. It is instructive to note that the same individuals gave over three times as much in benefactions to Hackney as to Manchester College. Richard Heywood was the only individual as generous to Manchester as to Hackney. Much more typical were William Russell who promised a subscription of 10 gns to Hackney and one of 3 gns to Manchester College, and William Shore with a benefaction of 40 gns for the former but a subscription of only 2 gns for the latter.

35. H. D. Roberts, *Hope Street Church, Liverpool and the Allied Nonconformity* (Liverpool, 1909).

36. Hunter, 'Familiae', pp. 23, 24, 39, 52, 54; Carter, *Warrington Academy*, p. 59.

37. Carter, p. 58; Manchester College, 'Minutes of the Proceedings of the Committee of the Manchester Academy', 1786–1810 [hereafter Minutes, A], p. 19.

38. Carter, pp. 58–9.

39. Minutes, A, p. 19.

40. G. M. Ditchfield, 'Manchester College and Anti-Slavery'.

41. A. Howe, *The Cotton Masters, 1830–1860* (Oxford, 1984), p. 303.

42. 'List of Subscribers' Hackney, where see Robert Newton, Esq.; Hackney Minutes, p. 110; H. McLachlan, 'Warrington Academy: Its History and Influence', *Chetham Society, ns* CVII (1943), p. 135; H. McLachlan, 'The Old Hackney College, 1786–1796', *Transactions of the Unitarian Historical Society*, III, no. 3 (1925), pp. 188–9; *Monthly Repository*, II (1807), p. 117. I have only been able to trace two donations of £500 each from Newton, though there was an anonymous gift of £500 recorded in the list of Hackney benefactions.

43. Harrison, *A Sermon*, p. 33; T. Barnes, *A Discourse Delivered at the Commencement of the Manchester Academy* (Warrington [1786]), p. 32.

44. Hackney Minutes, pp. 95–9, 100, 122, 126.

45. For a description, see Davis, *Manchester College*, pp. 61–2, 64.

46. Minutes, A, pp. 21, 43.
47. *The Works, Literary, Moral, and Medical of Thomas Percival M.D.* (London, 1807), I, p. lxxxii, n*. The total subscriptions for the three years 1794 to 1796 was £529 4s., an average of £176 8s. p.a. Admittedly, the two surviving sets of accounts both record small surpluses, and the College had other sources of income besides subscriptions, but the rents and fees could fluctuate markedly from year to year and congregational collections were only made on an irregular basis. Since in both cases the accounts are only a partial record, they may provide a misleading picture of the correct financial position. See Minutes, A, p. 71; 'Cash Account of New College Manchester, 22 February 1799–1800'.
48. Minutes, A, pp. 28, 31, 101–2. For the very similar pattern at Hackney, see Hackney Minutes, p. 122.
49. Minutes, A, pp. 47, 48–51.
50. It seems likely that this sum represents, at least in part, a transfer of subscriptions from the by then defunct Hackney College.
51. Minutes, A, pp. 65, 67–8, 72–3, 75–6, 78–80, 83–4, 61.
52. G. M. Ditchfield, 'The Early History of Manchester College', *Transactions of the Historic Society of Lancashire and Cheshire*, CXXIII (1972), pp. 87–8; Minutes, A, p. 95.
53. Minutes, A, pp. 118, 123–8, 130.
54. *Ibid.*, p. 128.
55. *Ibid.*, p. 129.
56. Ditchfield, 'Manchester College, pp. 86–7, 89.
57. Manchester College, Wellbeloved Correspondence, Charles Wellbeloved to William Wood, 14 Jan. 1798; Ditchfield, 'Manchester College', p. 87; Minutes, A, p. 69; Wellbeloved Correspondence, Joseph Astley, Chesterfield, to Charles Wellbeloved, York, 16 Dec. 1797.
58. Further indications of the lack of zeal comes from the number of inquorate meetings held in the mid-1790s, see Minutes, A, pp. 53, 55, 57.
59. Minutes, A, pp. 38, 40, 54, 56.
60. Timothy Kenrick, Exeter, to his father, see Mrs. W. Byng Kenrick, ed., *Chronicles of a Nonconformist Family: The Kenricks of Wynne Hall, Exeter and Birmingham* (Birmingham, 1932), p. 125; A. Brockett, *Nonconformity in Exeter, 1650–1875* (Manchester, 1962), pp. 154–5.
61. J. Seed, 'Jeremiah Joyce, Unitarianism and the Radical Intelligentsia in the 1790s', *Transactions of the Unitarian Historical Society*, XVII (1981), pp. 97, 103; I. Sellars, 'Unitarians and Social Change', *Hibbert Journal*, LXI (1962–63), pp. 16–7; J. Kenrick, *A Biographical Memoir of the Late Rev. Charles Wellbeloved* (London, 1860), p. 44.
62. McLachlan, 'Old Hackney College', pp. 199–201; McLachlan, *English Education*, pp. 252–3.
63. Wellbeloved Correspondence, Astley to Wellbeloved, 16 Dec. 1797. The shock felt over the collapse of Hackney, so soon after the loss of Warrington, was considerable. See Samuel Kenrick, Bewdley, to his nephew Timothy Kenrick, n.d., in Kenrick, ed., *Chronicles*, p. 115.
64. Ditchfield, 'Manchester College', pp. 90, 91, 96–7, 92.
65. This appears to have been the situation at Warrington, see McLachlan, 'Warrington Academy', pp. 91–4.
66. See *Roll of Students Entered at Manchester Academy, 1786–1803 . . .* (Manchester, 1868).
67. McLachlan, 'Warrington Academy', p. 99. There were 53 divinity students out of a total of 393, of whom 13 were either intended for the church or

subsequently conformed. At Hackney in October 1789 the number of exhibitions had to be restricted to seven due to the size of the debt, see Hackney Minutes, pp. 122, 140.

68. Minutes, A, pp. 11, 31, 39, 71.

69. See 'Cash Account'.

70. Davis came to the same conclusion, see Davis, *Manchester College*, p. 99.

71. Analysis of 'A List of Students educated at the Academy at Daventry . . .' (1752–1788), *Monthly Repository*, XVII (1822), pp. 163–4, 195–8, 284–7.

72. Ditchfield, 'Manchester College', pp. 82–4.

73. British Library, London, Add. MS 24, 442 Joseph Hunter, 'Collectanea Hunteriana Vol. VIII being Memoirs to Serve for a History of Protestant Dissenters', f 7$^{v}$; A. Ruston, 'Radical Nonconformity in Hackney, 1805–1845', *Transactions of the Unitarian Historical Society*, XIV, no. 1 (1967), p. 6.

74. Minutes, A, p. 1, Printed address and resolutions (1786); Barnes, *Discourse*, p. 31.

75. Thomas Percival's eldest son was a divinity student at Warrington (1781) while two of his younger sons were lay students at Manchester (1786, 1796). Likewise the eldest son of Thomas Butterworth Bayley was at Warrington (1782) and two other sons at Manchester (1790), though he apparently considered sending his two younger sons to Hackney, see Hackney Minutes, p. 121 (21 Sept. 1789). It seems likely that John Eaton of Chester, a student at Warrington (1782), was a brother of Joseph Eaton, one of the first students at Manchester (1786). Carter, pp. 78, 79; *Roll of Students*. The dates in parentheses which follow the names of students refer to their year of entry to the College.

76. Minutes, A, p. 1; Barnes, *Discourse*, p. 31. Much the same remarks were made about the need for an Academy in London, Hackney Minutes, p. 13.

77. John Aikin, *A Description of the Country from Thirty to Forty Miles round Manchester* [1795], p. 184; John Moore, 'Recollections of the Manchester Academy, its Tutors and Students' in J. Harland, ed., 'Collectanea Relating to Manchester and its Neighbourhood, at Various Periods', Volume II, *Chetham Society*, LXXII (1867), p. 239. The identification of Mortier with the Napoleonic Marshal has been questioned, see *Roll of Students* under 1799.

78. Pipe-Wolferstan's diary is the only record of Robinson as a student at the College (1801), Ditchfield, 'Manchester College', p. 86.

79. Joseph Hunter identifies the complex relationship, see Hunter, 'Familiae', pp. 275, 280, 302; E. Axon, 'The Bayley Family of Manchester and Hope', *Transactions of the Lancashire and Cheshire Antiquarian Society for 1889*, VII (1890), pp. 197–8, 212–3.

80. Axon, 'Bayley Family', pp. 204, 217; *Roll of Students*.

81. Ditchfield, 'Manchester College', pp. 83–5, 99.

82. *Ibid.*, p. 93.

83. McLachlan, *English Education*, p. 209. Eleven of the 53 divinity students proceeded to Oxford and Cambridge and took holy orders, including a future Irish bishop. A further six conformed or took holy orders including four who had followed the lay course: ultimately 17 entered the Church. There were, in addition, at least three Quakers. Carter, pp. 54, 56, 61, 62, 65, 66, 70, 71, 73, 74, 78, 80.

84. Davis, p. 64, in 1794 they evidently included a Quaker; *Works . . . of Thomas Percival*, I, p. lxxxi; Ditchfield, 'Manchester College', pp. 84, 86.

85. Ditchfield, 'Manchester College', p. 85. See also Timothy Kenrick's account of the victimisation suffered by the radical schoolmaster, Charles Lloyd. Lloyd was forced to quit Ditchling because of the prejudice of the people 'who withdrew

their children from his school as soon as they discovered he was a friend of the French Revolution & was a heretic in Politics', Timothy Kenrick, Exeter, to his father, 6 Mar. 1793, Kenrick, ed., *Chronicles*, p. 68; see also H. J. McLachlan, 'A Curiosity of Welsh Unitarian Literature', *Transactions of the Unitarian Historical Society*, XVII (1981), pp. 132–4.

86. The median period at College for future businessmen was one-and-a-half years, and for medicine and law two years, see Table 2.

87. *Works . . . of Thomas Percival*, pp. vii, viii, xi; Thomas Heywood, *A Memoir of Sir Benjamin Heywood, baronet with Two Chapters of Domestic Life and Letters, 1840–1865* (Manchester, n.d.), pp. 16–7.

88. Musson and Robinson, *Science and Technology*, p. 94, note 2.

89. P. L. Robertson, 'The Finances of the University of Glasgow before 1914', *History of Education Quarterly*, XVI (1976), p. 458; J. B. Morrell, 'The University of Edinburgh in the Late Eighteenth Century: Its Scientific Eminence and Academic Structure', *Isis*, LXIII (1971), p. 167, note 23; W. M. Mathew, 'The Origins and Occupations of Glasgow Students, 1740–1839', *Past & Present*, no. 33 (1966), pp. 74–94.

90. Musson and Robinson, *Science and Technology*, *passim*; Inkster & Morrell, eds., *Metropolis and Province*, *passim*; Sanderson, *Education*, pp. 33ff.

91. See J. Money, *Experience and Identity: Birmingham and the West Midlands, 1760–1800* (Manchester, 1977), chapters 4–6; A. T. Patterson, *Radical Leicester: A History of Leicester, 1780–1850* (Leicester, 1954), pp. 13f, 235ff.

92. Sanderson, *Education*, p. 26.

93. Thackray, 'Natural Knowledge', p. 678.

94. Barnes, 'Plan . . . of Liberal Education', p. 35; Harrison, *Sermon*, p. 10; Barnes, *Discourse*, p. 24 and above. Though it must be noted that literary and philosophical societies, and other public lecture courses, gained part of their audiences from those 'youths whose formal educational careers had been cut short by family pressures and who were forced to find a less conventional route to satisfy their ambitions', R. O. Day, *Education and Society, 1500–1800* (London, 1982), p. 211. See above the example of William Gardiner.

95. See Carter, *passim*, with additions from the original Warrington Academy admissions' register at Manchester College.

96. S. D. Chapman, *The Early Factory Masters* (Newton Abbot, 1967), *passim*.

97. Wilson, *Gentlemen Merchants*, pp. 243, 244, 247.

98. Carter, p. 58.

99. Hunter, 'Familiae', pp. 65–6.

100. The various printed authorities are good on their coverage of the careers of students who entered the professions, see Carter, *passim*; McLachlan, 'Warrington Academy', pp. 104–6.

101. For William Robinson (c. 1801) and Stanley Pipe-Wolferstan (1801) see above. The others included (John) Sparrow Stovin (1788), the son of James Stovin of Doncaster (JP for Lincolnshire and the West Riding) and a grandson of John Sparrow of Wincko Bank near Sheffield, both early College subscribers: John Sparrow Stovin was later a student at Daventry (1788), see Hunter, 'Familiae', pp. 319, 1244; 'List of Students . . . at Daventry', p. 287. And Joseph Ashton (1796), the son of Nicholas Ashton of Woolton Hall near Liverpool: Nicholas Ashton's sister married the Rev. John Yates, whose son John Ashton Yates (1795) had entered the College the year before his cousin, Hunter, 'Familiae', p. 360; Roberts, *Hope Street Church*, p. 217.

102. Axon, 'Bayley Family', pp. 217, 224–6; Hunter, 'Familiae', pp. 1047–8; Baker, pp. 105–6.

103. *Burke's Commoners* (1838), IV, pp. 500–1.
104. *The Inquirer*, 26 Jan. 1856, 21 Nov. 1863.
105. Musson and Robinson, *Science and Technology*, pp. 89ff. For a different interpretation of the same phenomena, see Thackray, 'Natural Knowledge', *passim*.
106. H. McLachlan, *The Unitarian Movement in the Religious Life of England*: I. *Its Contribution to Thought and Learning, 1700–1900* (London, 1934), p. 144; McLachlan, *Essays and Addresses* (Manchester, 1950), p. 64; H. J. McLachlan, 'John Thomson, M.D.: Unitarian Layman, 1782–1818', *Transactions of the Unitarian Historical Society*, VIII (1946), p. 141.
107. Hackney Minutes, pp. 80, 86; McLachlan, 'Old Hackney College', p. 205.
108. Davis, p. 65.
109. See above.
110. Harrison, *Sermon*, Appendix II, p. 10; Minutes, A, p. 56. It was still 30 gns in December 1795, see *ibid.*, p. 89.
111. Robertson, 'Finances', p. 458.
112. Prospectus of Hackney College, 24 June 1788; L. Stone, 'Size and Composition of the Oxford Student Body, 1580–1910' in L. Stone, ed., *The University in Society*, I, *Oxford and Cambridge from the 14th to the Early 19th Century* (London, 1975), pp. 43, 44; S. Rothblatt, *The Revolution of the Dons* (London, 1968), p. 66: though it was possible for persons of limited means to attend a college and pursue a university education at Cambridge, 'the *necessary* expenses of residence in college being small', see E. E. Rich, ed., *St Catherine's College, Cambridge, 1473–1973* (1973), p. 183.
113. Ditchfield, 'Manchester College', p. 97. The total cost advertised for the same facilities adds up to just under 70 gns. See Prospectus issued with 'Cash Account' (1800).
114. Davis, p. 64.
115. See the comments by J. B. Morrell, 'Science in Manchester and the University of Edinburgh, 1760–1840' in D. S. L. Cardwell, ed., *Artisan to Graduate* (Manchester, 1974), pp. 44–5; J. B. Morrell, 'Medicine and Science in the Eighteenth Century' in G. Donaldson, ed., *Four Centuries: Edinburgh University Life, 1583–1983* (Edinburgh, 1983), pp. 43–4.
116. Barnes, *Discourse*, p. 29; Minutes, A, pp. 119–20.
117. Hugh Worthington jun., *A Sermon Delivered on Wednesday 6th of May, 1789 . . . To the Supporters of a New Academical Institution among Protestant Dissenters* (London, 1789), p. 49.
118. Minutes, A, pp. 129, 120.
119. Ditchfield, 'Manchester College', pp. 85, 89, 97.
120. Dr. Seed appears to undervalue the significance of London and the South for lay students, J. Seed, 'Manchester College, York: An Early Nineteenth-Century Dissenting Academy', *Journal of Educational Administration and History*, XIV, no. 1 (1982), p. 13.
121. The three individuals who entered as lay students but subsequently changed to the divinity course have been excluded.
122. Joseph Roberts (1834) of Madras.
123. H. P. Roberts, 'Nonconformist Academies in Wales, (1662–1862)', *Transactions of the Honourable Society of Cymmrodorian for 1928–29* (1930), p. 83.
124. Wellbeloved Correspondence, Wellbeloved to Thomas Robinson, Manchester, 7 May 1807; *Monthly Repository*, II (1807), p. 441; 'Minutes of the Proceedings of the Committee of the Manchester New College removed to York, 1810', pp. 188–9. Printed Address concerning lay students, August 1814.

125. Wellbeloved Correspondence, Wellbeloved to Robinson, 7 May 1807; Wellbeloved to G. W. Wood, 23 Dec. 1813; *Monthly Repository*, II (1807), p. 441. VIII (1813), p. 482; XII (1817), p. 497.
126. Seed, 'Manchester College', p. 13.
127. Dr. Seed incorrectly identifies Marshall's eldest son as a student at York, Seed, 'Manchester College', p. 13.
128. R. Watts, 'Manchester College and Education, 1786–1853'; 'A Friend to the Permanence of Unitarian Dissent' [John Kenrick], Manchester, 31 Mar. 1815, *Monthly Repository*, X (1815), p. 287. For the identification of Kenrick see Kenrick Correspondence, letter to G. W. Wood, undated [March 1815].
129. Kenrick Correspondence, Kenrick to G. W. Wood, 23 Dec. 1831, to W. R. Wood, 30 Nov. 1833. See also the testimonies and acknowledgements of the students themselves: W. R. Wood, York, to his parents, 2 May 1830; 'The Late Mr Samuel Robinson', *The Inquirer*, 20 Dec. 1884, pp. 817–8; 'Obituary. Richard Martineau, Esq.', *The Inquirer*, 26 Aug. 1865, p. 550; 'Obituary. John Cooke, Esq.', *Christian Reformer* (1855), p. 390.
130. Baker, *Memorials of a Dissenting Chapel*, pp. 129–30; F. Boase, *Modern English Biography* (London, 1965), III, p. 607.
131. Evidence on the earlier schooling of York students is available for the period 1803 to 1816, Hunter, 'Collectanea Hunteriana', ff 7$^{v}$–28$^{r}$.
132. Minutes, A, p. 193; Manchester College, Treasurer's Correspondence E/63, Samuel Shore, Meersbrook, to Wood, 30 Sept. 1817.
133. See Wellbeloved's comments to Wood on 'embryo divines', undated [Feb. 1817], 15 Mar. 1817; Treasurer's Correspondence E/47, Wellbeloved to Thomas Robinson, Manchester, 14 Aug. 1817.
134. Brockett, *Nonconformity in Exeter*, p. 183; *Christian Reformer* (1837), p. 503; C. G. Bolam *et al.*, *The English Presbyterians* (London, 1968), p. 265.
135. Seed, 'Manchester College', p. 15.
136. Treasurer's Correspondence, E/11, Thomas Rankin, Bristol to Wood, 24 Feb. 1817.
137. *Memoirs of the Late Mrs Catherine Cappe, written by Herself* (1821), p. 387.

3

# MANCHESTER COLLEGE AND EDUCATION 1786–1853

RUTH WATTS

*Sometime, occasional Lecturer*
*Warwick and Leicester Universities*

In its first sixty-seven years, 1786 to 1853, Manchester College was, for the most part, a unique educational institution—open to all men irrespective of belief, at a time when most other institutions of higher education in England insisted on subscription to articles of faith. The founders of the Academy instituted at Manchester on February 22nd, 1786, stated clearly that the Academy was to be:

> on a plan affording a full and systematic Course of Education for DIVINES, and preparatory instructions for the OTHER LEARNED PROFESSIONS, as well as for CIVIL AND COMMERCIAL life. This Institution will be open to young men of every religious denomination, from whom no test, or confession of faith, will be required.[1]

The latter point was very important. The basic reason for the formation of Dissenting Academies was, after all, the exclusion, since Restoration times, of Dissenters from the two English universities of Oxford and Cambridge.[2] In order to obtain higher education Dissenters had either to go to universities in Germany, Holland or Scotland, with the attendant difficulties of language, expense and travel, or to provide institutions of their own. There were private secular academies in England in the eighteenth century but even the best were fully or partly vocational in character, two thirds of them were in London and they catered mainly for the lower middle-class.[3] The first Dissenting academies were established to ensure a continuing supply of ministers. The best of them, such as Warrington, educated to university level and can now be seen to have been the chief glory of English education in the eighteenth century. The more liberal increasingly took laymen as well, stressed their freedom from all restrictive subscriptions and upheld the right of liberal enquiry in all matters, especially religion. Their growth coincided with the spread of Arianism and subsequently, militant Unitarianism, which infected the academies. The growth of evangelicalism challenged such 'rational Dissent' and more orthodox Dissenters, in alarm, closed 'hotbeds' of heterodoxy and restricted their remaining academies to intending ministers, eventually establishing articles of subscription themselves.[4] The heirs to Warrington and the liberal tradition—Manchester, Hackney and Exeter Colleges—all the more stressed their openness of faith and belief in free enquiry after religious truth but from 1805 Manchester College was the only Dissenting academy remaining, and, indeed, almost the only institution of higher education in England drawing its students from the whole country, which did not require subscription.[5] In this period, when the new industrial and commercial middle-classes were fighting their way to economic and political power, their backbone of Dissenters persistently and vigorously opposed the laws which sought to repress them, not least those which excluded them from the universities. Unitarians, so often comprising a major part of the radical and intellectual elite both of the new middle-class and Dissenters, were to the fore in these struggles, as is shown by George William Wood's attempt to have a

Universities' Admission Bill passed in 1834 and by James Heywood's initiative both in securing Royal Commissions to investigate the old universities in 1850, and in achieving their admittance of Dissenters to first degrees in 1854.[6] Both these men were from families which constantly supported Manchester College: George Wood was treasurer and chief adviser to the College's hard-worked tutors for over thirty-five years, whilst James Heywood was one of the most munificent of the College's benefactors, long closely involved in its affairs and President 1854 to 1858.[7]

Similarly, Unitarians were among the trustees and supporters of Owen's College in Manchester in the 1850s and among the supporters of University College, London in the 1820s, both of which opened their doors to all men without subscription.[8]

It is little wonder, therefore, that all who were connected with the College from 1786 to 1853, emphasised so strongly and so consistently its policy of no subscription and of free enquiry for this was an educational and religious ideal which Rational Dissenters especially regarded as the glory of their academies. Thomas Barnes, the first principal, dedicated the College 'To TRUTH! to LIBERTY! to RELIGION!' as a chief reason for its existence.[9] The Revd. William Turner (Junior), a former student at the College and a tutor for eighteen years, in 1840 deplored the ancient universities demanding formal subscription:

> on their first entrance, from boys, who cannot be supposed to have given even the most cursory and superficial attention to the variety of disputed points which these acts involve.[10]

Unitarians alone, he added, had acted uniformly and consistently in the defence of free enquiry and at their academies every effort was made in the running of them, in their curriculum and methods of study, to promote genuine openness of mind and free enquiry.[11] The 1833 Report stressed that the College provided:

> for the education of a learned ministry, without any subscription to articles of religious faith . . . This recommendation it possesses in common with no Institution of the same kind in England, and on this account alone it is entitled to the support of those who think that the influence of Christianity and just conceptions of its nature and design keep pace with the rapid increase of knowledge and intelligence on other subjects.[12]

As the 1813 Report stated:

> The great and primary object of the institution is the education of youth for the exercise of the Christian ministry among that class of Dissenters usually denominated Presbyterian.[13]

Manchester College, however, was also in the Warrington tradition and differed from most orthodox Dissenting academies in its stress on a cultured, highly educated ministry. Evangelicalism emphasised emotion and sudden conversion in religion rather than reason and intellectual faith and tended to reinforce prejudices against academic learning. Even where it did not, usually the curriculum was not so wide as at Manchester College whilst the load of preaching and pastoral work was heavier.[14] The supporters and officers of Manchester College on the other hand, stressed that a wide and deep education was vital for a Christian minister. Unitarianism, after all, was based on reason, on knowledge requisite to examine the Scriptures critically and probe their true meaning. To continue the tradition of men like Priestley, to defend their beliefs against attack, especially from Anglican clergy educated at the universities, a thorough theological education was necessary.[15] Furthermore, not only theology but, as Thomas Barnes said, everything which added to the knowledge of God and man was relevant and useful. Only a minister thus educated with a wide general knowledge could bring the 'noblest culture and improvement' to the poor and be respected by the rich and influential.[16] As the 1833 Report said, provided that the intending minister was properly nurtured in character and spirit:

> literature and science will furnish new and wider views of the nature and application of religions truth, and enable the faithful teacher to speak with a confidence and authority, which he could not otherwise possess . . . the understanding of a Christian pastor cannot be too much enriched with knowledge, or too highly cultivated with the most enlarged philosophy . . . The character of the Dissenting minister is mainly determined by the nature of its academical education.[17]

Other tutors reiterated this theme.[18] John Kenrick, at the first Jubilee of the College, bitingly condemned the Church of England, for having 'first of all injured the Dissenters' by excluding them from the universities 'and then insulted them for the inferiority in learning which is the consequence of her own injustice.' Kenrick wished, therefore, to educate future ministers as far as possible, for whilst he thought it absurd to try and rival the highest peaks of Oxbridge learning the College could:

> give to those who were educating for the ministry among us, such a portion of sound and accurate knowledge as should prevent their being exposed to the imputation that their faith was the result of their ignorance:[19]

Celebrating the same occasion, James Martineau urged that since the idea of a priestly order was losing its influence, that influence must go to men of proven intellectual and moral power, particularly when fading belief in the plenary inspiration of the Scriptures called for knowledgeable and understanding minds to interpret the Gospels. Besides there were now other disseminators of ideas to compete with the man in the pulpit:

> Among those classes which form our worshipping assemblies . . . the whole sphere of life and action has become enlarged.[20]

This latter point was constantly stressed by leading supporters of the College, well aware that, despite the growth of Unitarianism among some of the less well-off, the principal congregations of Unitarianism, and certainly those from which Manchester College drew much of its support, were drawn from the elite of Dissent socially, economically and culturally.[21] Coming predominantly from the new commercial and industrial middle-classes, liberal in politics, pioneering in industry and commerce, often reformist in social matters as well as daring in religion, such Unitarians would not want ignorant preachers. Ministers needed to be educated in the new interests of their age, able to explain their rational religion and, not least, considering the low salaries such highly educated men were likely to receive, capable also of running a school up to the standard desired by many Unitarian parents.[22]

Furthermore, Unitarians generally had a deep interest in education. This stemmed from their respect for the power of reason and interest in new knowledge and from the Hartleian psychology propagated by their eminent eighteenth century leader, Joseph Priestley, and taught to and disseminated by the students of Manchester College.[23] Certain that intellectual, moral and physical education were interdependent, that real virtue was neither blind assent to incomprehensible tales, nor 'a wild fervour of excited feeling', but the result of reflection and deliberation, and that education was a lifelong process, affected by every circumstance and needing the fullest development of each faculty, Unitarian leaders were determined to achieve the best education possible at Manchester College. As John Kenrick contended in 1835, intellectual powers were God-given as were the means of improving them; all subjects could serve religion, for example, natural philosophy showed the simple and comprehensive laws of the universe—'an expression of an Infinite wisdom', whilst history showed the progress of the human race—'the gradual unfolding of a wise and benificent plan'.[24]

Since good education was seen to be so important throughout this period the College asserted its desire to educate laymen too. It only relinquished this plan in 1853 when it was obvious that many of the laity preferred the greater advantages offered by University College, London, which, after all, held a similar philosophy of education, and to which Manchester College had been affiliated since 1840.[25]

Doubtless, the constant advertising for lay students partially stemmed from the fact that the College was not viable without them. Most of the divinity students (generally expected to be of poorer parentage financially)[26] had their education paid for on the foundation. It was the fees of the lay students which largely raised the otherwise inconsiderable salaries of the tutors.[27] It was the patronage of the laity stimulated by the respect they had imbibed for learning and culture which would engender support and status for both the college and the ministers it sent out. Nevertheless, it would be cynical to deduce from this that the College's only interest in lay students was financial. In the tradition of Warrington and, like Hackney, Manchester College wanted, very positively, to educate Dissenting laymen. One supporter at least believed that this was 'greatly a more important object'.[28] From the first, College prospectuses offered places to those aiming at professional or civil and commercial life, and annual reports reiterated the College's claim to offer the completion of a liberal education 'with more enlarged and varied knowledge than is attainable at school, and guarded by a superintending discipline from the danger of having morals corrupted'.[29]

This emphasis on an education, both extensive and moral, was not only because of fears such as Charles Wellbeloved's on the depths of depravity into which untutored youths might fall[30] but also because of the roles which it was hoped a virtuous and enlightened laity might play. Unitarian academics were acutely aware of the new society of which Unitarians were so much a part. They appreciated its possibilities but feared the impact of the new industrial age on man's moral development. Thus they wished to ensure a modern, liberal education not only to educate future industrialists in scientific principles but also to educate future citizens to direct new developments for the good and not the detriment of the individual and society. The movement which had produced both William Roscoe and his writings on the cultured merchant princes of the Italian Renaissance and Joseph Priestley the eighteenth century 'universal man', and which was so involved in the thrust of the new middle class to dominance and power, was keenly conscious of the need for enlightened leadership. Thomas Barnes a co-founder of the short-lived College of Arts and Sciences in Manchester before he became principal of Manchester College in 1786, wanted to educate cultured businessmen to:

> contradict the disgraceful idea that a spirit of merchandise is incompatible with liberal sentiment, and that it only tends to contract and vulgarise the mind.[31]

At Manchester College he wanted to give both future professional men and intending merchants and industrialists a wider knowledge and view of life, not condemning the latter to ignorance and insipidity.[32]

It was because Unitarians were so conscious of the philistinism of many of their class that their ministers especially urged so strongly for a wide liberal and scientific education 'even' for businessmen, and sought to avoid the type of condemnation later poured on the majority of their class by historians such as E. J. Hobsbawm who wrote so bitterly—'even today the heart contracts at the sight of the landscape constructed by that generation'.[33] They were not asking, therefore, for a specifically commercial education, (though Priestley's lectures on commercial education were followed by Barnes, in the first Manchester period) but a liberal one which led commercial men like the other students to become useful, rational and progressive leaders. In addition, studies in the evidences of natural and revealed religion would enable lay students to sustain and defend rational religion. Educating lay and divinity students together would be beneficial to both.[34]

Barnes wished the new academy to be a 'Seminary of LIBERAL EDUCATION', that is, to give a wide education which would inculcate wisdom and a spirit of liberty, both of which he said were necessary successively for the welfare of mankind and British liberties and laws, for the honour of the Christian religion and for the means of salvation.[35]

Ralph Harrison echoed such sentiments and argued that because all wisdom required:

> the right exercise of and improvement of the intellectual powers, the foundation thereof must be laid in KNOWLEDGE.

Knowledge not only gave dignity, superior power and happiness to individuals, and made things 'subservient to our use', it extended civilisations, brought good government and liberty, was the basis of the useful arts, helped commerce and banished superstition and 'enthusiasm'. 'Liberal and extensive erudition' were necessary to professional men and would make merchants and manufacturers more respectable and useful and qualified for public service. Even the hereditarily rich and powerful would look insignificant and wretched without such.[36]

What was this vital 'liberal and extensive erudition'? Certainly it was not merely an aping of the narrow, classical curriculum which pervaded Oxford or Cambridge. As John Relly Beard, an ex-student of Manchester College said derisively of the old universities:

> . . . in the circle of what they teach, how much that is antiquated, how much that is useless, how much that is injurious is found, and how much of what would be the greatest service in cultivating the mind, expanding the heart, fitting for the intercourses of actual life—how much that would conduce to render their students the benefactors of their country and their kind, is altogether omitted!
>
> Thus does it happen that the universities which ought to be the light and glory of the country are wrapped in the darkness of a barbarous age, stand not as beacons, bearing the torch before advancing civilisation, but as monuments of the antique, the obsolete, the disallowed, the effete.[37]

Such criticism summed up much of what Dissenters generally, liberal Anglicans and progressive educationalists such as the Philosophical Radicals were increasingly saying about Oxford and Cambridge. Apart from attacking the structure, exclusiveness and expense, the aristocratic and licentious spirit of the universities, they centred on castigating them for perpetuating a curriculum, suitable for the sixteenth century, but anachronistic in more scientific and modern times.[38]

There was some truth in this. It is now generally agreed that, despite some reform in the early nineteenth century, the ancient universities were at their lowest ebb scholastically and morally. Although there was a wide range of university chairs, the universities were, in fact, dominated by wealthy and indolent colleges who concentrated on a narrow range of subjects, a limitation which was exacerbated by the growth of compulsory examinations. Both universities were predominantly clerical, and Oxford concentrated almost exclusively on classics and theology, although even in these, the great German advances in historical criticism and philology were all but ignored except by a handful of scholars in the 1820s.[39] Cambridge became famous for its prestigious tripos course in mathematics and theoretical physics, but despite some exceptional reformist mathematicians, the course, like the 1822 classical tripos, was an insular and a highly specialised training in reasoning for future lawyers and statesmen not a modern training for professional mathematicians and scientists.[40]

Defenders of the system, such as Edward Copleston of Oxford, condemned any specialised training in university studies or any intellectual fragmentation of the common culture of the upper-class elite, a condemnation paradoxical in reformers' eyes since they saw the rigidly classical education which Copleston termed 'liberal' as highly specialised.[41] Furthermore, basing a liberal education on classics hardly suited the Cambridge emphasis although at Cambridge mathematics was similarly defended because it was a 'permanent' completely defined subject, an interesting conclusion at a time when continental thinkers were revolutionising mathematical thinking.

Critics of the universities usually accepted the claims for the liberalising qualities of classics but believed they should be only part of the curriculum and should be taught in a less narrowly grammatical way. Modern studies should also be taught as being more enjoyable, more profitable, more relevant and more useful to those going into public life. Originality of thought and the extension of knowledge should be encouraged. Professional training could follow a first degree.[42]

Unitarians from Priestley onwards, propogated such sentiments and extended the argument to include the needs of commercial and industrial interests, and to advocate both progressive teaching methods and content relevant to a country involved in much social, economic and political change. Supporters of the College such as William Shepherd and James Yates, thus generally upheld the worth of all those subjects pioneered and stimulated by Joseph Priestley.[43]

Influenced also by the more 'modern' universities of Scotland and Germany at which many of them studied,[44] the promoters and tutors of Manchester College thus promulgated a very different curriculum from that of contemporary Oxford and Cambridge. The curriculum, indeed, and changing demands true to the principle of adapting to new knowledge did not remain static.[45]

In 1786, three main courses were offered, that is, the various branches of theology and its related subjects, Latin and Greek classics plus polite literature, and a course of mathematics and natural philosophy. Other subjects, such as history, geography, theory of language and oratory were, however, subsumed under these headings. The history and principles of commerce, its laws, regulations and ethics were also taught and extras included French and external science lectures. The first three years for theological students and the three year courses for laymen were all very similar except that the latter had no Hebrew but did have short courses on moral philosophy and the evidences and principles of natural and revealed religion in their third year.[46] The basic course with subtle variations was maintained in the York period. In 1833 a long-desired precedent was created of a divinity student extending his course to six years and this was made mandatory in 1848.[47]

In 1840 the curriculum was redrawn to fit the matriculation and degrees requirements of the University of London but this really meant, as the 1840 Report stated, 'a more minute division of the departments of instruction' rather than any essential change. Professors were appointed in classics and English language; history; mental and moral philosophy and political economy; pure and mixed mathematics; physical science and natural history; critical and exegetical theology; biblical archaeology and the evidences of natural and revealed religion; pastoral theology and the Hebrew, Chaldee and Syriac languages; and ecclesiastical history. French language and literature were given a lectureship. English literature was not in a distinct department but in 1846, with a reorganisation of some of the departments, this was rectified and a separate Chair of English history and literature was established.[48]

This then was the curriculum which, hopefully, would produce enlightened, progressive liberal men, with rational, enquiring minds, well able to take advantage of the new discoveries and changing ideas of the age. This education differed from that of Oxford and Cambridge and from most remaining Dissenting Academies: it was influenced to some extent by the Scottish universities, and, in essence (apart from theology), was similar to University College, London which opened in 1828.[49]

How far did the College fulfil the aims of its founders and supporters? Certainly, its advertisements and reports show clearly that the College remained publicly faithful to the principles of non-subscription and free enquiry.[50] For example, the report (probably by William Turner) of the Revd. Dr Toulmin's sermon on behalf of the College in 1807, stated that:

> youth, educated for the ministry in this seminary, are not and *ought* not, to be considered as *pledged* to support, in future life, a scheme of sentiments which may suit the taste and views of its patrons.[51]

Charles Wellbeloved, was highly gratified in 1809, to hear that some people thought that the College was insufficiently Unitarian in its teaching:

> . . . I considered their censure as the highest praise—I do not, I will not teach Unitarianism—or any Ism but Christianism. I will endeavour to show the students how to study the Scriptures—and if they find Unitarianism there—well—if Arianism—well—if Trinitarianism—well —only let them find something for themselves—let it not be found for them by their tutors.[52]

Such sentiments were generally proudly approved[53] and any suggestion that the liberal principles of the College might be being departed from in any way aroused angry opposition,[54] though John Kenrick, whilst fully upholding the principle of free enquiry, was honest enough to remark drily:

> With three Unitarian tutors, supported by Unitarians, receiving none but

> Unitarian students and sending out none but Unitarian preachers, we may disclaim as we please Unitarianism or Dissent.[55]

In fact, there were at times both non-Unitarian students and tutors, and, conversely, some students who later conformed.[56] Although, undoubtedly, the overwhelming predilection of the College, not least on its very stress on non-subscription and free enquiry, was not only Protestant and Dissenting but Unitarian, real efforts were made to avoid the inculcation of any particular system of belief. Wellbeloved, for example, principal and theological tutor 1803 to 1840 (and Robert Wallace, principal, 1840–1846), adopted Dr Taylor of Warrington's exhortation to students, counselling them to give no weight to his opinions unless proved by their own examination of the Scriptures.[57] Wellbeloved stuck to critical and philosophical examination of the texts[58] and was so impartial that, later, James Martineau recalled:

> the impatience with which, out of very homage to his wisdom, we almost resented his impartial love of truth in giving us the most careful epitome of other opinions with scarce a suggestion of his own . . . he set up within us a standard of Christian scholarship to which it must ever exalt us to aspire.[59]

Such praise echoed the heartfelt sentiments expressed at the first Jubilee of the College in 1836 and at Wellbeloved's retirement in 1840.[60] Wellbeloved's great theological learning was evinced not only in his own writings[61] but in the number of his students who became similarly renowned theological scholars of their age, for example, George Vance Smith,[62] John James Tayler[63] and James Martineau,[64] all later Principals of Manchester College. The leadership that Unitarians gave in England to biblical criticism and rational theology[65] stemmed to some considerable degree from the work of Manchester College. This was further stimulated by awareness of German advances in philological, historical and philosophical scholarship[66] and Manchester College played a significant role in developing such scholarship in England as the work of tutors such as John Kenrick, John James Tayler and George Vance Smith, all of whom studied in Germany, illustrated. Kenrick, however, who made his own thoughtful contributions to higher biblical criticism, did not believe that a year in Germany could *replace* one at Manchester College in theology.[67] The importance of such developments was accentuated in 1840 by the creation of three distinct chairs in theology instead of one.[68] The students did not take the London theological examination, Kenrick and others insisting that in no way could it compare with that of Manchester College.[69] When the ambitious Manchester experiment of 1840 to 1853 failed, the College's Committee did not consider that the theological department could be abandoned even if the literary and scientific departments could be provided elsewhere.[70] John James Tayler the new principal, in London, in 1853, firmly upheld the need for a 'thorough and scientific cultivation of theology' and the principle of free enquiry.[71]

A similarly high standard was reached in other subjects. Athough most

Unitarians derided the exclusive claims of classics in education they valued them as a mental discipline and training in style and taste, and for their use in the reading, understanding and accurate criticism of the Scriptures.[72] The one subject which was studied daily throughout the three year course, and from 1815, for the extra two years of the divinity course, too, was classics; the ability to read Homer and Horace was an essential part of the entrance requirements for students on the foundation from 1810, requirements which obviously were hoped for from lay students, too, and which were made more stringent in 1825, and actually reduced slightly in 1840 for students entering with a view to a London degree.[73] Classics were also encouraged by various prizes given at the annual examinations.[74]

How high the standard in classics was is difficult to judge. William Shepherd privately had reservations about the students' standard in Greek in 1810[75] but their general competence and interest was indicated by their letters, orations, and essays.[76] For example, three essays out of seven in the book of College Essays of 1816 to 1819, preserved at Manchester College, Oxford, are based on knowledge of the ancient languages, two of them significantly linked with biblical studies. The third, written completely in Latin, on Lucretius, was by John James Tayler who acted as classical tutor for one year. Tayler was an excellent latinist though admittedly so even before he had entered the college, a fact true of other Unitarians who had attended his father's school in Nottingham or other excellent schools run by Unitarians such as Lant Carpenter.[78] John Tayler who was allowed to concentrate on classics at college, greatly admired his tutor, John Kenrick, whom he described as 'a man of excellent talents, and uncommon diligence . . . a very elegant and accurate scholar' a 'very conscientious and indefatigable tutor' exacting high standards and reaching them himself; sentiments he obviously endorsed twenty years later.[79] Indeed, Kenrick, classical tutor 1810 to 1840, stands out in the succession of able classical tutors at Manchester College, 1786 to 1853. Charles Wellbeloved was convinced by 1818 that the college's reputation was chiefly owing to Kenrick's exertion and talents[80] and James Martineau, in later years, gave warm testimony to Kenrick's scholarship and teaching, contrasting the dry, grammatical pounding so common to contemporary classical teachers with Kenrick's full, clear and absorbing exposition of the literary history of the text and any other related matter, civic, legal, domestic or personal. Furthermore 'Mr Kenrick was in the front rank of the pioneers of improvement'.[81] Following his studies in Germany his highly popular translations of Zumpt's *Latin Grammar* and other works, culminating in his edition of Matthiae's *Greek Grammar*, made him widely known, as Edward Tagart, a former student of his, boasted in 1829.[82]

Kenrick's successor in 1840, Francis Newman, the radical, lovable and eccentric brother of the future Cardinal, later described as an 'intellectual giant', similarly poured a wealth of learning into his classical teaching. His enthusiasm was balanced by his recognition of the vast importance of modern knowledge and of English literature, a balance that enabled him to be well received at Manchester College.[83]

Opportunity to take modern languages was always considered necessary though at first modern languages were extras, usually to be procured from masters outside. John Kenrick taught some French and, after his stay in Germany, 1819 to 1820, also German, which was important for advances in both biblical criticism and in chemistry and other sciences. The need for modern languages for those training for commercial life was also increasingly recognised at the College and from 1826, when the Chevalier Pecchio arrived in 'high spirits' to teach Italian and French, all lay students were required to take lessons in one or both languages, though expenses for these were charged separately. In 1827, Pecchio added Spanish to his teaching and his reports 1827 to 1828 indicate a high proportion of divinity as well as lay students taking modern languages. After Pecchio left in 1838, there was no new appointment of a full-time teacher though Kenrick continued to teach German and approved masters in York were available. In 1840, however, the need to meet London degree requirements led to the appointment of a lecturer (though not 'professor') in French language and literature.[84] Modern languages were, therefore, given a respect as yet lacking from the ancient universities[85] but were not a major part of the curriculum.

European literature, however, inluding English, was always studied under the guise of belles-lettres or 'polite literature', taught by the classics tutor until 1840 and thence the history tutor. It was considered that the best way to study literature was:

> to view every distinguished writer of ancient or modern times in connexion with the circumstances in which he lived and the people among whom and for whom he wrote. Literature is thus exhibited in its proper combination with history, as serving to complete the picture of the people to whom it owed its birth: . . .[86]

Kenrick, the professor of history from 1840 to 1850, saw literature as a most important facet of general history:

> more intellectual than art, more popular and universal in their [sic] influence than mere science or abstract philosophy . . .[87]

Attention to the English language and composition was always included in the curriculum and from 1846 became part of the new course of English literature and language. The appointment of William Gaskell as the new professor was an apt one by a community which had pioneered the study of English literature in higher education. Gaskell was an excellent scholar and writer, with a wide, thorough knowledge and a relish for fine words (and a beautiful reader too).[88]

The College was similarly progressive in education in its teaching of modern history as an academic subject, taught by Barnes as part of the commercial course when the College was established in 1786, and as a separate subject at York. In the first year ancient history, including a view of the materials and sources of history and the principles of historical criticism, was studied, and in the second, modern history, which in particular compared the development of England and France and emphasised the history and principles of the English constitution.[89] From 1810 John Kenrick taught history and in 1840 he became the new professor. His chief reason for visiting Göttingen in 1819 was to enable him to establish a similar history lecture system at York. He wrote many historical articles and books including his *The Egypt of Herodotus* which earned him fame at the ancient universities despite their ostracism of 'heretics'. In 1840 Kenrick rejoiced to think that an English university, London, had at last given history a leading place among academic subjects. Although circumstance and the regulations of London demanded a chronological outline for the two year course, Kenrick wanted to teach his students a philosophical view. He did not claim to be completely impartial but hoped to be fair.[91] Yet James Martineau said of him:

> More than anyone we have ever met in life, he surrendered himself, unconditionally to objective evidence; would accept anything, where this was cogent; nothing where it failed.[92]

Martineau termed his history lectures a 'model of selection, compression and proportion' and greatly respected the largeness, the depth and rare balance of his mind. Others fortunate to study under him testified their admiration and respect.[93] No wonder the Revd. Charles Wicksteed said of him in 1877:

> he became at length one of the most exact and accomplished scholars in England, and certainly without a rival or a compeer, the first in the ranks of English Nonconformity.[94]

The provision of mathematics and science is discussed more fully elsewhere in this book. It appears to have been variable in its teaching and standards though the appointment of two scientists later eminent in their own field, John Dalton, 1793 to 1800, and an ex-student, William Hincks, 1827 to 1839, showed that the commitment to science was genuine.[95] The study of science was recognised by tutors and supporters of the college as important to all but vital to the lay students and essential if lay patronage was to be won.[96] Apparatus was secured, including that of Warrington and Hackney, and both in Manchester and York repeated references were made to the use students could and did make of the scientific lectures at the local philosophical societies in which Unitarians, not least the tutors of the College, figured so prominently. The College's dedicated visitor 1808 to 1853 was William Turner who so successfully lectured on science at the New Institution, Newcastle, 1802 to 1833 and there stressed the importance of science for 'commercial youth' who could apply science, particularly chemistry and mechanical philosophy, to local industries.[98] From 1842 to 1845, James Heywood liberally provided for a chair in civil engineering.[99]

The entrance requirements at York did require a certain amount of mathematical knowledge—admittedly not a great amount—but the syllabus covered the whole Cambridge mathematical course from Euclid to

Newton as James Martineau gratefully remembered.[100] Other students were not always so keen and it would seem that a certain amount of learning by heart took place: questions in the 1823 examination included: 'Demonstrate the forty-seventh proposition of the first Book of Euclid.'[101] W. R. Wood was sometimes dubious about Hincks's mathematical teaching but Hincks was, of course, primarily a botanist.[101] George Walker, at Manchester Academy had been a renowned mathematician. In 1840 there were separate chairs for mathematics and science and although the course for mathematics was little different from before, more was covered in science.[102] A truly Baconian (and Unitarian) enthusiasm for science was exhibited by Professor Phillips in stating that 'Here all is knowledge, and this knowledge is power' and that the study of science led to true religious belief in a 'supreme intelligent Author'. From the 1843 to 1844 session, however, following a change in the regulations of London University, natural philosophy reverted to the Professor of Mathematics.[103]

The recognition of the value of science in higher education showed that those who developed the curriculum at Manchester College were in the forefront of educational thinkers, many years ahead of the public and endowed schools, the colleges at the ancient universities, and, interestingly, many industrialists and businessmen of the day who were not convinced of the need for such education for their sons. Unitarian interest in science was also stimulated by their realisation of the implications of scientific discovery for rational theology—implications which John Kenrick was delighted to see troubled Anglican theologians.[104]

From 1809, the mathematical and science tutors at York were also responsible for mental philosophy, logic and ethics and political economy, subjects which had previously been taught by the theological tutor.[105] Lectures in mental philosophy covered the English and Scottish Schools and, by 1834, the 'leading doctrines of the most eminent philosophers of Germany and France'.[106] The chief concentration, however, was on David Hartley and the latest thoughts on Hartley were keenly followed, James Mill's *Analysis of the Human Mind* being purchased for the College Library in 1829, the year it came out. There is no doubt that the students were much influenced by these environmentalist and associationist ideas, a factor which reinforced the progressiveness of Unitarian education.[107] Many orations were given at the annual examinations on mental philosophy and on education[108] as they were indeed on political economy which was considered vital by the tutor for future leaders of commercial, industrial and civic life. Examination questions debating how political economy could be vindicated illustrate how seriously the College took this subject, as did orations such as W. R. Wood's paper at the College's Literary and Scientific Society in 1830, on 'The tendency of machinery to increase the products of human labour and the sum of human happiness as exemplified in the manufacture of cotton' and another in 1831 on 'The effect of commerce in promoting the civilisation of mankind'.[109]

In 1840, mental and moral philosophy and political economy were elevated to a separate department under James Martineau who justified these studies on the ground that only men 'thoroughly acquainted with the facts and laws of their own intellectual and moral being' could resolve the deep problems of speculative philosophy.[110] Although Metaphysics was hardly a new subject in higher education, Martineau was so far in the vanguard of nineteenth century philosophy that he even had some difficulty in retaining the lectureship in these studies after 1853.[111] His inaugural address in 1840 so impressed John Stuart Mill that he offered to publish in the *Westminster Review* any article written by Martineau on the free teaching and learning unique to Manchester College.[112]

This progressive curriculum was strengthened by many societies —Shakespeare, Belles Lettres, History, Modern Languages, and Debating, for example.[113] The last was highly significant as oratory was considered of prime importance not only because of the continuous pressure put on the College to produce eloquent and inspiring preachers (not always common among the more academic Unitarians, apparently) but also of its use to future leaders in public life.[114] Pole-leaping, cricket, boating, walking, political and other activities, provided lawful relaxation and change from constant study.[115]

That the curriculum was very wide there is no doubt and as such it was open to criticism similar to that received at Hackney and other Dissenting academies.[116] John James Tayler, when first a student, believed it impossible for students to master either the wide variety of subjects or the 'enormous quantity' of material within them that tutors, even the 'very judicious and sensible' Kenrick, taught:

> . . . in order to get done, they are obliged to gallop through so fast, that most of them drop behind at every step, what they picked up, at the preceding; so that when they come to their journey's end, most of them are as light as when they set out.[117]

Remarks by other students, such as William Holt in 1822 and William Wood in 1829 on the amount of time they needed to copy out lectures[118] raise the question of how far students could be learning to think for themselves, amid their efforts to set down another person's words. The fact that some lay students did the three-year course in two did not help.[119] On the other hand, students' complaints of being overloaded with work are hardly rare. The general unavailability of a variety of suitable books made the lecturers' words precious and shorthand was often used to help note-taking.[120] Furthermore, it was obviously not the intention of the tutors to encourage mere note-learning as Newman's letter to the Committee on behalf of the professors in 1841 showed.[121] The three students mentioned above certainly remained enthusiastic enough about their studies and the College.[122]

More importantly, the tutors and the supporters of the College never claimed to be doing more than awakening the students' minds to the various subjects which would both sharpen and develop their mental faculties and would prove useful to them in their future lives.[123] As at the universities, many of the students were between sixteen and eighteen on entrance and would not expect to follow a specialised course, though reformers argued that the much narrower Oxbridge curriculum was highly specialised. Charles Wellbeloved defended the 'extensive' course as necessary for a 'liberal' education in the contemporary widening state of knowledge and as suiting the need of rational Dissenters and the liberal supporters of the College. Kenrick pointed out that although some criticised them for teaching too much, others wanted them to teach more.[124] On a positive note, James Yates remarked in 1827, that Manchester College:

> probably yields to no seminary in England, either in the extent or accuracy of its literary and scientific pursuits[125]

One of the chief difficulties of the extensive curriculum, however, was having the requisite number of tutors to teach it competently. Robert Wallace, in 1840, lamented that in the past Dissenting Colleges, limited to the support of 'a small section of the Christian community', had had to expect one man to do the work of many as the case of George Walker, Principal of Manchester College, 1798 to 1803, exemplified.[126] It was, indeed, as well George Walker had 'the greatest variety of knowledge . . .' for as he complained so bitterly:

> I am every day so harrassed and exhausted by having for this year imposed upon me the whole duty of three tutors, that I seldom retire in the evening with strength or spirit to encounter the least exertion. My present labours are fitter for a Hercules in his youth than for an old man.[128]

Such weariness was echoed by Charles Wellbeloved in the early years at York and his repeated illnesses from over-exertion made the appointment of three tutors vital.[129] With improved finances the situation was never so bad again but even up to 1840, the workload remained heavy.

These difficulties of the tutors were exacerbated by the periodic disciplinary and financial crises of the College. Disciplinary problems, especially among lay students, undoubtedly worried would-be principals in 1798, caused Wellbeloved many a headache, nearly led the young John Kenrick to resign, eventually caused William Turner Junior to leave, and dogged the work of William Hincks when he was resident tutor.[130] For a college that distinguished itself from the 'corrupt' universities, both by the moral care of its students, and, in the York period, its domestic character, such interruptions were far from satisfactory.[131] George Wood, having been personally upset by a noisy, drunken party and an illicit, night-time theatre-goer, understandably feared that rumours of such carryings-on would frighten away would-be patrons.[132] This was by no means the whole picture[133] and often the difficulties were caused by one or two students only. Such problems are not uncommon in colleges or universities at any time, yet the tutors, whatever their principles and desire to make rational, enlightened and moral leaders of the middle-classes, could hardly regard lay students as an unmixed blessing.

Yet, in addition to the need for a steady inflow from subscription and congregational collections, lay-students were vital for the financial stability of the College, a stability which sometimes failed and was thus a major cause of the various moves of the College.[134] According to the College Roll 135 students were educated 1786 to 1803 (6 others are known also to have been at the College), 235, 1803 to 1839; 50, 1840 to 1853: of these 121, 113 and 32 respectively were lay students. There were also occasional students 1840 to 1853.[135] There was a periodic lack of lay students[136] possibly caused by rumour of disciplinary lapses, and by the economic depression of the 1840s, certainly by external factors such as involvement with political radicalism in the 1790s and the rivalry of London University from the 1830s. The ostracism of Unitarians by other Dissenters, particularly over the Lady Hewley case, cut off grants which would have assisted the students, as well as ensuring that the College remained primarily Unitarian.[137] This was an important factor. Unitarians did give substantial amounts to fund Manchester College, but the Unitarian body was comparatively small in number, not always firmly united, and many congregations had their own educational concerns to support, although some, admittedly, like the New Meeting, Birmingham, were outstanding for their contributions.[138]

All these factors affected support for and numbers at the College, a result which could seriously depress the remuneration of the already underpaid tutors and decrease the number of students on the foundation.[139] York was not the ideal situation to which to attract large numbers of students, particularly before the railway opened up the country. This might account for the fact that commercial families like the Potters used the College chiefly in the two Manchester periods.[140] Even the huge increase in donations and subscription and the enthusiastic propaganda generated by the move back to Manchester in the 1840s did not attract the expected increase in lay students, thus leaving the College dependent on resources too slender to support its high ambition.[141]

Unfortunately, the very lack of lay students could be self-perpetuating as parents doubted there could be any type of emulation. On the other hand, some students apparently worried that the standard of the public examination was too high.[142] Also the cost, eighty guineas at York, rising to one hundred in 1814,[143] and somewhat less at Manchester, made the College prohibitive to the less wealthy, especially many ministers, unless their sons followed in their fathers' footsteps, whereby they could have all their board and tuition fees paid on the foundation—another heavy expense for the College. Thomas Fletcher had wondered why with:

> the excellence of the plan of study, and the acknowledged qualities of the tutors . . . so few, so very few, of the youth of an opulent body of Dissenters should be found to take advantage of them.[144]

It is clear, however, that for many opulent Unitarian families the type of liberal education at Manchester College was what they wanted. The College was enthusiastically backed by a number of wealthy, commercial and industrial Unitarian families, for example, the Philips, Crompton, Strutt, Shore, Yates, Ashton, Potter, Hibbert, Kenrick, Paget and Heywood families, and this both by their money and by their presence.[145] William Strutt, for instance, not only delighted in his son Edward's chance to gain 'real knowledge' from which, hopefully he could advance his knowledge himself, but sought through him to tap his tutor, William Turner Junior's knowledge for his own mechanical invention.[146] But not all Unitarian industrialists used Manchester College in the same way. The Gregs did not, for example, although they had connections with the College. They chose Lant Carpenter's school in Bristol and Edinburgh University in preference, at both of which they could obtain a similar liberal and scientific education. Other Unitarian industrial and commercial families similarly patronised Unitarian schools and sympathised with the College to the extent of giving money and service.[147] Others of the middle-class were clearly not attracted by the educational ideals of the College. It is true that such generally took their time to be persuaded of their need of such an education, preferring one of a more immediately practical use and not continuing beyond fourteen. Schools of this type abounded in Manchester.[148] The commerce, mechanics and book-keeping of the first Manchester period did seem fairly popular, but the College's aims, as has been shown, were to produce enlightened, widely educated leaders of the commercial and industrial world, not narrowly trained men of business. Many Unitarians, however, increasingly chose to send their sons to London University for such higher education and it was for this reason that Manchester College so eagerly announced its affiliation with London in 1840 and eventually decided to move to London as a theological college, co-operating with University Hall and using University College for its secular education.[149]

The affiliation with London University did give an opportunity to test the standard of the College, albeit there were problems in judging the standards at London. Prior to this, apart from taking entrance requirements seriously, the College's summer examinations were open to supporters of the College and publicly reported. The examinations, in tune with developments elsewhere, changed from being entirely oral to largely written. There is much evidence to show that competition, both in these examinations and for the various prizes donated by patrons of the College, was keen.[150] That the College was certainly on a par with London was shown in 1840, when before the new structure was established, three students gained B.A. degrees in the first division. Two successes followed in 1841. By the time of the move to London in September, 1853, thirty more students had followed suit, as well as two who gained their degrees before entering and after leaving the College, respectively. Four, including John Adyss Scott, grandson of Charles Wellbeloved, moved on to an M.A. and won the University Gold Medal, and two gained their LL.D. From the students of this second Manchester period, three took London B.A.s in 1855 and two in 1854. Thirteen of the thirty-five B.A. degrees gained were taken by laymen. In this Manchester period twenty-eight divinity and thirty-two laymen were regular students.[151]

The College was clearly up to London standards. How far it fulfilled its liberal aims can be further judged by the type of men its students turned out to be and what their achievements were, though obviously previous schooling and home education also played a part. That the College did produce ministers who were capable of defending Unitarianism, defending rational theology and earning esteem for their learning is amply proved, not least in the examples of John Relly Beard, James Martineau, John Gooch Robbards, the eloquent minister at Cross Street, Manchester, William Gaskell, his co-pastor, and John James Tayler, their neighbour for so many years at Mosley Street and author of *A Retrospect of the Religious Life in England* among other writings.[152] All these were also concerned in various educational ventures including Manchester College.

Other writers in this book have assessed the contribution made to business, science and medicine. Many influential and powerful business, industrial, professional and political men were educated at Manchester College. Edward Strutt and Mark Philips, for example, both sons of wealthy manufacturers became M.P.s in 1830 and 1832 respectively. Strutt; a friend both of Robert Owen and John Stuart Mill, held various important posts and in 1856 became the first Baron Belper, and in 1860, F.R.S. Amongst other things he supported Lancasterian education, the establishment of Mechanics Institutes and London University. Philips fought hard to extend civil and religious liberties and made munificent gifts to Manchester such as a public park.[153] Other examples of civic leadership include William Enfield who became the solicitor and town clerk of Nottingham, was a manager of the Mechanics Institute, a promoter of the School of Art, of decent homes for the poor and of healthful places of recreation, and was a governor of the Institute for the Blind, the lunatic asylum and the Town and Country Hospital.[154] Similarly, H. W. Crosskey, Minister of the Church of the Messiah in Birmingham from 1869 was a foremost promoter of popular education and of a new civic gospel.[155]

Unitarian social concern was tempered by adherence to political economy, also fostered at Manchester College. Mark Philips, like many Unitarians, opposed factory legislation, though Samuel Fielden, another ex-student, upheld his father's eager fight for it.[156] Laissez-faire in economic and industrial matters would come easily to many merchants and manufacturers, yet belief in economic 'truths', often so harsh and uncompromising in their effects, had to be balanced by their Unitarian humanitarianism and equally firm belief in social service. That many Unitarian industrialists were famed for their paternalist benevolence as factory owners cannot be directly attributed to Manchester College since many of the most famous such as the Gregs and Thomas Ashton did not go there although they had connections with the College and with ministers who had been educated there.[157] Such industrialists, who retained their economic ideas yet sought to ameliorate the lot of their workforce in other ways, particularly by education, found that these conflicting ideals brought them less than success in their ventures. For example, Samuel Robinson, who was an ex-student of the College and was a popular writer on Persian poetry, discovered that his benevolent intentions in his village library, were partially baulked by his stand on industrial relations.[158] The liberating ideas permeating Unitarian educational philosophy were thus countered by suspicion that they were seeking social control. On the other hand, John Ashton Nicholls, a Manchester cotton-spinner, who opposed strikes and told workmen so, nevertheless worked for their betterment to the extent that the working men of Manchester erected an obelisk in Great Ancoats to his

> untiring zeal and earnestness for the elevation of their class intellectually, politically, socially and morally . . .[159]

Among those who modified their ideas on political economy was James Martineau (who turned to more paternalistic ideas reminiscent of Disraeli). His political economy lectures at Manchester College in the 1840s were so popular that they were repeated in evening classes.[160]

Former Manchester College students were well-known leaders in other ways. Robert Scott Taylor became editor of the *Manchester Guardian*, for example, whilst Richard Holt Hutton became editor first of *The Inquirer* and then of the *Spectator* and in his many articles illustrated the social and educational concerns common at Manchester College.[161] Robert Dukinfield Darbishire became a solicitor and prominent in local life. A trustee, active manager and munificent patron of Owens College, a founder of the Manchester High School for Girls, and a trustee of the Whitworth Trust, he promoted female education, and science and education generally.

Education, indeed, was the field where many former students of Manchester College worked tirelessly and endlessly, thus diffusing in an immediate way the ideal advanced at the College. A short list from the many examples shows the extent of their concerns. There were those like Revd. S. A. Steinthal and J. R. Beard and H. W. Crosskey who campaigned for State elementary education or who, like Edward Higginson, ran schools of their own.[163] Many ran Sunday Schools, a prime example being the Lower Mosley Street Sunday School in Manchester where, in the 1840s, J. G. Robberds, J. J. Tayler, and William Gaskell held evening services and many of the students taught, especially Travers Madge who was first editor of the Sunday School Magazine in 1848. This magazine illustrated the breadth of knowledge taught in Unitarian Sunday Schools and had articles by leading writers of the day such as Harriet Martineau and Elizabeth Gaskell. Madge would teach young male factory workers as early as four or five in the morning and helped in a mutual improvement society amongst other educational activities.[164] Samuel Robinson, Edward Strutt, William Bayley, J. A. Nicholls, James Martineau, are a few of those who founded, supported or taught at

Mechanics Institutes.[165] Many were similarly involved with opening up education for the middle-classes, whether through informal agencies, such as the literary and philosophical societies mentioned above,[166] or more formal institutions such as the universities, where, for example, James Yates in London and Charles Beard in Liverpool played such important roles.[167]

John Relly Beard was a prime example of one who was involved in multifarious educational activities. A prize student in 1821, awarded an honorary D.D. from the university of Giessen in 1841, he ran an excellent school of his own at Stony Knolls, Salford, attended by many of the sons of the leading industrialists and citizens of Manchester and district.[168] His interest in Pestalozzian education was typical of many Unitarians. In particular W. H. Herford, one of his admiring pupils who also attended Manchester College, pioneered Froebelian ideas in England and established Ladybarn School in Manchester, a coeducational school where Beard's granddaughter, Mary and Herford's daughter Caroline were headmistress in turn, in the early twentieth century.[169] Beard also established an infant school at Salford, had a flourishing Sunday School for three hundred children within seven years of his ministry, belonged to the Manchester Literary and Philosophical Society, lectured to the Manchester Mechanics' Institute and helped the fight to reform Manchester Grammar School. He was a fervent member of the Lancashire Public School Association which agitated for elementary schools, supported by local rates and under local control, largely on the plan of the Unitarian Horace Mann in Massachusetts.[170]

Beard wrote many books to help those dependent on teaching themselves and was a corresponding tutor to hundreds of young men who studied his English, Latin and Greek lessons in Cassell's *Popular Educator*. He was the principal founder and first theological tutor and principal of the Unitarian Home Missionary Board which sought to educate for the ministry less wealthy men than those who could attend Manchester College and who would then serve the more working-class congregations.[171] Beard had long argued the case for such a college, always having wished to extend a full education to all regardless of sex or class, having no fear of the effects of knowledge but dreading those of ignorance.[172]

Many alumni of Manchester College were involved in U.H.M.B. including James Yates, John Ashton Nicholls and Thomas Hincks. W. H. Herford taught German there in 1872 and from 1874 when Beard resigned, the theological tutor was T. Elford Poynting, a labourer's son, who had excelled in Hebrew as a mature student at Manchester College. Poynting, like Herford and Beard wrote books on education.[173]

The principal of U.H.M.B. from 1874 was William Gaskell, in turn student, English tutor, Chairman of the Committee and Visitor at Manchester College. Gaskell had lectured on 'The Poets and Poetry of Humble Life' to enthusiastic audiences of working-men, and in English Literature at the new Workingmen's College in Manchester from 1858. He helped his wife with her writing even when it upset some of his congregation; a refreshing attitude towards women also evinced by Gaskell's involvement in the education of his daughters and other young women,[174] and in similar attitudes shown by others such as J. R. Beard, James Martineau and S. A. Steinthal. Martineau's lectures in Liverpool to women such as Anna Swanwick, later a famous translator, gave them their first taste of higher education, whilst those in ethics at Manchester College in the 1870s paved the way for the College to open itself to women theological students, the first English college so to do.[175]

Unitarians from Manchester College were rarely wanting complete change in gender or class roles yet in their genuine desire to make available the best modern education to whomsoever they could, they were being revolutionary in fact. Many of those intimately connected with the College, though not students there, were similar, for example, William Turner, the Visitor for fifty-one years, a man involved in many educational activities whose name, with that of Wellbeloved, was feelingly recalled in 1859 by William Gaskell, who hoped that Manchester College would continue to ensure that Liberal Christians should have 'clear insight and large and generous culture' and leaders 'who were prepared to take up their position fairly before the world'.[176]

The College, therefore, though small, made a valuable contribution to English education. In its very existence as an institution of higher education open to all regardless of creed, it was unique for many years. In its curriculum and methods it pioneered a new type of higher education for the modern world. Through the ministers it trained it did supply the Churches of Liberal Christianity with men both learned and cultured. Through its alumni, both lay and theological, it disseminated a liberal, reformist message in many aspects of life. Kenrick's belief in 1840 that many parents were now seeking a 'higher and more enlarged education' for their sons was too sanguine but perhaps it could be said that his hope of seeing the labours of the College diffusing:

> through the whole mass of society which surrounds us, sound knowledge and virtuous principle

was, at least, partially realised.[177]

## NOTES

All books published in London unless otherwise stated.

All manuscript and document material to be found at Manchester College, Oxford unless otherwise stated.

References:

| | |
|---|---|
| M.A. | Manchester Academy |
| M.C. | Manchester College |
| M.C.Y. | Manchester College, York |
| M.N.C. | Manchester New College |
| C.W. | Charles Wellbeloved |
| G.W.W. | George William Wood |
| J.K. | John Kenrick |

| | |
|---|---|
| Roll | Roll of Students, 1786 to 1867 |
| M.R. | Monthly Repository |
| N.S. | New Series |
| D.N.B. | Dictionary of National Biography |
| D.W.L. | Doctor Williams' Library |
| T.U.H.S. | Transactions of the Unitarian Historical Society |
| T.H.S.L.C. | Transactions of the Historic Society of Lancashire and Cheshire |
| U.C.L. | University College, London |

1. Report of the Committee of M.A., 22.2.1786, p. 1.

2. Oxford required subscription to the 39 Articles from candidates entering matriculation, Cambridge from those taking a degree.

3. N. Hans, *New Trends in Education in the Eighteenth Century* (1951), pp. 63–116.

4. E.g. H. A. Bright, 'A Historical Sketch of Warrington Academy' *T.H.S.L.C.* XI, Nov. 1859, p. 2; J. Priestley, *Autobiography* (1970 ed.) pp. 75–7, 91; H. McLachlan, *English Education under the Test Acts* (1931), pp. 75, 124, 164, 166, 169; J. William, *Memoirs of the Late Thomas Belsham* (1833), pp. 300, 421.

5. In the 1820s a number of local nondenominational collegiate institutions were established, e.g. in Bristol—Bristol Central Library 23363, *Prospectus of a College for Classical and Scientific Education*, 1829. Possibly these were more akin to sixth-form colleges e.g. Philip Carpenter attended Bristol, then went to M.C. for four years *D.N.B.* IX, p. 162; Roll 1837.

6. E.g. see *M.R.* XVI (1821), p. 357; I. Sellars, *Nineteenth Century Nonconformity* (1977) pp. 65–8; R. W. Davies, *Dissent in Politics*, 1780–1830 (1971) pp. 148–186, 199–203, 216–44; R. B. Aspland, *Memoir of the Life, Work and Correspondence of the Revd. Robert Aspland of Hackney* (1850) pp. 260–8, 281, 467; A. Ruston, 'The Non-Con-Club . . .' *T.U.H.S.* XIV no. 3 (1967) p. 151; MSS. *J.K. IV*, J.K. to G.W.W. 17.3.1834, 11.4.1834, 20.4.1834, 11.5.1834, 28.6.1834, 7.7.1834; *James Heywood*, typescript of the Church of the Divine Unity, Newcastle upon Tyne; R. V. Holt, *The Unitarian Contribution to Social Progress in England* (1952) pp. 61, 242–3.

7. *M.N.C. 1844 Report*, p. 3; *M.N.C. Report* 1841–1854; *M.N.C. Proceedings 1853*, pp. 33, 35, 37, and Report, pp. 5, 43.

8. *Letters, papers etc. re second M.N.C., 1840–53*, 9.3.1848, 6.4.1848, 30.5.1848, Extract from John Owen's Will; *Printed Papers and Addresses, 1838–53*, M.N.C. Report of the Committee of Inquiry 30.6.1848, pp. 26–9; J. Yates, *Thoughts on the Advancement of Academical Education in England* (1827); *D.N.B.* LXIII, p. 295; H. H. Bellot, *University College, London, 1826–1926* (1929) pp. 27, 80–6, 96–102, 187, 210–14, 256–8, 261–5, 382–3; R. S. Fitton and A. P. Wadsworth, *The Strutts and the Arkwrights, 1758–1830* (1958) pp. 180–1; ed. T. Saddler, *Diary, Reminiscences and Correspondence of Henry Crabb Robinson* (1872) vol. II, pp. 54, 125, 208, 258, 285, 335, 339–401; *James Heywood, op. cit.*; *M.R.* N.S. I (1827), 161–71, 254–6, 468–70; N.S. 2 (1828), pp. 195–6, 283, 411, 632, 771–7, 864; N.S. 3 (1829), pp. 129–30, 806, 877–9; H. Morley, *A Lecture Introductory to the Fifty-first Session, U.C.L.* (1878), pp. 5–22.

9. S. T. Barnes, A discourse delivered at the Commencement of the Manchester Academy, 1786, p. 73, in *Report on the Proceedings of the Hundredth Anniversary, M.N.C., 22.2.1866*.

10. W. Turner, Jun., *Lives of Eminent Unitarians* (1840) pp. 347–8. (See also note 2 above.)

11. *Ibid*, pp. 351–3.

12. *M.C.Y. 1833 Report.*

13. The evolution of Unitarianism from primarily Presbyterian origin (though with important exceptions) is succinctly described in C. G. Bolam, J. Goring, H. L. Short and R. Thomas, *The English Presbyterians* (1968). Unitarians frequently

referred to themselves as Presbyterians—with good reason before the 1813 Act relieved them from penalties against anti-Trinitarianism.

14. H. McLachlan, *op. cit.* pp. 91–9, 192–7, 237–43. Homerton from 1801, and Blackburn (1816–43), both Independent, did have wider curricula *ibid.* pp. 181–7, 270–2.

15. W. Turner, *A Sermon preached at the chapel in Hanover Square, Newcastle for the support of the New College, Manchester, 1800*; MSS High Pavement Papers Nottingham University *Sermons . . . on behalf of M.C.Y.*, HiY7, HiY5; *M.R.* XXI, 1826, pp. 554–7.

16. T. Barnes, *op. cit.* pp. 60–6.

17. *M.C.Y. 1833 Report.*

18. *Christian Reformer* 1841 pp. 473–8; J. J. Tayler, 'Inaugural Address' pp. 10–19, *M.N.C. Addresses 1853–81*; M.R. XIX, 1824, p. 427; *Christian Reformer* 1834, p. 571.

19. *Christian Reformer* 1836, p. 198.

20. J. Martineau, *Essays, Reviews and Addresses* IV (1891) 'The Need of Culture for the Christian Ministry' Cross Street Chapel 24.1.1836, pp. 360–8.

21. The rather bitter comments of John Tayler in 1822 and John Kenrick in 1843 deprecating the low value set on literary accomplishment by Unitarians might have been in reference to the less wealthy congregations—ed. J. H. Thom, *Letters of John James Tayler* 1 p. 52; MSS *J.K. IV* J.K. to G.W.W. 23.2.1843.

22. W. Turner, *op. cit.*

23. R. Watts, 'Joseph Priestley and Education', *Enlightenment and Dissent* No. 2 1983 pp. 83–100; J. E. Carpenter, *James Martineau* (1905) pp. 35, 119–20.

24. J. Kenrick, *The Union of Religion with Intellectual Culture . . .* Dublin, 16.8.1835.

25. *M.N.C. Proceedings 1853* Petition 31 clause 98.

26. W. Turner, *op. cit.* pp. 16–20; *1797 Prospectus*; *1853 Proceedings*, Petition 14.

27. *M.C.Y. 1829 Report*, p. 4. See however D. Wykes, Sons & Subscribers: *TRUTH, LIBERTY, RELIGION, ESSAYS celebrating two hundred years of Manchester College*. 1986.

28. *MSS J.K. IV* W. Turner to G.W.W. (including letter of Heywood to Turner) 7.11.1809.

29. E.g. *Letter-book, cuttings etc. M.C. 1824–80*, p. 17, Prospectus 1817; M.C.Y. Reports 1823, p. 6; 1828, p. 5.

30. C. Wellbeloved, *Objects of pursuit Proper for Young Persons who have received a Liberal Education*. Sermon St. Saviourgate, York, 1810 (1811) pp. 11–12.

31. T. Barnes, 'A Plan for the Improvement and Extension of Liberal Education in Manchester', *Memoirs of the Manchester Literary and Philosophical Society*, vol. 11, p. 29.

32. T. Barnes, 'A Discourse . . . 1786', *op. cit.* p. 66.

33. E. H. Hobsbawm, *The Age of Revolution* (1977) Abacus Paperback p. 230—though even Hobsbawm allows some exceptions which point to Unitarians, *ibid.*

34. *Prospectus M.N.C. 9.8.1797*; *M.C.Y. Report* 1831; *Unitarian Chronicle* 1833 p. 167; *1853 Proceedings*, p. 32, Affidavits of Wellbeloved, Kenrick, Martineau, Smith, Tayler etc. pp. 39, 41–2.

35. T. Barnes, *op. cit.* p. 55.

36. *Sermons and Tracts on Education, 1763–1841*, John Rylands Library, University of Manchester, R. Harrison, 'Sermon preached at . . . Cross Street, Manchester, March 26, 1786, on the occasion of the Establishment of an Academy in that town' pp. 3–10.

37. *M.R.* N.S. 5, 1831 p. 831.
38. B. Simon, *The Two Nations and the Educational Structure, 1780–1870* (1974), pp. 87–94; M. M. Bowery, *William Turner's Contribution to Educational Developments in Newcastle upon Tyne (1782–1841)*, M.A. Newcastle University 1980, pp. 188–9; ed. L. Aikin, *The Work of Anna Laetitia Barbauld* (1825), vol. II, p. 365; T. Barnes, 'A Plan for . . .' *op. cit.* p. 20.
39. G. Haines, *German Influence upon English Education and Science, 1800–66*, Connecticut College, Monograph 6 (1957) pp. 13–14, 19; B. Simon, *op. cit.* pp. 86–7.
40. *D.N.B.* LX, pp. 455–6. D.S.L. Cardwell, *The Organisation of Science in England* (1972) pp. 14–15, 39–45.
41. Edinburgh Review vol. XVI No. 31 (April 1810) pp. 158–187; B. Knights, *The Idea of the Clerisy in the Nineteenth Century* (1978) pp. 10, 190–7. See also *Apologia Academica, Oxford* (1831) pp. 1–28 passim.
42. B. Simon, *op. cit.* pp. 87–8, 89.
43. R. Watts, *op. cit.*; W. Shepherd, J. Joyce and L. Carpenter, *Systematic Education* (1817) vol. I pp. 16–18; J. Yates, *op. cit.* pp. 71–97.
44. G. Haines, *op. cit.* especially pp. 94–6; D. Cardwell, *op. cit.* pp. 20–5; *Roll*, passim.
45. E.g. see *M.C.Y. 1834 Report*, 4.
46. Sermons and Tracts, *op. cit.* 1886, Appendices I and II: Prospectus . . . 1797; J. W. Ashley Smith in *The Birth of Modern Education, the Contribution of Dissenting Academies* (1954), p. 170, stated that no modern languages were taught at Manchester Academy but French and Italian were definitely intended and Pipe-Wolferstan's son certainly studies French there from 1801–2 at a cost of 8 guineas—G. N. Ditchfield 'The Early History of Manchester College', *T.H.S.L.C.* vol. 123 (1972), p. 92.
47. E.g. MSS. C.W. 11, C.W. to T. Robinson 7.5.1807; *M.R.* Vol. II (1807) pp. 118–19, 441; (1810) pp. 605, XXI (1826) p. 497; Letter Book . . . 1824–80, pp. 17, 28, 25; *M.C.Y. Reports* especially 1834 pp. 4–5, 6; *York Letters*, 1811 G.W.W. to C.W. 3.1.1813; *C.W. II*; C.W. to G.W.W. 21.12.1813; *Letters, Papers re 2nd M.N.C. 1840–58*, 1848 Address of the Committee to the Trustees, pp. 1–3.
48. *M.N.C. Reports* 1840, pp. 4–5; 1841, pp. 3, 6, 8–11; 1847, pp. 4–5; M.C. Theology was not examined at London—see note 69.
49. H. H. Bellot, *op. cit.* pp. 77–9.
50. See note 9.
51. *M.R.* II (1807), p. 283.
52. MSS *C.W. II*, C.W. to C.W.W. 6.4.1809.
53. E.g. *M.R.* VI (1811), pp. 369–71, 441; *MSS York Letters*, 1811, G.W.W. to C.W. 8.6.1811.
54. *Letter book . . . 1824–80*, p. 2; *Letter book, cutting M.C. 1842–53*, pp. 177–8.
55. *MSS J.K.* III, J.K. to G.W.W. 10.8.1814. Compare 1813 Annual Report in *M.R.* IX (1814) p. 250, yet see also *J.K. IV* J.K. to G.W.W. 15.7.1832.
56. *Roll* passim.
57. V. D. Davies, *A History of Manchester College* (1932) pp. 39, 76n, pp. 2, 111.
58. J. Kenrick, *A Biographical Memoir of the late Revd. Charles Wellbeloved* (1860) pp. 99–110
59. J. Martineau, *op. cit.* IV, p. 54.
60. *Christian Reformer* 1836, pp. 196–203; 1840, pp. 542–7; see also R. Wallace, *Inaugural Lecture Critical and Exegetical Theology*, pp. 20–1, 1840. Some scholars did dispute Wellbeloved's teaching of Hebrew without points—M. McLachlan *Essays and Addresses* (1950) pp. 188–9.

61. C. Cappe, *Memoir of the late Mrs Catherine Cappe* (1822) pp. 441–2; J. Kenrick, *op. cit.* pp. 59, 77–9, 145–54, 229–30.
62. *Ibid.* pp. 231–2; D. G. Wigmore-Beddoes, *Yesterday's Radicals* (1971) pp. 38–9; V. D. Davies, *op. cit.* p. 116.
63. *D.N.B.* IV pp. 399–400; J. Martineau, *op. cit.* vol. 1. 'In Memoriam John James Tayler'; ed. J. H. Thom, *op. cit.*; D. G. Wigmore-Beddoes, *op. cit.* pp. 39–40, 55–6, 58, 99, 116–17.
64. *Ibid.* pp. 57–8, 95–9, 101, 116–19; J. E. Carpenter, *op. cit.* passim; J. Drummond and C. B. Upton, *The Life and Letters of James Martineau* (1902) passim.
65. D. G. Wigmore-Beddoes, *op. cit.*, passim; J. E. Carpenter, *The Bible in the Nineteenth Century* (1903) passim.
66. Unitarians such as William Taylor and Henry Crabb Robinson had spearheaded the introduction of German work into England and many Unitarians in the 1820s were keenly interested in German educational ideas—J. W. Robberds, *A Memoir of the Life and Writings of the late William Taylor of Norwich* (1843); ed. T. Saddler, *op. cit.*, vol. I pp. 39ff., vol. II p. 53ff.; M. R. Parnaby, *William Johnson Fox and the Monthly Repository Circle of 1832–1836*, unpublished Ph.D. thesis Australian National University (1979), pp. 153–62, 228–9, 413.
67. D. G. Wigmore-Beddoes, *op. cit.*, pp. 34–6, 70; *Inquirer* 19.5.1877, pp. 321–3; *Letters re M.C. early 19th century, Times* 26.5.1877 'A Latin Scholar'; J. Martineau, *op. cit.* vol. I. 'In Memoriam: John Kenrick'; ed. J. H. Thom, *op. cit.* pp. 105–69; *M.N.C. 1853 Report*, p. 4; J. Drummond and C. B. Upton, *op. cit.* vol. I, pp. 182–9; MSS *J.K. III* J.K. to G.W.W. 16.4.1826.
68. *Inaugural Lectures*, 1840–Theology–Wallace, Tayler and Robberds.
69. MSS *J.K. IV* J.K. to G.W.W. 23.2.1841.
70. *Printed Papers and Addresses*, 1839–53, Report of the Special Committee M.N.C. 8.12.1852.
71. J. J. Tayler, *Inaugural Lecture 1853*, especially pp. 7–9, 16–19.
72. E.g. *M.R. VII* (1812) pp. 430–1; XI (1816) pp. 119; XII (1817) p. 497; XIII (1818) p. 462; XXI (1826) pp. 431, 557; High Pavement Sermons *op. cit.*
73. *M.R.* V (1810) p. 605; X (1815) p. 448; XX (1825) p. 375; *MSS York Letters* 1815, Thomas Fletcher to G.W.W. 12.2.1815 (N.B. J. R. Wreford in *Statistics on Dissenting Colleges* has the Fletcher brothers entering Manchester College in 1813) *Letters re M.C. early 19th C.*, William Holt to his father 5.11.1822; *MSS J.K. III*, J.K. to G.W.W. 30.3.1825; *M.N.C. Report 1841*, p. 8.
74. E.g. see *M.R.* XI (1816) p. 119; XII (1817) p. 496; XIII (1818) p. 462; XXI (1826) p. 431; N.S. (1829) p. 584; and the *Reports* of the College throughout the period here studied.
75. MSS *Shepherd Papers* VI, p. 83.
76. E.g. *M.R.* IX (1814) p. 432; MSS W. R. Wood *Letters to his parents*, 1829–31, 18.4.1830 (21), to 6.6.1830 (28) passim.
77. MSS *College Essays*, 1816–1819.
78. *D.N.B.* IV, p. 399; IX, pp. 157–9 ed. J. H. Thom *op. cit.* I, pp. 3–7, 12, 14, 19–21, 25–6 and 233, 299; II, p. 172; R. L. Carpenter, *Memoir of the Revd. Lant Carpenter LL.D.* (1842) pp. 339–52.
79. *DWL 24 102* (1), J. J. Tayler to cousin W. Tayler 5.11.1814. See also MSS *Wellbeloved Letters*, J. J. Tayler to John Kenrick 14.12.1836. Those who did not reach Kenrick's exacting standards might suffer from his 'keen sarcastic wit'—W. R. Wood *op. cit.* 14.11.1830 (35).
80. MSS *Wellbeloved Letters*, T. Robinson to C.W. 10.10.1818.
81. J. Martineau *op. cit.* vol. I, pp. 408–9.
82. *Ibid.*; *Inquirer* 19.5.1877, pp. 321–2 (Kenrick himself believed that every

classical teacher should have studied in Germany—MSS *J.K.* IV J.K. to G.W.W. 17.11.1839); 24.11.1839 (to J. J. Tayler). *M.R.* N.S. 3 (1829) p. 878.

83. G. Sieveking *Memoir and Letters of Francis W. Newman* (1909) pp. 108–9; F. Newman *Introductory Lecture to the Classical Course, 1840; M.N.C. Report 1847*, p. 4.

84. *Report of the Committee of M.A. 22.2.1786*, p. 2; *Letter re M.C. . . . early 19th C.* W. Holt to his father 5.11.1822; MSS *J.K. III*, J.K. to G.W.W. 6.4.1826; 7.5.1826; *J.K. IV* 28.2.1834; *Letter book . . . 1824–80*, pp. 24, 28, 35, 42–3; *M.C.Y. Reports* 1828, 1829, 1834; *Roll* 1826–9 *M.N.C. Report* 1841, pp. 6, 8, 9; 1842, p. 6.

85. E.g. an honours course in modern languages was only open to men at Oxford in 1908 after women had pioneered the subject as a university degree.—V. Brittain, *The Women at Oxford* (1960) pp. 90, 122.

86. *M.C.Y. Report 1834*, p. 5.

87. J. Kenrick, *Inaugural Lecture on Ancient and Modern History and the History of Literature*, 1840, p. 12. See also J. Martineau *op. cit.*, vol. I, p. 411.

88. W. Gérin, *Elizabeth Gaskell* (1976) pp. 45–52, 63.

89. *Sermons and Tracts . . . op. cit.* Appendix II, p. 8; MSS C.W. II to T. Robinson C.W. II 7.5.1807; *Letter book . . . 1824–80*, pp. 17, 28, *M.C.Y. Report* 1834, p. 5.

90. *Inquirer op. cit.* pp. 321–3.

91. J. Kenrick, *op. cit.* pp. 3–20.

92. J. Martineau, *op. cit.* p. 413.

93. *D.W.L. Letters to Kenrick 24.81. (15)* J. Martineau to Mrs Kenrick 24.5.1877; W. R. Wood *op. cit.* 1.11.1829 (4); *Wellbeloved Letters* J. J. Tayler to J.K. 14.12.1836.

94. *Inquirer op. cit.* pp. 322–3.

95. H. E. McLachlan, *Essays and Addresses* (1950) pp. 62–9; *D.N.B.* XXVI p. 441.

96. MSS *C.W. II.* C.W. to T. Robinson, 26.2.1805; to G.W.W. Feb. 1809; 25.2.1809; 6.4.1809; *MSS J.K. III*, J.K. to G.W.W. 23.4.1827; *J.K. IV* J.K. to G.W.W. 22.10.1824; P. E. Musson and E. Robinson, *Science and Technology in the Industrial Revolution* (1969) pp. 93–6, 113–14.

97. E.g. MSS *CW II*, C.W. to G.W.W. 25.1.1810; 11.4.1810; *M.R.* V (1810) p. 605, VI (1811) p. 558; *Letter book . . . 1824–80*, p. 125; *Letter book . . . 1842–53*, p. 153.

98. *Letter book . . . 1824–80*, p. 35; F. Nicholson, 'The Literary and Philosophical Society, 1781–1851', *Proceedings of the Manchester Literary and Philosophical Society*, vol. 68 part 1 (1923–4), pp. 98–100, 108–11, 140–3; A. D. Orange, 'Philosophers and Provincials: The Yorkshire Philosophical Society from 1822–44', *Yorkshire Philosophical Society* (1973) pp. 23–4, 26, 46, 51–2, 56–9; M. M. Bowery, *op. cit.* pp. 227–245.

99. *M.N.C. Report* 1842, p. 6; *Printed Papers and Addresses 1839–1853*, Advertisements for civil engineering course and evening classes in practical chemistry.

100. J. Drummond and C. B. Upton, *op. cit.* p. 34; see also MSS *Shepherd Papers* VI, p. 83.

101. MSS *York Letters*, C.W. to G.W.W., 13.2.1817; *Letters to M.C. early 19th C.*, 1823 mathematical paper; W. R. Wood, *op. cit.* 1.11.1829 (4), 7.2.1830 (14); 16.5.1830, (25); 31.10.1830, (33); in the second year, however, Wood gave his attention principally to mathematics, *ibid.* 19.6.1831 (62). In 1833 when the maths class was not doing very well, Robert Phillips was allowed to drop mathematics for political economy—MSS *J.K. IV.* J.K. to G.W.W., 7.3.1833.

102. *Unitarian Worthies* (1876) pp. 239–240. Compare *M.N.C. Reports* 1834, 1835 and 1841, pp. 8–9.

103. *Introductory Lecture in Physical Science and Natural History*, 1840, p. 26; *1844 Report*, p. 4.

104. MSS *J.K. IV*, J.K. to G.W.W. 8.5.1834.

105. *Sermons and Tracts . . . op. cit.* p. 8; *Prospectus 1797; MSS C.W. II,* C.W. to T. Robinson, 7.5.1807; *M.R.* V (1810), p. 605. Commerce became subsumed into political economy in the York period, logic into mental philosophy, e.g. see *1834 Report*, p. 5.
106. *Ibid.*, p. 5; J. E. Carpenter, *op. cit.* pp. 34, 35. See also *M.R.* VII (1812) p. 625; N.S. 2 (1829) pp. 31–40.
107. J. E. Carpenter, *op. cit.* pp. 35, 119–20, 123; J. M. Connell, 'Dickens' Unitarian minister Edward Tagart', T.U.H.S. VII, No. 2, 1944, p. 78; *Letter book . . . 1824–80*, p. 50. See also W. R. Wood, *op. cit.* 16.1.1831 (39).
108. On education e.g. *M.R.* VI (1811) p. 439; X (1815) p. 448; XI (1816) p. 416; XII (1817) p. 496; XIII (1818), p. 462; XVI (1821), p. 427; XX (1825) p. 420; XXI (1826) p. 430.
109. *Letters re M.N.C. . . . early 19th C.*, 1823 examination paper. W. R. Wood, *op. cit.* 2.5.1830 (23), 24.4.1831 (51); *M.R.* XX (1825) p. 420; XXI (1826) p. 430; N.S. 4 (1831) p. 567.
110. J. Martineau, *op. cit.* vol. IV, pp. 1–17. Significantly, the London examination in mental philosophy concentrated on those problems familiar in Unitarian education and had questions on Hartley and James Mill—*Printed Papers and Addresses* 1843 Mental Philosophy Examination, Junior Class.
111. 1854 *Report*, 9. J. Drummond and C. B. Upton, *op. cit.* pp. 252–60.
112. *Ibid.*, III.
113. *Letters re M.C. . . . early 19th* C. William Holt to father, 1822; W. R. Wood, *op. cit.* 8.11.1829 (5); 2.5.1830 (23).
114. E.g. *ibid.* 17.4.1831 (50); 29.5.1831 (59); *M.C.Y. Report*, 1823, p. 4; MSS *C.W. II* passim; MSS *J.K. III* passim; *J.K. IV.* 1.7.1825; *Letters re M.C. . . . early 19th C.*, Missionary Project; *Christian Reformer* 1836, pp. 555, 582.
115. *Letters re M.C. . . . early 19th* C. W. Holt to father, 1822; W. R. Wood *op. cit.* 13.12.1829 (9); 27.3.1831 (46); H. McLachlan *op. cit.* pp. 200, 207, 211.
116. E.g. G. Wakefield *Memoirs* vol. I (1792) pp. 352–375. William Turner Junior recognised that there was some basis to Wakefield's criticism but believed that more recent academies (probably M.C.) had tried to rectify such mistakes—W. Turner (Jun.) *op. cit.* p. 263.
117. *D.W.L. 24 102(1) J. J. Tayler* to cousin 5.11.1814.
118. *Letters re M.C. . . . early 19th C.*, W. Holt to father, 5.11.1822; W. R. Wood, *op. cit.* 1.11.1829 (4); 14.11.1829 (6); 25.4.1830 (22); 28.11.1830 (36). But see also *ibid.* 20.3.1831 (45).
119. MSS *J.K. IV* J.K. to G.W.W. Dec. 1830; *Letter book 1824–80*; p. 28; *M.R.* VIII (1813) p. 482.
120. E.g. W. R. Wood, *op. cit.* letters p. 15ff . . .
121. *Letter book re M.C. early 19th* C. Newman to Committee, 20.10.1841.
122. William Wood became treasurer, 1844–52; J. J. Tayler was on the staff 1840 69; for William Holt see 1847 *Report*, p. 30, for example.
123. E.g. T. Barnes, *op. cit.* pp. 60–2; *M.R.* VII (1812) pp. 8–9; *Christian Reformer* 1841, pp. 476–8.
124. MSS *C.W. II*, C.W. to T. Robinson, 7.5.1807; *J.K. III*, J.K. to G.W.W., 10.8.1814.
125. J. Yates, *op. cit.* 57.
126. R. Wallace, *Introductory Lecture . . . Theology*, 1840, pp. 6–9.
127. *Ibid*, Wakefield's comment.
128. G. M. Ditchfield, *op. cit.* p. 90.
129. *M.R.* II (1807) pp. 117–20; MSS *C.W. II* C.W. to Revd. W. Wood 14.8.1805, 30.11.1807; to T. Robinson 10.4.1807, 5.5.1807, 5.3.1808; to G.W.W. Feb. 1809, 6.4.1809, 10.6.1809, 19.8.1809, 14.12.1809.

130. E.g. *Letters re M.C. . . . early 19th C.* J. Astley to C.W., 16.12.1797; MSS *C.W. II* to Revd. W. Wood, 14.1.1798, 23,10.1827–14.3.1828; G. M. Ditchfield, *op. cit.* p. 86; *York Letters* 1816, C.W. to G.W. 4.6.1816, 1.4.1817, 15.3.1817 to 23.1.1828 passim; *Wellbeloved Letters* W. Turner Jun. to C.W., Nov. 1818, *M.R.* XI (1816) p. 419, XIV (1819) p. 449; MSS *J.K. III*, J.K. to G.W.W. 18.1.1817, 2.3.1817, 19.3.1817, 2.4.1819; *J.K. IV*, J.K. to G.W.W. 21.11.1827; *Letter book . . . 1824–80*, pp. 32, 33, 35; W. R. Wood, *op. cit.* 24.1.1830 (12), 6.6.1830 (28), 14.11.1830 (35), 16.1.1831 (39), 13.2.1831 (43), 5.6.1831 (60).

131. *Wellbeloved Letters*, W. Turner Jun. to C.W., 27.8.1818, W. Turner to C.W. 3.12.1818.

132. *Ibid.* G.W.W. to C.W. 7.1.1828, 17.1.1828, 23.1.1828, 19.11.1828. See Lucy Aikin's comments in *Shepherd Papers II*, p. 221.

133. E.g. MSS *J.K. III*, J.K. to G.W.W. 10.10.1820, 15.3.1822; W. R. Wood, *op. cit.* 5.6.1831 (60).

134. *M.R.* II (1807) pp. 117–21; *Letter book . . . 1824–80*, pp. 65–151 passim; M.C. *Reports* 1820, 1828, 1830, 1834, 1844, 1845; *Printed Papers and Addresses* 1839–53, 1853 Report of Committee. Such also put off prospective tutors in 1798—*Shepherd Papers* IV; pp. 69, 73. 21.5.1798; R.L. Carpenter, *op. cit.* p. 33; J. Williams, *op. cit.* pp. 479–80.

135. *Roll*; There are one or two discrepancies between this and other Rolls e.g. Kenrick's in his appendix to his biography of Wellbeloved. For reference purposes here the College Roll is used.

136. *M.C. Reports* 1829, Special Report 1844, 1846, 1852, p. 4; *Printed Papers and Addresses* Report for the Special Committee 1852, p. 4; *1853 Proceedings*, Petition 31.2; MSS *J.K. IV*, J.K. to W. R. Wood, 21.3.1834.

137. *1844 Special Report*, p. 4; A. Prentice, *Historical Sketches* (1851) pp. 1–21; J. Kenrick, *op. cit.* pp. 178–94; For Lady Newley's Charity Fund to M.C. see MSS *C. W. II* 14.8.1805, 3.4.1807, 5.3.1808, 25.8.1808, 3.10.1810, 8.8.1826, 22.12.1830, 10.12.1833; *Letter book M.C. . . .* 1824–80 p. 69.

138. MSS *J.K. IV*, J.K. to G.W.W., 17.6.1838; MSS *High Pavement Papers* Nottingham University, HiM2, 22.11.1840, 25.3.1849; *M.R.* II (1807) p. 283; IV (1809) p. 301; XI (1816) p. 118; XVIII (1823) p. 553; *M.C. Reports* 1823, pp. 13, 14; 1847, pp. 24–5.

139. MSS *C.W. II*, 1812 passim, 23.12.1813, 14.12.1815; *Letter book . . . M.C.* 1824–80, pp. 48, 49, 54–5, 63, 64, 65, 71, 72; *M.R.* XVI (1821) pp. 59–60; XVIII (1823) p. 411; XIX (1824) pp. 373, 375; MSS *J.K. IV* J.K. to W. R. Wood, 18.1.1836; *M.C. Report* 1845, pp. 5–6.

140. *Roll*, Thomas Henry Potter attended 1815–17.

141. *M.C. Report* 1840, p. 6; 1841, pp. 28–30; 1844 Special Report; *Letter book M.C. . . . 1824–80*, pp. 137–51. Between 1840–4 9 new divinity students registered and 15 lay. There were also 37 one year students but 25 of these were 1840–2—*Roll; MSS List of students M.C. 1840–9*.

142. E.g. MSS *York Letters* 1814, T. Fletcher to G.W.W., 11.1.1815, 12.2.1815; *J.K. III*, J.K. to G.W.W. 25.2.1815.

143. MSS *York Letters* C.W. to G.W.W., 25.5.1816; *Report 1814*. Fees at Manchester were £22 for a divinity student, board and lodging £35–£40; *1847 Report*, pp. 14, 17.

144. *Roll* passim; *Letters re M.C. . . . early 19th C.* A List of Benefactions, 1780–2 (show Warrington connection), Benefaction from Life Trustees deceased; *Reports* 1823 pp. 11–2; 1841, 28–9, 1847, p. 21. Note too that many appeals for funds were quickly answered e.g. *Reports* 1821, 1833, 1834, 1840, p. 6.

145. MSS *York Letters*, 1814 T. Fletcher to G.W.W., 11.1.1815.

146. R. S. Fitton and A. P. Wadsworth, *op. cit.* pp. 171–2. Both William and Edward became F.R.S. . . .

147. *1853 Proceedings*, Petition, p. 35; *M.N.C. Reports* 1840, p. 2; 1841, pp. 28, 29; 1853, p. 3. R. H. Greg was married to Mary Philips and this might have stimulated his interest in the College. A number of powerful Manchester industrial families also had members serving on the Committee of the College but no students in the first half of the 19th C. e.g. the Kennedy, McConnel and Ewart families.

148. *1844 Special Report 4*; A. E. Musson and E. Robinson, *op. cit.* p. 115.

149. *Inaugural Lectures*, 1840, Preface iii–iv; 1853 *Proceedings*. Petition. 26–36. A principle reason against Owen's College was that it was not yet firmly established—see e.g. *Report for the Special Committee, 1852*, p. 8. It had also decided to include religious instruction which Unitarians feared might become Anglican in time—H. McLachlan, *The Unitarian Home Missionary College*, 1915, pp. 3–5.

150. *Annual Reports*; *Christian Reformer*, 1836, vol. III, pp. 554–5, 581; W. R. Wood, *op. cit.* 17.1.1830 (11), 25.4.1830 (22), 23.5.1830 to 6.6.1830 (26–8), 12.6.1831 (61).

151. MSS *J.K. IV*, J.K. to G.W.W., 11.6.1840; 1854 *Report*, p. 25 plus *Roll*, 1835–55. The first three successes were sons of a past tutor, an occasional tutor and a past visitor of the College. J. M. Tayler's, R. D. Darbishire's, R. Halley's, R. H. Hutton's B.A.s are omitted on the 1854 list as are J. H. Hutton's and G. Heap's. Before 1840 many students took degrees in other countries particularly at Glasgow often before they took the divinity course at Manchester College. J. J. Tayler is an example of this and John Davies in 1842. There were also 50 extra one year students, 1840–9, not on the Roll compiled by the trustees in 1868—see MSS *List of students M.N.C., 1840–9.*

152. *D.N.B. II* p. 14; J. H. Carpenter, *op. cit.* passim; J. J. Tayler, *Memoir of J. G. Robberds* (1855) reprinted from *Christian Reformer*, June 1854; J. Martineau, *op. cit.*, vol. I, 'In Memorian John James Tayler'; B. Brill, *William Gaskell 1805–84 (1984 Manchester Literary and Philosophical Publications Ltd.) passim.*

153. *R. S. Fitton and A. P. Wadsworth, op. cit.* pp. 171–3, 189; J. S. Mill, *Autobiography* (O.U.P. paperback 1971) pp. 48, 63, 72; A. Briggs, *Victorian cities* (Penguin 1968) p. 135; *Record of Unitarian Worthies* (1876) p. 244.

154. R. A. Armstrong, *In Memoriam: William Enfield*, pp. 22–7 (privately printed).

155. Briggs, A., *op. cit.* pp. 198, 202, 206.

156. R. V. Holt, *op. cit.* p. 196. For Samuel Fielden as a student see MSS *J.K. IV*, W.R.W. to G.W.W. 29.6.1834.

157. E.g. Thomas Ashton served on the General Committee and collected subscriptions—*M.N.C. Reports*, 1841, 1845, 1853.

158. M. Tylecote, *The Mechanics Institutes of Lancashire and Yorkshire before 1851* (1957) pp. 121–6, 252–3, *D.N.B.*, XLIX, pp. 44–5; *Roll, 1811.*

159. R. V. Holt, *op. cit.* pp. 41–2, 141, 187, 204, 225. R. Wade, Nonconformity in Manchester (1880) p. 64.

160. J. Drummond and C. B. Upton, *op. cit.* p. 155; J. E. Carpenter, *op. cit.* pp. 287–9.

161. J. A. Drummond and C. B. Upton, *op. cit.* p. 193; e.g. *Spectator*, 14.6.1862, pp. 665–6; 11.7.1874, pp. 334–6; 23.6.1877, pp. 786–8; 22.3.1884, pp. 374–5. See R. N. Tener, *Victorian Periodicals Newsletter* No. 20, June 1973.

162. G. M. Ramsden, *A Record of the Kay Family . . .* Gift to Manchester College, pp. 59–61.

163. S. E. Maltby, *Manchester and the Movement for National Elementary Education* (1818) pp. 112, 113, 154, 155; R. V. Holt, *op. cit.* pp. 265–7; *D.N.B.* XXVI, p. 372.

164. L. Burney, *Cross Street Chapel Schools, Manchester, 1734–1942* (1977) pp. 40–1, 46–7. See also A. Marcroft, *A Historical Account of the Unitarian Chapel, Oldham* (1913) pp. 86, 92–4.

165. M. Tylecote, *op. cit.* pp. 121–5, 252–9; R. S. Fitton and A. P. Wadsworth, *op. cit.* p. 186; S. Harrop, *The Place of Education in the Genesis of the Industrial Revolution with particular reference to Stalybridge, Dukinfield and Hyde*, unpublished M.A., Manchester University, 1976, p. 160; R. S. Holt, *op. cit.* pp. 71, 76–7.

166. See above p. 14 and note 98.

167. H. H. Ballot, *op. cit.* pp. 210–11, 264–6, 355, 382–3; *D.N.B.* XXII, Supplement, pp. 154–5.

168. For biographical details see James Rait Beard, *Collection of Notes and Materials for the life of J. R. Beard, D.D.*, duplicate typescript D.W.L.; D.N.B. II; p. 14; for later connection with Manchester College see Manchester College *Reports* 1840, pp. 2, 10; 1847, pp. 3, 8, 9; *Letters . . . 1840–53*, Address to the Trustees 16.3.1848 p. 8; J. J. Tayler, *op. cit.* vol. 1, p. 277.

169. H. MacLachlan, *Records of a Family* (1935) p. 98; S. Harrop, *op. cit.* p. 152; H. McLachlan, *The Unitarian Home Missionary College* (1815) p. 49.

170. J. R. Beard, *The Abuses of Manchester Grammar School* (Pamphlet 1837). S. E. Maltby, *op. cit.* p. 154; D. K. Jones, 'Lancashire, the American Common School, and the Religious Problem in British Education in the 19th C.' *British Journal of Educational Studies* p. 15, 1967.

171. H. McLachlan, *op. cit.* pp. 3–12. James R. Beard, *op. cit.*

172. *Ibid.* 1833.

173. H. McLachlan, *op. cit.* pp. 28–31, 49, 57–8.

174. *Ibid.* pp. 22, 57; J. A. V. Chapple and A. Pollard, *The Letters of Mrs Gaskell* (1966) pp. 20, 27, 33, 134–7, 217, 220–6, 758–9; W. Gerin, *op. cit.* pp. 89, 92–3, 137–41, 187, 258–69; B. Brill, *op. cit. passim.*

175. H. McLachlan, *Records of a Family . . .* pp. 104–19; J. E. Carpenter, *op. cit.* pp. 159–60; R. V. Holt, *op. cit.* p. 152; MSS *Letters re M.N.C.—early 19th C*: J. Martineau—Occasional students, Ethics; MSS *J. E. Carpenter to J. Martineau* (probably between 1885–9) on women at Manchester College; L. Burney, *Cross Street Chapel, Manchester and its College* (1983) p. 41.

176. M. M. Bowery, *op. cit.*; *Inquirer* 25.6.1859 p. 552—William Gaskell at the annual examination.

177. J. K. Kenrick, *Inaugural Lecture on History*, 1840, p. 22.

# 4
# MANCHESTER COLLEGE AND ITS BOOKS

PAUL MORGAN
*Formerly Senior Assistant Librarian*
*Bodleian Library,*
*Fellow of St Cross College, Oxford*

It is obvious that any institution concerned with the education of the young needs some means of providing books, the tools of the trade, for both teachers and students. This fact was well appreciated by the Committee of the Manchester Academy whose proceedings on 22nd February 1786, printed as the initial appeal, included: 'Manchester contains one of the largest public libraries in the kingdom, to which access may be had at stated times' and 'Resolved: That a common hall and convenient lecture rooms be erected, with provision for a library.' The public library mentioned is a reference to Chetham's Library[1] founded in 1653, then 'the greatest of all the early town libraries'[2] and, though its use was implied, the Committee appreciated that the proposed Academy would also need books of its own and somewhere to house them. It is proposed to outline here how Manchester College acquired, administered and arranged its own Library during the last two centuries as far as can be ascertained from the surviving records, the annual reports and the actual books.[3]

As in other institutions, a library in its growth and activity or inactivity reflects the history of the parent body to result in that peculiar amalgam of a residue from former curricula combined with the specialist benefactions and bequests of past members characteristic of the older Oxbridge colleges. Manchester College is no exception, but as its books, the actual survivors of its peripatetic history, rich as they are, have been described in general terms more than once,[4] they will receive only incidental mention here.

To satisfy the need for books, action was swiftly taken by the founding Committee, whose chairman, Thomas Percival, was asked on 31st March 1786 to apply to John Stubbs for the loan of his late brother Samuel's library then deposited at Warrington Academy. This was followed by an appeal, dated 20th May 1786, to the Trustees of the Warrington Academy asking for the loan of the books and apparatus 'now lying useless in your possession'. Decisions were soon made, for at the Committee meeting on 13th July it was reported that the Warrington Trustees had agreed on 29th June to give to Manchester its library and half of the money raised from the sale of their buildings. The Warrington minutes[5] record 'that the Library shall on the same Trust [as the sale money] be sent to the Academy at Manchester and the apparatus to the Academy at London[6] on the same Trust. Resolved that Mr. [Ellis] Bent be authorised to deliver the books . . .' At the same Committee meeting it was reported that a letter from John Stubbs of Longdon, Staffs., dated 8th July, had been received agreeing to continue the loan of his brother's books on the same terms as to the Warrington Academy providing he could be consulted if the Manchester Academy ceased to function. The books of Samuel Stubbs (1715–1753) ranged widely in subject matter and are today identifiable from the presence of his signature and frequent extensive marginalia, the latter revealing 'considerable learning and curious research'.[7] At the

Committee meeting on 3rd April 1788, Mrs. Elizabeth Stubbs, wife of John, was thanked for 'presenting' [*sic*] the books and for adding a further 95 volumes; the loan was finally converted to a gift in 1813.[8]

The library of Warrington Academy, built up by the tutors and purchases from 'a benefaction of not less than half a guinea' on admission[9] has received much attention and has been described as possibly the most extensive academy library in England[10] catering for a wide range of subjects. The books had no label nor ownership inscription and can only be identified today from the distinctive shelf-marks written in the front. The actual contents when transferred to Manchester Academy are revealed in a catalogue printed by William Eyres in 1775, arranging 674 titles under twelve subject headings.[11] A manuscript shelf-list of the library, made possibly a decade later, has also survived, but with only ten subject headings. Since the classification scheme adopted a system of capital and lower-case letters followed by a numeral used in the College Library until the 1870s, they are given here with percentages based on rough estimates of the number of titles to show the proportions of the various subjects represented. For comparison, percentages adapted from the printed catalogue variant subject headings, again based on the number of titles, are also given.

| *Symbol* | *Subject heading* | *% in MS, c. 1785* | *% in printed catalogue, 1775* |
|---|---|---|---|
| Aa-Cc | Greek and Roman classics | 8 | 10 |
| Da-Ei | Grammar, philology and antiquities | 9 | 12 |
| Ga-Gi | Biography | 5 | 7 |
| Ha-Ii | History, chronology, geography, voyages and travels | 11 | 12 |
| Ka-Li | Evidences of Christianity and ecclesiastical history | 8 | 10 |
| Ma-Nh, Xa-Yc | Belles lettres and miscellaneous | 13 | 12 |
| Oa-Oi, Ri, Si, Ti | Mathematics, natural philosophy, natural history | 7 | 12 |
| Pa-Qi | Sermons, morals and metaphysics | 8 | 6 |
| Rb-Yg | Theology and Scripture criticism | 26 | 13 |
| Zd-Zi | Politics, commerce, law, etc. | 5 | 6 |
| | | 100 | 100 |

The decrease in the proportions of the natural sciences and the increase in the theological sections during the last decade at Warrington are perhaps significant. As the Library grew after the transfer, the symbols 'aa'-'ci' were added, judging from a later classified catalogue. The source of this scheme has not been traced[12] and was probably home-made, as so often happens in small libraries, though it is interesting that Exeter Academy used a similar scheme of capital and lower case letters from Aa to Q, omitting P. However, although no outline survives, it was different from the Warrington system. From a shelf-list it can be deduced as

| | |
|---|---|
| A–C | General works and philosophy |
| D | History |
| E | Classics |
| F–L | Various types of theology |
| M–O | Biblical studies and commentaries |
| Q | Orientalia |

Of course, the book cases in the rooms used as libraries must have influenced arrangements.

The fledgling Manchester Academy had thus acquired a good, basic collection of possibly 4,000 volumes, but a living, efficient library must keep up-to-date and acquire new books as they are published. So, in September 1787 it was resolved that students should pay entry money at the beginning of each session for the use of the Library. How it was administered is not clear, but in October 1792 T. Nichols, the mathematics tutor, was 'desired to purchase such modern mathematical and philosophical books as he shall approve not exceeding £10 in value'. At the same time he was appointed Librarian at a salary of £20, presumably in addition to his tutorial stipend, and to be responsible for the books. At the same meeting, the Library was insured for £800 and a rule made that students could only be admitted when a tutor was present, suggesting that there had been losses or misdemeanours.

Nichols left in 1793 to be succeeded by John Dalton, who in February 1794 wrote to his cousin Elihu Robinson: 'Our Academy is a large and elegant building . . . It consists of a front and two wings; the first floor of the front is the hall where most of the business is done; over it is a Library with about eight thousand volumes . . . There is in the town a large library, furnished with all the best books in every art, science and language, which is open to all, gratis'[13] so evidently both Chetham's and the Academy libraries were appreciated. Perhaps the latter's books were used more for class purposes and the former for the specialist interests of the tutors.

During the troubled years of 1794–1799, for which accounts are recorded in the Minute Books, an average of £18.17*s*.3*d*. was spent on books and apparatus, representing 5% of the total expenditure. The fresh appeal for funds for the 'Academical institution or New College at Manchester' issued in August 1797 called attention, as in 1786, to 'one of the largest public libraries in the kingdom' near at hand, and that Warrington Academy had transferred its 'large and valuable' library. However, the advertisement for students placed in newspapers and magazines in May 1798 contained no mention of book provision.

Although Dalton remained at the College until 1800, he apparently did not oversee the Library for very long, as in May 1798 it was resolved that the 'office of Librarian be revived' and that the Rev. Mr. [W.] Shepherd have £21 in addition to his £52 salary. In August the Committee decided to charge each student two guineas on admission for the use of the Library during the whole period of residence, but at the September meeting for some unexplained reason this fee was reduced to one guinea only.

The Library was obviously much in the Committee's thoughts in 1798, as at the October meeting it was decided that application be made to the Trustees of the 'late Exeter Academy' for the loan of their Library, 'now lying useless at Hackney', the earliest mention of a project that did not come to fruition until 1813. The motive for this proposal was not stated, but it is interesting that a catalogue of the Exeter Library made in August 1800 survives in Manchester College archives for which the inspiration may have been this enquiry.

A prospectus issued in 1800 concludes by mentioning that students have 'access to and the free use of, a large and valuable Library, with direction and assistance in the course of reading'.[14] This presumably refers to the College's own books, and not Chetham's Library. The need for proximity to a large, public collection was apparently not felt at this time, for the move to York in 1803 meant that for the first and only period in the College's history it had to be self-sufficient so far as provision for reading and reference material was concerned, a condition that lasted until the return to Manchester in 1840.

At the time of the move to York there were possibly about 5,000 volumes in the Library.[15] It certainly impressed Benjamin Silliman of Yale during his visit in 1805–1806 when he over-estimated the stock at 15,000 volumes.[16] The earliest borrowing records date from the York period and show that books were taken out by classes, not individuals. A single ledger records loans firstly during 1804–1809 and secondly for 1828–1843. But as only the classification symbols and numbers are entered, as 'Ae 140' for example, with the tutor's initials, it is neither easy to discover what was borrowed nor by whom. The hiatus may indicate a change of tutor-librarian rather than a missing document, as this ledger includes a list made in June 1828 of books not returned from the 1804–1809 period.

Charles Wellbeloved, the theological tutor in whose York house the Library was then kept, certainly took an interest in it, and in April 1805 obtained permission to dispose of 'any duplicates in the academical library in exchange for new books' provided he kept a record of those so exchanged. Then in March 1812 he reported that Marmaduke Constable had given ten guineas to buy books, though in the published appeal of July 1812 for funds for new buildings there was no mention of books nor library. £10 was spent in 1813 at Todd's shop at the Sign of the Bible, 23 Stonegate, the site of a bookshop for several centuries until 1983. Wellbeloved must have been feeling the lack of books rather severely at this time, for during 1813 not only did John Simpson present 182 volumes, including some early printed books such as Brian Walton's *Biblia*

*Polyglotta* of 1657 and *Bibliotheca Fratrum Polonorum quos Unitarios Vocant* of 1656, but at the Committee meeting in August he revived the suggestion that application be made for the Library of the 'late Exeter Academy' and that the cost of the move be borne by the College. A favourable reply from the Exeter authorities was reported in September, but asking for a bond of £500 for security and an insurance against fire of £500 also. This must have reminded the Manchester New College Trustees of their own responsibilities, as in December 1813 the College Library was insured with the Sun Life Office for £1,000. The Exeter Academy books came north by sea to Hull at a cost of £14.9*s*.6*d*., arriving in York on 29th April 1814 at the further expense of £10.5*s*.6*d*. In addition shelving to house them cost £28.4*s*.5*d*. in 1814 and 1815. Books from this source can be identified by a distinctive printed label on the inside front covers with 'Exeter Library' within a border, probably printed towards the end of the eighteenth century.

With the Exeter books came various handwritten lists of funeral and ordination sermons, works on certain controversies and persons, none later than 1791, but as no shelf-marks were included their usefulness was limited. The Exeter classification, as already mentioned, had similarities with that used at Warrington, but instead of the numeral following the letters, it was placed underneath, as $\frac{\text{Oi}}{33}$ or $\frac{\text{Sd}}{15}$ for example. The different symbols and system of marking were no doubt reasons why the Exeter collection was shelved separately at first until the books were re-classified before 1830 and incorporated into the Manchester New College system of a capital letter, a lower case letter and a number, with full-stops between, such as 'E.a.16'. A folio catalogue came with the books; the later shelf-marks have been added and the missing items marked 'wanting'.

At a meeting of the Committee on 24th April 1817, a new set of thirteen Laws for the Regulation of the College were approved and concluded with the following eight separate Laws relating to the Library:

1. The students who have finished the two first years of their course shall act as Librarians in rotation; each student undertaking the office for half the session. If he have performed his duty at the expiration of his office he shall receive *One Guinea* as a compensation for his trouble.
2. The Librarian for the time being shall attend for half an hour in the Library on Monday, Wednesday & Friday in every week immediately after the latest lecture in the forenoon of each day, for the purpose of delivering and receiving books.
   The Librarian is empowered to lend the key of the Library-room to any student who has passed through the two first years of his course, & who may be desirous of consulting any book or books in the Library, but no books shall be taken out, unless the Librarian be present under the penalty of two shillings & sixpence.
3. Students of the first & second years shall not be permitted to take any books from the Library but such as are recommended or allowed by one of the tutors.

4. The Librarian, upon delivering a book from the Library, shall enter, in a book provided for that purpose, the number of the book delivered, the name of the student who receives it, and the date of its delivery: and when the book is returned he shall mark the date of its return, signing the whole entry with the initials of his name. For every neglect to do so he shall forfeit sixpence.
5. If any student take a book from the Library without having it first regularly entered by the Librarian, or by one of the tutors, he shall forfeit two shillings & sixpence.
6. If a book shall be found on being returned to have received any injury the Librarian shall report it to a tutor. If the injury be considerable the book shall be replaced by one in good condition, or a sum equal to its value shall be paid by the student who has injured it. Any student convicted of writing or scribbling in a book belonging to the Library shall for every such offence forfeit one shilling.
7. If any book be left in a lecture room, the dining room or any other improper place, the student in whose name it is entered shall forfeit sixpence.
8. No student shall have more than four volumes from the Library at one time, besides those books to which references are given in the lectures. All the books belonging to the Library shall be returned and the Library examined by the Librarian in the presence of one of the tutors on the last Saturday in every month.
   All forfeits shall be expended for the use of the Library.

These laws show how the Library was administered and do not present any unexpected features for a small college without a permanent librarian. They remained in force until revised in 1899. Of the tutors it was Charles Wellbeloved who took the greatest interest in this part of the College and who purchased a miscellaneous selection of books, though in 1828–1829 these included a Ptolemy's *Geographia* of 1605 and a 1735 edition of the *Antonine Itinerary*. The forfeits (what are styled fines nowadays) were used mainly to defray binding costs—£10 in 1826–1827 for instance. Although not specified in the laws, from 1827 to the end of the Wellbeloved era in 1840, annual certificates from each June or July survive, stating that the Library had been examined and found complete, though occasionally missing books get mentioned. They were signed by a tutor, often Wellbeloved, and the student librarian, presumably the one in his final year whose tour of duty coincided with the end of the academic year. For example, Henry Wreford signed in 1830 and Thomas Hincks in 1839; the latter was paid five guineas for his pains, a sum that apparently remained unaltered until the move to Oxford. In his last report Wellbeloved estimated that there were about 5,500 volumes in the Manchester and 2,400 in the Exeter collections. However, his proposal of 1820 to print an 'arranged catalogue' of the 'aggregate library' for the use of both students and the public was never put into effect.

After the move back to Manchester in September 1840, the Library was housed in rooms either side of the entrance, with the College collection to the left and the Exeter books still shelved separately on the right.[17] J. H.

Ryland, assistant classical tutor from 1838, who had acted as tutor Librarian until moving to Bradford in 1843, sent a detailed report on the Library to S. D. Darbishire, the Committee's Secretary, in January 1844 which provides a valuable account of the situation then existing. He first stated that he had arranged by subject the pamphlets which the Committee had ordered to be bound in January 1843, and that journals had been tied up ready for binding. He then gave the following statistics:

| | | |
|---|---|---|
| Additions catalogued | 552 | volumes |
| General library, arranged and catalogued | 6,352 | |
| 'Extra books' | 417 | |
| 'Mr. Bartlett's donation' | 175 | |
| Exeter Library | 2,335 | |
| Exeter Library 'extra books' | 133 | |
| Extra valuable books, 'locked up' | 25 | approx. |
| Unbound reviews, pamphlets, etc. | 175 | approx. |
| Total | 9,622 | approx. |

What he meant by 'extra books' is not clear; possibly they were works waiting for processing. While joiners had been putting 'protecting strips of glazed calico' round the shelves, he had checked the books and found many previously thought to be missing; probably they had not been surveyed thoroughly since the move from York. Ryland considered the shelf catalogue, presumably used as a subject guide, inadequate and repeated the suggestion that a printed catalogue was desirable—incidentally something that has never been achieved to this day. He pointed out that only £20 a year had been given for purchases at York and raised the perennial problem for librarians of whether continuations should be paid from this allocation or dealt with on a separate account; the *Encyclopaedia Metropolitana* was cited as an example. Finally, Ryland called attention to the necessity of maintaining the chronological and donation catalogues (of which no early examples have survived) and the need to mark the books to show ownership and to enforce the rules.

Whether it was a result of Ryland's representations or not, that the Trustees were aware of the importance of an efficiently run book-service became evident from the introduction of lists of Library benefactors in the published Annual Reports covering 1843 onwards (also entered in the Minutes), and in 1845 and 1846 from the detailed reports of two tutors, F. W. Newman and Robert Wallace, acting as Library curators, on the state of repair of the bindings, the need to weed the old class-books and dispose of duplicates. By June 1846 'nearly all' the pamphlets were bound. After this, the Library gets little mention except for the lists of donors in the annual reports.

During the whole of the London period, from 1853–1889, the College was accommodated in University Hall, an academic residence for students associated with University College, Gower Street, which had been founded in 1846 to commemorate the passing of the Dissenters'

Chapels Act of two years earlier and opened in 1849 in a building in Gordon Square now occupied by Dr. Williams's Library. The College Library was kept in a large upper room, also used for lectures, throughout the period, for which a rent of £100 a year was first paid, increased to £150 in 1857.[18] How exactly it was administered and the relationship with University Hall's own Library is obscure, but some re-arrangements were made so a new shelf-catalogue was compiled. The system of annual certificates being sent to the Committee that all was well continued and were invariably signed by James Martineau up to 1883, when they either ceased or have not been preserved. The notable absence of detail and unchanging formula suggests that Library administration was taken for granted, though the contents were not neglected; in 1859, for instance, an appeal was made for funds to keep the Library 'on a level with the scholarship of the age', and so a special grant of £100 was given.

During the 1860s the Library continued working in its usual way. There were some notable benefactions, such as the gift of a Complutensian Polyglott Bible, paid for in 1862 by seven friends: Thomas Abison, Thomas Ainsworth, R. D. & S. D. Darbishire, W. J. Lamport, Mark Philips and Edmund Potter. In 1860 Dominik Simén from Transylvania came to the College and the connection with Hungary that has lasted until today is regularly reflected in the lists of donors: Simén himself in 1863 and 1869, Dénes Peterfi between 1877 and 1907, István Györfi in 1914, for example.[19]

The next decade saw more changes than the 1860s. Apart from notable bequests such as twenty selected early works from W. J. Lamport in 1875, and the libraries of J. R. Beard in 1878 and John Colston in 1879, a re-arrangement of the books began in 1873, continuing to feature in the annual accounts until 1883, while paper for the catalogue was specially bought in 1884 and 1885. The new classification was to give each book a number to indicate the press followed by a lower case letter for the shelf. This new arrangement was not fully completed until after the move to Oxford, and was used until after the Second World War. About 1911, nos. '1a' to '165h' had been used, with the Beard collection on '80f' to '89h', and the J. J. Tayler collection on '27b–f, 23a–f'.

While in London, students from other colleges began to make use of the Library, no doubt a tribute to its efficiency and its contents, so in 1883, after the re-organisation, a fee of 10*s*.6*d*. a term was charged; it is significant that more money was received from these outsiders than from the Manchester students. The re-classifying was nearly finished in 1887, and in 1888 it was reported that 'The College Library has recently been thoroughly overhauled and re-arranged, and the Professors, with the assistance of Mr. Felix Taylor [a final year student] have given much time and labour to the work. The cataloguing and classification of the pamphlets have been completed and they prove, upon examination, to be a rare and valuable collection'. This last phrase is even truer today; it is a regular refrain during the last hundred years, possibly demonstrating that each generation has to make the discovery for itself. During reorganisation, duplicates, including some formerly in the Warrington and Exeter academies, were sold to the Unitarian Home Mission Board for a nominal £5 in 1874 and for £8 in 1887. The card and shelf catalogues, for which a cabinet had been bought in 1886, were completed by Hubert Clarke in 1888, in time for the transfer to Oxford in 1889, three years after the Congregationalists had moved from Birmingham to the re-named Mansfield College.

The first notable occurrence after the move was the arrival in 1890 of a further 1,040 volumes on Luther, the Reformation in Germany, and Port Royal from the widow of Charles Beard, and about half of the Library of University Hall, London, whose buildings had been sold, with financial gain to all parties, to Dr. Williams's Trustees. The next year saw the start of the building of the new Library designed by Thomas Worthington of Manchester[21] and paid for through the munificence of Sir Henry Tate. The main room, measuring 80 by 30 feet, with a large bay window, is dominated now by Hope Pinker's statue of James Martineau. At the opening in October 1893 it was estimated to contain about 17,000 volumes.

With a new Library in a new place, the authorities must have reconsidered how it should be run; perhaps they were influenced by the methods of neighbouring, established Oxford colleges, who, though like Manchester usually had a teaching fellow as librarian, employed, in the majority of cases, a full-time clerk to perform the actual day-to-day duties. Anyhow, in 1894 Lucy Toulmin Smith was appointed Librarian and clerical assistant to the Principal at a salary of £120, the first woman in England to be appointed head of a public library.[22] She was then 56 years old and held the post until November 1911, a month before her death. Like many Oxford librarians at that time and today, she had neither library experience nor qualifications, but she was a distinguished scholar who had acted as her equally distinguished father's amanuensis and has justly earned a niche in the *Dictionary of National Biography*; she became a well-known Oxford hostess and gardener. Her influence on the Library is difficult to trace though she initiated the inclusion of books bought as well as presented in the annual reports in 1896, but these had to be reduced to selections only from 1909. In 1899 new Library regulations were promulgated and 'surplus books' were again sent to the Unitarian Home Mission in 1901, and others to Dr. Williams's Library.

If Lucy Toulmin Smith was content with the existing Library arrangements, her successor, Champlin Burrage, was not. An American from Portland, Maine, he had come to Oxford in 1906 and took his B.Litt. in 1909; he later published many archaeological and historical books. At Manchester College, he promptly succumbed to the perpetual temptation felt by so many Oxford college librarians during the last two centuries to re-arrange and re-catalogue the libraries in their charge. It is possible that the Arlosh bequest of 1904, which included a large general collection, had caused problems of accommodation. Unlike many who begin such tasks he completed his in 1914, but he apparently did not try to change the classification; at the conclusion he reported that Library planning was required to prevent it becoming congested again. In 1915 Burrage left Oxford to become Librarian of the John Carter Brown Library in Providence, Rhode Island. Presumably on account of war-time exigencies, the lists of gifts were omitted from the annual reports for 1915 onwards, and since that date only major benefactions have been recorded.

Burrage was succeeded by Lachlan Macrae, with D. C. Simpson as temporary librarian in 1915–1918 while Macrae was serving with the Cameron Highlanders. His salary in 1919–1920 was put at £155, but the following year it was reduced to £100, being regarded as in the days before Lucy Toulmin Smith's appointment, as a supplement to a tutorial salary. Henry Gow was Librarian from 1922 until 1927, and in the first year of his stint, J. E. Carpenter's notable collection of books on comparative religion arrived, so a special grant of £100 was made for Library rearrangements, followed by a further £25 in 1923. Another 1,500 volumes were received after Carpenter's death in 1927; this important collection is housed separately; its administration was absorbed into the main library in 1977. R. V. Holt followed Gow as tutor and Librarian in 1927, remaining in office until 1943.

Mrs. Dora Higginson of Edgbaston gave the College in 1930 a copy of the first edition of Walt Whitman's *Leaves of Grass* to dispose in whatever way the College liked, so it was sent for auction at Sotheby's and fetched £515, though it was not recorded whether this welcome gift was put to Library use or not.

As on previous occasions, R. V. Holt felt that the scholarly value of the Library in his charge was not fully appreciated by his contemporaries; the 1932 annual report included 'The Library is a rich inheritance. It needs continuous thought and planning to preserve it for use and to extend it judiciously. The Library is used in increasing measure by our own students. It is used also by others, chiefly research students sent to us by tutors of other colleges.' From this period until 1939 there are frequent references to re-arrangement, weeding the stack books and changing the catalogue from cards to sheaf—a change that might have been regarded as a backward step by some. In 1935 Holt estimated the Library to contain about 35,000 volumes, but lamented that fewer gifts were being sent by old students and friends, possibly a reflection of the general economic condition of the country. Though the change-over from cards to sheaf was stated to be 'nearly complete' in 1937, re-cataloguing was still going on during 1938–1939, during which year the Tower Room was taken over for Library use.

The years of the Second World War affected the College very markedly with consequences that are very apparent in the Library today. In 1941, parts of the College were taken over by Government departments, including various Library rooms, so the sixteenth, seventeenth and eighteenth century books were deposited in the Bodleian Library. Many difficulties arose over ordinary usage; the Ministry of Works, for instance, allowed students into the Library for half-an-hour daily to get books, and those most frequently consulted were transferred to the Hostel. H. John McLachlan succeeded R. V. Holt as Librarian and in 1944 was obliged to send more books on deposit to the Bodleian and others into the Tower Room. In 1945, it was reported that the Tate Library was quite inadequate in size and was still occupied, this time by the Admiralty, but preliminary steps were being taken to tackle the problem, so shelf re-arrangement and re-cataloguing began once again the next year. The Library was then described as being 'like Gaul' with its contents split in three parts between the Hostel, the College and the Bodleian.

The older books returned from evacuation during 1946–1947, together with those transferred to the Hostel. The former at some stage had got completely out of their classified order, so they were re-arranged in the Tower Room and upper corridors in chronological order in sequences according to size, an order that remains to this day, creating problems in locating items recorded in the various catalogues. £100 was received from the Ministry of Works towards the cost of re-arrangement together with another inadequate sum of £150 for repairs.

Between January 1947 and 1949, Miss Emily Blomfield re-classified the books, including the pamphlets, and began a subject catalogue. Duplicates were sent to Carmarthen College in 1947–1948, and once again to the Unitarian College, Manchester, in both 1947–1948 and 1949–1950, and to Dr. Williams's Library in the latter year as well.

During the 1950s H. John McLachlan began work on a catalogue of the College's manuscript collections which his father, Herbert, had exploited so admirably and efficiently in his several historical publications, and work continued on cataloguing the older books, especially after H. L. Short became Librarian in 1956. His appreciation of their value was evident when he wrote in 1960, 'the Library is one of the College's greatest assets'. After he was appointed Principal, Library fees for students were re-introduced in 1966 and were fixed at 10 guineas in 1970, and subsequently these fees have been levied as part of the general fees; visitors are asked for a donation. The post of Librarian was combined with that of Principal, a practice continued under his successor, but as elsewhere in Oxford and Cambridge, assistants are responsible for the practical administration. In this respect, Manchester College has been fortunate in having the services of Mrs. Katherine Swift from 1972 to 1974, and Mrs. Barbara Smith from 1974 to 1985. Apart from efficiently supplying the bookish needs of current generations of students they have made available to the scholarly world the accumulations built up in the Library over the last two centuries, to a large extent through the generosity of benefactors who include many former members. The appreciation of the value of the Library among scholars was demonstrated in 1978 by the British Library's financial grant towards repair of the older books. Research workers are also attracted to the Library as its holdings become more widely known through union catalogues, such as the Oxford Inter-Collegiate Catalogue available in the Bodleian Library, the Eighteenth-Century Short-Title Catalogue based at the British Library and other specialist guides such as B. R. Crick's *Guide to manuscripts relating to America*.[23] There are also special research tools kept in the Library itself, such as the Johnston *Index of obituaries in Unitarian periodicals*, while the wealth of Joseph Priestley material owned by the College was amply demonstrated in 1983 by an exhibition held in the Bodleian Library for which a catalogue was published.

Let us hope that Manchester College Library will continue to serve its own community and the republic of letters for the next two centuries as well as it does today.

## APPENDIX I

Select list of manuscript collections in Manchester College Oxford abstracted from P. Morgan: Oxford Libraries outside the Bodleian 2nd Ed. 1980; Appendix II. Select list of manuscript collections in Oxford Libraries, not in H. O. Coxe (1852).

| | |
|---|---|
| Allsop, Thomas (1795–1880) | 28 letters from Charles Voysey |
| Armstrong, George (1792–1857) | Papers |
| Aspland, Robert Brook (d. 1869) | Notes on dissenting history |
| Belsham, Thomas (1750–1829) | Lecture notes |
| Bowring, Sir John (1792–1872) | Papers and letters |
| Carpenter, Joseph Estlin (1844–1927) | Papers |
| Carpenter, Lant (1780–1840) | Papers and correspondence |
| Dickenson, Thomas | Shorthand notes of sermons, 1694–96 |
| Doddridge, Philip (1702–1751) | Lecture notes |
| Fox, Arthur William (1863–1945) | Papers, verse |
| Heinekin, Thomas (1763–1840) | Notes taken at lectures |
| Henry, Philip (1631–1696) | Sermons |
| Kenrick, John (1788–1877) | Papers and letters |
| Lindsey, Theophilus (1723–1808) | Sermons |
| Lingard, John (1771–1851) | Papers |
| Martineau, Harriet (1802–1876) | Papers |
| Martineau, James (1805–1900) | Papers |
| Munro, Alexander (1697–1767) | Lecture notes |
| Odgers, James Edwin (1843–1925) | Papers |
| Odgers, John Collins (d. 1928) | Historical notebooks |
| Palmer, Thomas Fysshe (1747–1802) | Letters |
| Priestley, Joseph (1733–1804) | Notebooks and letters |
| Seddon, John (1725–1770) | Correspondence |
| Shepherd, William (1768–1847) | Papers |
| Tayler, John James (1797–1869) | Papers |
| Taylor, John (1750–1826) | Papers |
| Voysey, Charles (1828–1912) | 28 letters to Thomas Allsop 1869–71 |
| Walker, George (1734?–1807) | Lecture notes |
| Warrington Academy | Trustees' minutes 1757–86 |
| Wellbeloved, Charles (1769–1858) | Papers |
| White, Joseph Blanco (1775–1841) | Papers |
| Wicksteed, Charles (d. 1885) | Papers |
| Wright, Richard (1764–1836) | Papers |

Manuscript notebooks containing 18th and 19th century codes of shorthand systems including those of Joseph Priestley and Samuel Greg.

Since the above index was compiled Manchester College has discovered or received several minor collections of manuscripts.

## NOTES

1. V. D. Davis, *A History of Manchester College from its Foundation in Manchester to its Establishment in Oxford* (1932), p. 65.
2. Thomas Kelly, *Early Public Libraries* (1966), p. 77.
3. Unless otherwise indicated, statements are based on the Minute Books of the Committee and the Annual Reports (printed from 1817 onwards), in the custody of the College. I should like to express my warmest thanks to Mrs. Barbara Smith for her help in the preparation of this paper. I should also like to put on record my appreciation of the way in which the late Rev. Dr. H. L. Short was always ready to share his expert knowledge of the College's history and its books.
4. P. Morgan, *Oxford Libraries outside the Bodleian; a Guide.* 2nd ed. (1980), pp. 72–9 and the references there cited.
5. Now in Manchester College archives.
6. *i.e.* Hackney.
7. H. McLachlan, *Warrington Academy; its History and Influence.* (Chetham Society, New Series vol. 1078, 1943) p. 34.
8. H. McLachlan, *English Education under the Test Acts; being the History of the Nonconformist Academies, 1662–1820.* (Publications of the University of Manchester, no. ccxiii; Historical Series no. lix, 1931), p. 269.
9. A Report on the State of the Warrington Academy by the Trustees, June 28th MDCCLXXIV, p. 4.
10. J. F. Fulton, 'The Warrington Academy (1757–1786) and its Influence upon Medicine and Science', *Bulletin of the Institute of the History of Medicine*, vol. 1 (1933), p. 64.
11. H. McLachlan, *Warrington Academy*, p. 35.
12. The system has not been identified with any of the numerous schemes listed in Edward Edwards, *Memoirs of Libraries*, vol. 1 (1859), pp. 759–831; Julius Petzholdt, *Bibliotheca Bibliographica* (1866), pp. 20–65; E. C. Richardson, *Classification*, 3rd ed. (1964), pp. 49–133.
13. V. D. Davis, pp. 64–5; H. McLachlan, *English Education*, p. 261 misquotes the number of books as 3,000.
14. McLachlan, *English Education*, p. 261.
15. G. M. Ditchfield, 'The early History of Manchester College', *Transactions of the Historic Society of Lancashire and Cheshire*, vol. cxxiii (1972), p. 86.
16. J. F. Fulton and E. H. Thomson, *Benjamin Silliman, 1779–1864* (1947), p. 47.
17. V. D. Davis, pp. 108–9.
18. V. D. Davis, pp. 123–4, 136.
19. A typescript list of some 25 Hungarian students and three temporary visitors, 1860–1934, is in the College archives.
20. H. McLachlan, *The Unitarian College Library* (1939), p. 20.
21. Jennifer Sherwood and Sir N. Pevsner, *Oxfordshire.* (Buildings of England, 1974), p. 233.
22. *Dictionary of National Biography.*
23. B. R. Crick, *A Guide to Manuscripts relating to America in Great Britain and Ireland.* Revised edition (1979), p. 208.

# 5

# THE NATURAL SCIENCES AND THE LEARNING OF THE ENGLISH UNITARIANS

## An exploration of the roles of the Manchester College

JEAN RAYMOND
*Recently Research Assistant in the History of Science at University of Manchester Institute of Science and Technology*

JOHN V. PICKSTONE
*Senior Lecturer in the History of Science, Technology and Medicine Manchester University*

In the beginning was Priestley—the father figure and radical hero for the Unitarians of industrial England; the exponent of a stern necessarian philosophy; a giant of pneumatic chemistry; a pioneer of history as a discipline, particularly history of science. Priestley learned and taught across a very broad front, to construct and propagate a philosophy in which the progress of natural sciences was central evidence of the unfolding of divine purpose.[1]

What followed, in rational philosophy and within the span of the natural sciences, was a fragmentation, a differentiation, a separation of spheres, often worked out within the formal and informal institutions to which Priestley had belonged: the Unitarian academies, the congregations, and especially the intellectual families of unitarianism, which made up so much of the social fabric of English science in the industrial revolution.

The continuing linkages of science and Unitarianism were omnipresent. Priestley left Warrington Academy in 1767 and it collapsed in 1783, but two of its former pupils helped organise a northern replacement. Dr. Thomas Percival and the Rev. Thomas Barnes were central to the intellectual life of Manchester. They helped bring to this city a young schoolteacher, John Dalton, who taught at their new Manchester Academy and came to dominate the Literary and Philosophical Society which Percival had founded. Dalton's atomic theory brought an international reputation and made him a folk-hero in Manchester. But he was not an isolated figure; his friend William Henry, son of a Unitarian colleague of Percival, was an experimental as well as a manufacturing chemist. Dalton's chief pupil was James Prescott Joule, an anglican now known for his work on the mechanical equivalent of heat and the idea of energy conservation. These men were the scientific core of a local culture whose institutional and political leadership came largely from Unitarian families: the Heywoods, the Potters, the Gregs.

Manchester Academy left this culture in 1803 when it moved to York. For the next 37 years it was a less 'northern', less industrial institution, but its scientific culture was no less exemplary. It was in York, in 1831, that the British Association for the Advancement of Science was founded, a parliament for a community of interest in natural science which linked industrial centres with metropolitan and Oxbridge savants, and which depended crucially on the vogue for polite science in centres like York, Newcastle or Bristol, to name but three cities where Unitarian families were pillars of local societies. The cousinhood of Unitarians provided many of the nodes and linkages in this diffuse, largely unprofessionalised community.

In 1840 the College returned to Manchester, the capital of the northern Unitarians, some of whom entertained hopes of a northern university to complement the recent initiatives in London. By the 1840s, chemists and engineers were established as scientific professions alongside a reformed medicine, less literary and more technical than the English physic of Percival's day. The college attempted to provide a university-level education in arts and sciences, and it experimented with professional education for engineers. For reasons to be explored it was unsuccessful. Those roles were left to purely secular institutions: University College London, alongside which Manchester College took up its new home, and Owens College, Manchester, which succeeded Manchester College as the chief 'university' of the north. Manchester College went to London to concentrate on a task which itself had undergone considerable development and professionalisation since the days of Priestley—the training of Unitarian ministers.

During its second Manchester period the college had employed sound, professional, teachers of science, but its intellectual reputation depended largely on James Martineau, the Liverpool minister and moral philosopher and his friend James Tayler, minister at Upper Brook Street chapel. Martineau's theology was grounded, not in the English tradition of natural philosophy but in German biblical criticism and ethics, especially in the work of Kant. Martineau and his associates took their intellectual standards from German universities, as did the leading Manchester chemists. All of them shared an ideal of university learning and professional training, but there was no necessary scholarly continuity between their disciplines. James Martineau, like John Henry Newman, had broken with the English tradition of natural theology. There was then little reason why aspiring ministers need have more than an elementary knowledge of science and mathematics. Neither was there much reason why lay students, even Unitarians, should seek scientific education in an institution which was, in part, the theological college of a heterodox and still suspect denomination. It was possible for natural science to play a much wider intellectual role, but it was dangerous. James Martineau's sister Harriet, like many young intellectuals, had taken the path of scientific naturalism and Comtean positivism: that way lay atheism and moral uncertainty. It was better for Unitarians to give to secular learning and science the title of high common culture as well as of utility. They would concentrate on the realm of morals and belief, hoping that here too, effort of mind would produce, at least, a secure theology for an advanced denomination.

### *The Warrington inheritance*

From its beginning in 1757, the curriculum of the Warrington Academy included mathematics and natural philosophy along with languages, moral philosophy and theology. The mixture was characteristic of the Dissenting Academy tradition which Warrington was intended to continue and in which its key personnel had been raised.[2] Such institutions were self-consciously 'modern' in orientation, but they also aimed to cover all that the English universities covered. Mathematics and Newtonian mechanics etc. scored on both counts. Throughout the history of

Warrington and 'Manchester College', someone was there to teach mathematics; but of those who did so, only Dalton is well-remembered as a scientist, and not for his mathematics or physics. Generally the instructor was a minister with mathematical interests and/or a former school teacher; often they were retiring men who failed to communicate; their material was found difficult and often proved unpopular, though some of the bright students appreciated the challenge.

The second element of the 'science' was less constant, less demanding, more varied and more subject to the changing circumstances of the college. This was the natural history, the chemistry and occasional ventures into anatomy/physiology or engineering. These might be taught by tutors other than the mathematical, or by visitors. Such courses were presented as broadening and as useful for future merchants, industrialists or professional men. It was especially in these areas that the curriculum of the relatively rural Warrington and York periods differed from the two periods in Manchester.

In surveying both mathematical and observational sciences we shall be examining courses and tutors, claims for utility and, to some extent, the responses of students. These were largely 'in house' matters. Beyond them lay the general questions of science, metaphysics and theology which concerned the Unitarian community at large. In these matters Warrington and 'Manchester College' was important because it employed and educated a high proportion of the movement's intellectuals, though not as science teachers. We can illustrate these general points from Warrington Academy before moving to the founding of Manchester College.

The intellectual core at Warrington comprised John Taylor and especially John Aikin. Both were well known as scholars and theologians. The first tutor in natural philosophy was John Holt, of whom little is known, either as a Unitarian or as a natural philosopher. Holt was, apparently, too retiring a man to be a successful minister. He had supported himself at Kirkdale, near Liverpool, by running a mathematical and commercial school, patronised by the merchant families of the rapidly growing port. At Warrington he seems chiefly to have taught mathematics, in a way which was not generally popular. Mrs. Barbauld described him as 'a sort of reasoning automaton' whose 'soul was absorbed by his science'. He lectured three times a day: at 9–10 am on Fluxions and Conic Sections, 11–12.30 on Natural Philosophy and at 1.30 pm on Roe's Fluxions. His course on natural philosophy included a regular series of experiments, which were rather more popular than his mathematics.[3] Holt, for his private school, had obtained a set of apparatus at the death of Caleb Rotheram, who from 1733 had kept a dissenting academy at Kendal. Rotheram had purchased it from John Horsley (1685–1732), a presbyterian minister and archaeologist of Northumberland, who in his later years had travelled as a lecturer in experimental philosophy. The equipment was eventually bought by the Warrington Academy from which it later passed to Hackney.[4]

Demonstrations in natural philosophy were popular and fashionable; provision was expensive, but courses would increase the attraction of the school. In 1760 the Annual Report recorded: 'a regular course of experiments' was intended 'to be established every year' if they could set up a complete set of apparatus. In 1762 'A set of lectures, principally of the commercial kind are intended to be given in the ensuing session'.[5] This last project was taken up, not by Holt himself, but by a fellow Liverpudlian, the surgeon and chemist Matthew Turner, one of the leading spirits in the cultural life of that city. He was interested in drawing and helped found the Liverpool Academy of Art; he supplied chemicals to Josiah Wedgwood's pottery manufactury; his lectures at Warrington were aimed chiefly at the commercial uses of chemistry. It was apparently these lectures which drew to chemistry the new tutor in languages and literature, Joseph Priestley. The connection continued, at least at an intellectual level, for it was Turner who, pseudonymously, debated Priestley's *Letters to a Philosophical Unbeliever*. Turner, like Priestley, was a strong sympathiser with the American republic; unlike Priestley he was an atheist.[6]

Priestley himself seems not to have taught chemistry or natural philosophy in the six years he was at Warrington, though he did offer courses on anatomy. But in the small community of polymaths he would certainly have discussed science. It was at Warrington that he wrote his *History of Electricity*, and he continued the experimental work he had begun when he ran a school at Nantwich. But it was after Warrington, chiefly when he was a minister at Leeds, that Priestley made the observations on gases for which he is remembered by chemists.[7]

When Priestley left Warrington the replacement language teacher was also an enthusiast for natural sciences. Johann Rheinhold Forster came from an English family settled in Prussia. He had been a minister in the reformed church, but from 1765, when he accepted an invitation to Russia, he devoted himself to science and letters. After he left Warrington, he and his son attained fame by accompanying Cook on his second voyage, and notoriety by the subsequent competition with Cook over published accounts of the exploration. At Warrington, Forster offered courses on mineralogy (on which he published); if enough students were interested he would teach fortification, gunnery and tactics; but his main scientific offerings were in natural history, which, we may note, was to be useful as well as ornamental:

> 'he particularly excels in natural history, on which very important and useful branch of knowledge he will give a compleat course of lectures every year wherein will be contained the natural history of all the principle materials of commerce'.[8]

Forster's stay at Warrington was brief. Thereafter the initiatives in science-related courses mostly came from John Aikin (Junior), the son of the divinity tutor. He had been elaborately educated for a medical career. He had studied at the Edinburgh medical school, then in its prime with

Black and Cullen. Three years as an apprentice of Charles White, Manchester's premier surgeon and man-midwife, was followed by a visit to William and John Hunter in London. He then tried to establish a practice in Chester, but failed and returned to Warrington, where he continued the chemistry lectures established by Turner, plus lectures in anatomy and physiology which Priestley had pioneered. Like so many of these teachers, Aikin (Junior) was trained for a profession but came to prefer teaching and literary work. From 1784 to 1792 he tried medical practice again, in Great Yarmouth, but lost custom over his advocacy of dissenters' rights. Thereafter he lived in London, spending most of his time on literary work, the centre of a family and a circle of friends which included several enthusiasts for science. His son, Arthur Aikin (1773–1854) abandoned his training for the Unitarian ministry, and was encouraged in chemistry by Joseph Priestley. He wrote on natural history, mineralogy, chemistry and chemical manufacture, and he was prominent among the founders of the Mineralogical Society, a group whose strongly utilitarian flavour was not carried fully into the Geological Society which succeeded it, Aikin again among the founders.[9]

This succession of lecturers and initiatives in empirical sciences accompanied the regular mathematical lectures and demonstrations of John Holt. When he died in 1772, he was replaced by another Unitarian minister, George Walker, whose education, like Holt's Warrington apparatus, had derived from Caleb Rotheram's academy at Kendal; later he had studied in Edinburgh and Glasgow universities. He was a very proficient mathematician, but he was also an able and experienced minister. Warrington Academy was in financial difficulties and Walker's income was inadequate. He therefore took up the ministry in Nottingham where he mixed mathematics with philanthropy and dissenting politics.[10]

When Walker left, the trustees needed another mathematical teacher. One of the closest and most competent in Unitarian circles was then a Liverpool minister, Nicholas Clayton (1733–1797), again educated in dissenting academies and Scottish universities. Clayton was later (1781–1783) to teach divinity at Warrington, but his immediate contribution to its mathematics was indirect. He gave a crash course to the Rev. William Enfield who was already teaching languages. Clayton also provided Enfield with apparatus, which he had made himself.[11]

We shall see again the mix of 'science staff' here seen at Warrington: the competent, dull mathematician—a minister who would have difficulty holding a congregation; the 'sons' of the College, trained for a profession but returning to teach; the 'visiting staff' and brief appointments—men of wide interests and many talents, but marginal to Unitarianism; and the Unitarian polymaths, like Walker, or above all, Priestley. The first two groups did most of the teaching; the third linked the college to its local communities; the last were the men who made science a central part of Unitarian culture.

*The first Manchester period, 1786–1803*

Compared to the Warrington Academy, that founded at Manchester was, as Wykes shows in this volume, more northern and more oriented to manufacturing and commerce. Here, and again for the second Manchester period, we are concerned not just with the role of Manchester in the development of a Unitarian academy, but with the place of that academy within the scientific and educational aspirations of the Manchester cultural elite. The historical conjunctures make this very clear: Manchester Academy was set up in 1786, three years after a College of Arts and Sciences, which it to some extent superseded. Manchester New College came back to the city in 1840, four years after public meetings to launch a northern university. The New College left Manchester for London when such a university, as Owens College, was just beginning to take shape. All three cases afford opportunities to consider how the education of divines and commercial gentlemen was meant to relate to industrial knowledge and to the education of other professionals.

The Manchester College of Arts and Sciences seems to have been a product of the Manchester Literary and Philosophical Society, formalised in 1781. As is well known, the chief protagonists of the Lit and Phil were all Unitarians: Dr. Thomas Percival and the Reverend Thomas Barnes were former pupils of Warrington Academy; their friend Thomas Henry was an apothecary. It is symptomatic of the cultural and commercial power of Cross Street Chapel in the late eighteenth century, that Thomas Henry, though not raised as a dissenter, attached himself to that congregation soon after his move to Manchester.[12]

The Lit and Phil had begun as Percival's dining club; no sooner was it formalised than his friends were advertising educational projects. Henry lectured to the Society on 'the advantages of literature and philosophy in general, and especially on the consistency of literary and philosophical with commercial pursuits'. Henry had wanted to attend Oxford as an undergraduate; instead he had lived there as an apothecary's apprentice; but his appeal was not only for liberality in the education of businessmen, or for rational amusements as an alternative to 'the tavern, the gaming table and the brothel'; Henry was particularly concerned with the uses of science. Manchester was being transformed by industry; the manufacturer needed to understand 'Mechanical Powers' and Chemistry.[13]

Thomas Barnes took up the cause a few weeks later, arguing for a museum—'a Publick Repository among us for Chemical and Mechanical Knowledge', where the superintendent could run a 'Mechanical School' which 'would properly finish the education of a young Tradesman or Manufacturer'. A year later Barnes had reduced the project to concentrate on lectures alone, and in autumn 1783 these were begun.[14] The College of Arts and Sciences, president Dr. Percival, gave its classes in the evening. Dr. Barnes lectured on commerce, Thomas Henry on chemistry, Mr. Bew (another medical man) on fine arts, and Mr. Henry Clarke on natural and experimental philosophy. The aim, in Henry's words, was 'to supply the youth of this very wealthy, commercial town with rational amusement and instruction'.

But even in the early 1780s, 'bigotry and party rage' were an obstacle to the cultural enterprise of the unitarian elite. The Lit and Phil lost members over the College scheme, and the College itself came in for criticism. One such criticism, from a colleague of Percival, Henry and the Whites at the Manchester Infirmary, illuminates the relationship with Warrington Academy, which had effectively closed in 1783, though not dissolved until 1786. In 1784, Alexander Eason wrote to a friend in Scotland:

> 'The foundation stone of the Academy is not yet laid . . . It is to be on a small footing, and if it fails, which I think it must the loss will not be great. To ensure success, very little more is required than able masters, scholars, money, and the ruin of the Warrington Academy, in most of which they will be disappointed.'[15]

The Lit and Phil had launched the College of Arts and Sciences, but as a non-sectarian body it had to distance itself from the Academy. The Society publicly 'declare(d) their independence; and that they do not afford any patronage to the above named Academy'.[16]

But the personal links between the three bodies were very close, and there was nothing to prevent the Academy advertising the complementary nature of the College of Arts and Sciences. Barnes and Percival had rebuilt at Manchester the secular functions of the Warrington Academy; these would now help support the theological activities of a dissenting academy.

> 'The friendly correspondence which subsists between the patrons of the College of Arts and Sciences and the supporters of our academy, is a circumstance mutually favourable to both establishments, and to the common cause which gave them birth. By this friendly co-operation the circle of studies which young men may attain among us is agreeably enlarged, and opportunities afforded which could not have been equally enjoyed in a single institution, or in a more confined sphere.'[17]

Perhaps because of this complementarity, there was at first no need for the Manchester Academy to give the whole range of courses attempted at Warrington. Initially the only tutors were Thomas Barnes and his co-minister at Cross Street, Ralph Harrison. Barnes taught theology and added lectures on commerce, presumably those developed for the College of Arts and Sciences. Harrison, who was also an ex-student of Warrington, taught languages and literature.[18] But by May 1787 the College of Arts and Sciences seems to have foundered. Mr. Clarke who had taught natural philosophy there, sold his electrical apparatus to the new Academy, and was asked to postpone the sale of the other part of the apparatus until the arrival in town of Mr. Davies, the Academy's new mathematical tutor.[19]

Like his mathematical predecessors at Warrington, Davies was a minister, a former student of Carmarthen Presbyterian College. He also, after two years, returned to the ministry;[20] he appears not to have pleased the trustees, who had asked Barnes and Harrison to find someone to fill his place. His successor, Mr. W. Nicholls, was hired at the same stipend—£90 p.a. including fees. He stayed until 1792, building up the philosophical apparatus, but nothing is known of his background or later career.[21]

The new Academy was hardly secure, partly because of heavy expenditure on a fine new building. Political and religious divisions deepened markedly from the end of the 1780s, partly as a result of the French Revolution. The Academy's staff were interesting men, but few stayed for long. When Harrison retired in 1790 through ill health, his replacement was Lewis Loyd, who had only just graduated from the college, and who went on to leave an estate worth three million pounds. He was followed by William Stevenson, who had left a tutorship at Bruges and whose varied later career included agricultural journalism and the fathering of the novelist Mrs. Gaskell.[22] Even Dr. Barnes grew unhappy, and in 1792 both he and Nicholls submitted their resignations. Barnes was persuaded to remain; Nicholls was worried about his future subsistence and he left.[23]

His successor in 1783 was John Dalton, a young teacher from Kendal. Barnes had sought the advice of John Gough, of Kendal, of whom Dalton had been a pupil. Dr. Edward Holme was another link recommending Manchester to Dalton; Holme was from Kendal, an ex-student of Warrington Academy, an ex-secretary-pupil of Percival, another notable in the Lit and Phil.[24]

Dalton was 26 years old in 1783, the year of his first publication—*Meteorological Observations and Essays*. He soon became an important member of the Manchester scientific community, taking advantage of the Academy's excellent facilities to expand his knowledge of chemistry. When he arrived in Manchester, Thomas Henry may still have been giving chemistry lectures at the Academy, as he had done from the foundation. But his son, Thomas Henry (Junior), was then entangled in a chemical manufacturing venture at the new copper mines of Anglesey; he found himself with heavy debts, and in 1794 left for America, following Joseph Priestley (Junior). and preceding Joseph Priestley himself. Thomas Henry (Senior) thought of going, but didn't. He recalled his younger son William from his medical studies at Edinburgh, so as to help with the family apothecary practice and chemical manufactory, but he gave up his Academy lectures; chemistry classes became the preserve of Mr. Dalton.[25] In 1797–9 Dalton's 'department' included: arithmetic and merchant's accounts, algebra, geometry and the various branches of mathematics, geography and the use of globes, natural philosophy and chemistry, theoretical and experimental.

Dalton, both as a teacher and as an exponent of atomism, moved to chemistry from a general interest in natural philosophy and meteorology. He was probably helped along the way by William Henry, whose time in Edinburgh had included lectures from James Black, a teacher whose interests in medical chemistry corresponded closely to those young Henry was himself to pursue as a doctor and manager of the family magnesia business. In 1797–9 William Henry gave some chemical lectures in Manchester, probably at the Academy, in which he introduced the new 'French' chemistry, on which he was to write a widely used textbook. He was then engaged in a wide range of ventures in industrial and medical chemistry at a time when Dalton had little experience of the science. Dalton spoke to the Lit and Phil on colour blindness, from which he suffered, and on meteorological questions, but by 1800 he had already begun the train of speculation and investigation which was to make him famous. The mode of this progress and Dalton's occupation at the Academy, were not without connection.

John Dalton was a competent mathematician but he was not an enthusiast for mathematics and certainly not for metaphysics. It is perhaps typical that his old teacher, John Gough, the blind mathematician, criticised Dalton's atomic theory for neglecting mathematical demonstrations; Dalton said mathematics was irrelevant, his was an inductive theory. But Dalton was neither a skilled chemist, nor a practitioner of industrial chemistry. He was a teacher with a gift for simplification. While still employed at the Academy, he guessed that the failure of air to separate into layers of its constituent gases might be due to the repulsion between atoms of each such gas. It was Dalton's good fortune that William Henry, as a manufacturer of soda water, gave support to this initially unlikely hypothesis by showing that any gas would dissolve in water to an extent determined by the pressure above the water of that gas alone; it was unaffected by the pressures of any other gases present. By then Dalton was shifting his theoretical ground, but had realised that the atomic theory could be used in chemistry to determine the relative weights of atoms of various combining elements. As was argued by the Farrars and Scott, it is unlikely that Dalton would have achieved much success in determining combining weights had he not had to hand the chemical expertise of William Henry.

One might then reasonably argue that the atomic theory in chemistry was born from the interaction of natural philosophy with the industrial and medical exploitation of the new chemistry; in other words from the two traditions of natural science which at Warrington seemed rarely to meet. Dalton was employed chiefly for mathematics and natural philosophy; the Henrys played roles like Turner, and John Aikin jr at Warrington, in providing empirical science of interest to aspirant doctors and manufacturers. These later influences were stronger and more immediate in Manchester, as an industrial and professional centre. In the Lit and Phil, Manchester had an arena for displaying good ideas in scientific fields. Dalton was not a minister; he had only the distractions of elementary teaching, which he turned to advantage. As the town's professional teacher of mathematics, he was well placed to play a key role in the practical and theoretical concerns of its business and professional elite.

By 1800 the Lit and Phil had its own purpose-built premises on George Street, where Dalton had a class-room and a laboratory, which may be one reason why he resigned from the Manchester Academy. The trustees were 'concerned', for at the same time they also lost their recently appointed classics tutor, William Johns (1771–1845) a Unitarian minister who returned to Manchester in 1804 to run a private school; he was then, for 26 years, John Dalton's landlord and friend.[26] The Academy was left with a single tutor, George Walker, who had taken over theology at Barnes' resignation in 1798. This was the same Walker as had taught mathematics at Warrington, but even his talents could not save an institution which was already failing in very troubled times.[27] The Unitarians had suffered badly in the repression of the 1790s; their ascendancy in Manchester local politics was at an end. Barnes had resigned because of recurrent discipline problems, and even then some supporters of the college were clear as to their remedy. 'The dissipation of Manchester is so serious an objection that the Committee cannot be too desirous of speedily removing it.'[28]

Dalton would remain in Manchester, based on the Lit and Phil. He would teach elementary (and not so elementary) science to budding industrialists and engineers.[29] One of them, Joule, like his master, would achieve fame for careful, unsophisticated reflection on the technology which so insistently surrounded them. The science of the Lit and Phil continued, in part because it could pass as apolitical. The Unitarians sought elsewhere a new basis for combining the education of ministers with the general education of their leading laymen.

### *The York years (1803–1840)*

In moving from Manchester to York the College sought a smaller, less threatening setting in which a house of learning might go about its business.[30] Charles Wellbeloved had ministered to the Unitarians of York since he had left the Hackney Academy in 1792. He had been a college friend of Arthur Aikin; he had been approached to succeed Barnes in Manchester in 1797–98; in 1803 he agreed to be director if the Institution was moved to York, where he was already teaching. He remained as director until 1840 when the college returned to Manchester.[31]

Initially he had only one assistant, Hugh Kerr, a Glasgow graduate, who taught classics, maths. and natural philosophy while Wellbeloved concentrated on theology, especially biblical exegesis. When Kerr left, following an attempt to reduce his salary, he was succeeded by the Rev. Theophilus Browne, a controversial man who left in 1809. It was from 1809–10 that Wellbeloved had two assistants; one of them, John Kenrick, became his son-in-law and remained with the College until after its move to Manchester. Kenrick taught classics, literature and history; he was referred to as the finest scholar of his denomination. Mathematics and natural philosophy were taught first by William Turner (Junior), newly graduated from the College and the son of the Unitarian minister of Newcastle. When Turner left for the ministry in Halifax, he was succeeded by William Hincks.[32]

At York the College was 'domestic'; nearly all the pupils lived in a boarding house under the care of one of the assistants. In general there were about a dozen theological students, often supported by Unitarian funds, and about as many 'lay' pupils, usually intended for careers in industry, commerce or law. In a sense, this was a return to the Warrington pattern—a small boarding establishment serving a wide geographical area, providing a broad but intensive general education supposedly under domestic discipline. The full general course lasted three years; intending ministers then studied for a further two years.

At York the College was remote from the chemical and mechanical concerns of Manchester. Students came from the industrial districts and Kenrick's brother founded a hardware company in West Bromwich, but York, at least until the coming of the railways, was noted more for agriculture and antiquities than for manufactures and commerce. In the scientific interests of the staff too, it was the countryside and ancient monuments which predominated. They shared the interests of the intellectually alert in many a county-town, and in Oxbridge—botany, geology, archaeology; these sciences could be linked to religion via natural theology; but increasingly, and especially for 'scholars', links were made through the study of language, scriptural exegesis and ancient history.

Wellbeloved did not claim to be a scientist, but he knew the Aikins well and was noted as a naturalist. He shared an interest in plants with his friend, the Rev. William Wood, Priestley's successor as minister in Leeds and a botanist of eminence.[33] He was a noted antiquarian, an expert on the history and monuments of York, and a keen 'conservationist' for York Minster. Kenrick's historical interests extended into pre-history and philology; as a student at Glasgow he had won distinction in physical science as well as in classics and logic.

Though most of William Hincks' teaching was, of course, in mathematics and natural philosophy, this was not where his main scientific interests lay; indeed his mathematical proficiency was doubted by at least one student.[34] He was keen on politics—an ardent radical who damned all institutions but the American Congress; he was especially keen on natural history. When he first attracted attention as a possible master for York, he had returned to England from his native Ireland, dreaming of a cottage in Wales, 'where he wished to live, but not alone, botanising and mineralogising'; so at least John Kenrick reported to George William Wood.[35] In 1824–5 when Hincks was in Liverpool as a minister, the staff and trustees at York discussed the possibility of his giving a course of lectures on botany.[36] It was eventually in natural history that Hincks obtained a fully professional post. After leaving York, he spent most of the 1840s in London, editing the *The Inquirer*, before being appointed in 1849 as Professor of Natural History at Queens College, Cork. In 1853 he moved further west, to a similar post at University College, Toronto. Thomas Henry Huxley had also applied for this post; Hincks' brother Francis (the Colbert of Canada) was then premier.[37]

None of these men were major figures in natural science. Those most professionally concerned—Turner and Hincks—were 'attendant lords';

Kenrick was a scholar of national stature, but only marginally involved with natural sciences. But all of them were interested and all took part in the network of local scientific organisations which by the 1830s was drawn into support of the British Association for the Advancement of Science.

Wellbeloved had been one of the founders of the subscription library in York (1794), which was as close as York came to organised science in the late eighteenth century. When liberal intellectual culture re-emerged about 1820, and 'philosophical' societies were organised in the second-league of provincial cities, York gained the Yorkshire Philosophical Society. The College staff were among its major supporters, but they were not its founders. These were an ex-military gentleman, a local solicitor and a local surgeon, respectively interested in geology, antiquities and the arts. The particular occasion of their collaboration was the finding of an extensive set of fossil bones in a cave at Kirkdale in the North Riding; this attracted the attention of the Rev. Wm. Buckland, Reader in Geology and Mineralogy at Oxford, and it stimulated the local geologists and antiquaries to think of founding a public museum. Their plan was brought to fruition, as a philosophical society and museum, by William Vernon (Harcourt), son of the Archbishop of York and former student of Buckland at Oxford. Vernon knew the leading chemists of Oxford and especially of London; back in York he retained a practical interest in chemistry as well as geology. It was Vernon who encouraged the contribution to the YPS of William Smith, the stratigrapher, and his nephew John Phillips, who in 1826 became the Society's paid curator. These two were men of humble background whose precarious and peripatetic existence as surveyors and geologists contrasted with the widespread recognition of their innovative science.[38]

In 1823 Wellbeloved became curator of antiquities for the Society and with characteristic persistence he held the post to his death, when he was succeeded by Kenrick, who had long been an active member. Kenrick and Turner had joined the Society together in 1823. Hincks joined in his turn, and was made curator of Botany in 1828. The links between College and Society also worked the other way round when Phillips arranged to admit college students to his public lectures free of charge.[39]

The 1820s, in York as elsewhere, were extra-ordinarily productive of broadly scientific organisations, for the working-classes as well as for their superiors. The mechanics institute movement was brought into York by Wellbeloved. The Unitarian involvement is hardly surprising; at Manchester it was Benjamin Heywood who took the lead; Heywood was a friend of Kenrick and his family must have been well known to Wellbeloved. The Visitor of Manchester College, William Turner (Senior), was involved in the promotion of the Mechanics Institute in Newcastle, as he was involved in most of that city's scientific and educational ventures. The examples could be multiplied for the growth of local and national organisations for science owed much to the broad intellectual culture of the Unitarians. In most of the provincial cities and in London, well-educated Unitarian ministers, industrialists or professional men were among the leaders of local scientific culture, sometimes themselves as notable practitioners, more often as keen supporters. The Aikins in London, Turner in Newcastle, Wood in Leeds, and Holme, the younger Woods, the Heywoods and the Philipses in Manchester, were all directly involved with Manchester College or its predecessor at Warrington.[40] To them can be added two remarkable families, the Carpenters of Bristol and the Martineaus of Norwich, with whom major tendencies in Victorian thought became matters of family history.[41]

Without the Unitarians, most of the provincial scientific societies would have been substantially weaker and several would not have existed. The Unitarians were probably the most important, in this respect, of the nonconformist denominations—out of all proportion to their total numbers. In the 1820s and the 1830s, in voluntary organisations and government reform, they gained leading places as representatives of a new middle-class culture. But in the establishment of that culture and its associated institutions they were joined by reformers of other backgrounds; their shared successes inevitably altered the conditions of existence for Unitarian scientific culture, as did the institutional achievements of continental intellectuals, especially in the German states.

These elements can be examined in the formation and early years of the British Association for the Advancement of Science, which also nicely illustrates the centrality of geology to British science, and to the emergent debates about science and religion. The first meeting of the B.A.A.S. was held at York in 1831. It was modelled on meetings of German naturalists and was prompted by deep discontent in some quarters with the record of the Royal Society and other established scientific institutions. The reformers, many in the Geological Society, sought a new means of promoting science by linking metropolitan reformers, Scottish savants and the regional scientific groupings of provincial England. York was chosen for the first meeting because it was midway between London and Edinburgh, it was near the northern cities of dissent, but itself the seat of an Archbishop. It had a thriving Philosophical Society, run by the Archbishop's son, aided by a geologist from 'humble life'.[42]

The principals in the early B.A.A.S. were not Unitarian; control soon lay firmly with liberal anglicans from Oxford, Cambridge, London, Bristol and York itself. But Unitarians were a significant presence. At the first meeting Dalton and Henry had headed a powerful Manchester contingent; William Henry gave public offence by praising Priestley; it was Dalton who persuaded the B.A.A.S. to remain 'ever provincial'—it would not meet in London. William Turner headed the Newcastle delegation; the Rev. T. D. Hincks, father of William, was the organisers' chief contact in Belfast. The Unitarians also supplied two key administrators: the treasurer of the B.A.A.S. from 1832 to 1861 was John Taylor, who came from a mercantile family in Norwich and had attained great wealth through mining enterprises in Britain and abroad; Taylor also had a long-standing interest in polite geology and was a key figure in the Geological

Society. The Secretary to the B.A.A.S. Council was the Rev. John Yates, son of a Liverpool Unitarian minister, student at Glasgow and at Manchester College, York (1808–10), then a noted antiquary and Unitarian controversialist.[43]

The teachers of Manchester College took an interest in the new Association, though the best known of them, Wellbeloved and Kenrick, were only marginally 'scientists'. In 1833 Kenrick suggested bringing forward the College examinations because he hoped

> 'to go to the Scientific meeting at Cambridge which I hear is expected to be splendid, numerous and highly interesting. I doubt what branch of science I profess, unless it be that respecting which Dr. Prichard makes communication in the Reports to the Oxford meeting—language and history—which hardly is honoured with the name of a science by the chemists and geologists but I shall enjoy the sight of so many illustrious men as will be congregated there'[44]

Kenrick may have been marginal to 'science' but that boundary with history and theology was of very considerable importance during the 1830s.

'Genesis and geology' was a hot issue for the B.A.A.S., many of whose founders were geologists and/or clergymen. At the Oxford meeting to which Kenrick referred, William Buckland used palaeontology in support of natural theology, so provoking the Oxford tractarians and evangelicals who objected to the concord of science and scripture if that meant subjecting belief to the tests of science. The arguments continued through the mid 30s, fuelled in part by the success of Charles Lyell's *Principles of Geology* in which he argued for a very old earth, and for geology as a science like any other, quite independent of scripture. Lyell's rejection of 'catastrophes' threatened the accommodation which Buckland and other liberal anglicans had found between geological and biblical records of 'floods'.[45]

Of the broad anglican responses to the evangelicals, the most liberal came from the Rev. Baden Powell, Professor of Geometry at Oxford. He argued that 'absolute contradictions' between geology and scripture were not 'arguments against the truth of relevation in general, or the Christian religion in particular; nor are the accordances which may be made out necessary to its support'. Kenrick was delighted and wrote to G. W. Wood: Powell's pamphlet was 'liberal to the verge of Unitarianism . . . It seems as if rational reform of Theology was to spring from the Geologists in the church at least'. After the 1835 B.A.A.S. meeting in Dublin, Kenrick himself joined the argument with a sermon in praise of science: in contemplating the laws of nature as expressions of infinite wisdom, the natural philosopher freed himself from sectarian bigotry.[46] It was a lesson already preached in the reports of Manchester College: 'literature and science will furnish new and wider views of the nature and application of religious truth, and enable the faithful leader to speak with confidence and authority'.[47]

Kenrick's views were to be made very clear in 1846, when he published his *Primeval History*. It was wrong to 'reconcile' science and scripture; Whewell was at best misleading when he spoke of 'investing the language of scripture with new meaning'; he ought to know that 'the interpretation of the Bible is governed by rules as little arbitrary as that of any other ancient book'. We know, through science and through historical–critical study that the biblical narrative is partly true and partly erroneous—the 'authority of relevation is not involved in the correctness of the opinions which prevailed among the Hebrew people respecting cosmology and primeval history'.[48]

The urge to truth is clear, the expectation that men could find a common basis of belief by the free exercise of scientific and literary criticism. But the problems must also have been clear to his listeners and to his fellow-workers at the College: scripture and science might support religious belief, but they did not necessitate it. The appeal was increasingly to the human spirit; and that ground was to be elaborated by Kenrick's pupil, James Martineau, when the College was back in Manchester. In its York years, the theological framework was still Priestleyan;[49] the College responded to the scientific debates around it in the firm assurance that the wider the range of the critical intelligence, the more likely it was that men and women would reach the Unitarian position.

The role of York as a seminary was clear, but its claims in lay-education became more problematic as competition developed. The founding of University College, London (1826), and of London University (1837) as a degree granting body, posed the problem acutely. University College was secular and open to all, unlike Oxbridge; it was provided by middle-class reformers from essentially the same culture as the Unitarians; compared to York, it could offer lectures from a wider range of specialised staff, and it could give degrees. University College aimed to provide, in London, the best elements of Scottish and German universities, in both liberal and professional education; it was bound to be a rival for the lay-functions of York.[50]

By 1829, the York Annual Report was complaining of diminished student numbers and financial support through competition with University College. The next year they regretted 'those fluctuations of opinion, which, in an age like ours of ceaseless change and excitement, acknowledged merit cannot always arrest, and amidst which old and tried institutions are perpetually abandoned for more brilliant and imposing schemes of public utility'. In response York stressed the advantages of educating lay-students with 'embryo divines', for mutual social and moral development.[51]

In 1834, George William Wood helped sponsor a bill to open Oxford and Cambridge to dissenters. Kenrick had suggested improvements to the draft bill, commenting that it would be some time before London would rival the ancient universities.[52] This bill did not pass. (Another two decades went by before such a measure succeeded, this time proposed by

James Heywood.) But Manchester College was already on the defensive, arguing that

> 'the mode of life pursued in these ancient and wealthy establishments is adapted to a different class of society, and their courses of study are directed rather to the high cultivation of the mind in a few branches, than to the communication of that knowledge by which a young man is fitted to discharge with intelligence the public and private duties of a middle station'.[53]

Kenrick allowed that the rich might follow fashion to Oxbridge, or to London University, which compared to York 'will be regarded as a splendid and fashionable institution'; Manchester College might aim for a lower class, but might have to reduce its fees accordingly.[54]

Yet an alternative path was already under discussion. By 1834, Kenrick, Wood and others were considering a move to London, where non-theological classes could be left to University College. The Annual Report of 1836 referred to pressure as to 'the desirableness of an important change in the situation and arrangement of the college'. This was probably a reference to a plan of James Heywood to set up a college in Manchester, which would take over the 'science and philology'. Kenrick thought this a good idea; two years later he precipitated a decision by proposing resignation.[55] With Hincks looking for a minister's position and Wellbeloved approaching seventy, it seemed time to re-assess the position. A report was to be drawn up by James Martineau and John James Tayler, both former pupils.

The majority of the College's supporters favoured a move and a link with a general college or university. The Scottish universities were considered, University College London was explored; eventually the majority favoured Manchester. James Heywood had offered his house and £500, if the College moved to Manchester; this seems to have been a way of using Manchester College to resuscitate his plan of 1836 for a general college. Even if Manchester had no college already in existence, re-siting there would not preclude formal affiliation to London University; and it would preserve the northern attachment which had been important since the College's beginning.[56]

### *Manchester College and Manchester science, 1840–1853*

The city to which Manchester College returned was considerably changed from that it had left in 1803, not least through the cultural activities of the Unitarian elite which had continued to support the College when it was in York. The population had grown from 70,000 to 250,000; new industrial and residential suburbs had been developed; the city was now recognised world-wide as proto-typically industrial. After the Napoleonic Wars and Peterloo (1819), middle-class radicalism had re-emerged and consolidated around campaigns for free trade and reform of central and local government. By 1840, Manchester had two MPs and a strong town council. One of the MPs was Mark Philips; G. W. Wood had been an MP for South Lancashire 1832–5; the mayor in 1839 was Thomas

Potter. This local prominence of the key unitarian families had been achieved in large part through cultural as well as directly political activities. The range of scientific and cultural institutions had expanded remarkably between 1820 and 1840, often on the initiative of younger Unitarians, some of them trained at Manchester College. These initiatives were the chief base of local plans for a general college or university, and thus the immediate context of the return of Manchester College.[57]

The cultural expansion had begun soon after Peterloo, when a Natural History Society and Museum was established, chiefly to house collections built up by John Leigh Philips, a Unitarian industrialist by then identified with the conservative wing of a large and influential family. The Museum was run initially by a taxidermist more skilled in stuffing than science; 'reformers' in the 1830s succeeded in installing as curator the young W. C. Williamson, then an apprentice surgeon but raised in the rich artisan stratum of Yorkshire geology to which we have already referred.[58] Further specialist societies were developed in the 1830s, catering for the hobbies of industrialists and gentlemen, but generally run by 'devotees' with some claims to national recognition in science. The Phrenological Society was founded in 1829 (Cobden was a great enthusiast); the Botanical Society was begun in 1830; the Geological Society opened in 1838 and originally intended to have its own museum.[59] All these societies had things to exhibit—stuffed birds, casts of criminal heads, exotic plants or specimens of local fossils. That was an important part of their public presence, and part of their difference from the austere Literary and Philosophical Society which continued, with closed membership, under the rather dry chairmanship of Dr. Dalton. Indeed if the Lit and Phil had anything to display, it was Dr. Dalton himself and his unwearied assiduity:

> 'His fine venerable appearance, surrounded by a variety of chemical apparatus,—his thoughtful countenance—the time, place and circumstance,—conveyed to the mind of the (guide book) writer the beau ideal of a philosopher'[60]

But the Lit and Phil, increasingly focussed on chemistry and the principles of engineering, was no place for cultural entrepreneurs wanting to lead a general elevation of the Manchester middle class. Hence the founding in 1832 of the Royal Manchester Institution for the cultivation of literature, science and the arts. The building, by Barry, was the finest in town; it functioned as an art gallery and James Heywood gave a prize for painting. The key protagonist behind this out-going institution was G. W. Wood, treasurer of Manchester College, York and one of the great committee men of Whig reform. He was much attached to the English Presbyterian tradition—the 'quiet aristocracy of talent and social influence' in which lay a safeguard 'for the tranquil and progressive improvement of human affairs'.[61]

The Manchester Institution raised the town's tone, housed many popular scientific lectures, and often provided meeting rooms for more specialised activities, such as the Medical Society, founded 1834. Even before its building was opened, a Wm. R. Whatton F.S.A. proposed to his fellow governors that the present plan be altered and extended 'for giving it the power and efficient form of a university'. Presumably this was Manchester's response to University College London.

The scheming came to nothing, to be renewed again in 1836 when the chartering of London University as an examining body allowed affiliation by provincial colleges. But meantime Wood and the Heywoods had been active at other levels. They were central to the formation of the Manchester Mechanics Institute (1824) which Benjamin Heywood long dominated. In 1837 the School of Design opened, again serving the artisan classes. About the same time, the Royal Manchester Institution spawned the Athenaeum to provide reading rooms and lectures for the younger elements of the middle class, who apparently were not attracted by the parent body. The Heywoods were also central to the Statistical Society (f. 1833) one of whose major early concerns was education.[62]

Thus were the elements in line for the initiative of 1836. James Heywood, educated at Glasgow University and since then a good friend of Kenrick, addressed the opening meeting of the Athenaeum and called for an establishment in Manchester to take up the work of the College of Arts and Sciences of 1783. Later in the year he sponsored an address to the Statistical Society and funded its publication as a pamphlet. The engineer Wm. Fairbairn, who was closely associated with the Mechanics Institute, produced schemes for town improvement which incorporated a university. One of the (proprietary) medical schools came forward as a prospective partner in the venture, hoping that a general college could raise the status of their own enterprise. A committee was set up, but the scheme failed, partly because of rivalry between the two medical schools. It was not easy for a college of general education to serve the fractious medics and the range of contending religious denominations. Most of the supporters of the 1836 plans were medics or dissenters; the Church of England interest tried to float a college but failed; this may have been a fore-runner of the Manchester Commercial Schools opened in 1845 by the Manchester Church Education Society.[63]

In 1837 the Manchester Society for Promoting National Education was founded, to help provide non-sectarian elementary education; this, of course, was opposed by Anglicans and by many fervent Congregationalists who favoured religious voluntaryism.[64] The Congregationalists were increasingly prominent among Manchester dissenters. In 1838 they decided to bring back to Manchester their seminary which had been for some years out at Blackburn. The Lancashire Independent College opened its splendid gothic buildings in 1845; it boasted a distinguished staff headed by Dr. Vaughan, a former professor of history at University College London. By then the Wesleyans had also opened a new seminary to the south of the city.[65]

These collateral developments highlight the double task which James Heywood and Kenrick undertook. At one level they were paralleling the Independents in moving a small seminary back to Manchester. But they were also trying to provide a general college of education for lay students of any denomination, including those intending careers in secular professions. It was Heywood's scheme of 1836, but without the medical interest and with an explicit Unitarian attachment.

In moving to Manchester and in affiliating to London University, the New College was recognising that certificates and the preliminary qualifications of professional bodies were now central to higher education; any future 'quiet aristocracy of talent and social influence' would want degrees.[66] Manchester New College, in its courses and tutors, had to equal University College London. Thus for classics, Kenrick wanted a public school and English university man or someone who 'should have supplied that deficiency with at least a year at a German university'.[67] They appointed F. W. Newman, former fellow of Balliol, of whose religious opinions they knew only that 'they are not in accordance with his brothers or our own'.[68] Kenrick himself continued to teach history. James Martineau taught mental and moral philosophy. It was a very strong team.

Officially the College was divided into three departments: theology, literature, and science; in fact, the latter two were almost always listed together, as having no denominational attachment. In mathematics, as in classics, the ancient universities had reputable standards. Tayler and Martineau hoped they could obtain a man 'of University training and name'. They were well aware of the difficulty of finding anyone competent across the whole range of the sciences. As Martineau wrote:

> 'The great difficulty in filling up the scientific department seems to me to arise from this; that you cannot find a person equally skilled in Mathematics and Physics [sic], on the one hand, and in what one may term, the science of Observation [sic] on the other, in which last phrase I include Experimental Natural Philosophy and Chemistry, and the several branches of Natural History, with Geology. If it were possible to make of these latter a separate department, the advantage would be incalculable, and would ultimately, I am persuaded, repay the venture. With a view to attracting attendance from lay students, especially medical, this arrangement would be of the utmost consequence'.[69]

For both assignments the tutors sounded out suitable informants —Thomas Thomson in Glasgow, Baden Powell in Oxford, James Prichard in Bristol; James Heywood was to make enquiries in Cambridge, where he had once studied. The Committee appears not to have advertised, but Thomson placed notices in the Scottish papers.[70] The resultant list of candidates for the mathematical post is not without general interest: most were present or past employees of Scottish colleges—St. Andrews, Inverness Academy, Glasgow Mechanics Institute, Glasgow Andersonian Institute.[71] Martineau recommended two of the teachers at Liverpool High School; Heywood, probably, recommended a Mr. Walton of Trinity College, Cambridge, from which there was also a second candidate.[72] The Committee interviewed two Cambridge men and Robert

Finlay, a graduate of Trinity College Dublin, then teaching at the Endowed School, Dungannon.[73] Finlay was eventually appointed to teach mathematics and the Committee looked for someone to teach experimental philosophy.[74] Bryden Jack, of St. Andrews, was unwilling to teach as elementary a course as required, so they appointed Montague Phillips, pleased with his account of his teaching at Liverpool High School.[75]

These appointments must have been rather disappointing for Martineau. He had looked with admiration to Liverpool High School, but his prime target there was Mr. Hartshorn, principal teacher of mathematics and a graduate of Trinity College Dublin. Hartshorn was a teacher of genius and breadth who had suffered in Ireland for his Unitarian convictions. He had written on mathematics and he was skilled in languages. It is not clear why this representative of a great tradition chose not to come to Manchester. His colleague Phillips knew more about experimental science but was far less sympathetic and imaginative. He took 'not the slightest interest in any but his own physical pursuits, and will not open his lips for hours, unless these are the topics of conversation'.[76]

One of the reasons why Martineau had wanted two posts was his hope that a chair in experimental philosophy would be filled by William B. Carpenter, son of Lant Carpenter (the minister at Bristol), and brother to two Manchester College students:

> 'the great reputation which he has already acquired, especially as a Physiologist, and a Philosophical Naturalist, would be of unquestionable benefit to the College. When he was here he drew up a plan of a course of study sweeping over the whole of the region of which I speak; and the sketch was very masterly. The testimonials which he produced from the very first men of scientific repute in this country were singularly hearty and very striking. He is an exceedingly ambitious man, and would not be content without winning some glories for the college'.[77]

Certainly Carpenter was on the look-out for a more remunerative lecturing post than he then held at the Bristol Medical School. He was trying to build a medical practice, but never liked practical medicine. He was a good friend of F. W. Newman, and indeed recommended him to Manchester College. Why he himself disappointed Martineau's hopes is not clear. Personal factors may have played a part—his father was drowned in 1840 and he married later that year. In 1842 he tried for the chair of the Institute of Medicine at Edinburgh, but was ruled out as a Unitarian; it was 1845 before he obtained a satisfactory post—as Fullerian Professor of Physiology at the Royal Institution. It may well be that Carpenter, though able to map a wide area of natural science, preferred to cultivate only a small part of it, and saw the writing of physiology texts as ultimately more rewarding than being a superior science-master.

This, one suspects, was the general dilemma of Manchester College. Its organisers knew that to rival London they would need more 'division of labour' and, for science, a lot of expensive equipment. Martineau saw that they were gambling, and aimed to 'follow the noble economy of *deserving and producing more,* instead of the poor frugality of *consuming and requiring less.*[78] Phillips' equipment cost more than the renovations to the house in Mosley Street which they were then using.[79] But they could afford only two science tutors; both had to teach some elementary material; neither was a recognised authority in science. No one could fail to recognise Kenrick and Martineau as national figures, but no history of Manchester scientific talent in the 1840s, would feature Finlay or Phillips. The college's chief lights were in the literature department, providing an excellent general education for Unitarian ministers, but likely thereby to attract suspicion among any non-Unitarian Mancunians who might want a general education for their sons. For most of this potential audience, 'sound education' meant sound religious principles; Manchester New College was either Unitarian or secular. Secular chemistry could be useful; secular moral philosophy was much more problematical, whatever the record of Scottish or German universities. Nor could the college easily tap the growing need for scientific professional education. The Scottish universities and University College London relied heavily on their medical schools; Manchester New College could not. They all had a finer division of scientific labour than Manchester New College and employed men of higher reputation. Heywood saw the difficulty and tried a solution in sponsoring teaching of civil engineering. Here surely was a real local need and a way of linking the College with the pre-occupations of Manchester's scientific elite.

In the summer of 1841 Heywood offered to pay the salary of a Professor of Civil Engineering for a year, with the possibility of extension for a further two: 'in three years a class of civil engineering which manifestly is of great local utility ought to support itself'.[80] William Fairbairn, who was to assist with the choice of tutor, was a local engineer of great distinction who, in collaboration with Eaton Hodgkinson, carried out important experimental studies on 'strengths of materials'.

In October 1841 the Committee appointed Edward Sang 'a gentleman well known to those who are familiar with this branch of science, for his union of theoretical knowledge and practical skill'.[81] He was probably the Mr. Sang of Edinburgh who had been a candidate for the chair of mathematics. In Manchester he was to teach a general engineering course with a bias to textiles. The classes were held in James Heywood's Mosley Street house at 8.00 pm, the fees were paid into a separate account, from which Sang was guaranteed £50 in addition to his £110 salary. The rest of the fees went to pay expenses, any deficit being made up by Heywood. Any profits went to Sang and to the College in the ratio of three to one. Sang was also free to do private work and planned to take apprentices for a full three year course at a fee of £210, which was to be divided between him and the college.[82]

Sang arranged his lecture course in five self-contained sections so that students could select what they wanted. The sections were:

1. Surveying
2. Roads, bridges and canals

3. On the sources and conveyance of force
4. On change of form
5. On disintegration,

and the fee for each section was two guineas.[83] He refused to lecture on all five nights, mainly because 'young men who are occupied in offices and works for ten hours every day are much too fatigued to devote every evening to such studies; and also that such attendance would prevent the prosecution of other branches of education'. He planned to lecture on Monday, Wednesday and Friday on 'simple matters' and devote Tuesdays and Thursdays to 'conversations with the more zealous or advanced students in regard to the difficulties that might occur'.[84] A fortnight later he asked if the fees might be reduced for needy cases and it was agreed 'that operative mechanics paying fees for two courses be allowed, in Mr. Sang's discretion to enter for the three remaining courses at half fee, on Mr. Sang's ascertaining from their Employers that their circumstances do not admit of their conveniently paying the full fee'.[85]

It is not clear what went wrong. In May 1842 Sang said that the number of students on the second course was greater than expected; he had 14 names already and expected three more. In November he was trying a preparatory class as an experiment, which indicates that some of his would-be students had difficulty with even the 'simple matters' he lectured on.[86] Finlay had to do the same for mathematics to occasional students 'who may not be prepared to enter and proceed with the regular classes with advantage'.[87] The regular students had to pass an entrance examination, but, of course, the 'casuals' did not. The civil engineering course was causing concern by January 1843.[88] In February Sang asked if he might resign 'on the ground that the Number of Pupils proved inadequate to give him sufficient encouragement to continue his classes', and he offered to leave on payment of £150 (a year's salary and fees). This was done with Heywood's agreement.[89] No attempt was made to appoint another professor. It may well be that the 'effective demand' in terms of money, inclination or educational attainment was not there and Heywood was forced to recognise it.

The executive committee made sure that the college's activities were well publicised, through advertisements, circulars, and the inaugural lectures. The professors themselves tackled the problem (it was in their interests to do so). They drew up a circular for schoolteachers, showing how parents might be persuaded to keep their children at school until the age of 16, before sending them on to a college like Manchester New College to prepare for London University examinations. Such a connection with the University would, they claimed, raise the status of the school and the schoolmaster.[90] Montague Phillips went out of his way to raise local interest in the science courses. He began an evening class in chemistry covering:

1. General principles of chemistry and manipulation of chemical apparatus.

2. Preparation and properties of elementary substances, organic and inorganic.
3. Application of chemistry to manufactures, manufactures of acids, alkalies, soap and other compounds. The theoretical principles of dyeing, calico printing and bleaching.
4. Inorganic chemistry, qualitative and quantitative analysis, organic and inorganic.

The course would cover two sessions of nine months, each including 78 lectures (two per week), and the fee would be three guineas per session.[91] It does not seem to have 'caught on'; in 1843 he reported that 'after considerable difficulty and by making personal application I have at length succeeded in raising a chemical class at the College'.

He had found ten students and was again charging three guineas of which he proposed to pay two guineas to the College and use the rest to cover the expenses. He said he did not want the money for himself and pointed out that Kings College charged seven guineas for 'this class'.[92] It seems as if this was an attempt to promote his subject, rather than to earn extra money for himself. Certainly this was the case in May 1843 for the lectures on Calico Printing he planned to give at the Athenaeum in the hope of attracting people to the college courses.[93] However, some of his outside work was undertaken to supplement his income. In January 1842 he was clearly hard up and partly dependent on outside earnings, for he wrote to S. D. Darbishire (one of the secretaries):

> 'I had made an engagement for a course of lectures at Warrington which the business of the times has deferred. I received a few pounds the other day for some chemical analysis which I performed for the Manchester and Birmingham Railway and in March I have some engagements which will make up the deficiency in my salary'.[94]

Three weeks later he wrote again, apologising for giving trouble and saying he had sold part of his library; he blamed his financial difficulty on the cost of removal from Liverpool to Manchester.[95]

Phillips seems to have been the most diligent of the professors in doing outside work. The others attacked the problem by identifying another market for the College's teaching and tailoring a course to suit it. This was a two-year, non-degree programme, entitled a Course of Modern Instruction. As they said:

> 'There are parents in Manchester who have a decided judgement against bestowing on their children a classical education, and who will on no account consent to their becoming students of our entire course. It is possible that they hardly know how to make a judicious selection from our lectures; and when invited to do so, rather imagine that such occasional teaching is to be supplementary to the counting house, than find in it an inducement to give their sons one or two years more time for intellectual improvement . . .'[96]

The course of Modern Instruction consisted of two self-contained years. In the first it covered

1. Ancient History and English Composition

2. Natural Philosophy, Chemistry and French or German
3. Political Economy or Moral Philosophy

and in the second

1. Modern History and English Composition
2. Natural Philosophy and Chemistry (continued), French or German
3. Moral Philosophy or Political Economy, Botany

This was simply a selection from the degree course syllabus.[97] The fee for the full degree course was twenty-five guineas per session (excluding French or German), while for the 'Abridged Course' the cost was fifteen guineas including the languages.[98] This looks like another example of 'pearls before swine': the fee for the abridged course was quoted in the next year's Report, but had disappeared the year after that (1844).

In its transition from York to Manchester the College underwent a complete change of style. In York the students lived with one of the three tutors; the time-table was not heavily crowded—young William Holt in his first year in 1822 had an average of three hours a day in lectures, and no teaching was done between one o'clock and five o'clock so that there was plenty of time for private study and getting to know fellow-students and tutors.[99] In Manchester not only was the teaching more intensive, but the students lived in lodgings so there was less opportunity for social contact with their tutors or each other, and they had the added problem of having to cater for themselves as cheaply as possible. Philip Carpenter, who was at the college over this transition period, did not like the change. Although York had the disadvantage of a 'dearth of society', the lack of community in Manchester, and the added pressure of having to make his money stretch to cover the costs of feeding himself, made Manchester a dreary place. On top of that, the pressure of the work intensified so that, as he said 'I am hurried on from one thing to another and have not a single hour to think'.[100]

It was not only Manchester New College who found the London University work over-demanding. Within five years of the establishment of the University, four of the affiliated colleges had asked for the removal of science from the curriculum, on the grounds that it was of limited use to Christian ministers. The Senate refused claiming that 'some knowledge of chemistry, botany and natural history, formed a necessary part of every liberal education'.[101] In 1842 only eight of the 21 affiliated colleges had sent students to the examinations and only 20 of the 35 students had passed:

> 'The Senate as at present constituted is you know swamped by Medical Men, who make no secret of their wish to discourage the study of the classics and mathematics and to introduce into its own colleges a more extensive cultivation of the Natural Sciences in their stead'.[102]

The Manchester College agreed that the course was 'too broad and superficial', and sent a memorial to London University to this effect.[103]

William Hincks, now in London, did not see it this way. He felt that the students should acquire a smattering of a wide range of subjects; deep study over a smaller range should be carried on in later life. He thought the problem of the high failure rate should be solved by giving the students a greater choice of questions in the examination. He defended 'that knowledge which is sometimes laughed at as a smattering, but is in reality what makes a well-informed mind'.[104] A decade later, J. H. Newman in *The Idea of a University* was famously to denounce such smatterings. General knowledge of plants and sea shells were an 'accomplishment', along with drawing, fencing, painting, stuffing birds and playing stringed instruments, none of which had a place in a university.[105]

The Manchester professors had their own ideas about what a B.A. should know. In a letter to Dr. Garrard of Bristol Baptist College Highbury, they suggested that a B.A. 'Should be competent in Classics, Mathematics, Natural Philosophy, Moral Philosophy and one of these remaining subjects

1. Logic
2. Chemistry
3. Animal Physiology
4. Vegetable Physiology and Structural Botany.'[106]

London University did change its regulations in 1843 and, it would seem, rather in line with the above suggestion, for the change meant that Phillips' professorship was 'rendered no longer necessary'.[107] He was given half his year's salary and dismissed. Finlay took over the Natural Philosophy, which became purely Physics. In 1843 the syllabus included 'Physical Science': for the first year, Elements of Mechanics, Chemistry, Heat and Electricity and of Natural History; second year, Mechanics, Pneumatics, Acoustics, Hydrostatics and Hydraulics, Chemistry; third year, The Steam Engine, Optics, Geology, Animal and Vegetable Physiology and Structural Botany, Chemistry. In 1844 we find 'Natural Philosophy' covering: first year, The Elements of Mechanics and Hydrostatics and of Light and Sound; second year, Statics, Dynamics, Optics, Acoustics; third year; Mechanics, Astronomy, the Steam Engine.[108]

The college authorities were probably not sorry to he able to dispense with Phillips' services, saving £200 a year (£150 salary plus a guaranteed £50 from fees).[109] In 1845, at the end of the five year experimental period, the professors were faced with the choice between a salary cut and a reduction in staff; they chose the salary cut.[110] A report on the state of the college towards the end of this first quinquennium put down the lack of success to five reasons 'of a temporary nature'

1. Problems over the Lady Hewley Case
2. Commercial and manufacturing distress
3. The value of the College was not fully recognised
4. Anti-Unitarian prejudice. (They had tried to separate the lay and theological sides and had attracted a few non-Unitarians, but the prejudice remained.)[111]

The Trustees welcomed the Owens bequest with relief. In the 1847 report they alluded to 'the establishment of an Institution in Manchester, to which the students of the college may hereafter resort, to receive at least a portion of their literary and scientific instruction'.

The College however was not to remain in Manchester. During Owens College's first session a committee from Manchester New College reported back with provisional approval, but decided to reserve final judgement, partly because of worries that Owens was going to give religious lectures in spite of its founder's explicit exclusion of all religious tests. The following year a movement for London was successful, though contested at law. The main factor in the switch was probably the availability of accommodation for the College and its students at University Hall, a residence which had been opened four years earlier as a residential and theological supplement for liberal dissenters attending University College London. Links with University College London were already close. Newman had gone there in 1846 as Professor of Latin and so renewed his friendship with William Carpenter, who by 1852 had a series of appointments in London University, including the Principalship of University Hall.

Both these men were close friends of A. J. Scott, Professor of English at University College London, who became the first Principal of Owens College. James Heywood was on the initial management committee of Owens College, but he was the only Unitarian. Owens, unlike Manchester New College, enjoyed Anglican and Congregationalist support. The Congregationalists had rather superseded the Unitarians as leaders of national dissent, and as the vocal party among the dissenters of Manchester.[112]

### *Science and Unitarian belief*

When Warrington Academy was established, England had offered no formal education for science, medicine or the ministry which could reasonably be called professional. By 1853, London University was setting standards of academic attainment in all three fields, and doing so without religious tests. As a result, England, with some difficulty, came to recognise a body of higher learning, available without religious discrimination, but allowing supplementation according to theological taste. This was not problematical in Scotland or Germany, but it was in this country, because the renewal of higher learning in the early nineteenth century coincided with the surge of evangelical anglicanism and orthodox dissent, and because arguments about higher education were entangled with bitter disputes about control of elementary schools. It is perhaps significant that compromise solutions over elementary education were being pioneered in Manchester as Owens College began to build a reputation as a non-sectarian but broadly religious establishment.

It was the pride of the English Presbyterians that they had provided academies free of religious tests and dedicated to the pursuit of reason in all fields of human knowledge. They had claimed simply to be non-sectarian and liberal, not requiring adherence to the Unitarian beliefs in fact held by most of the teachers. This was, of course, a claim both tolerant and grand: that their position could withstand opposition, it being the end-result of reason in theology. This claim meant that natural sciences, in as much as they served as a paradigm of free enquiry, were of peculiar concern to Unitarians. Their Priestleyan model of man, as a knowing and worshipping being, had been central for their science and for their rational theology. It was on this central question that a 'shift in intellectual temper' came to interact with the growing specialisation and professionalisation of knowledge.

Priestley and his considerable following had preached a creed based on a materialist account of man. Nature was an infinite system of linked causes, created by God. It extended through man, to whom the system became progressively clear, though never fully knowable. Suffering was but incomplete knowledge; to know more was to rise above pain in the contemplation of an ultimately benevolent system. Thus was the rational inextricably linked with the moral. Science was not just a cultural ornament increasing in value during the eighteenth century; it was not just a part of the debating equipment of ministers; its pursuit was integral to moral progress; its growth was evidence of man's increasing identification with the Divine order. Science provided the Evidence of God.[113]

When a later generation of unitarians came to reject that view, they thereby altered intellectual priorities and the perceived relationships of now separable bodies of knowledge. R. K. Webb has highlighted the point with a quotation from J. J. Tayler:

> 'I do not believe the Evidences ever tell, till the inner man is previously touched and won by a deep feeling of spiritual want. Yet I hardly ever met with a Unitarian of the old school who did not regard such a statement as mystical and almost incomprehensible; whilst to my mind it flashes with all the conclusiveness of the clearest light.'[114]

It is important to realise that this shift was common to Unitarians expert in several particular disciplines, at least if we may judge from those in and around Manchester College. The problem, of course, was most acute for those, whatever their particular expertise, who still sought a wide synthesis; much less for such as John Dalton, a Quaker whose antipathy to metaphysics and to theological doctrine, allowed a 'practical Christian' to pursue a Newtonian 'natural philosophy' without worrying unduly about their links.

Perhaps that was, in part, because Dalton was not a social philosopher, nor did he ever seem to worry about the morals or morale of Manchester, which were problematic for men such as J. J. Tayler and James Martineau. They shared the 'romantic' reaction against utilitarianism as a doctrine and against contemporary industry as a social practice and mode of life. In terms of general intellectual movements, the growth of romanticism and of German idealism is a familiar enough theme, but one perhaps still too little explored in detailed social history or in the history of science.

Certainly it seems to us to shed some light on the general meaning of Manchester College's science.

Among the first romantics in Manchester was the adolescent Thomas de Quincey, precocious, presumptious and enormously impressed with Coleridge and Wordsworth. It is revealing that he spent a holiday in 1801 at Everton, exposed to that fading neo-classical culture of Liverpool dissent which had helped provide support and teachers for Warrington Academy. He was contemptuous of its doggerel verse, for he knew of the coming men. De Quincey felt no conflict; he was anyway an instinctive Tory with no sympathy for Whig reformers or their cities;[115] but for other young men the rejection of associationist and broadly materialist doctrines was much more traumatic. Coleridge himself had been a disciple of Hartley and had intended to become a Unitarian minister, instead taking up Kantian idealism. Perhaps the best known case is John Stuart Mill's reaction against the utilitarianism which his father had so carefully instilled.

In Liverpool, in the 1830s, James Martineau along with J. J. Tayler and J. Thom seem to have undergone a similar transition. As detailed elsewhere in this volume, Martineau, long a romantic if judged by attachment to the Lake District, dropped the Hartleyan doctrines he had learned from Lant Carpenter at Bristol; by 1840, when he joined Manchester College, Martineau had found in Kant a means of bringing philosophical rigour to his fundamental conviction that motives not results were the essence of ethics. It is of great significance for this chapter that Martineau wanted rigour in Christian moral philosophy, and that he denigrated the natural theology through which science and religion had been customarily linked in England.[116]

The link through natural theology had still been important at Manchester College York, where, as we have seen, geology and natural history were more to the taste of the teachers than were physics and chemistry. It was important to Sedgwick and Whewell and other Cambridge broad churchmen with whom Martineau also came to disagree over ethics. It was fundamental, in a paradoxical way, to Darwin's evolutionary theory; but by then Martineau had rejected standard natural theology as condescending to God.

In this connection the developing Unitarian position can be well illustrated from the writings of William Carpenter, who of all the professed Unitarians was the best known for biology. He was well versed in geology and anthropology from his days in Bristol; by the late 1840s he was established in London as a physiologist; he was a friend of Lyell and Darwin. When Manchester College moved to London, Carpenter, as Principal of University Hall, was very much involved.[117] In 1844, he had been suspected of authoring the anonymous *Vestiges of Creation*. The hypothesis of evolutionary development, of a law-governed unfolding rather than special creations, was one with which he sympathised and he soon became a friend of the real author, Robert Chambers. Thus Carpenter had no difficulty with the general idea of evolution when Darwin popularised it after 1859; it was no more difficult to suppose that all forms of animal life had developed from simple creatures, than to suppose that a complete man had developed from an egg. But he did have difficulty with 'natural selection' as a mechanism—that was too wasteful and too little a matter of design. He clung to the hope that variation was not accidental—the course of evolution would thereby be determined. This was shaky ground: comforting for one who had long believed, but of little persuasive power.[118]

The links Carpenter wanted between his science and his faith were plausible only because he had already adopted a psycho-physiological dualism in those areas of study which were his own particular specialty. Influenced by Martineau, he had come to believe that mental force could be construed as producing physical consequences, and vice versa. Our experience of 'will' was the root of our concept of force; behind the forces of the world was the mind of God; there was no contradiction between discussing physical causation and discussing the divine intelligence and moral purposes which lay behind the physical. In such a scheme, one's direct knowledge of God was immune from physical arguments and unsupportable thereby, though as we have seen, Carpenter clung to directed variation as evidence of a creative purpose. He was sensitive to music and played the organ in chapel and at home; he was responsive to landscapes and to personal relationships. But he worried that, in spite of his metaphysics, he lacked a real experience of the Deity; his religion was based on Christ as a 'moral image of supreme beauty'. Martineau and his other spiritual doctors told him not to worry.

As R. K. Webb had pointed out in a paper to which we are indebted, Unitarians were not conspicuous in the religious reaction against Darwinism. They had learned from Kenrick and others that science did speak of primeval history and that philology could interpret ancient speech; there were conflicts between natural science and scripture. For necessarians like Harriet Martineau, Darwin, in removing the need for design, had greatly enlarged the range of science at the expense of revelation. But her brother and her teacher's son were no longer necessarians. William Carpenter would have abandoned theology if Calvinism were its only form; but he was not asked to adhere to a necessarian, materialist, theology; idealism of one kind or other was to the fore; Coleridge and Kant had saved at least some Unitarians from Harriet Martineau's necessarian progress to secularism.

But where did that leave their science? It remained an adornment, a means of establishing intellectual competence and authority, but it was no longer central to the argument for liberal dissent. Martineau and Carpenter were keen to claim 'no conflict', keen to bring natural philosophy and moral philosophy into the same picture; but in discussions of religious conviction, the latter was primary. The nature of God's creation was evident through science; the limits of his revelation were to be explored through history and philology; but the key to religion lay in the spirit of man, which was directly known. Thus moral philosophy became central and could be advertised as a non-denominational base for theology. That such a base was possible is of general relevance for later nineteenth century religion; it is particularly relevant to the Unitarians and their use of 'science'.

That denominational seminaries could be attached institutionally and intellectually to colleges of secular learning became evident in London, in Manchester, and eventually in Oxbridge. When Manchester College was in London, it tended to be seen as a denominational college, though many disliked the description. Had it stayed in Manchester, it would have been seen alongside the Lancashire Independent College, drawing on Owens for courses in science and literature. The sensitive question, as the debate about the Manchester to London move showed, was whether 'theology' could be non-sectarian, part of the common ground. At Owens, A. J. Scott gave some very general lectures in religious philosophy, which proved acceptable as an option for students; later a Faculty of Theology was established which served several seminaries, including the Unitarian College.[119]

That such 'common ground' became available suited denominations in search of educated ministers, but it was much more to Unitarians than a matter of convenience. This is clear from the discussion over the move to Oxford. One major reason for going was to establish there, in the reactionary heart of the English university tradition, that theology could be treated as a science. Even Oxford had accepted that natural sciences, philology etc. could be free of religious tests. In a sense, the Unitarians went, not to be a 'college', but to be a substitute faculty of theology; to bring to theology at Oxford their long and proud tradition of free inquiry.[120] This would seem a good indicator of where they felt the intellectual frontier to lie. By 1880 or so, no one in or around universities needed the intellectual elite of the Unitarian ministry to argue for the independence of inquiry in natural sciences. There was, of course, much debate as to where that freedom led and what were its consequences for religion, but the independence of inquiry from revelation or scripture was accepted. Unitarians could promote their position by being open to science and accepting of its results, but to advertise one's commitment to free enquiry it was necessary to choose an area where that commitment was not forced or taken for granted. That is perhaps another key to the shift to moral philosophy. In the early nineteenth century the Unitarians could identify themselves with reason by supporting natural sciences; they and others had won those battles; later they identified with reason in matters of morals and psychology.

In a recent article on natural theology, John Hedley Brooke drew attention to a contemporary analysis of this shift, which would seem to extend the point. In 1870 J. B. Brown, an early graduate of University College London, wrote of 'a growing belief that the relation of God to the world is less fairly set forth by the relation of a king to his subjects, than by that of a father to his household'. God was no longer the legislator of physico-theology, he was a presence and a model which 'moulded life'.[121] One is reminded again of the social roots of the idealism of Tayler and Martineau, of John Seed's recent article on Unitarian social doctrines,[122] and indeed of the fact that the place of Manchester College in Manchester was, in a way, filled by the Unitarian Home Missionary College. The general shift to idealism was bound up with an increase in social concerns, a rejection of utilitarian political economy and an emphasis on interpersonal relations.

In a broad historical perspective, we can again see the results of victories by Unitarians and their allies. Their business successes, their ability to represent the provincial middle-classes, and their escape from discrimination, all meant that by 1850 or so, they were no longer an 'outsider' group. This is a fact which has been used in explanation of their loss of interest in natural science, but it may well explain much more.[123] They were moving away from a particular approach to science as they were moving towards a particular kind of alternative.

R. K. Webb, in the article we have used so much, mentions the public presentation of necessarian arguments in the Unitarian criticism of national days of fasting etc. Priestley's system allowed no place for special pleading and special interventions of the kind hoped for. Certainly, in their reaction to the first cholera epidemic (1831–2), Unitarians scorned providentialism, followed anti-contagionist doctrines about environmental causes, and argued for cleaning up the cities. As R. J. Morris has shown, these were the arguments one would expect from a group with relatively high status but relatively little political power. They were a means of criticising existing political arrangements; necessarian natural science extended into political economy and allowed a detailed critique of traditional, 'arbitrary' power; such beliefs were important in motivating such key anti-contagionists and public health reformers as Thomas Southwood Smith.[124] But by the 1850s, anti-fast-day agitation was no longer pertinent: the dominant educated culture was no longer providential in this way; moreover, the Unitarians were no longer outsiders—they were strongly identified with local government in the key cities. It is not surprising that many Unitarians preferred to concentrate their sentiments and their critical intellects on moral rather than natural philosophy.

Of course, the Unitarians continued to promote education and indeed science. Several major scientists and engineers in the later century came from their intellectually fertile stocks: two of W. B. Carpenter's sons were scientists, his grandson was an important metallurgist.[125] Another son, of course, was J. Estlin Carpenter, who pursued ancient history and comparative religion, becoming the Principal of Manchester College, Oxford. But Manchester College, after about 1850, no longer mattered for natural sciences; there had been a separation of spheres.

The college had never sponsored 'original trains of research' in science; in that sense science had always been secondary to theological scholarship; but the College had been an instrument through which the Unitarians of the industrial provinces had used and developed natural science as a major intellectual and social form. After 1850, the scepticism of Unitarians was but a minor part of a general, positivistic scepticism which they had helped to develop. As a dissenting denomination, they were now less prominent than the Congregationalists, and much less 'ideological'. Under such conditions, 'science' belonged in the much-increased domain of higher secular culture; Unitarians, neither needing it nor fearing it, had little incentive to engage in natural theology. Priestley's cosmos had undergone dissociation: science could be left to professional scientists, who might, or might not, see God behind the phenomena of their domain.

## NOTES

1. We are indebted to Manchester College, Oxford for financial support of archival research. Unless otherwise stated, all our archival sources can be found at the College. It is a pleasure to thank Barbara Smith for skilled guidance, enthusiasm and forbearance. Professor R. K. Webb helped through discussion and by sending us a copy of his excellent paper: 'The Faith of Nineteenth Century Unitarians: A Curious Incident'. Kathleen Farrar also gave early assistance.

2. The standard source on the academies is Herbert McLachlan, *English Education under the Test Acts* (1931); also Nicholas A. Hans, *New Trends in Education in the Eighteenth Century* (1951). On Warrington, William Turner, *The Warrington Academy* (1957). Also see John F. Fulton, 'The Warrington Academy (1757–1786) and its Influence upon Medicine and Science,' *Bulletin of the Institute of the History of Medicine*, i, 50–80 (1933).

3. Turner, *Warrington Academy*, pp. 5–6, 41; McLachlan, *English Education*, p. 219.

4. See 'John Horsley' (1685–1732) in *D.N.B.*

5. Warrington Academy Annual Reports, 1760 p. 2, 1762, p. 3.

6. Turner, *Warrington Academy*, p. 42; *D.N.B;* Annual Reports 1763, 1766.

7. Turner, *Warrington Academy*, pp. 23–8; *D.N.B; Dictionary of Scientific Biography.* For interpretations of Priestley's science, theology and metaphysics see especially John G. McEvoy and J. E. McGuire, 'God and Nature; Priestley's Way of Rational Dissent,' *Historical Studies in the Physical Sciences*, vi, 325–404 (1975) and John G. McEvoy, 'Enlightenment and Dissent in Science: Joseph Priestley and the Limits of Theoretical Reasoning,' *Enlightenment and Dissent*, ii, 47–67 (1983) which volume also contains several other useful studies of Priestley.

8. Turner, *Warrington Academy*, p. 29; *D.N.B*; Annual Report 1767 p. 8.

9. Turner, *Warrington Academy*, pp. 42–3; *D.N.B*; Annual Report 1773.

10. Turner, *Warrington Academy*, p. 42; *D.N.B.*

11. Turner, *Warrington Academy*, pp. 42–3; *D.N.B.* (Enfield and Clayton); McLachlan, *English Education*, p. 229.

12. W. V. Farrar, Kathleen R. Farrar & E. L. Scott, 'The Henrys of Manchester,' *Ambix*, xx & xxi (1974), esp. Part I pp. 183–208. This paper gives useful detail on the College of Arts and Sciences. See also the major paper on Manchester science and the industrial revolution: Arnold Thackray, 'Natural Knowledge in a Cultural Context: the Manchester Model,' *American Historical Review*, lxxix, 672–709 (1974).

13. Thomas Henry, 'An Essay on the Advantages of Literature and Philosophy in General, and Especially on the Consistency of Literary and Philosophical with

Commercial Pursuits,' *Memoirs of the Manchester Literary and Philosophical Society*, i, 7–29 (1785).

14. T. Barnes, 'On the Affinity Subsisting Between the Arts, with a Plan for Promoting and Extending Manufactures, by Encouraging those Arts, on which Manufactures Principally Depend,' *Memoirs of the Manchester Literary and Philosophical Society*, i, 72–89 (1785); T. Barnes, 'Plan for the Improvement and Extension of Liberal Education in Manchester,' *Memoirs of the Manchester Literary and Philosophical Society*, ii, 16–29 (1783).

15. Farrar, Farrar & Scott, 'The Henrys,' xx, 195.

16. Farrar, Farrar & Scott, 'The Henrys,' xx, 196–7.

17. See Joseph Thomson, *The Owens College, its Foundation and Growth and its Connection with the Victoria University, Manchester* (1886), pp. 9–10.

18. V. D. Davis, *A History of Manchester College* (1932), pp. 53–63.

19. Manchester Academy Minutes, May 2, 1787.

20. McLachlan, *English Education*, p. 257.

21. Minutes, March, 1789; Sep, 1790; Feb, Mar, Oct, 1792.

22. Davis, *Manchester College*, pp. 63–7; *D.N.B.*

23. Minutes, volume A, Special Meeting of Trustees, December 26, 1792.

24. On Dalton see E. C. Patterson, *John Dalton and the Atomic Theory* (1953); D. S. L. Cardwell, ed., *John Dalton and the Progress of Science* (1968).

25. Farrar, Farrar & Scott, 'The Henrys,' esp. xx, 195; xxi, 179–188.

26. *D.N.B.*

27. *D.N.B*; Davis, *Manchester College*, pp. 67–9.

28. Letter, Charles Wellbeloved to William Wood, 14 Jan, 1798. A useful account of adolescent Manchester around 1800 is given in Grevel Lindop's *The Opium Eater. A Life of Thomas de Quincey* (1981, 1985). It was said of Manchester Grammar School that 'The resorting to taverns and intercourse with women of the town becomes a fashion amongst the Boys in the higher classes of the school, which no vigilance of the masters can suppress' (p. 49).

29. A useful bibliography on Manchester science is provided by Terry Wyke in A. J. Kidd and K. W. Roberts, eds., *City, Class and Culture. Studies of Cultural Production and Social Policy in Victorian Manchester* (1985).

30. William Turner, then the college visitor, countered accusations about neglect of lay students, insisting that they were welcome, *provided* they were well-behaved. The college wished to avoid 'that promiscuous admission of West Indians, wild Irish, and forlorn hopes from other seminaries who were the destruction and ruin of discipline both at Warrington and Hackney'. Letter, Turner to William Wood, November 7, 1809.

31. *D.N.B.*

32. *D.N.B.* (Browne, Kenrick, Hincks).

33. *D.N.B.*

34. George William Wood's son, William Rayner Wood, was a lay student between 1829 and 1831. His letters to his father give useful detail on courses and teachers. See esp. Oct 30, 1830 for doubts on Hincks' competence.

35. John Kenrick to G. W. Wood, January 17–18, 1817.

36. Minutes, September 9, 1824; January 12, 1825; February 21, 1825.

37. *D.N.B.*, and Prof. R. K. Webb, personal communication.

38. See A. D. Orange, *Philosophers and Provincials: The Yorkshire Philosophical Society from 1822 to 1844*, Yorkshire Philosophical Society (1973).

39. Minutes, June 26, 1830, letter William Rayner Wood to Geo Wm Wood, Mar 21, 1830.

40. On Manchester see n. 24 and n. 29, plus R. H. Kargon, *Science in Victorian Manchester: Enterprise and Expertise* (1977). Also Michael Neve, 'Science in a Commercial City: Bristol 1820–60,' Derek Orange, 'Rational Dissent and Provincial Science: William Turner and the Newcastle Literary and Philosophical Society,' J. N. Hays, 'The London Lecturing Empire, 1800–50,' and Paul Weindling, 'The British Mineralogical Society, a case study in Science and Social Improvement,' all in Ian Inkster and Jack Morrell, eds., *Metropolis and Province. Science in British Culture, 1780–1850* (1983).

41. *D.N.B*; other essays in this volume; R. K. Webb, *Harriet Martineau. A Radical Victorian* (1960); and see below.

42. For a recent analysis, as sophisticated as it is empirically rich, see Jack Morrell and Arnold Thackray, *Gentlemen of Science. Early Years of the British Association for the Advancement of Science* (1981). Unless otherwise stated, the biographical information on the B.A.A.S. and Unitarians is derived from this source.

43. *D.N.B.*

44. Kenrick to W. R. Wood, May 1833; see also Kenrick to G. W. Wood, April 16, 1833. Prichard was a Bristol physician noted for his interests in anthropology and psychiatry. He was a Tory Anglican, but associated with the Carpenters in various scientific ventures.

45. See Morrell & Thackray, *Gentlemen*, esp., pp. 224–5; C. C. Gillispie, *Genesis and Geology: A Study in the Relations of Scientific Thought, Natural Theology, and Social Opinion in Great Britain, 1790–1850* (1959); and S. F. Cannon, *Science in Culture: The Early Victorian Period* (1978).

46. Morrell & Thackray, *Gentlemen*, pp. 235–6; for context also see N. C. Gillespie, *Charles Darwin and the Problem of Creation* (1979), and more generally the excellent recent survey by Peter J. Bowler, *Evolution. The History of an Idea* (1984); letter Kenrick to G. W. Wood, May 8, 1834.

47. Annual Report 1833.

48. J. Kenrick, *Primeval History* (1846) esp., XVI, XXI.

49. See R. K. Webb, 'The Faith of Nineteenth Century Unitarians: A Curious Incident,' given at a conference on the Victorian crisis of faith, Toronto, Nov 1985.

50. See, for example, D. S. L. Cardwell, *The Organisation of Science in England* (1957, 1972), pp. 47–8.

51. Annual Reports, 1828, 1829, 1830.

52. John Kenrick to G. W. Wood, March 17, 1834.

53. Annual Report 1835.

54. Common Hall Minute Book F, May 6, 1835.

55. See Davis, *Manchester College*; Kenrick to W. R. Wood, Mar 26, 1838; Common Hall Minute Book G, Jan 17, 1838.

56. Davis, *Manchester College*, pp. 95–9.

57. The best summary of Manchester politics in this period is V. A. C. Gatrell, 'Incorporation and the Pursuit of Liberal Hegemony in Manchester 1790–1839,' in D. Fraser, ed., *Municipal Reform and the Industrial City* (1982).

58. W. C. Williamson, *Reminiscences of a Yorkshire Naturalist* (1896). Between Philips' death and the founding of the Museum, the collections had been owned by a former student at Manchester College, York (T. H. Robinson), Kargon, p. 14.

59. James Heywood was one of the founders of the Geological Society. Eddowes Bowman, classical tutor at Manchester New College, 1846–1853, was one of its keenest members.

60. Love and Barton, *Manchester As It Is* (1839), p. 113.

61. On the Royal Manchester Institution see Kargon, *Science;* on G. W. Wood, Obituary in *Christian Reformer* (1843), pp. 726–9.
62. Kargon, *Science;* Thomson, *Owens College; D.N.B.*
63. Thomson, *Owens College*, p. 19.
64. See S. E. Maltby, *Manchester and the Movement for National Elementary Education 1800–1870* (1918).
65. M. G. Duffield, *The Stranger's Guide to Manchester* (1850).
66. J. Kenrick to G. W. Wood, August 15, 1840.
67. J. Kenrick to G. W. Wood, November 17, 1839.
68. James Martineau to William Gaskell, Jan 15, 1840, Special Committee Minutes, p. 9.
69. *ibid.*
70. Special Committee, March 4, 1840.
71. *ibid*, April 1, 1840. The full list reads as follows: (1) David Grey, Rector of Inverness Academy. (2) David Mackie, teacher of Natural Philosophy in Glasgow Mechanics Institute and private Mathematics teacher. (3) Mr. Thompson, Tutor in the family of an Irish Baronet and an ex-pupil of the Dean of Ely. (4) Sang of Edinburgh, ex-candidate for the Belfast Maths. Chair. (5) Wilson, Professor of Mathematics and Natural Philosophy in Glasgow Andersonian Institute and University. (6) Mr. Adam, an elderly gentleman, formerly Rector of Inverness Academy. (7) Thomas Aikin of Edinburgh.
72. *ibid*, Jan 15, 1840; April 22, 1840.
73. *ibid*, April 27, 1840.
74. *ibid*, June 10, 1840, Common Hall Minute Book, June 26, 1840.
75. Special Committee Minutes, July 13, 1840; August 6, 1840.
76. *ibid*, Jan 15, 1840.
77. *ibid*, Jan 15, 1840.
78. *ibid*, Jan 22, 1840.
79. Annual Report 1842.
80. Common Hall Minute Book, May 5, 1841.
81. Annual Report 1842.
82. Executive Committee Minutes, Jan 12, 1842; May 25, 1842; Common Hall Minutes, Oct 29, 1841; Rough Minute Book, Dec 29, 1841.
83. Annual Report 1842.
84. Executive Committee Minutes, Feb 9, 1842.
85. *ibid*, Feb 23, 1842.
86. *ibid*, May 25, 1842; Nov 2, 1842.
87. Common Hall Minute Book, Jan 13, 1841.
88. *ibid*, Jan 25, 1843.
89. Executive Committee Minutes, Feb 15, 1843.
90. Volume of miscellaneous correspondence etc., 1840s (Misc. MCO) n.p., n.d.
91. *ibid.*
92. Executive Committee Minutes, Feb 8, 1843.
93. *ibid*, May 3, 1843.
94. Misc. MCO, Jan 2, 1842.
95. *ibid*, Jan 25, 1842.
96. Board of Professors' Minute Book, Nov 17, 1841.
97. *ibid.*
98. Annual Report 1842.
99. Wm Holt to his parents, Nov 5, 1822.

100. Russell Lant Carpenter, *Memoir of the Life and Work of Philip Pearsall Carpenter* (1880), p. 29.
101. Editorial, *The Inquirer*, Dec 31, 1842, p. 2. The editor was William Hincks, formerly tutor in Natural Philosophy at Manchester College, York. We are grateful to Professor R. K. Webb for this reference.
102. R. A. Platt, St. Cuthbert's College, Ushaw, to John Kenrick, Nov 10, 1842.
103. Board of Professors Minutes, April 26, 1843.
104. Editorial, The *Inquirer*. Dec 31, 1842, p. 2.
105. J. H. Newman, *The Idea of a University*, ed., I. T. Ker (1976) pp. 127–9.
106. Board of Professors Minute Book, April 26, 1843.
107. Executive Committee Minutes, Sep 27, 1843.
108. Annual Reports 1843 & 1844.
109. Common Hall Minute Book, August 21, 1840.
110. Annual Report 1845.
111. Report to the Subscribers and Friends of the College, 30 Oct, 1844.
112. On Owens and Manchester College see Thomson, *Owens*, esp., pp. 125–32; Davis, *Manchester College*, pp. 124–9; on W. B. Carpenter, see *D.N.B.* and J. E. Carpenter's 'Introductory Memoir' to his father's scientific and philosophical essays, *Nature and Man* (1888).
113. On Priestley see n. 7 and R. K. Webb's article in this volume.
114. Tayler to J. H. Thom, September 6, 1859, quoted in R. K. Webb, 'John Hamilton Thom: Intellect and Conscience in Liverpool,' in P. T. Phillips, ed., *The View from the Pulpit: Victorian Ministers and Society* (1978).
115. Lindop, *De Quincey*, pp. 52–3.
116. See the useful essay on James Martineau in this volume.
117. See n. 112.
118. Carpenter had inherited a Priestleyan outlook from his father. Between 1845 and 1847 he moved to a new conception of 'mental force', stimulated by Mr. Groves on the 'Correlation of Physical Forces,' Dr. Noble on phrenology, and 'an anonymous critic' (James Martineau) writing on ethics,

> 'But if such a correlation really exists between Mental and Vital and Physical Forces, that the one may even indirectly produce the other, may we not regard all the physical forces of the universe as the direct manifestation of the Mental force of the Deity.'

See *Nature and Man*, pp. 49–57, esp. p. 52.
119. Thomson, *Owens*, pp. 126–133.
120. Davis, *Manchester College*, pp. 156–7.
121. J. H. Brooke, 'The Natural Theology of the Geologists: Some Theological Strata,' in L. J. Jordanova & R. S. Porter, eds., *Images of the Earth: Essays in the History of the Environmental Sciences* (1978). Cambridge University Press have recently published Robert M. Young's seminal and stimulating essays: *Darwin's Metaphor, Nature's Place in Victorian Culture*, 1985, which remains the best introduction to natural theology and its viscissitudes.
122. John Seed, 'Unitarianism, Political Economy and the Antinomies of Liberal Culture in Manchester 1830–50,' *Social History*, vii, 1–26 (1982).
123. For the ideological uses of middle-class science in the industrial revolution see Thackray, 'Manchester Model,' Inkster and Morrell, *Metropolis and Province*, esp. introduction; also Inkster's PhD thesis: 'Studies in the Social History of Science in England during the Industrial Revolution,' Sheffield University (1977).
124. R. J. Morris, *Cholera 1832; The Social Response to an Epidemic* (1976).
125. *D.N.B.*

6

# THE MANCHESTER MEDICAL REVOLUTION


CHARLES WEBSTER

*Wellcome Unit for the History of Medicine*
*Oxford*

JONATHAN BARRY

*Department of History*
*The University of Exeter*

Taken in isolation Manchester College has not made a particularly significant contribution to medicine or to medical education. However, when considered in the broader context, taking account of its association with the Warrington Academy, and when viewed as a component of the wider process of medical innovation taking place in Manchester in the late eighteenth century, Manchester College assumes much greater importance. Indeed the Manchester Academy emerges as part of an heroic enterprise aimed at meeting the crisis of health associated with the industrial revolution.

Manchester was at the heart of the process of industrialisation. Its population faced massive problems of ill-health occasioned by urban squalor, and the imposition of the inhumane regime of the factory system. Traditional medical institutions were ill-adapted to meet this challenge, but Manchester was the one place where a concerted effort was made to deal with health and environmental problems in a comprehensive manner. Unitarian intellectuals were the vanguard of this effort, and the individual most responsible was Thomas Percival (1740–1804), who provides a direct personal link between virtually all the agencies of enlightenment—Warrington Academy, Manchester Academy, the Manchester Literary and Philosophical Society, the Manchester Board of Health and the Manchester Infirmary. Percival was in some respects the nearest English equivalent to Condorcet. These two thinkers and planners were united in their faith in the capacity of the critical scientific imagination to bring relief to the disastrous condition into which the human estate was sinking.

In the sphere of medicine Manchester Academy stood in the shadow of its predecessor, the Warrington Academy. The importance of Warrington in providing one of the vehicles for directing the dissenting elite towards medicine should be set against the almost terminal decline of the medical faculties of the English Universities. By the mid-eighteenth century medical teaching had effectively ceased, and even the function of granting degrees on the performance of token acts was sliding into abeyance.[1] From the point of view of medicine Oxford and Cambridge were educational backwaters in which the few advocates of innovation such as Nathan Alcock or Thomas Beddoes met with fierce opposition on account of alleged religious non-conformity or political radicalism.[2]

The vacuum left by Oxford and Cambridge was filled by private medical schools in London, and by the medical faculties at Leyden and Edinburgh. All of these agencies were at the height of their reputation when Warrington Academy was established in 1757.

Warrington added to the momentum of the already strong dissenting tradition within British medicine.[3] Indeed it is arguable that dissenters reached the peak of their influence in medicine and related activities in the second part of the eighteenth century. Somewhat prophetically, Thomas Percival was the first student to be registered at Warrington

Academy and the first of 21 medical practitioners educated there between 1757 and 1777.[4]

Although Joseph Priestley taught at Warrington, the science teaching was conducted by other tutors, especially by Priestley's friend, the physician Matthew Turner.[5] Little specifically medical instruction was provided until John Aikin (1747–1822) returned in 1770 to teach at the Academy where his father was principal. The younger Aikin epitomised the ethos of his generation at Warrington, becoming a prolific writer, editor and translator, polymath, and also an inveterate reformer and improver.[6] One of Aikin's first publications dealing with hospital organisation contained a contribution by Percival, his contemporary at Warrington and lifelong friend.[7]

Warrington-educated doctors played a leading role in provincial medical affairs, for example Bostock in Liverpool, Chorley in Doncaster, Farr in Bristol and Martineau in Norwich. As in the case of Aikin and Percival their contribution to provincial medical culture was by no means narrow and technical. Warrington-educated doctors were bound together by numerous ties of family association and personal loyalty, and these ties extended to the wider fraternity of dissenting medical practitioners, including such figures as John Lettsom and John Fothergill in London, John Haygarth in Chester and James Currie in Liverpool. At the centre of this network was Thomas Percival who, after studying in Edinburgh and obtaining his MD in Leyden, spent a brief time in Warrington before settling in Manchester in 1767.[8]

Percival's move from Warrington coincided with Priestley's departure to Leeds. Percival no doubt sensed the greater potentialities of Manchester, already twice the size of Warrington, and also one of only two towns in Lancashire possessing an infirmary. But he could scarcely have predicted that this small town would be transformed into the cotton metropolis by 1800. Between Percival's arrival and his death in 1802 there occurred a fourfold increase in population, taking the population of Manchester and Salford to about 100,000.[9] Manchester had by then become the 'heart of this vast system' of commerce in the region.[10] By 1800, Manchester had evolved a model concentric settlement pattern. Already in 1795 Aikin noticed that the prosperous classes were abandoning the centre of town in favour of villas situated out of range of insalubrious working class housing.[11] Manchester was the victim of overcrowding, pressure of commerce, smoke and water pollution and general deterioration of the physical environment. The town also became notorious for civil disturbance, crime and dissoluteness. By the time of the removal of the Warrington Academy to Manchester the town was well on the way to becoming the classic modern manufacturing slum town so eloquently described by Engels and subsequent social commentators.[12]

Forty years before Engels, Aikin noted that Manchester 'vies with, or exceeds, the metropolis, in the closeness with which the poor are crowded in offensive, dark, damp, and incommodious habitations, a too fertile source of disease!'[13]

Thomas Percival was caught up in a vortex of social change taking place in the Manchester region. One of the prime objectives of his intellectual circle became the investigation of industrialisation and urbanisation from a medical point of view. Together with his associates, John Aikin in Warrington, John Bostock and Matthew Dobson in Liverpool, and John Haygarth in Chester, Percival made suggestions for improving the quality of local Bills of Mortality. Percival and his co-workers in Manchester also conducted in 1773 a precise enumeration of the population of Manchester and Salford. Aikin undertook a similar exercise in Warrington.[14] Their primary efforts were directed towards assessing the impact of industrialisation on the health of the poorer classes. These studies constitute one of the important, albeit neglected, foundations of modern epidemiology.

Summing up their observations of spectacular population growth Percival's associate, Thomas Henry moderately concluded that 'great towns, it must be allowed, are unfavourable for the duration of human life'.[15] Observers were particularly struck by the severe impact of epidemics of smallpox, measles, and especially typhus on these populations. Henry concluded that 'contagious fever has proved very destructive, and its virulence has been, probably, increased, by the crowded and uncleanly manner, in which the poorer people have been lodged'.[16] Percival himself, on the basis of an officially instigated study of an outbreak of fever at the Radcliffe Bridge Mill of Sir Robert Peel, firmly identified mills as the focus for infection, a conclusion which scandalised local mill owners when it was forcibly presented in print, and associated with a demand for strict control of the conditions of work of child labour.[17] Percival also noticed a rapid increase in pulmonary complaints, for which he blamed the smoke from local factories. Percival told Benjamin Franklin that he would appeal to local JPs to take urgent action to purify the air of Manchester 'for they are guardians of the health, as well as the morals, of their fellow citizens. And though works, which are essential to the prosecution of trade, ought not to be deemed nuisances, the persons who are engaged in them should be induced or compelled to conduct them in a manner, as little injurious as possible, to the public'.[18]

The above commentary indicates that Percival and his associates were not merely passive onlookers, but were concerned to translate their findings into social action. Their conclusions were by no means welcome to the vested interests. However Percival's opposition to unscrupulous factory owners, like his opposition to the slave trade, or sympathy with the American colonists, won him allies as well as creating opponents.

In Manchester Percival's particular non-professional allies were Thomas Barnes, who was educated at Warrington and became Minister at Cross Street in 1779, and Thomas Butterworth Bayley, Vice-President of the Warrington Academy and Trustee of the Cross Street Chapel. Percival's primary professional colleague was Thomas Henry (1734–1816), who settled in Manchester in 1764. Best known as a chemical manufacturer, he was also a scientific writer of major repute, and a medical practitioner supporting Percival's social causes.[19] Although originally, like Percival, an Anglican, Henry joined the Cross Street congregation. As noted below, the names Barnes, Bayley, Henry and Percival became almost inseparably linked in the Manchester movement for medical reform.

Restoration of the Warrington Academy in Manchester should be seen against the background of the grand design of Percival and his associates for the creation of a comprehensive range of institutions in Manchester capable of providing the intellectual infrastructure for the ambitious reforms they had in mind.

Crucial to this development was their scheme for the Infirmary. At the time of Percival's arrival in Manchester there was little to distinguish the Infirmary from its provincial counterparts.[20] As in the case of Birmingham, the Manchester Infirmary was unusual in being located in a new centre of population growth, rather than in a county town. Manchester gradually moved to the head of the pack, being one of the first to establish a Lunatic Hospital (1763) and Public Baths (1780). Of the Honorary Staff during the early years only Samuel Kay (1708–1784) was a Unitarian, serving as Honorary Physician from 1752 to 1782, and continuing as Physician Extraordinary until his death.[21] More important, Thomas Henry acted as Visiting Apothecary between 1778 and 1812, while Percival, after only a short time as Honorary Physician (1779–1780), was promoted in 1782 to become Physician Extraordinary, in which capacity he served until his death. Such rapid elevation was an exceptional act, almost certainly indicative of Percival's very special standing in the Manchester medical community.

In association with their allies among the Trustees Percival and Henry used their positions at the Infirmary to press for further development. Already by 1780 the Out-patient work of the Infirmary was highly developed. In 1781 the *Rules* were modified to allow necessitous patients to be visited in their homes, work which was assigned to the newly appointed assistant physician, George Bell.[22] The latter was a well-qualified dissenting physician and a keen botanist, supported by Percival and James Currie of Liverpool, but his impact on Infirmary affairs was precluded by premature death in 1784.[23] The Home-patient commitment was expanding, onerous and ultimately dominant, in the first year involving 357 patients, in the second 652, in the third 1,032, and 2,500 in 1792.[24] This service to Home-patients was unique to Manchester among the voluntary infirmaries and controversy over further expansion of the Infirmary revolved around this aspect of care.

The initial campaign for expansion involved the appointment of two additional physicians specially responsible for Home-patients. As in the case of Bell, the appointees, John Ferriar (1761–1815) and George Bew (d.c. 1813) were associated with Percival.[25] Ferriar quickly established himself as one of the most formidable intellectuals in Manchester.[26] The existing honorary medical staff, who were predominantly Anglican and anti-expansionist, sensing a shift in the balance of forces within the

Infirmary, were aroused into opposition. However the entrenched honorary medical staff and their outside supporters achieved nothing but a slight delay in the expansion of the Home-patient service. This episode demonstrated that Percival's group controlled the majority necessary to impose substantial changes on the Infirmary.

Pickstone and Butler have given a lucid and detailed account of the ensuing manoeuvring within the Infirmary in 1790 in all of its religious, political, and medical ramifications.[27] The result was a minor revolution, effectively terminating the influence of families of physicians and surgeons which had dominated the Infirmary since its inception. At various points in the 1790 controversy the resignations took place of the six honorary staff, by far the most distinguished of whom was Charles White FRS. They were replaced by twelve successors, among whom the newly arrived Bew and Ferriar were the most senior. The whole ethos of the Infirmary was changed. It was now ordained that all members of the medical staff should undertake the care of every class of patient. Out-patients would now be seen on six days of each week instead of one.[28] These changes meant not only a quantitative increase in the responsibilities of the Infirmary, but also more active confrontation with the problems of poverty and destitution. Also, without major physical changes, the Infirmary was likely to become a focus for the spread of infection. Consequently the first priority adopted was provision of a largely separate Dispensary, which was opened in 1793 to deal with the Out-patient and Home-patient side to the Infirmary's work, as well as containing isolation wards to house fever patients on an emergency basis, along the lines pioneered by Haygarth in Chester.[29] Consistent with the new status of the Infirmary, a Library and Museum were established and plans were made to introduce a novel and economical system of medical education.[30] Under this 'New System' it was claimed that 'not only a strict attendance on the Patients is secured but every disorder that the human Frame is subject to, whether of the Body or Mind finds compleat assistance at these Charities'. The new rules of the Infirmary were circulated elsewhere to demonstrate the 'universal benefit to our fellow Creatures' attained in Manchester.[31]

The direction of events within the Infirmary suggests that the momentum of the reform movement depended on the creation of a corps of doctors and trustees sharing common goals, in particular accepting the analysis of social change evolved by Percival and his associates. It was therefore inevitable that the movement to change the face of the Infirmary should become associated with a larger campaign of intellectual enlightenment and with a concerted effort to attract right-thinking youth into the medical profession. Formation of an Academy in Manchester was integral to this plan.

The first practical manifestation of these broader aspirations was the creation of the Manchester Literary and Philosophical Society, which took place in 1781, simultaneously with the start of the Home-patient experiment at the Infirmary. Traditionally the 'Lit and Phil' has been noted for its links between science and commerce, but Thackray rightly points out the medical predominance in the early society, which is not surprising considering that it originated from informal weekly meetings taking place at the home of Thomas Percival.[32] The latter's medical and lay accomplices dominated the affairs of the early Lit and Phil. Fourteen of the twenty-four founders of the Society were medical men. Nine were associated with the Infirmary in 1781.[33] Twenty-three of the first fifty-seven papers given at the Society were contributed by medical men.[34] During its early years, the offices of the Lit and Phil were also monopolised by medical men. About half the first group of honorary and corresponding members were drawn from the medical profession. After this initial demonstration of medical assertiveness there occurred a slow but steady decline in medical dominance beginning around 1800, largely brought about by the increasing ascendancy of merchants and manufacturers within the Society. Foundation of a Medical Society in 1834 reflected a further drift of medical men away from the Literary and Philosophical Society.

The Unitarian element within the Lit and Phil was 18% at the outset, and this level was exceeded among subsequent cohorts of recruits until the 1830s.[35] The influence of this group was disproportionate to their numbers. Of the main officers at the sparklingly successful opening decade of the Society, Thomas Percival and Thomas Henry were Unitarian medical men, while Thomas Barnes of Cross Street Chapel was actively involved in medical affairs, and Nathaniel Heywood the Treasurer was the son-in-law of Percival. Three Unitarians involved in the affairs of the Infirmary (Bayley, Henry and Percival) were among the four Fellows of the Royal Society involved in the foundation of the Society. Finally, many of the leading figures in the initial phase of the Society were drawn from Percival's circle of medical friends (e.g. John Ferriar), while Percival's influence extended to a later generation owing to the activity of two of his secretaries Edward Holme (1770–1847) and William Henry (1774–1836). Holme attended Manchester Academy between 1786 and 1789, while also acting as Percival's private secretary and reader. Renowned for his encyclopaedic range of scientific interests, Holme was President of the Lit and Phil between 1844 and 1847.[36] William Henry was the second and most distinguished son of Thomas Henry. After studying at Manchester Academy (1787–1798) he succeeded Holme as secretary to Percival, in which capacity he served for five years, eventually marrying the daughter of Thomas Butterworth Bayley. William Henry soon became a leading figure in a variety of scientific organisations in England.[37] Both Holme and Henry studied at Edinburgh, while Holme also went to Göttingen and Leyden; and soon they were both appointed Honorary Physicians at the Manchester Infirmary.

The Literary and Philosophical Society was valuable for purposes of intellectual cohesion and prestige, but it left unsolved the problem of recruitment. What was required was a centre for lectures and instruction, a place where the educational practices of Warrington Academy would be universalised. Following the example of Albrecht von Haller in Switzerland, the reformers established the first British College of Arts and Sciences in the summer of 1783.[38] This institution was largely the creation of Thomas Barnes, with active support from Thomas Henry, and with Thomas Percival as the first President. Although, as in the case of the Lit and Phil, the College is primarily remembered on account of its role in commercial education, the medical element was significant.

In 1786 Charles and John White, 'joint praelectors in Anatomy and Midwifery to the College of Arts and Sciences', were offering lectures on anatomy and physiology, while Thomas Henry lectured on chemistry, stressing its importance to 'medicine and pharmacy'. The Whites offered to repeat their lectures triennially, possibly interspersed with courses on midwifery and surgery. Manchester was portrayed as an ideal centre for those interested in medicine but unable to travel to London or Edinburgh, and for young persons preparing for a university education. Medical students could participate in special classes on the nature and cure of venereal diseases, and also were offered the opportunity of attending the 'excellent Hospital'.[39]

The College Prospectus of 1786 also noted the 'recent institution of an Academy where courses of lectures will be delivered by able professors in the several departments of the sciences necessary to a Liberal Education'. The fading of Warrington Academy had long been evident, and Aikin's presence had not revived its fortunes in medical education, as only one medical student was registered there after 1777. In 1784 Bayley resigned as Vice-President, perhaps to prepare the ground for a new Manchester Academy.[40] In 1786 the Warrington library, with its useful collections of medical and scientific books, was transferred to Manchester, although the scientific apparatus was lost to Hackney Academy. Percival became first President of the Manchester Academy, while Barnes was the principal.[41] The Academy aims agreed in February 1786 listed amongst the many advantages of Manchester the presence of the Literary and Philosophical Society (which the senior students would probably be allowed to attend), the College of Arts and Sciences, and the Hospital. The College would offer 'both practical and theoretical knowledge of chemistry, anatomy, physiology and other branches of science', while 'STUDENTS OF MEDICINE' could also attend 'the Hospital'. Sounding a note of considerable optimism, in October 1786 Percival told Franklin that 'we have now established here an institution on a plan similar to the late Academy at Warrington and in conjunction with this a medical school is formed, which seems to bid fair for eminent success'.[42]

Clearly the Academy and the College were seen as reinforcing each other, completing Manchester's pre-eminence in provincial intellectual life, founded on the Lit and Phil and the Infirmary. In practice the partnership was short-lived, since by 1788 the College had collapsed. The reasons for this are unclear, and may simply relate to financial and organisational factors. But it might also reflect the dissatisfaction of Barnes and his colleagues with the diffuse educational circus of lectures the College offered, and a decision to concentrate their efforts on the

Academy. In addition from the outset strains were evident in the various organisations due to religious differences and rival social philosophies. The disagreements over Infirmary expansion were merely the sharpest expression of this friction. Some members of the Lit and Phil had resigned in 1783 over the Society's support for Barnes' College. Any scheme jointly involving Henry and the Whites, like the 1786 lectures, would have been quite impossible by 1790, when the Infirmary upheavals caused the White faction to resign en masse. A medical lecturer in London, Charles Este, who had trained in Manchester with the Whites, was disgusted at the 'unnecessary innovations' at the Infirmary, and the threat posed by the enforced resignations to the standard of medical training and care at the hospital.[43] No longer able to call on the same range of external lectures, the Academy had to provide its own scientific teaching, conducted from 1793 by the young John Dalton. Some sources associate Dalton's appointment at Manchester Academy with Edward Holme, his close friend, and also a fellow Quaker from Kendal.

The exact status of the 'students in medicine' at Manchester Academy is also difficult to establish. In his *Discourse delivered at the Commencement of the Manchester Academy*, Barnes discussed the value of the establishment for those going on to the 'higher regions of professional science', as a transitional stage after the Grammar School and before the technical study of medicine or law, offering the advantages of cultivated understanding, improved taste and more general science, and preventing pedantry or narrowness.[44] The 1783 College *Proposals* had sounded very much the same note, stressing a liberal education, including natural and experimental philosophy as well as more standard humanistic subjects.[45] There was no avowed attempt to challenge the provision of specific medical training in London or Edinburgh, and to have plunged students too young into such a technical training would have violated the image of the medical practitioner held by Percival and his friends and implicit in Percival's famous *Medical Ethics* (1794). Despite their scientific interests and progressive social and medical aims, they modelled themselves very much on the classical physician building his medical practice on the broadest basis of moral and natural philosophy. Therefore, although one might speculate that Manchester could have pioneered development of provincial medical schools which emerged two decades later, it seems unlikely that the Academy's Students in Medicine were intended to pursue their medical course so thoroughly.[46]

The lectures of White and Henry probably bore the same relations to Manchester Academy as John Aikin's 'course of private instruction preparatory to the regular study of physic' which he offered at Warrington Academy in 1779. Like White and Henry Aikin conducted lectures on chemistry and anatomy. At an early stage in his career Aikin had been apprenticed to Charles White. In 1786 the links between White and the Unitarians were still sufficiently strong for him to become a trustee of the Manchester Academy.

The unusual practice of enrolment of students specifically in medicine, adopted at Manchester as at Warrington, indicates the importance of the medical profession in the minds both of dissenting parents and the school's trustees, but the education these students were to receive was basically the same as the other pupils. The unusual concentration on chemistry in the scientific teaching at both Warrington and Manchester may, however, have appeared particularly appropriate for future medical practitioners.

During the early years of the Manchester Academy medicine played about the same proportionate part as at Warrington. Compared with 92 students of Commerce, and 20 students of Divinity, 10 students of medicine were enrolled between 1786 and 1798.[47] The medical side of the Academy was in fact stronger than this figure suggests, because certain students of Commerce and Divinity attended lectures on subjects preparatory to medicine. This wider medical catchment perhaps contributed towards turning some ex-Manchester students to medical practice at a later stage in their education or in their careers. However, the rate of recruitment was only sufficient to establish a viable medical presence at Manchester College for the limited period extending from 1786 to 1790. At the outset five medical students were in residence, but this number gradually declined until between 1791 and 1797 there were no more than one or two formally enrolled at any time. In 1800, coinciding with the resignation of Percival and Dalton, the Academy suspended its plan for teaching medicine.[48]

Effective teaching of medicine was in practice limited to two intakes of four students, the first in September 1786 at the opening of the Academy, and the second in 1789, coinciding with the drive to expand the Infirmary. Once again the Manchester experience contains an echo of the Warrington pattern, where two waves of recruitment took place, the first coinciding with the opening of the Academy (1757–1758) when four medical students were enrolled, and the second occurring with Aikin's arrival (1770–1772) when four more medical students were taken in.

Of the five medical students enrolling in 1786 and 1787 four were connected with Thomas Percival and Thomas Henry. The Academy was entrusted with Percival's second son James, and with Edward Holme, who was Percival's secretary, and with Thomas Henry's two sons Peter and William. The fifth was the unknown Joseph Eaton of Chester. James Percival and Peter Henry became casualties of their chosen professions. The former died in 1793 of 'malignant fever' as a medical student in Edinburgh. Peter Henry deserted medicine for a military career and died in India in 1808.[49] As noted above Edward Holme and William Henry fulfilled Percival's expectations, returning to Manchester after qualifying in medicine, and enjoying successful careers at the Infirmary as well as becoming pillars of the Literary and Philosophical Society.

Nothing is known of the three medical students enrolling in 1789 except their place of origin: Joseph Mason Carpenter (Bristol), Thomas Coupland (Ormskirk), John Serle (Winchester). In addition one of the Divinity students, Robert Lewin (d. 1851), went on to study medicine in

Edinburgh, after which he became a physician at the Liverpool Dispensary.[50] Once again the above pattern mirrors the experience of Warrington, where the 1757–1758 intake (containing Percival, Aikin and Farr) was noticeably more distinguished than the 1770–1772 intake, when the only notable figure was Caleb Hillier Parry.

Only three more medical students were enrolled at Manchester Academy between 1792 and 1796. Of these, two went into medicine, Thomas Bland practising in Suffolk, Edward Percival in Dublin and Bath. The latter attained a minor reputation as a medical writer, but is primarily remembered as the editor of his father Thomas Percival's works.[51] The third, John Taylor, left medicine for commerce.

Paradoxically the best known medical practitioners emanating from Manchester Academy in its latter years were enrolled in Commerce or Divinity. Samuel Hibbert (1782–1848) was a student of Commerce at Manchester (1796–1797), but he also developed a strong interest in chemistry. After the death of his father, who was a linen yarn manufacturer, Hibbert moved to Edinburgh, where he qualified in medicine and established a reputation as a medical practitioner, geologist and phrenologist. He also shared Ferriar's interest in demonology and apparitions.[52] Joseph Astley briefly studied divinity at Manchester (1793), but later became a manufacturing chemist. John Thompson also studied Divinity (c. 1799–1802), became a minister, but later turned to medicine, becoming a practitioner in Halifax and Leeds. William Winstanley (1772–1852) followed the same path, but with greater distinction. Winstanley's educational career suggests that the Manchester Academy achieved a good reputation under Barnes, because he and William Stephenson were attracted to Manchester from Northampton in 1793. Winstanley's obituary noted that his first preference was medicine. After a brief spell in the ministry, Winstanley studied medicine at Edinburgh and then served as Honorary Physician at the Manchester Infirmary from 1808 until 1817, before moving into the country on health grounds.[53]

In 1796 Percival led a drive to revive the fortunes of their flagging academy, but his own son, Edward, was the only new medical student enrolled before Percival resigned as President in 1800. This marked the end of the formal involvement of the Manchester Academy in medical studies, although, as noted above, a new trend was emerging whereby Lay or Divinity students were later turning to medicine, thus perpetuating a long tradition of the movement of the dissenting clergy into medicine, two of the most notable earlier examples being Richard Baxter and John Wesley.

The transfer of the Academy to York in 1801 did not mark a complete break with the earlier tradition, although it was not until 1810 that experimental natural philosophy was re-established as a major part of the curriculum, which flourished under the talented William Turner.[54] Nine York Academy students have been identified as taking up a career in medicine. They studied at York between 1808 and 1828, about half being enrolled as Lay students and the other half in Divinity. Most became minor medical practitioners in the south of England. Their careers suggest that the Academy's continued stress on a broad liberal education was producing standard physicians with wide cultural interests, but without the devotion to social progress through science of the earlier generation. The experimental natural philosophy taught by Turner was directed towards natural theology rather than practical application, and the Library was not replenished with the latest scientific and medical works necessary to keep up with an increasingly specialised medical training.[55] Nevertheless, three students obtained some medical reputation. Henry Lee (d. 1870) became physician to the General Dispensary, Birmingham and later to the Farringdon Dispensary, London.[56] Gilbert Wakefield Macmurdo FRCP & FRS (d. 1869) was a surgeon at St Thomas's Hospital, London and a leading ophthalmologist.[57] George Hunsley Fielding FRS (d. 1871) practised in Hull and later in Kent, being primarily known for his meteorological investigations and for identifying 'Fielding's membrane' in the eye.[58]

The York Academy kept alive a connection with medicine, but neither this institution nor its predecessor in Manchester generated a sustained influx of talent into medicine, and they exerted little influence on medical care locally. The strongest concentration of influence was exercised by the three Manchester Academy students (Henry, Holme and Winstanley), who returned to Manchester and became leading medical figures in the town.

The limited impact of Manchester Academy on recruitment to Manchester medicine, taken together with the failure of the College of Arts and Sciences, the drift of the Literary and Philosophical Society away from association with more radical social objectives, and finally the continuing campaign against the medical expansionists, added to the difficulties of sustaining medical reform in Manchester.

The successes of 1790 left Percival's grand scheme seriously incomplete. It was appreciated that the 'New System' at the Infirmary, even in its most extended form, was incapable of addressing the basic health problems of Manchester. Indeed, the degree of amelioration offered by the Infirmary seemed futile unless a simultaneous effort was made to deal with the health crisis at its source.

The trend of thinking of Percival's group is indicated by a tract by Ferriar calling for the Police Commissioners to play a more active part in public health reform, particularly with respect to the regulation of housing. In an annotation, Ferriar called for more systematic provision of fever wards, and for special hospitals for incurable lunatics.[59] Percival had tried long but unsuccessfully to influence the Police Commissioners. The 1792 appeal by Ferriar and a similar one made from the Infirmary in December 1794 were also unsuccessful.[60] Opportunity for further action arose during a renewed fever scare in 1795, when a violent outbreak at Ashton-under-Lyne threatened to engulf Manchester. Percival and his colleagues now tried to achieve by charity what had proved impossible through official agencies. In January 1796 at a public meeting they established a Board of Health to deal with the control of fevers among the manufacturing poor. Almost predictably, Thomas B. Bayley was elected President of the Board.[61] The immediate goal of the Board of Health was the establishment of fever wards to house the poor afflicted with fever. A small committee, headed by Bayley, and including Ferriar and Holme, was established to discuss this proposal with the Infirmary. The Infirmary Weekly Board welcomed this ancillary charity and it appointed a committee, chaired by Percival, to give guidance on technical questions. This committee introduced the term 'House of Recovery' or 'House of Reception' for the new institution for fever patients.[62] After delay occasioned by a fresh outburst of opposition headed by the disaffected former Infirmary medical staff, the House of Recovery was opened in May 1796 in houses on Portland Street adjacent to the Infirmary and made available by the Trustees for this purpose.[63]

The initial Committee of the Board of Health constitutes a roll call of radicalism and dissent in Manchester.[64] The Board of Health took credit for containment of the fever epidemic and its House of Recovery not only prospered, but also became the model for similar institutions established elsewhere. However the Board was totally unsuccessful in its broader objectives to set up machinery for easing the 'calamitous state of the poor in this town'.[65] Memoranda stemming from S. A. Bardsley, Ferriar and Percival dwelt on such abuses as cellar dwellings, insanitary housing, overcrowded lodging houses, and especially the exploitation of child labour. Extensive proposals for sanitary regulations were offered, in the course of which it was recognised that effective action was dependent on legislative interference. Percival in particular hazarded bold conclusions concerning the impact of factory work on health. Percival's 'Resolutions' on this social problem have been eulogised as 'at once a famous landmark in the history of sanitation, and the source of the Factory Acts and of the movement for the intervention of the State on behalf of children'.[66]

Consistent with his 1784 pamphlet, factories were firmly identified by Percival as the source for the contagion responsible for fever, and accordingly as the focus for spread of disease into neighbouring residential areas. Factory work was in its essence inimical to a healthy mode of existence, the most pernicious evils being associated with 'untimely labour of the night, and the protracted labour of the day' by children, who were thus debarred from all opportunities for education, and moral or religious instruction. Percival appealed for the establishment of a 'general system of laws for the wise, humane, and equal government of all such works'.[67]

The more ambitious sentiments of the Board of Health were crowded into the first few months of its activities. Very quickly the Board restricted its activities to the maintenance of the House of Recovery. Ironically, soon after the death of Bayley (1802) Percival's old adversary Sir Robert Peel the elder succeeded to the Presidency of the Board of Health.

The extraordinary difficulties in achieving public health reform or even extension of voluntary hospitals elsewhere illustrate the inertia of the system as a whole. The successes of the expansionists in Manchester might seem modest in retrospect but they were revolutionary for the times. Percival's contribution in particular has been applauded by recent commentators on account of its telling premonitions of key elements in modern social legislation.

The high expectations and modest success of the reformers in Manchester were made possible by the special circumstances prevailing there. It has rightly been pointed out that health reform was sustained at a crucial moment by a tide of events associated with other causes, such as the anti-slavery movement, agitation for repeal of the Test and Corporation Acts, or broader movements associated with the American and French Revolutions.[68] But the forces which ensured the success of the Infirmary expansionists in 1790, were largely dissipated by 1800, with the inevitable consequence that the broader ambitions of such agencies as the Board of Health or the Manchester Academy were consigned to the world of utopian dreams.

## NOTES

1. C. Webster, 'The Medical Faculty and the Physic Garden' in *History of the University of Oxford, the Eighteenth Century* (forthcoming), pp. 684–723.
2. Webster, 'The Medical Faculty', pp. 705–706, 711.
3. J. F. Fulton, 'Warrington Academy (1757–1786) and its Influence on Medicine and Science', *Bull. Inst. Hist. Med.*, i, 50–80 (1933); R. Guest-Gornall, 'The Warrington Dispensary Library', *Medical History*, xi, 285–296 (1967); H. McLachlan, *Warrington Academy and its Historical Influence*, Chetham Society Remains, cvii (1943); W. Turner, *The Warrington Academy* [1813], ed. G. Carter (1957).
4. Between 1757 and 1777 the Register of Warrington Academy includes the following names specifically identified as medical students: William Acklam (1758); John Aikin (1758); John Bostock (1763); Timothy Bentley (1760); Edwood (or Edward) Chorley (1777); Richard Codrington (1777); Thomas Crompton (1776); George Daniel (1775); . . . Dickson (1772); Robert Dukinfield (1764); Samuel Farr (1758); Philip Holland (1777); . . . Moorhouse (1773); Philip Meadows Martineau (1765); Caleb Hillier Parry (1770); Thomas Percival (1757); Edward Rigby (1761); John Taylor (1759); John Vize (1772); John Wadsworth (1765); Snowden White (1763). After 1777 one other medical practitioner is recorded, Peter Crompton (1781).
5. McLachlan, *Warrington Academy*; J. W. Ashley Smith, *The Birth of Modern Education: The Contribution of the Dissenting Academies 1660–1800* (1954), pp. 152–168.
6. R. Frankenberg, 'John Aikin—Doctor and Philosopher', *Memoirs of the Manchester Literary and Philosophical Society* (hereafter 'Manchester *Memoirs*'), cvi, 74–93 (1963–1964).
7. Aikin, *Thoughts on Hospitals with a Letter to the Author by Thomas Percival* (1771), signed Warrington 30 November 1771. Dedicated to John Haygarth. Percival's letter (pp. 85–98) is dated 1 October 1771.
8. Edward Percival, *Memoirs of the Life and Writings of Thomas Percival M.D.* (1807); E. M. Brockbank, *The Honorary Medical Staff of the Manchester Infirmary* (1904), pp.

83–107; R. B. Hope, 'Dr. Thomas Percival: A Medical Pioneer and Social Reformer, 1740–1804' (Unpublished Manchester University M.A. Dissertation, 1947).

9. W. H. Challoner, 'Manchester in the Latter Half of the Eighteenth Century', *Bulletin of the John Rylands Library*, xlii, 40–60 (1959–1962).

10. John Aikin, *A Description of the Country from 30 to 40 Miles round Manchester* (1795), p. 3.

11. Aikin, *A Description*, p. 205. For a modern confirmation of this picture see R. Dennis, *English Industrial Cities of the Nineteenth Century: A Social Geography* (1984), p. 73.

12. F. Engels, *The Condition of the Working-Class in England in 1844* (Engl. trans. New York 1887, London 1892).

13. Aikin, *A Description*, p. 192.

14. Aikin, *A Description*, p. 192; Percival, 'Observations on the State of the Population in Manchester, and other Adjacent Places', *Phil. Trans.* lxiv., 54–66 (1774); lxv, 322–335 (1775) [reprinted (as revised in 1789) in B. Benjamin (ed.), *Population and Disease in Early Industrial England* (1973)]; Hope, 'Percival', pp. 48–77.

15. Thomas Henry, 'Observations on the Bills of Mortality for the Towns of Manchester and Salford', Manchester *Memoirs*, iii, 159–173 (1790), written 25 August 1788, p. 168.

16. Henry, 'Observations', p. 160.

17. Anon., but probably by Percival, *A short essay written for the service of the proprietors of cotton mills and the persons employed in them* (1784); Anon., 'The Putrid Fever at Robert Peel's Radcliffe Mill', *Notes and Queries*, cciii, 26–37 (1958); A. Meiklejohn, 'Outbreak of Fever in Radcliffe Cotton Mills', *British Journal of Industrial Medicine*, xvi, 68–69 (1959); S. E. Maltby, *Manchester and the Movement for National Elementary Education 1800–1870* (1918), pp. 12–15.

18. Letter from Percival to Franklin, 27 October 1786, American Philosophical Society, Philadelphia, Franklin MSS xxxiv, Part II, letter 163.

19. A. E. Musson and E. Robinson, *Science and Technology in the Industrial Revolution* (1969), pp. 231–246; W. V. Farrar, K. V. Farrar and E. L. Scott, 'The Henrys of Manchester, Part I: Thomas Henry', *Ambix*, xx, 183–208 (1973); Brockbank, *Honorary Staff*, pp. 72–82.

20. E. Lyon, 'Sketch of the Medical Topography and Statistics of Manchester . . . Part III', *North of England Medical and Surgical Journal*, August 1830–May 1831, pp. 133–148; W. Brockbank, *Portrait of a Hospital 1752–1948* (1952); J. Woodward, *To do the Sick no Harm: a Study of the British Voluntary Hospital System to 1875* (1974); C. Webster, 'The Crisis of Hospitals during the Industrial Revolution', in E. Forbes (ed.), *Human Implications of Scientific Advance. Proceedings of the XVth Int. Congress of the History of Science, Edinburgh 1977* (1978), 214–223.

21. Brockbank, *Honorary Staff*, pp. 22–25.

22. Manchester Infirmary, Quarterly Board Minutes 21 June and 23 August 1781.

23. Brockbank, *Honorary Staff*, pp. 115–117; James Currie in Manchester *Memoirs*, ii, 381–393 (1785) (submitted 1784).

24. Lyon, 'Medical Topography', p. 135.

25. Manchester Infirmary, Special Board 8 October 1789, Quarterly Board 24 December 1789.

26. J. E. M. Walker, 'John Ferriar of Manchester: His Life and Work' (Unpublished UMIST M.Sc. Dissertation 1973); Brockbank, *Honorary Staff*, pp. 127–156; *idem*, *John Ferriar. Other Essays and Verses* (1950), pp. 1–16.

27. J. V. Pickstone and S. V. F. Butler, 'The Politics of Medicine in Manchester

1788–1792: Hospital Reform and Public Health Services in the early Industrial City', *Medical History*, xxviii, 227–249 (1984); Pickstone, 'Ferriar's Fever to Kay's Cholera: Disease and Social Structure in Cottonopolis', *History of Science*, xxii, 401–419 (1984).

28. Manchester Infirmary, Quarterly Board, 23 September 1790.

29. Lyon, 'Medical Topography', pp. 137–142.

30. Manchester Infirmary, Quarterly Board, 23 September 1790 to 23 June 1791; Lyon, 'Medical Topography', pp. 136–137.

31. Manchester Infirmary, Quarterly Board, 22 December 1791.

32. A. Thackray, 'Natural Knowledge in Cultural Context: The Manchester Model', *American Historical Review*, lxxix, 672–709 (1974). For the alternative view, Musson and Robinson, pp. 88–100.

33. Thackray, pp. 684–688, 694–695.

34. Brockbank, *Honorary Staff*, p. 94.

35. Thackray, p. 697.

36. *Christian Reformer*, pp. 61–64 (1848); W. C. Henry in *Transactions of the Provincial Medical and Surgical Association*, xvi, 97–116 (1849). Brockbank, *Honorary Staff*, pp. 191–199; R. H. Kargon, *Science in Victorian Manchester* (1977), pp. 14–16, 42–44.

37. *Christian Reformer*, pp. 743–746 (1836); W. C. Henry, 'A Memoir of . . . the late Dr. Henry', Manchester, *Memoirs* vi, 99-141 (1842); Brockbank, *Honorary Staff*, pp. 235–240; W. V. Farrar, K. Farrar and E. L. Scott, 'The Henrys of Manchester: Parts II & III' *Ambix*, xxi, 188–228 (1974).

38. R. B. Hope, 'Education and Social Change in Manchester, 1780–1851' (Unpublished Manchester University M.Ed. Dissertation, 1955), pp. 22–29; Musson and Robinson, pp. 92–93. See also Manchester College, Volume of printed ephemera 1783–1800: includes Proposals for College of Arts and Sciences, 23 April 1783.

39. *College of Arts and Sciences Manchester, 26 May 1786 Anatomical and Chemical Lectures*, Bodleian Godw. Pamph. 1808 (4).

40. McLachlan, *Warrington Academy*, p. 102.

41. V. D. Davis, *A History of Manchester College from its Foundation in Manchester to its Establishment in Oxford* (1932); McLachlan, *Warrington Academy*, pp. 128–137; Hope, 'Education and Social Change', pp. 30–44; Musson and Robinson, pp. 94–96.

42. Printed Report on the Academy, 22 February 1786, Manchester Academy, Minute Book A. See also Minute Book A, 31 March 1786 (students able to attend White and Henry lectures gratis) and T. Barnes, *A Discourse delivered at Commencement of Manchester Academy* (1786), Appendix p. 9. See Note 18 (above) for Percival's letter

43. Charles Este, Printed letter, 1790, Bodleian Godw. Pamph. 1808 (4).

44. Barnes, *A Discourse*, p. 21.

45. *Proposals for College of Arts and Sciences*, printed 23 April 1783.

46. Manchester's first two medical schools, Pine St. and Marsden St. were both started in 1824. See E. M. Brockbank, *The Foundation of Medical Education in England and of the Manchester School in Particular* (1936).

47. *Roll of Students entered at the Manchester Academy, 1786–1803; Manchester College York etc.* (1868).

48. Manchester Academy, Minute Book A, 15 May 1800.

49. For James Percival, *Transactions of the Provincial Medical and Surgical Association*, xvi, 99 (1849); for Peter Henry, W. V. Farrar, K. Farrar and E. L. Scott, 'The Henrys of Manchester: Part II', *Ambix*, xxi, 187–188 (1974).

50. Lewin studied at Manchester 1789/90.

51. See Note 8 above. Thomas the eldest son of Thomas Percival became an Anglican Minister, who at one stage worked in St. Petersburg.

52. Mrs Hibbert-Ware, *Life and Correspondence of the late Samuel Hibbert-Ware* (1882).

53. *Christian Reformer*, p. 636 (1852); *Medical Directory*, p. 561 (1853); Brockbank, *Honorary Staff*, pp. 236–245.

54. York Academy, Minute Book B, 3 March 1813; Minute Book C, 24 April 1817, 12 March 1818.

55. George Chetham (U.S.A.) and Brooks Crompton (Essex) both became surgeons, but Nathaniel Lister (London), Samuel Nicholson (London), William Gordon Peene (Kent) and Thomas Saunders Watson (Bath) were all physicians. See Nicholson's obituary in The Inquirer p. 462 (1893). For the natural theology emphasis see Manchester Academy Minute Book B fol. 127, 180, 214 (annual visitations); Manchester New College, *Introductory Discourses* (1841), especially M. L. Phillips on 'the Physical Sciences'; York Library Shelf Catalogue (N.D. ?1843) sections X–Z.

56. *Medical Directory* p. 1037 (1870); W. Munk, *Roll of the Royal College of Physicians*, (1878) iii, p. 194.

57. F. G. Parsons, *History of St Thomas' Hospital* (1936), iii, pp. 87, 94, 122, 157.

58. J. A. R. Bickford and M. E. Bickford, *The Medical Profession in Hull 1400–1900* (1983), p. 43.

59. John Ferriar, *To the Committee for the Regulation of the Police, in the Towns of Manchester and Salford* (1792) (with manuscript additions Bodleian, Gough Lancs. 30 (11)). See also *Medical Histories and Reflections* 3 vols. (Warrington and London, 1792–1798), ii, pp. 177–214, an expanded version of *To the Committee*, but does not include points raised in annotation. First volume signed 30 April 1792 and dedicated to Percival.

60. R. B. Hope, 'Percival', pp. 98–99.

61. *Proceedings of the Board of Health in Manchester* (1805), includes memoranda and letters relating to the Board of Health from 1796 to 1804.

62. Letter from Board of Health, Manchester Infirmary, Weekly Board, 13 January 1796, 6 February 1796; *Proceedings of the Board of Health*, pp. 44–48.

63. Hope, 'Percival', pp. 138–159.

64. In addition to the physicians* of the Infirmary, the committee included John Barton, T. B. Bayley*, Richard Barlow*, Rev. Thomas Barnes*, C. F. Brandt, Rev. Rowland Broomhead*, Rev. John Clowes, Samuel Greg, Robert James, Rev. Samuel Hall, Nathaniel Heywood, George Lee, George Lloyd*, Samuel Marsland, Richard Meadowcroft, George Philips*, Robert Philips*, Thomas Robinson*, John Simpson, James Touchet and Charles Wood. *Proceedings of the Board of Health*, pp. 53–54. (* denotes having served on the 1790 Committee of the Infirmary which had set in motion plans for expansion).

65. Report of the Committee of the Manchester Infirmary, *Proceedings of the Board of Health*, pp. 44–48.

66. Maltby, *Manchester and National Education*, pp. 16, 121–122.

67. Percival, 'Heads of Resolutions', 25 January 1796, *Proceedings of the Board of Health*, pp. 33–35.

68. See above, Note 27. For the direct legacy of the medical reformers, see J. Seed, 'Unitarianism, Political Economy and the Antinomies of Liberal Culture in Manchester 1830–1850', *Social History*, vii, 1–25 (1982), and the brief exposition of his forthcoming book, *A Cultural Geography of Industrialisation*, in M. Billinge,

'Hegemony, Class and Power in late Georgian and Early Victorian England', in A. R. H. Baker and D. Gregory, *Explorations in Historical Geography* (1984), pp. 28–67.

The authors would like to thank Margaret Pelling, Jean Loudon and Dr I. S. L. Loudon for their assistance in preparing this paper, and also Mrs Ann Cheales for help with the typing.

# 7
# MANCHESTER COLLEGE AND ANTI-SLAVERY[1]

G. M. DITCHFIELD
*University of Kent at Canterbury*

> 'The Liberty which you claim for yourselves, you extend with equal latitude to others. The burden to which you will not submit, you will never impose.'
>
> THOMAS BARNES
> *A Discourse delivered at the Commencement of the Manchester Academy, 14 September 1786*, p. 8.

A scholarly enterprise dedicated to the celebration of the bicentenary of Manchester College provides an almost embarrassing range of opportunities for specialist studies of the College's history and traditions. The particular theme of this essay is the connection between the College and the British Anti-Slavery movement during the years 1786 to 1833, with specific reference to the campaign for the abolition of the Slave Trade. It will seek to examine the role of Manchester College, and the religious values for which it stood, in the most successful and widely-supported humanitarian cause of the late eighteenth and early nineteenth centuries. In doing so, it will proceed in the belief that the issue of Anti-Slavery serves the valuable added purpose of illuminating the nature of the College in its most obscure and least appreciated period. Even at first glance, the conjuncture of the two is obvious. One cannot but note the close chronological proximity between the foundation of the College in Manchester two hundred years ago and the beginning of the local and national campaign against the British Slave Trade. The heyday of British Anti-Slavery, moreover, coincided almost exactly with the first Manchester and the York periods of the College's history. What, it may be asked, could they offer to each other?

It is proposed to conduct this inquiry in three stages. The first section focuses upon the contribution of Manchester College to the campaign for the abolition of the Slave Trade between 1786 and 1807; the second discusses the ideological background to the abolitionist attitudes of those connected with the College; the third considers the later commitment to the cause and assesses its significance for Manchester College and for Unitarianism more generally.

## I

The main emphasis of this essay will be placed firmly upon the first seventeen years of the College's existence. The present writer has suggested elsewhere that this early period of the College has been seriously under-rated and that its achievements in the city of its birth were not inconsiderable.[2] Here the same theme will be pursued, but the aim will be to ask what, in this context, could the fledgling Manchester College contribute to the early abolitionist movement? It could certainly offer more than might be supposed if some of the more dismissive accounts of its early years are accepted. For several reasons the College occupied a position in late eighteenth century Manchester which was topographically central and highly respectable. It could accordingly be of value to a religious, moral or even political cause with which it sympathised.

Firstly, it must be emphasised that Manchester College between 1786 and 1803 was solvent. That it experienced financial alarms and excursions in this period is, of course, true. But their extent should not be exaggerated. It has been stated, for instance, that the annual income of the College was in the region only of £220 to £250, that it never reached £300 and at times fell below £200.[3] This, however, is only true of income from subscriptions, which was by no means the only source of funds available. A list of College accounts for 1794–6 in the Manuscript Minute Book reveals that in these three years, total annual income averaged £405 and included rents and fees as well as subscriptions, which averaged £176.8s. In the same years the average annual expenditure was £373.[4] So gross average annual income did exceed £300 and left a small surplus. Figures such as these help to explain how the library was augmented and 'philosophical apparatus' built up during the 1790s.[5] Even in 1799–1800, a particularly low point in the College's fortunes, when the beleaguered George Walker struggled on almost alone, when there were barely a dozen students and when the names of new entrants were unrecorded, all was far from lost. A printed balance sheet for that academic session indicates gross income of £618.12.1, and expenditure of £661.13.10. There was indeed a small excess of expenditure over income, but this was covered by reserves; £310 'in the Treasurer's hand' in February 1799, £267 a year later.

The College, moreover, enjoyed the security of physical assets. The newly erected buildings were held as freehold property and could provide facilities for unofficial as well as official intellectual activity: Robert Owen recorded his religious and scientific discussions with John Dalton in the latter's College rooms.[7] The debts on the College buildings were cleared by 1799: the buildings were valued at £3200 in the accounts of 1799–1800 and at £4000 in 1803 they were sold for £14,065 in 1861.[8] The College also owned a small amount of land, together with academic equipment. The library was insured for £800 and 'philosophical apparatus and other furniture' for £200 in 1792.[9] The acquisition in subsequent years of the York property and the Exeter Academy library adds further evidence of the ability of the College to raise funds and to prove itself a worthy repository for academic benefactions.

One important reason for the College's solvency lay in its ability, in the first Manchester period, to attract sufficient, if not abundant, numbers of lay students, the financial lifeblood of a dissenting academy. In fact Manchester College drew by far its highest proportion of lay students in the first Manchester period. No less than 115 of the 135 enrolled between 1786 and 1797 were destined for lay professions, compared with 113 of 235 in the York period, when the numbers fell away markedly in the 1830s.[10] The contrast emerges more starkly when one observes that in Manchester the College attracted an annual average of about ten lay students compared with a figure of barely three at York. Nor were the fees and incidental expenses abnormally low, as Samuel Pipe-Wolferstan, whose son Stanley attended the College for eighteen months in 1801–2, discovered with some pain.[11]

The College's main financial problem was the absence of a permanent fund to guarantee continuity and subsidise the divinity students who might otherwise be unable to afford the fees. It was this lack of provision for divinity students which influenced Thomas Belsham's decision to decline the divinity tutorship in 1797.[12] There was no formal attachment to the traditional dissenting educational funds, such as the Presbyterian Fund or the Coward Trust, although grants from these funds were made regularly to individual students at Manchester College.[13] 'If there were a permanent fund, no doubt concerning the success of the institution could be entertained', wrote the Rev. Charles Wellbeloved in January 1798, as uncertainty over the future of the College temporarily deterred him from taking over its management.[14] He recognized, however, that the potential for such a device existed, and it was soon realized. For in a group of powerful and prosperous friends the College possessed another asset. A substantial section of the mercantile and professional elite of Manchester, including the Hibbert, Phillips, Potter and Rigby families, gave financial support, served as officers on the Committee and sent their sons to the College. Indeed Lewis Loyd, assistant classical tutor in the early 1790s, married into a local banking family, became a partner in the firm, and achieved considerable wealth. He contributed £100 and remained a subscriber to the College long after professional demands removed him to London.[15] Dr. Thomas Percival, the first president, harnessed this goodwill and by his personal commitment ensured the survival of the College in the turbulent decade of the 1790s. It is small wonder, then, that Wellbeloved had found it surprising that 'among so many rich men who support it . . . a subscription for the purpose of forming a fund is not entered into.'[16] Once the location of the College had been settled, the deficiency was met. In 1808 the banker Samuel Jones, whose connection with the College was enhanced by the fact that Loyd was his brother-in-law, inaugurated the permanent fund with a donation of £100. Its subsequent growth was steady if not spectacular. The *Annual Report* of 1817 gave its standing as £1082; by 1820 it had risen to £1803.[17] Thereafter there was a healthy list of annual subscribers, despite some falling off in the later years at York.[18] Hence the number of divinity students in the York period rose in absolute terms and as a proportion of the total. When the supply of lay students dwindled to the point of disappearance in the mid-1830s, University reform was in the process of altering the entire *raison d'être* of the College, leaving it to concentrate more heavily upon the training of ministers, a task for which it was primarily equipped, and which, in the longer term, it was well able to afford.

Secondly, it should perhaps be re-affirmed that the early Manchester College possessed a remarkably distinguished staff and a wide curriculum. It is not necessary here to dwell upon the high pastoral and preaching reputation of Thomas Barnes, or upon his work for social improvement in Manchester.[19] The musical talents of Ralph Harrison, together with the mathematical gifts of Walker and Dalton have also received due recognition. One might add, however, that there were no failures among the other tutors, most of whom achieved respectability or distinction in the academic, pastoral or other professional fields.[20] The one obscure figure among them is Mr. T. Nicholls, who preceded Dalton as Mathematics tutor between 1789 and 1793. Although little is known of him, there is ample evidence that he gained the confidence of the Committee soon after his arrival, and in November 1792 the post of librarian with the additional salary of £20 per annum was created for him.[21] Charles Sanders, the Anglican cleric who was classics tutor in 1798–9 also served as librarian with a salary of ten guineas.[22] All the eleven tutors in the first Manchester period reinforce that impression of powerful intellectual activity with which rational dissent has long been associated. Indeed one must regard the fidelity of the early tutors as a crucial factor in the College's progress. A recent study of the York period indicates that the same was true in the early nineteenth century.[23]

The width of the curriculum is easily illustrated. Apart from the theological, literary and classical studies which formed the basis of the five year divinity course, and the commercial subjects which seem to have attracted lay students, the College was proficient in at least two other areas. It offered a remarkable range of lectures in various branches of science. Immediately after 1786 access to scientific lectures was possible at the transient 'College of Arts and Sciences' in Manchester, which Barnes had helped to establish. After that institution became defunct in 1788, scientific lectures were available via the Literary and Philosophical Society of Manchester and through a series of eminent local and visiting lecturers.[24] Some of them, like Thomas Henry and Charles White, were already friends and subscribers to the College, which was strategically placed at the very centre of one of the most progressive scientific and technological communities of late eighteenth century Britain, and its students and visitors were alike impressed. Manchester College continued and indeed enhanced the elevated reputation of dissenting academies for scientific study.

The College also offered its students the opportunity of acquiring proficiency in modern languages. Here its efforts have not been appreciated. Modern languages at Manchester were 'a striking omission' according to one authority and Dr. McLachlan suggests that they received less prominence than had been the case at Warrington Academy.[25] Yet the surviving prospectuses for the first Manchester period repeatedly mention the availability of French, Italian and (at times) German. Although a languages tutor was not appointed at this stage, private masters in Manchester were clearly employed in a part-time capacity. An advertisement in 1788 stated 'A Master regularly attends the Academy to instruct the students in French and Modern Languages', and Samuel Pipe-Wolferstan, paid eight guineas for his son's tuition by a French Master in

1801–2.[26] Much the same practice seems to have been followed at York, [27]where John Kenrick taught German and where even Spanish was briefly offered. Indeed in the York period, the College actually appointed to the post of languages tutor the Milanese exile Chevalier Giuseppe Pecchio (1785–1835), another forgotten figure in the College's history, who will feature later in this essay.[28] In short there is evidence from such independent sources as the diary of Pipe-Wolferstan that what was offered in the curriculum was in fact delivered.

None of this, of course, is to deny that in its first twenty-five years the College experienced several severe and almost fatal crises. The Committee encountered enormous difficulty in replacing Barnes in 1797–8 when the office of divinity tutor was offered to, and declined by, no less than five dissenting ministers.[29] The years 1800–3, when Walker was alone, ageing and aggrieved over financial promises which he believed had been made to him, gave rise to the most pessimistic speculations over the future of the College.[30] On Walker's resignation in 1803 there was doubt as to whether the College would be continued at all and the move to York, together with Wellbeloved's willingness to step into the vacant place, was far from automatic. The latter's reservations seemed quickly to be justified when overwork and lack of assistance drove him to the point of breakdown, and this latest crisis was only resolved with the appointment of two new tutors in 1810.[31]

Behind these episodes lay the recurrent theme of indiscipline amongst at least some of the students. During the 1790s it had reached serious and unacceptable proportions. Indiscipline evidently played some part in the resignations of Dalton and William Johns as tutors in 1800; the latter in particular had to face insults and insubordination which caused one pupil to be expelled and another to be severely reprimanded.[32] Irregularity of conduct, moreover, was one reason why Pipe-Wolferstan removed his son from the College two years later.[33] In 1797 this problem obliged Barnes to relinquish his office, in accordance with his promise eleven years earlier, when he had declared that he could 'not continue to endure in this Academy the commission of enormities, which, whenever they prevail, poison the minds of youth, and destroy all the good effects of liberal education'.[34] Certainly his triumphalist tone at the inauguration of the College was not maintained. But indiscipline was hardly peculiar to Manchester College: it was all too common a feature of dissenting academies (and, for that matter, public schools) in this period. One's surprise is not that it happened, but that its consequences did not prove fatal to the College. Nor were all the circumstances which produced it entirely within the College's own control. Wellbeloved and his friend Rev. Joseph Astley agreed in 1797–8 that the 'dissipation of Manchester' and the opportunities which the town offered for the 'commission of enormities' by the young men were the most important obstacles to the College's well-being.[35] This is admittedly an irony when one recalls that the founders of the College in 1786 had given assurances that the 'well-regulated police' and 'serious attention to the duties of public worship' of the people of Manchester would prevent any repetition of the disorderly conduct which had characterised the later years at Warrington, although the removal to the much smaller city of York did not eliminate disciplinary troubles.[36]

But endurance in these circumstances was an achievement in itself and these early crises must be seen in that context. Unlike Hackney or Warrington, which could not sustain the initial promise, or so many other dissenting academies, which could not survive the death or migration of an individual tutor, Manchester College was highly unusual of its type in that it actually outlived, and ultimately triumphed over, its difficulties. It possessed underlying sources of strength and, after the closure of Hackney in 1796, had the negative and accidental advantage of lack of alternatives. But while the mere fact of survival might, baldly stated, appear banal, it was the *sine qua non* of any contribution to the wider society to which it belonged. The first answer, then, to the question, what did Manchester College contribute to British Anti-Slavery must be, that it remained alive, and that it did so for a respectable, and respected, academic purpose.

It is possible to trace three profound influences which surrounded the College's foundation and which help to explain, not only its survival but also its commitment, from the very start, to Anti-Slavery. The first was the concept of 'religious liberty' inherited from Warrington Academy. This was an ideal which evoked considerable loyalty among rational Dissenters and which was capable of a much wider application. Warrington had been obsessed with hostility to, and its own freedom from, the imposition of religious creeds and tests. Its whole purpose, in the words of John Seddon, had been 'to further the progress of true religion and religious liberty'[37] and, indeed, Warrington had flourished at the time of the publication of Blackburne's *Confessional* and the attack on clerical and university subscription. This obsession was fully shared by Manchester College and it was constantly reiterated in a manner which did not entirely exclude a measure of self-righteousness. The College's advertisement in the *Monthly Magazine* for 1797 boasted of a 'liberal and comprehensive plan . . . without distinction of party or of religious denomination, and exempt from every political test and doctrinal subscription,' and this theme is present in successive *Annual Reports* of the early nineteenth century.[38] Although it cannot be stated too often that Warrington and Manchester College were distinct institutions, Warrington's influence over its fledgling successor, in this and other respects, was undoubtedly very strong. This was particularly true in the period 1786 to 1803, when there was still much continuity of curriculum and personnel. Without the closure of Warrington it is difficult to believe that such a successor would even have been regarded as necessary. Seventeen trustees of Warrington signed the invitation to Barnes and Harrison to undertake the new venture in 1786, and twelve were members of the Committee of Manchester College.[39] Barnes and Harrison themselves were alumni of Warrington, as was Percival, the first president of the

College, while George Walker had served there as a tutor. Even the library was inherited from Warrington. Above all, moreover, this legacy to Manchester College of religious liberty was associated with a Whiggish, abolitionist ethos. The Warrington tutors were, according to Dr. McLachlan, 'Anti-Slavery to a man', a generalisation which is easily justified.[40] It was certainly true of the family of John Aikin, who presided over Warrington's most prosperous years: his daughter, Mrs. Barbauld, dedicated some of her literary work to abolitionism and boycotted West Indian sugar in protest against the Slave Trade.[41] A significant number of Warrington alumni found their way into Anti-Slavery circles and at least two of them attained national prominence in that field: Henry Beaufoy, M.P. became one of the leading parliamentary advocates of abolition between 1784 and 1795,[42] while J. P. Estlin stood at the centre of the influential abolitionist group in Bristol.

The second formative influence which was present, and indeed dominant, at the birth of the College, was the rational dissent of Cross Street Chapel. Its congregation was sufficiently respectable and prosperous to confer immediate material advantages upon its protégé. The original land for the College was provided by the trustees of Cross Street;[43] the chapel room was used for the first and several subsequent meetings of the College Committee and the chapel itself remained the practical as well as the spiritual headquarters of the College for many years thereafter. At least fourteen of the forty-five signatories to the Address of 7 February 1786, urging the establishment of the College, were Cross Street trustees, while many others were chapel members.[44] Barnes and Harrison were joint ministers of the chapel as well as College tutors. As Wellbeloved accurately observed in summarising his view of the College's prospects in 1798, 'the most zealous friends to the institution are his [i.e. Barnes's] friends and the leading men in his congregation'.[45] The connection was further developed during the second Manchester period in the persons of J. G. Robberds and William Gaskell.[46] Although it is perhaps something of an over-simplification to assert that Cross Street Chapel 'turned Unitarian' under the ministry of John Seddon (1741–69),[47] it undoubtedly succoured a type of Arian theology which was akin to, and in later years moved further towards, Unitarianism. This process was not without political implications. As a recent historian of early industrial Manchester has noted, 'the correlation between association with Cross Street and commitment to liberal causes was almost inevitable in the late eighteenth century and the first four decades of the nineteenth century'.[48] Chief among these causes was Anti-Slavery, to which the liberal Christianity of Cross Street was attracted from the start. Most of the fourteen trustees mentioned above subscribed to the Manchester abolitionist campaign of 1788. This commitment will require elaboration later in this essay: at this point it is necessary to say only that it was shared by many other trustees and members, including some, like the magistrate and social reformer Thomas Butterworth Bayley, who became 'loyalist' and 'Tory' in the later 1790s.[49] This transmission of liberal ideas to the

College was strengthened by a close proximity to Mosley Street Chapel, founded in 1789 as a supplement, rather than as a rival, to Cross Street.[50] Its minister, Rev. William Hawkes, shared many of these values: he subscribed to the *Sermons* of George Walker in 1808, joined the Manchester campaign against the Slave Trade and contributed to the rational dissenting ethos which Cross Street Chapel bestowed upon Manchester College. Much the same is true of the smaller chapel at Dob Lane, Failsworth, which had also adopted Arian worship in the later eighteenth century, and which the College supplied with a series of preachers between 1790 and 1803.[51]

The third formative influence, which of course was inextricably bound up with the first two, might best be described as the liberal intellectual ethos of the Manchester Literary and Philosophical Society. Although the Society was institutionally separate from Manchester College and predated it by five years, the two were dominated by the same individuals and were the joint recipients of the mantle of Warrington. The founding fathers and principal tutors of the College held high office in the Society: Percival and Walker were presidents, while Barnes, Harrison, Johns and Dalton were prominent members. Intellectually, College and Society were inseparable: they even shared many of the same lectures. It is, accordingly, odd to find the claim, in a recent biography of Dalton, that its subject disliked the political atmosphere of the College, while finding inspiration in that of the Society. Since the two were practically identical in terms of personnel and commitment to liberal inquiry it is difficult to see how Dalton was able 'to reject the one organisation while rising steadily in the other'.[52] Nor is there any evidence to suggest that Dalton resigned his College tutorship in 1800 because he was 'dissatisfied with the College's radical posture'.[53] On the contrary, Dalton was on close terms with Robert Owen, whom he was in the habit of meeting, together with other associates, in the College to discuss moral, religious and scientific questions.[54] It is unlikely that the friend of Owen would have been offended by 'political radicalism'.[55] After all, Dalton remained for seven years in the employ of the College and the *Minutes* repeatedly speak well of him.[56] He remained also a close friend of his fellow-tutor William Johns and both retained links with associates of the College after their departures. Like Johns himself, Dalton appears to have left the College as a result of indiscipline among the students.[57] Johns at least was still a member of the College Committee as late as 1820,[58] he and Dalton served as joint secretaries of the Literary and Philosophical Society, and Dalton ultimately became its president.

The Manchester Literary and Philosophical Society represented the type of provincial intellectual elite which was springing up in several towns of the north and midlands. Like its counterpart in Newcastle, over which William Turner presided, it involved 'a marriage between liberal politics, liberal religion and useful knowledge'.[59] Turner in fact was the Newcastle equivalent, in terms of social and intellectual improvement, of Thomas Barnes. Although the Manchester Society placed a formal ban upon discussion of current politics at its meetings, the liberal sympathies of most of its members were not concealed. Common to all these societies was a marked sympathy towards Anti-Slavery.[60] One of the strongest abolitionists of the later eighteenth century, Gilbert Wakefield, was made an honorary member of the Manchester Literary and Philosophical Society in 1784.[61] It is noteworthy that fifteen of the thirty-one members of the Anti-Slave Trade Committee of Manchester in 1788 belonged to the Literary and Philosophical Society and that their liberal politics were so far recognized in the 1790s that several members were singled out for surveillance and possible prosecution by local loyalists.[62]

With each of these formative influences there were two common factors: a powerful influence over Manchester College in its early years and an inclination towards a state of mind which led easily towards Anti-Slavery. It is significant that many individuals laboured diligently in the service of each and that Thomas Percival was the most important individual link between all three.[63] It is against this background that the involvement of Manchester College in the early abolitionist movement must be placed.

The origins of popular abolitionism in England may be traced to the mid-1780s. At the national level a decisive step was taken in April 1787 with the formation in London of the Abolition Committee, which was itself an enlargement of a long-standing Quaker organization. There was immediately a rapid process of canvassing and cultivation of grass roots in the country as a whole, in which the efforts of Thomas Clarkson were prominent.[64] But at precisely this time a significant local initiative was taken in Manchester, where abolitionism was already stirring.

The commitment of Manchester College to abolitionism might be said to have begun, as it were, at the top. A central figure in Manchester and, to some extent, indeed, British abolitionism was Thomas Percival. The 'Biographical Memoirs' penned by his son in 1807 neatly summarize the outline of his contribution and that of his native town:

> To a mind habitually disposed to cherish the strictest notions with regard to the rule of justice and humanity, it may readily be conceived, that the negro trade of Africa, and slavery in the West-Indies, would appear in a high degree iniquitous. The impolicy of the traffic was indeed matter of serious and dispassionate enquiry; in which Dr. Percival engaged with more than common assiduity . . . But what particularly directed his interest to this enquiry, was a circumstance which reflects honour on the town where he resided; the inhabitants of Manchester having afforded the first example of presenting a Petition to Parliament for the *Abolition of the Slave Trade*. Among the earliest movers and most zealous supporters of this measure (by which the sentiments of a large and respectable part of the community were made known to the legislature) was the Subject of these memoirs.[65]

As the popular campaign for abolition began in the winter of 1787–8, Percival was already in contact with several writers on the Slave Trade and with others who were to become prominent abolitionists, including

Joseph Priestley, Bishop Watson of Llandaff, Bishop Porteus of London, Thomas Burgess, a future bishop of St. David's, and even Madame Necker.[66] His purpose was to encourage them to give full support to the growing abolitionist movement and, whenever possible, to use their literary gifts to augment the rapidly increasing number of anti-slavery pamphlets of the type which the Abolition Committee in London was beginning to circulate in substantial numbers.

Following Percival's active commitment at the very start, the most direct role of those connected with Manchester College belonged to the first years of abolitionist campaigning in 1787–92, when circumstances were at their most propitious, and before popular, extra-parliamentary agitation, even of the most respectable kind, had been overtaken by wider political events. The first Anti-Slave Trade Committee in Manchester was formed as early as the autumn of 1787, under the leadership of the cotton merchant Thomas Walker who became its chairman, and the radical writer and lawyer Thomas Cooper. Both drew on their recent experiences as parliamentary reformers in the Society for Constitutional Information.[67] Several months of active preparation and solicitation of support led to the publication in the *Manchester Mercury* of 15 January 1788 of an impressive list of 'Subscribers against the African Slave Trade'. It consisted of 231 separate subscriptions, from individuals, a few business firms and several chapels, mostly of one, two or three guineas, amounting to a total pledge of almost £300.[68] The list is of considerable interest to the historian of abolitionism.

For in this activity Manchester College was very well represented, and those concerned gave help of a practical and financial kind to abolitionism in Manchester. Of the twenty-one members of the College Committee in 1786 two (Percival and James Touchet), together with Thomas Barnes, were also members of the abolitionist committee in Manchester which was formed in December 1787 and which represented a wide variety of local political opinion.[69] A further ten members of the College Committee appear in the abolitionist subscription list of January 1788. They included the principal lay officers of the College, notably Percival (President), George Duckworth (Secretary) and James Touchet (Treasurer), the former two each subscribing one guinea and the latter two guineas. Similarly, of the 45 signatories of the College Address of 7 February 1786, four (Percival, Touchet, Titus Hibbert and William Rigby junior) belonged to the abolitionist Committee, while twenty may be found in the abolitionist subscription list.[70] The sympathies of these lay supporters were matched by those of the most prominent tutors. Barnes, like Percival, was a founder of the abolitionist movement in Manchester, a member of the local committee from December 1787 and a subscriber in 1788. Even earlier than that, in November 1787, he brought his eloquence to bear on the subject:

> On Monday Evening the Rev. Dr Barnes delivered a Sermon at the Dissenting Chapel, in this town, in favour of the poor African slaves, from xviith Chapter of Acts, and the former Part of the 26th Verse. The

arguments brought to support that iniquitous Traffic, were considered and very satisfactorily answered. The impolicy and cruelty of the Trade were exploded with a Spirit that did honour to his Feelings as a Man and a Christian. Many Persons who, for want of Information, were not present on this Occasion, are in hopes of being gratified with a future Discourse on the same subject.[71]

The local press provides ample testimony to the willingness of large audiences to attend anti-slavery sermons in the later 1780s and Barnes on this occasion preached only two weeks after Thomas Clarkson's celebrated visit to Manchester.[72] His views were shared by his coadjutor Ralph Harrison who, like Barnes, subscribed one guinea to the abolitionist efforts in 1788 and whose published sermons leave no doubt as to his abolitionist sentiments.[73] Although most of the other eight tutors of the first Manchester period held their College offices after the main initial burst of abolitionist campaigning, Walker had already established a reputation in this field, whilst it should not be forgotten that Dalton was a conscientious Quaker in a period when Quakers had made the first serious protests against the Slave Trade. Those men of science who also contributed to the tuition of the College, moreover, offer confirmation of the same impression. The very first College prospectus announced, with justifiable pride, the availability of medical lectures by Charles White and chemical lectures by Thomas Henry. Both men subscribed to the College and both were prominent in local abolitionist circles. Thomas Henry was a member of the Manchester abolition committee of 1787 and the names of both may be found in the subscription lists which were inserted in the *Manchester Mercury* by the local abolitionists.[74] To their names can be added that of Dr. John Ferriar, a medical man who became co-secretary of the Literary and Philosophical Society in 1790, and whom Pipe-Wolferstan encountered on his visit to the College in 1801; he belonged to the committee of 1787 and subscribed one guinea to the Manchester abolitionist cause in 1788.[75]

A glance at the earliest lists of benefactors and annual subscribers to the College in 1786, moreover, also reveals a significant abolitionist presence. Four of those 48 individuals who made benefactions to the College at its foundation were also members of the Manchester abolitionist committee of 1787, while a further 22 subscribed to abolition the following year. Of 58 annual subscribers in the Manchester area, five belonged to the Committee and eighteen feature among the abolitionist subscribers.[76] The annual subscribers from outside the Manchester area also included prominent abolitionists: Richard Slater Milnes, M.P. for York and identified by Professor Anstey as a leading parliamentary abolitionist,[77] subscribed ten guineas to the College, Josiah Wedgwood who in 1787 produced his celebrated anti-slavery medallion 'Am I not a man and a brother?' subscribed three guineas, and the Rev. J. P. Estlin of Bristol subscribed two guineas. The Liverpool abolitionists of the early period also feature prominently in the list of annual subscribers: Dr. James Currie and the Rev. John Yates, for instance, each subscribed three guineas. Other members of that circle were closely associated with the College and none more so than Rev. William Shepherd of Gateacre. A friend of William Roscoe and at the centre of Liverpool abolitionism, he subscribed to the College from 1797 until his death fifty years later, was offered the classical tutorship in May 1798, endowed the College with a prize and preached to the assembled tutors and students in the York period.[78] His associate in that group, William Rathbone IV, almost sent his son to the College in 1802 and subscribed to the *Sermons* of George Walker in 1808.[79] Nicholas Clayton, William Enfield and the Nicholson family into which they both married also help to underline one's impression of the strength of the link between sympathisers with the College and active abolitionism.[80]

Of course, appearance in the published lists of the abolitionist ranks was by no means the only type of involvement in abolitionist activity, although it is the type of involvement for which firm evidence tends to survive. Subscription lists, moreover, were themselves a form of propaganda, designed to strengthen the cause by displaying the eminence and worthiness of its principal adherents. Many rank and file abolitionists remain unrecorded in this kind of source, and abolitionist activity on the part of all those connected with the College cannot now be conclusively demonstrated. What we do not have, however, is significant evidence of opposition to abolition among supporters of the College.[81] Moreover, something positive can be said about the collective efforts of those who, following the lead of Percival and Barnes, committed themselves to abolitionism in Manchester. Their work included preaching, attending meetings and canvassing for signatures, as well as raising funds, both for the expenses of their own organisation and for those of the Abolition Committee in London. They used their private friendships to propagate the movement: Percival, for instance, despatched the resolutions of the first Manchester meetings to William Robertson and Dr. Beattie and urged both of these luminaries of the Scottish Enlightenment to write in the abolitionist interest.[82] The Manchester resolutions were advertised in the press in a successful attempt to persuade other towns to follow their example, and local M.P.s were pressed to give the matter their favourable attention in the House of Commons.[83] Just as the leading Manchester merchants, notably Thomas Walker, had recent experience of this kind of organization in their successful agitation against the Fustian Tax, so those associated with Manchester College could draw on their own experience in the use of meetings, addresses, press advertisements and subscriptions to launch their new academic enterprise. The techniques used in 1786 to promote the College and those employed in the interests of abolitionism were remarkably similar: the difference was one of scale.

The Manchester campaign against the Slave Trade reached two early climaxes. The petition to Parliament of 1788 secured, according to the local press, 10,639 signatures, while the petition of 1792 achieved no less than 20,000.[84] One important reason for these impressive results lay in the political radicalism of the most energetic group on the local abolitionist committee. It was the radical members, led by Walker and Cooper,

PLATE I

Thomas Barnes

George Walker

Charles Wellbeloved

John Kenrick

John James Tayler

PLATE II

James Martineau

Joseph Estlin Carpenter

John Dalton

William Gaskell

Philip Henry Wicksteed

who took the initiative independently of Clarkson and the London headquarters, in launching a petition and thereby providing abolitionism with a more popular base. Barnes, Percival, Thomas Henry and their friends did not share all these radical attitudes but they formed the vital Whig faction on the Manchester committee which allied with the radicals and allowed the latter to dominate the Committee and use that dominance to pioneer and spread the idea of abolitionist petitions. Manchester was the only provincial town where the abolition committee was dominated by radicals: this helped to give Manchester abolitionism a more popular and 'democratic' hue and a wider political appeal. By 1792 the radicals were in almost complete control locally.[85] Those connected with Manchester College were as well represented on the local Committee in 1792 as in 1788 and feature in comparable proportions in the rather shorter abolitionist subscription list of April 1792.[86] Barnes and Percival, however, tended to draw back from some of the more dramatic forms of radicalism embodied in the Manchester Constitutional Society and among sympathisers with the French Revolution. By the end of the decade they, along with others of their ilk, had felt obliged to make public professions of loyalism, while Thomas Henry, according to his son, was 'perhaps [disposed] to allow more than its due weight to the aristocratical part of our mixed government'.[87] But their Whiggish libertarianism permitted them to make common cause with the radicals in the interests of anti-slavery and in that conjunction lay decisive results, and important achievements, for British abolitionism. These achievements are worth examining in a little more detail.

In the first place observant contemporaries, as well as modern historians, recognized the crucial role of Manchester in pushing British abolitionism into political agitation and a national petitioning campaign. In January 1789 a Bristol shipper wrote 'I at first laughed at the attempt of the Manchester fanatics, but now find it is a serious business, taken up warmly by Mr. Wilberforce and others'.[88] Manchester was in the vanguard of public opinion over the Slave Trade and the Manchester College members of its abolition committee helped to incline, first local and then, as an immediate result, British abolitionism into a significantly new and ultimately successful direction. As Manchester's example was endorsed and followed by other towns and as the London Committee came to accept it, so abolitionism acquired a most potent political weapon. No less than 508 abolition petitions were presented to Parliament in the spring of 1792.[89] In the longer term, the petition was the spearhead of the Anti-Slavery Society and the Agency Committee during the years leading up to Emancipation itself in the 1830s.[90] Secondly, these efforts could show tangible results even in the short term. Following the decisive winter of 1787–8 the progress of abolition was not as rapid as its most optimistic luminaries had hoped, but much was achieved. There were major inquiries into the Slave Trade, first by a Committee of the Privy Council, then by a Committee of the House of Commons; there was a national debate over the whole issue, with the proponents of the Slave Trade increasingly on the defensive: there was the Act of Parliament, sponsored by William Dolben in 1788, to limit the number of slaves which could be carried per ship, followed by other ameliorative measures; and finally there was the historic vote by the House of Commons in March 1792 for gradual abolition which, despite subsequent failure in the House of Lords, carried the cause significantly forward. Thirdly, popular abolitionism was responsible for an elevation in the status of the petition itself. Between 1787 and 1833 petitioning underwent an enormous qualitative and quantitative change. Its respectability was enhanced, its volume massively increased and its status as firm evidence of the state of public opinion greatly augmented. By 1833, when the Anti-Slavery movement produced thousands of petitions with hundreds of thousands of signatures, it was no longer possible to dismiss petitions (as Dr. Johnson, for instance, had done, with some justification, in *The False Alarm* sixty years earlier) as sponsored from above and not really representative of widespread feelings. As James Walvin had written, 'It was the abolitionists who first established both the legitimacy and the political effectiveness of the petition'.[91] The founding fathers of Manchester College played some part in the initiation of this process and in so doing helped to set in motion a political development of significance far beyond the issue of Anti-Slavery.

After 1792–3, however, this sort of activity sustained a temporary but severe setback, especially in Manchester. The loyalism of the early and mid 1790s made mass petitioning much more difficult, especially when so prominent an abolitionist as Thomas Walker was the target both of mob violence and official suspicion. If radicalism discredited abolition nationally after the shock of the French Revolution and of the slave uprising in Haiti, then this was bound to be particularly true of Manchester, since nowhere else was abolitionism so firmly associated with radicalism. There was accordingly much less abolitionist agitation in the remaining years of the first Manchester period of the College, and indeed the abolition of the British Slave Trade itself in 1806–7 was achieved without mass petitioning. But for the College the pattern was set and the image created. Its Anti-Slavery sympathies were thereafter displayed, if less obviously paraded, in other ways.

It was, for instance, a sign of the liberal, abolitionist ethos of Manchester College that George Walker should have been chosen as Divinity tutor in 1798 and a measure of the College's reputation that he should have accepted, at some cost to himself. Although Walker was sixth choice for the office, he was even more distinguished than some of the earlier candidates, who were themselves, of course, abolitionists. Walker maintained the Warrington legacy. While minister at the High Pavement Chapel, Nottingham, he had devoted 'a considerable portion of his attention' to abolition, alongside his dedication to parliamentary and religious reform.[92] His abolitionist endeavours, moreover, were well known in Manchester: the *Manchester Mercury* of 24 January 1792 carried a report of an Anti-Slave Trade meeting at Nottingham and listed Walker and the Rev. Gilbert Wakefield as members of the local committee.[93] Walker brought with him to Manchester a considerable reputation as a reformist speaker, organiser, writer and author of the highly praised *Dissenters' Plea* (1790). He was very well regarded in reforming circles, especially by his friend Major John Cartwright.[94] His friendship with Cartwright and association with him in causes dear to them both continued during his period of service to the College.[95]

Other connections of the College in the early period point clearly in the same direction. It is noteworthy that when seeking extra subscriptions in 1797 the College applied to many rational dissenting ministers and congregations with known abolitionist inclinations.[96] The abolitionist ethos and allied liberal values of the College helped to attract Samuel Pipe-Wolferstan, whose diary does so much to illuminate the principalship of Walker. Pipe-Wolferstan himself was a staunch abolitionist who boycotted West Indian sugar and was acquainted with Wilberforce.[97] A vital figure in the background of the College during the early years was the Rev. William Wood, minister of Mill Hill Chapel, Leeds; Visitor in 1806–8 and counsellor of Wellbeloved, it was Wood who argued against closure in 1803 and advocated the move to York. As early as 1781 he had denounced the Slave Trade in his published *Sermon on Universal Benevolence* and remained a committed abolitionist, notably from the pulpit, until his death in 1808.[98] Admirers of the College from a greater distance included Gilbert Wakefield, whose *Memoirs* testify to the vehemence of his abolitionist convictions, and Samuel Kenrick of Bewdley, whose unpublished correspondence provides ample evidence of the same kind.[99] Inasmuch as the College was known to the wider public it was at least in part through individuals such as these, and there is a remarkable uniformity about their views on the Slave Trade and in the image of the College which they presented.

## II

In this section it is proposed to investigate the motivation behind this commitment to abolitionism and to indicate the ways in which it helps to illuminate the political ethos of Manchester College.

In *The Atlantic Slave Trade and British Abolition*, Roger Anstey identified the evangelical impulse as a central factor in promoting the important changes in public and private attitudes which made the Slave Trade appear increasingly unacceptable to British opinion. According to this analysis evangelicalism produced through its theology a reforming dynamic of its own, especially in the field of humanitarian reform. The most obvious evangelical theological priorities, notably a heightened sense of an intervening providence, a concern with the law of love and a consequently heightened sense of the duty of benevolence, a positive response to the depiction of evil, whose solution could be presented as redemption from bondage, and a powerful sense of the millenium, could all easily be translated into hostility to the Slave Trade and to Slavery itself. In particular the evangelical focus upon the individual's salvation and redemption from sin led rapidly to a view of the Slave Trade as detestable in the eyes of God and lent urgency to attacks upon it. The rapid international spread of evangelicalism in the eighteenth century may thus be regarded as a fundamental reason for the growing criticism of the Slave Trade and the evangelical motivation, accordingly, as a major religious pressure which propelled abolitionism to the very centre of the political stage.[100]

This is a highly convincing thesis and its claim that the main pressures which fuelled abolitionism were religious ones is well sustained by the overwhelmingly religious tone of the vast bulk of abolitionist polemic. It is by no means inconsistent with this argument, however, to suggest that evangelical theology was not the sole religious dynamic at work in British abolitionism (even if it was the main one) and that other religious traditions had something to contribute to Anti-Slavery. Here it will be suggested that the reasons which explain the Unitarian and rational dissenting gravitation towards Anti-Slavery were fundamentally different from those which inspired the evangelicals in that direction. For the abolitionist commitment of Manchester College originated in what were essentially non-evangelical considerations, and one must look elsewhere to find its source.

Progress in this search may be facilitated if two issues are resolved at the outset. The first is the familiar question as to whether it is appropriate to apply the term 'Unitarian' to Manchester College. There is little point in raking over the embers of this controversy: it has been fully discussed elsewhere.[101] Instead it will be accepted for the purposes of this essay that the strict insistence of the College upon freedom from sectarian alignment did not entirely conceal a strongly Unitarian undercurrent, especially after 1803. The best and most realistic verdict is perhaps that of Catherine Cappe, who was closely involved in the fortunes of the College during the early York period. 'For as Unitarianism is the known sentiment of the tutors, and the avowed principle on which their worship is conducted', she wrote, 'how is it possible that a prejudice should not be excited in its favour, in the minds of the pupils, antecedent to this declared impartiality of examination?'[102] The *Annual Report* of 1828 frankly acknowledged that the College's 'practical connexion with the Unitarian body . . . is neither denied nor concealed.'[103] At the same time the College, under Barnes and Walker, and even under the more decidedly Unitarian Wellbeloved, undoubtedly achieved a genuine eclecticism which was untypical of contemporary Unitarianism and the very antithesis of the aggressive Socinian rigour of the Unitarian Society which was founded in 1791.[104] Nevertheless, the answer to the question as to whether the College may be described as Unitarian must be an affirmative one, albeit a heavily qualified affirmative, and this is not without significance for the College's Anti-Slavery values.

The second issue is not quite so depressingly familiar as the first. It has been argued recently, and in a most able fashion, that some prominent Unitarian thinkers of the early nineteenth century shared a sufficiently wide range of evangelical characteristics to make possible a direct comparison between evangelical and Unitarian support for Anti-Slavery. In his identification of a species of religious thought which may be termed 'evangelical Unitarianism', the author placed most emphasis on the period after 1830 and on Unitarian attitudes towards American, rather than British imperial, slavery.[105] But the implications of this thesis should not pass unnoticed here, since they offer an explanation of the Unitarian commitment to Anti-Slavery which invokes evangelical as well as rational dissenting origins.[106] In addition to other reservations about this thesis,[107] however, it needs to be stressed that 'evangelical Unitarianism', even if its existence in a later period can indeed be satisfactorily demonstrated does not explain the initial Unitarian participation in British abolitionism, which pre-dated 'evangelical Unitarianism' by more than a generation. For substantial evidence of such a phenomenon can hardly be detected in the pre-1833 period (and still less in the pre-1807 period) and it exerted no serious influence on the teaching or research of Manchester College in these years. The College arose from and continued to be sponsored by those branches of English Dissent which were least affected by the evangelical revival and its subscription lists indicate no measure of evangelical endorsement. As far as slavery in the British Empire was concerned, Manchester College drew its support for abolition and, later, for emancipation, from a religious mentality which owed little or nothing to evangelicalism and Professor Anstey has drawn attention to the distinctiveness in the Anti-Slavery movement of Unitarians from those Protestant sects which had been fashioned or transformed by evangelicalism.[108]

For early nineteenth century Unitarianism was increasingly inclined to reject the evangelical stress upon an intervening providence and the concept of salvation from sin as a redemption from bondage. This was a natural corollary of the tendency of Unitarian theology, in the heyday of Priestley and Belsham, in the direction of an acceptance of the simple humanity of Christ, as Arianism moved towards Socinianism at the end of the eighteenth century. These views did not become dominant at Manchester College before 1803 and even in the time of Wellbeloved they were not imposed with dogmatic insistence.[109] But the general emphasis was unmistakable. At York the College embraced a necessarian doctrine of will and a utilitarian theory of ethics: this was translated into the academic prominence accorded to materialism, political economy and constitutional history.[110] This was the prevailing ethos when James Martineau was a pupil and it was many years before he and others repudiated the materialist legacy of Priestley.[111] It was also the way of thought which informed the religious, ethical and political attitudes of the young Harriet Martineau, enabling her biographer to argue that the role of evangelicalism, with its 'insistence on the insignificance of the individual' in the shaping of the principal features of the Victorian age has been 'somewhat overdone'.[112] The next passage of the same work is of particular importance for the Anti-Slavery question, since Professor Webb indicates 'how the same ideals of activity and service could emerge from a context which bore not a trace of evangelicalism and which, far from stressing the insignificance of the individual, raised him to the towering pinnacle of mastery of his own fate through mastery of the laws of the universe'.[113] Similarly, it was possible for a religiously inspired commitment to Anti-Slavery to emanate from other than evangelical sources.

Unitarians of the later eighteenth century were attracted towards Anti-Slavery primarily because they conceived of abolition as an extension of that religious liberty to which they themselves aspired and of which they were still partially deprived. Popular abolitionism began to develop at precisely the same time as the revival of the campaign by Protestant Dissenters for the repeal of the Test and Corporation Acts. In this campaign many rational dissenters were involved and Unitarians provided much of the intellectual leadership. Those connected with the College were warm and active supporters of repeal. Over this issue, however, they did not enjoy that co-operation with evangelicals, or indeed with many other of their fellow-citizens, which they experienced in the abolitionist movement. This was hardly surprising. For in the repeal campaign rational dissenters applied arguments which were fundamentally different from those employed by evangelical theology against the Slave Trade. Local as well as national evidence indicates that arguments for repeal were decidedly secular and political, embracing a 'rights of man' philosophy. As in the agitation against the Slave Trade, Manchester was an important centre of dissenting pressure for repeal of the Test laws, but without the broad consensus achieved by abolitionism. Instead of the widely based abolition committee, with its Anglican and Tory members, the dissenters could muster only a relatively narrow and increasingly isolated group. Only a few leading abolitionists in Manchester espoused repeal, and they tended to be prominent radicals like Thomas Walker and Thomas Cooper, or dissenters connected with Manchester College. Thomas Percival was as early a local champion of repeal as he was of abolition and his correspondence includes pro-repeal sentiments as early as 1787, the year of the first unsuccessful parliamentary repeal motion.[114] Barnes became chairman of the 'Meeting of ministers in Cheshire and Lancashire' in the dissenters' national organization.[115] In May 1789, he presided over a pro-repeal meeting at the 'Dissenters' rooms', Cheapside, Manchester, which passed a series of resolutions including the following:

> That we shall ever consider the Repeal of Penal Laws respecting Religion as an ABSOLUTE RIGHT: and as a matter of Grace and Favour—only to the Reputation of our Country.[116]

In the national context George Walker was an even better known repealer than Barnes. He was not only chairman of the 'associated dissenters' of nine Midland counties but also author of the highly praised *Dissenters' Plea*. After the narrow defeat of the second repeal motion in the House of Commons in May 1789, Walker was responsible for the preparation of resolutions from his own counties which indicated the extensive nature of religious reform envisaged by his branch of opinion:

> That though the particular grievance of the Corporation and Test Acts has been the means of convening us, as part of the body of dissenters, we think it our duty, to use our utmost endeavours to procure the repeal of all penal statutes in matters of religion, as this is clearly comprehended within our just rights; and are persuaded, that in this we meditate nothing new, as religious liberty ever will and must be defective, while one such penal law is suffered to exist.[117]

There could be no doubt as to what was meant by 'all penal statutes in matters of religion': laws against Unitarians were the target and, indeed, remained in force until 1813. But these were unpopular causes, especially after the French Revolution and injudicious observations from Priestley. The crushing defeat of the third repeal motion in March 1790 brought the repeal campaign in Manchester and elsewhere to a halt and exposed its supporters to counter-attack.

In such circumstances the legal disabilities of dissenters in general and Unitarians in particular encouraged them to identify with those causes which appeared to promote the moral, constitutional and political liberty of the individual. This, however, proved highly divisive in a political nation suspicious of constitutional change and regaled with accounts of the horror of the practical application of such notions across the Channel. Although there were exceptions, evangelical supporters of abolition did not on the whole seek to democratize the political system and tended to be hostile, or at least lukewarm, towards repeal. Wilberforce himself strongly opposed repeal in Parliament and engaged in acrimonious correspondence with dissenting ministers (including William Wood) in the West Riding of Yorkshire who had pressed him to give it his support.[118] Evangelicals were even more hostile to the Unitarian petition of 1792; they loathed Unitarian theology and did not accept rational dissenting arguments for toleration. Wilberforce disliked the Unitarian petition and believed that links with such radical causes would damage the prospects of abolitionism.[119] But rational dissenting and Unitarian supporters of abolition did seek to democratize the political system, in however limited a way, and saw abolition as a means to this end. To them Anti-Slavery was one of a series of necessary political and constitutional reforms, of which reform of the system of parliamentary representation had the highest priority.

In Manchester it was the Unitarian petition which emphasized the divisive nature of the dissenters' aspirations. Writing of the petition Theophilus Lindsey noted:

> I was sorry to hear Dr. Priestley say, that whilst Dr. Barnes of Manchester was very hearty for the thing, Mr. Hawkes declined to sign it: so much it is said had he been intimidated since the outrages at Birmingham.[120]

Hawkes had good reason to feel 'intimidated'. Unitarians were unpopular nationally and in Manchester in and before 1792. In Manchester a 'Church and King' Club became increasingly aggressive towards dissenters who engaged in politics and its broadsides were encouraged by several local newspapers.[121] At the very time when abolition was uniting these groups behind a petition which carried 20,000 signatures, Unitarians in Manchester were the victims of violent attack. On 4 June 1792 a mob celebrating the birthday of King George III stormed Mosley Street Chapel and battered its doors with trees uprooted from St. Ann's Square.[122] There were also attacks upon members of Dob Lane Chapel as well as the more spectacular Walker riots.[123]. Loyalism, both magisterial and popular, was especially strong in Manchester during the early 1790s and Unitarians were frequently singled out as its targets.[124] If even so broadly based a cause as abolitionism was cautious about public campaigning after 1792–3, this was much more true of dissenting aspirations for civil liberties. There is no doubt but that Manchester College kept a low political profile after the early 1790s. But the sense of persecution only encouraged Unitarians to identify more closely with groups which, like them, lacked full constitutional liberty. Abolition was a source of encouragement to them in their own struggles, both before and after 1807. The ultimate success of abolitionism justified their own continued endeavours and, in the words of a correspondent of the *Monthly Repository*, provided 'eternal evidence of the value of small beginnings and of many and repeated exertions, to work good impressions upon the minds of even an enlightened society'.[125]

Evangelicals tended to conceive of 'liberty' in highly personal terms, involving a direct, immediate relationship between the individual and God, *via* repentance and the atoning sacrifice of Christ. Rational dissent saw 'liberty' in much more secular terms, based on political and constitutional concepts. For of all the religious groups and traditions which contributed to British abolitionism, Unitarians alone did not enjoy full legal toleration of their own worship.[126] Matters of legal status were, accordingly, of considerable importance to them and led them to look in politics towards those who might remedy their legal and constitutional grievances. Such a concern with constitutional reform effectively excludes Manchester College and its Unitarian background from that type of motivation towards abolitionism which may be termed evangelical and places it firmly within the Whig category of attitudes to abolition, although without always carrying it quite into the radical camp. And indeed there is overwhelming evidence to show that, in its attitudes and connections, Manchester College between 1786 and 1833 evinced a political ethos which was unmistakably Foxite Whig.

The Whiggish inclinations of the Warrington tutors in the age of the American Revolution have been recognized by Dr. McLachlan.[127] A Whiggish advocacy of significant, albeit cautious, measures of constitutional reform within the framework of the existing social order was transmitted *via* Percival, Barnes and Walker to Manchester College, York.

The principal tutors of the York period—Wellbeloved, Kenrick, Turner—as well as most of their associates,[128] were Whigs to a man. The re-emergence of sharpened party divisions in British parliamentary and electoral politics in the early nineteenth century facilitates their identification as such. Wellbeloved belonged to the Whig Club in York, earned the approbation of Henry Brougham with his controversial writings and enthusiastically projected a visit to Paris on the conclusion of peace with France in 1801.[129] John Kenrick was steeped in Whig nostrums from youth: he sympathised with continental liberalism since his studies in Germany in 1819–20 and admired Hallam's constitutional history.[130] It is accordingly not surprising to find him an ardent champion of the legislative reforms of the Whig ministry of the early 1830s, especially when several of his friends notably George William Wood, had secured election to the House of Commons as supporters of that ministry. His hopes of reform included 'some modification in the national church . . . and also in the present system of the Universities.'[131] He also applauded the Great Reform Bill, but in a manner which marks him out clearly as a Whig rather than a radical: 'I am for the ballot in towns where bribery cannot otherwise be prevented', he wrote in 1830, 'but against it in counties because I do not wish to see the influence of the aristocracy there annihilated'.[132] The same ethos is evident in the syllabus, with its emphasis on science, political economy and constitutional history as well as the usual theological subjects. The *Annual Report* of 1834 claimed that the 'course of modern history' at the College 'shows by an instructive contrast the opposite influence and tendency of constitutional and arbitrary monarchy,' and students were clearly brought into close contact with Whiggish libertarian values.[133] This ethos is equally clear in the commitment to Whig candidates in successive parliamentary elections in the City of York and County of Yorkshire, from 1807, when students canvassed energetically for Lord Milton, to the early 1830s.[134]

The Whiggery of Manchester College, however, was of a moderate kind which accepted the leadership in politics of the aristocratic grandees of the party. Here indeed the connection went back many years: Lord George Cavendish, for instance, had donated ten guineas to the College funds as early as 1788.[135] The political figure most idolized by those connected with the College in the first fifty years of its history was undoubtedly Charles James Fox—Whig, abolitionist and, assuredly, not evangelical. Wellbeloved and William Wood held Fox in the highest esteem while George William Wood, College Treasurer from 1808–43, and M.P. successively for South Lancashire and Kendal, was described as 'a Whig of the School of Charles James Fox' who possessed 'what many deemed an undue confidence in the leaders of the great Whig aristocracy, as the hereditary conservators and constitutional champions of English freedom'.[136] The *Monthly Repository*, which belonged to precisely the same type of dissent as the College and which publicised its activities, gave lengthy and favourable coverage to the collected edition of Fox's

*Speeches* in 1815, while Fox's closest dissenting friend and fellow-Whig, Samuel Heywood, subscribed to the College from 1809.[137]

Nor do the Whig connections end here. The Milanese languages tutor Chevalier Pecchio was precisely the sort of liberal foreign exile whom early nineteenth century English Whigs admired. Having held 'an administrative office in the department of finance in the abortive Kingdom of Italy from 1810 to 1814' he became 'a staunch advocate of the constitutional cause in his native land and ultimately an exile for freedom'.[138] He arrived in England in 1821 and was lionized almost as General Paoli had been fifty years earlier. His tutorship at the College lasted for only two years but that was sufficient for him to comprehend and to align himself with what he conceived to be the Unitarian ideal in politics: as stated by him it has the ring of impeccable Whig sentiments.[139] At the same time the College attracted the support of James Losh, one of the leading Whigs in the north-east and friend of Grey and Brougham. A subscriber from 1815 and a member of William Turner's congregation in Newcastle, Losh warmly admired the work of the College and drew it to the attention of his Whig friends.[140] Undoubtedly the preaching at Turner's chapel by College students and alumni helped its reputation in his eyes: on 16 August 1812, for instance, he was impressed by a sermon of John Kenrick.[141] Losh was also a prominent lawyer on the northern circuit and deeply involved in politics. He campaigned actively against Slavery in the 1820s, chairing several Anti-Slavery meetings in Newcastle. But his other political aims, alongside Anti-Slavery, were repeal of the Test and Corporation Acts and parliamentary reform, an association of issues far more likely to be made by a rational dissenter than by an evangelical.[142] In many ways Losh was representative of the political attitudes to be found among those who succoured Manchester College and his career reveals much about the non-evangelical nature of its political priorities.

In recognizing the power of religious influences which lay behind Anti-Slavery one also accepts that these influences were many and varied. In its crusade against Slavery, in other words, evangelicalism had some rather unlikely allies. For all the temporary odium incurred by rational dissent in the 1790s, in the longer term, the involvement of Manchester College in British abolitionism and, subsequently, endeavours for slave emancipation, underlines (albiet in a small way) the validity of recent claims as to the 'unusually wide constituency' of British abolitionism.[143] The best conclusion might be that in the history of the Anti-Slavery movement Manchester College was as significant for what it was as for what it did, since it helps to illustrate the variety and breadth of Anti-Slavery support and, hence, perhaps its ultimate success.

## III

Progress towards the abolition of the Slave Trade and its accomplishment in 1806–7, amounted to an untypically favourable item of political news for Unitarians at the turn of the century. Historians of Unitarianism speak with one voice of a sense of persecution, weakness and discouragement in the last decade of the eighteenth century and the first decade of the nineteenth.[144] This assessment is confirmed by a great deal of contemporary evidence and such attitudes are fully reflected among those connected with Manchester College. The French revolutionary years, the exile of Priestley, the revival of aggressive high churchmanship and the painful memories of mob hostility all helped to give Unitarians—at least temporarily—a feeling of isolation. A month after Waterloo, for example, J. T. Bache wrote from Shropshire:

> Bridgnorth containing more than 6000 inhabitants does not afford me an unitarian Frd. By the religious the cause of Unitarianism is dreaded as a dangerous heresy[145] & by the irreligious not known.

Twenty-one years later the *Annual Report* of the College, in a particularly self-pitying mood, referred to 'the almost unprecedented situation in which our body of Dissenters is now placed, hemmed in as it were between an exclusive Establishment on one hand, and the still bitterer and more intolerant spirit of persecuting sectaries on the other'.[146] In the light of testimony of this kind it is hardly surprising that a recent student of the subject observed that 'Unitarians were a tiny minority in a deeply hostile culture'.[147] Even after the Trinity Act of 1813 had removed the stigma of illegality from their worship and the repeal of the Test and Corporation Acts in 1828 had breached the Anglican constitution, the isolation of Unitarians was far from over. The Unitarian delegates seceded both from the Body of Protestant Dissenting Ministers and from the lay Protestant Dissenting Deputies in the 1830s; there were challenges to their use of the name 'Presbyterian' and they faced a serious threat to their church property as a result of the Lady Hewley Case.[148] Their numbers, moreover, remained small, even in the rapidly expanding population of early nineteenth century England. Between 1800 and 1851 there were only slightly more than two hundred avowedly Unitarian congregations in England and Wales, while the religious census of 1851 recorded no more than 28,483 attenders at Unitarian morning worship on 30 March of that year.[149] This relative paucity of numbers carries further implications for the main themes of this essay. The number of pupils educated at Manchester College between 1786 and 1840 was slightly in excess of 370 (some two-thirds of them lay students), and they were not, of course, all drawn from Unitarian backgrounds.[150] Compared, moreover, with the enormous volume of petitions, with thousands of signatures against Slavery from other Protestant denominations in 1833, the Unitarian petitions were few in number.[151]

But two significant qualifications to this portrayal of gloom are necessary. Firstly, the counting of heads alone would be a crude and inaccurate method of measuring the Unitarian presence in contemporary British politics and society. Unitarian influence was out of all proportion to numerical strength. If one considers financial wealth, the solid basis of mercantile and professional families, parliamentary and other political contacts and intellectual prowess, a whole range of real and potential assets becomes apparent. Manchester College was without doubt one of those assets and it helped to enhance, rather than retard, the ability of Unitarians to communicate effectively with their fellow-ci''zens. Secondly, in the age of slave emancipation, one can begin to detect a greater measure of self-confidence among Unitarians than before. In 1834 John Kenrick, recalling the leadership of William Smith M.P. over the previous generation, commented:

> I know the unpopularity of Unitarianism—in name—it is nothing more—but no greater odium attaches to it now than in the days when W. Smith was its champion and surely it can now make itself formidable, whereas then it was utterly powerless.[152]

In the longer term, of course, there was to be material justification for such confidence, as the Dissenters' Chapels Act secured the church property of Unitarians, as further endowments were obtained and as the sense of insecurity faded in the mid-Victorian period. But with its continued interest in Anti-Slavery, Unitarianism possessed a further asset and one which helped it to harmonise with society as a whole. For this, Manchester College deserves some of the credit. For the commitment to Anti-Slavery on the part of those connected with the College was a continuing one and it was strongly sustained during and indeed beyond the first forty years of the nineteenth century. Anti-Slavery attitudes during the College's York period are evident among pupils, tutors, parents and subscribers. Denunciations of slavery featured among the orations delivered by students at the annual College examinations which were held in June: Mark Philips, the future M.P. for Manchester, for instance, delivered an oration upon this subject in June 1818.[153] John Kenrick undoubtedly spoke for all the tutors when he expressed the hope that the slave emancipation bill of 1833 would 'get through with much less virulence of opposition than at first seemed likely'.[154] His colleague William Hincks, himself a former divinity student at the College, subsequently became editor of *The Inquirer* and in the 1840s turned that organ into a propaganda vehicle for the radical, Garrisonian brand of abolitionism which helped to draw the attention of the British public to the persistence of American slavery.[155]

Early in the York period William Smith M.P., a leading parliamentary advocate of dissenting liberties and of Anti-Slavery, sent his third son Samuel to the College as a lay student.[156] This combination of sympathy with Unitarianism and support for Anti-Slavery runs through the list of subscribers to the College in the early nineteenth century. They include several eminent members of the Liverpool Anti-Slavery group, including William Roscoe, William Rathbone, John Cropper, William Shepherd and several members of the Yates family.[157] It was this group, and in particular Cropper's father James, who led the campaign for the ending of the privileged entry of West Indian sugar to the British market and helped to revive the movement for the final assault on the institution of slavery itself in the early 1820s.[158] The Anti-Slavery interest in Bristol was similarly well represented, with John Estlin, Rev. John Rowe and Lant Carpenter all listed as subscribers in 1817.[159] The latter indeed was on more than one occasion offered a post at the College.[160] The earlier Wedgwood connection continued with 'Miss Wedgwood' of Parkfield, near Stone, Staffordshire, a subscriber from 1807.[161] As in the first Manchester period the College drew much of its support from provincial dissenting intellectual elites in the large cities of the north and midlands: Manchester, Liverpool, Nottingham, Leeds and Newcastle upon Tyne provided the largest groups of subscribers. These, not surprisingly, were among the areas which had succoured the College in its earliest years, where dissent in general was strong and where Anti-Slavery received particularly powerful support with the revival of the petitioning campaign after 1822.

Anti-Slavery attitudes, moreover, are evident among those pupils and supporters who entered Parliament in this period. One such M.P., John Ashton Yates, a Commerce student in 1795–7, friend of Dalton and M.P. for Carlow between 1837 and 1841, produced a tract denouncing colonial slavery in 1824.[162] At the time of the emancipation bill of 1833 there were six sitting M.P.s directly connected with Manchester College: two were former pupils, Mark Philips (Manchester) and Edward Strutt (Derby), while four were annual subscribers, Rawdon Briggs junior (Halifax), G. W. Wood (South Lancashire), Richard Potter (Wigan) and Daniel Gaskell (Wakefield).[163] In the House of Commons these members voted consistently with the 'abolitionist opposition', which strongly favoured emancipation but thought the terms too generous to the West Indian planters and hence voted against the clauses setting out details of the compensation scheme and the period of apprenticeship. On 11 June 1833, for instance, Richard Potter made a speech criticizing the proposed £20 million compensation as too high, and he and Gaskell voted for an unsuccessful amendment to substitute £15 million instead.[164] On 24 July, Briggs, Gaskell and Philips joined other critics of the bill, led by T. F. Buxton, in a vote against proceeding to the committee stage on the grounds that the bill did not go far enough.[165] Six days later, in committee, Gaskell, Briggs, Philips and Strutt all voted for Buxton's unsuccessful amendment to withhold half of the compensation until the expiry of the period of apprenticeship.[166] Their purpose was not to frustrate the principle of emancipation, which they strongly supported, but to amend the bill in such a way as to bring an earlier, and less qualified, liberation to the slaves. As a recent study has shown, M.P.s who voted for this 'abolitionist opposition' tended to represent large, often newly-enfranchised, English urban constituencies with a high proportion of dissenting voters.[167]

These M.P.s in their parliamentary voting help to illustrate a wider theme. Anti-Slavery attracted Unitarians towards the mainstream of British political and social thought, instead of separating them from it.

However different their motives, Unitarians could co-operate with other groups in this, as in few other issues. Hence Priestley had been able to join ministers from other churches in Birmingham in 1788 in devoting a particular Sunday to preaching against the Slave Trade.[168] In the same spirit, the Unitarian William Smith M.P. was able to work closely with the evangelicals of the Clapham Sect in the Anti-Slavery cause.[169] It was in such a joint enterprise that Manchester College had participated between 1787–92 when it had been at the centre of the earliest popular abolitionist movement. As Samuel Bradburn, a local Methodist preacher, noted at the time:

> In Manchester we signed the [abolitionist] petition in common with our neighbours, deeming it a less pompous way, than sending a distinct petition of our own.[170]

Collaboration of this kind between groups from opposite ends of the religious spectrum which otherwise distrusted each other was summed up by the Unitarian Samuel Kenrick in 1792 when he wrote 'The Methodists are the most violent anti-revolutionists we have, & yet we all join for the abolition of the Slave Trade'.[171]

It was highly unusual in Britain between 1780 and 1830 to find Unitarians involved in other than minority and unpopular causes. The same was true of those academies where their doctrines received sympathy. Warrington students irritated the local citizens by supporting the American colonists; Hackney brought disrepute upon itself by excessive enthusiasm for the French Revolution. Manchester College, on the other hand, in espousing Anti-Slavery, touched upon the great exception. For here was an issue which was not unpopular and which had a unifying rather than a divisive effect upon British society. Of course, by the middle, and even more by the later, nineteenth century, other issues helped Unitarians to emerge from their 'isolation'; free trade, political economy and temperance were among them.[172] But this was a much later development. Abolitionism was virtually the only such issue in the later eighteenth century, when Manchester College was founded, and during the French revolutionary period. Moreover it was an issue central to the Unitarian perception of its own role in society and its unsatisfactory legal status. As late as the 1840s a Unitarian minister could identify his religious convictions with hostility to American slavery:

> Until there was more education, we, amongst others, should not enjoy the full benefit of toleration and Christian charity: we were treated as a sort of theological negro—our humanity was just acknowledged, and no more; but our Christianity was denied. He would not be a slave in England any more than in America.[173]

Anti-Slavery on the part of Unitarians may indeed be regarded as an understandable attitude for those with such a strong sense of persecution. It is also possible that some, perhaps consciously, had a tactical purpose in hoping to improve their 'heretical' and 'unchristian' image by participating in a cause which drew so many Christians together.[174] But at all events the favourable effects were unmistakable. They can be seen in the way in which Unitarians were accepted in Anti-Slavery circles when they were shunned elsewhere. There are signs that their display of Anti-Slavery attitudes did indeed help to 'soften prejudices', as Theophilus Lindsey had hoped as early as 1788.[175] Soon after his arrival in England, Guiseppe Pecchio, a future tutor at Manchester College, had his anxieties about Unitarians eased when he heard a Unitarian minister preach on the abolition of slavery:

> He laid politics aside and treated his subject exclusively in a religious point of view . . . Are these, then, said I to myself, those Unitarians who, because they do not believe in the divine nature of Jesus, although they believe in his divine mission, are by some treated as atheists, by others considered as Mahometans? So indeed it is: the greater part of the Trinitarians,[176] of whatever sect, regard them as creatures to be avoided.

It was Anti-Slavery, above all, which launched Unitarians upon the escape-route from 'cultural isolation' and allowed them to participate in what was becoming almost a national consensus. Professor David B. Davis has observed that the triumph of Anti-Slavery also represented the triumph of those liberal, humanitarian and above all middle class values which were to influence strongly, and some would say to dominate, British political and social thought in the nineteenth century. 'Abolitionists,' writes Professor Davies, 'succeeded in making a sincere humanitarianism an integral part of class ideology, and thus of British culture . . . such philanthropic causes as prison reform and anti-slavery provided a meeting ground for Utilitarians and Christian "Saints" '.[177] Unitarianism, too, was present on this 'meeting ground', both nationally and in the formation of what has been termed the 'liberal hegemony' in mid-nineteenth century Manchester politics.[178]

If indeed Unitarianism may be said to have emerged from 'isolation' in and after the first third of the nineteenth century, then its commitment to abolitionism from the 1780s onwards must be regarded as a vital factor in that process. Support for abolitionism, and, after 1807, for ending Slavery itself, was given its crucial intellectual and practical impetus by the academies, whose role was naturally vital in a sect so dominated by intellect. In turning out a highly educated ministry and lay elite which propagated Anti-Slavery attitudes, academies played a much greater part in the Unitarian, than in the Quaker or evangelical, contribution to Anti-Slavery. Of the academies concerned, Manchester College was not only in the forefront but at times almost alone. It might be suggested, therefore, that in its support for this cause Manchester College rendered an important service to Unitarianism as well as to Anti-Slavery.

## NOTES

1. I wish to thank Manchester College, Oxford, for providing me with access to its splendid archives, and with generous hospitality, in the course of my research

for this paper; I am particularly indebted to the Principal, the Rev. Bruce Findlow, and the Librarian & History Tutor, Mrs. Barbara Smith. I am grateful to Mr. F. C. Pipe-Wolferstan, of Statfold Hall, Staffordshire, for permission to make use of the diary of Samuel Pipe-Wolferstan, and to the Librarian and Trustees of Dr. Williams's Library, London, and the John Rylands University Library of Manchester for permission to quote from manuscripts in their possession. Professor Seymour Drescher, Dr. John Walsh and Mr. David Wykes kindly read a draft of this essay and made many helpful suggestions.

Two expressions which are used frequently in the essay require further definition. Firstly, I have used the term 'Manchester College' to cover the whole of its history, although between 1786 and 1803 it was usually known as 'the Manchester Academy' or 'The New College at Manchester', while between 1803 and 1840 the regular appellation was 'Manchester College, removed to York'. A convenient summary of the various changes of name may be found in V. D. Davis, *A History of Manchester College from its Foundation in Manchester to its Establishment in Oxford* (London 1932) p. 53 note 1. Secondly, 'Anti-Slavery' is used here as an 'umbrella' term to denote the campaign for the abolition of the Slave Trade before 1807 and the movement for slave emancipation thereafter.

2. G. M. Ditchfield, 'The Early History of Manchester College', *Transactions of the Historic Society of Lancashire and Cheshire*, vol. 123 (1972) pp. 81–104.

3. *The Works, Literary, Moral and Medical of Thomas Percival*. (4 vols, London 1807), I, p. lxxxi; H. McLachlan, *Warrington Academy. Its History and Influence* (Manchester 1943) pp. 136–7. In 1786 benefactions of £801 and annual subscriptions of £243.12s. were raised; Davis, p. 59 n.1.

4. 'Minutes of the Proceedings of the Committee of the Manchester Academy', Vol. I, 1786–1810 (hereafter cited as 'Minutes') p. 71; Manchester College, Oxford. (M.C.O.)

5. On 29 February 1792, for instance, the Committee authorized the expenditure of a sum not exceeding £100 for purchase of a 'Philosophical Apparatus'; *ibid*, p. 44.

6. Printed sheet headed 'Cash Account of the New College, Manchester, from the 22nd February 1799 to the 22nd February 1800'; M.C.O.

7. G. D. H. Cole, *The Life of Robert Owen* (London, 3rd edition 1965) pp. 78–9.

8. Davis, *Manchester College*, p. 71. See the contribution to this volume of David Wykes, 'Sons and Subscribers: Lay Supporters and the College', *passim*.

9. 'Minutes', p. 45. The land was valued at £400 in the accounts of 1799–1800.

10. Davis, pp. 62, 101.

11. Ditchfield, 'Manchester College', p. 97.

12. John Williams, *Memoirs of the late Reverend Thomas Belsham*, (London 1833) pp. 479–80.

13. The printed accounts of 1799–1800 reveal four grants from the Presbyterian Fund, two from the Coward Trust and one from Lady Hewley's Fund.

14. Wellbeloved to the Rev. William Wood, 14 January 1798; M.C.O.

15. Loyd married Sarah Jones, only daughter of John Jones, banker, of Manchester, and sister of Samuel and William Jones. See R. C. Michie, 'Income, Expenditure and Investment of a Victorian Millionaire: Lord Overstone, 1823–83', *Bulletin of the Institute of Historical Research*, Vol. LXVIII (1985), pp. 59–77; Leo H. Grindon, *Manchester Banks and Bankers: Historical, Biographical and Anecdotal* (Manchester 1877) pp. 56–63; obituary of Loyd in *Christian Reformer*, New Series, Vol. XIV (1858), pp. 414–22 and 602–7. As late as 1846 Loyd donated £20 towards new school buildings at Dob Lane Chapel; Alexander Gordon, *Historical Account of Dob Lane Chapel, Failsworth, and its Schools* (Manchester 1904) p. 46. One must

record, however, that his own son, Samuel Jones Loyd, the future Baron Overstone, was educated at Eton and Cambridge.

16. Wellbeloved to Wood, 14 January 1798. George Walker, too, complained in 1801 of tardiness in raising funds for this purpose; Ditchfield, 'Manchester College' p. 87.

17. *Manchester New College Annual Reports, 1817–1841* (bound volume, M.C.O.); *Report*, 1817 p. 7.

18. The *Reports* of 1817 to 1820 show that, although fluctuating slightly, annual subscription income averaged just over £700 in these years. This takes no account of other benefactions.

19. See, for instance, the obituary of Barnes in *Gentleman's Magazine*, Vol. 80 pt.ii (1810) pp. 105–8. It is a matter for considerable regret that his papers were evidently destroyed at his death; McLachlan, *Warrington Academy*, p. 136.

20. Two tutors who created successful lay careers were the banker Lewis Loyd, and William Stevenson, who moved to London and became Keeper of the Records of the Treasury.

21. 'Minutes', pp. 38, 46.

22. *Ibid*, p. 106. Although Paul Morgan in *Oxford Libraries Outside the Bodleian. A Guide* (Second Edition, Oxford 1980) p. 73, correctly notes that a salary for a librarian (of two guineas per annum) appears in the accounts published in the first printed reports of the College in 1816–17, the post in fact existed, and was paid for, at a much earlier stage.

23. John Seed, 'Manchester College, York: An Early Nineteenth Century Dissenting Academy', *Journal of Educational Administration and Research*, Vol. XIV (1982) pp. 9–17.

24. College advertisement in *St. James's Chronicle*, 14–17 June 1788; A. Clow, 'The Industrial Revolution and John Dalton' in D. S. L. Cardwell (ed), *John Dalton and the Progress of Science* (Manchester 1968), p. 131. When Samuel Pipe-Wolferstan visited the College in 1801 he attended a scientific lecture: Ditchfield, 'Manchester College', pp. 95–6.

25. J. W. Ashley Smith, *The Birth of Modern Education* (London 1954) p. 170; H. McLachlan, *English Education under the Test Acts; being the History of the Nonconformist Academies, 1662–1820* (Publications of the University of Manchester no. ccxiii; Historical series no. lix, 1931) p. 259.

26. *Manchester Mercury*, 16 December 1788; Ditchfield, 'Manchester College', p. 97.

27. Seed, 'Manchester College, York', p. 13.

28. *Report 1827* p. 4. Chevalier Pecchio served as languages tutor from 1826 to 1828. His manuscript report on attendance at French, Italian and Spanish classes in 1827–8 can be found in 'Manchester College Letterbook', pp. 42–3. M.C.O. It is odd that Pecchio is mentioned neither by Davis nor Seed.

29. The five were William Turner, Thomas Belsham, Charles Wellbeloved, Timothy Kenrick and Joseph Bretland. Not all of their refusals were solely determined by the state of the College; Belsham, for instance, feared that his Socinian theology would be unacceptable to the Lancashire Arians and Turner was reluctant to leave the pastoral and intellectual scene which he was helping to create in Newcastle; Alexander Gordon, *Addresses Biographical and Historical* (London 1922), p. 294; Derek Orange, 'Rational Dissent and provincial Science: William Turner and the Newcastle Literary and Philosophical Society', in Ian Inkster and Jack Morrell (eds), *Metropolis and Province, Science in British Culture, 1780–1850* (London, 1983), p. 223.

30. Ditchfield, 'Manchester College', pp. 86–90. There is an account of Walker in

these years in Lucy Aikin, *Memoir of John Aikin, M.D.* (2 vols. London 1823), I, 411–12.

31. Seed, 'Manchester College, York', p. 10.

32. Obituary of Dalton by William Johns, *Christian Reformer*, N.S., Vol. XI (1944) pp. 1001–4. The 'Minutes' record that in March and April 1800, Mr. Savery was expelled and Mr. Bull suspended (though subsequently reprieved) as a result of complaints by Johns; 'Minutes', pp. 124, 126–7. *The Roll of Students entered at the Manchester Academy* (Manchester 1868; pages un-numbered) mentions Bull and Savery as pupils in this period and notes that they feature in the 'Minutes' although tactfully refraining from explaining why. Bull subsequently adopted the name Bristowe and became dissenting minister at Mansfield; Gordon, *Dob Lane Chapel*, p. 50.

33. Ditchfield, 'Manchester College', pp. 97–8.

34. Barnes, *Discourse* . . . p. 36. However a former pupil of the College, Joseph Astley, gave different, and less damaging, reasons for the resignation of Barnes, in a letter to Wellbeloved, 16 December 1797: envelope marked 'Letters re. M.N.C. York, etc, early 19th C.' M.C.O.

35. Astley to Wellbeloved, 16 Dec. 1797: Wellbeloved to William Wood, 14 Jan. 1798; M.C.O.

36. Davis, p. 59; Seed, 'Manchester College, York', pp. 13–14.

37. Quoted in McLachlan, *Warrington Academy*, p. 16.

38. *Monthly Magazine*, Vol. IV (1797) p. 105.

39. Davis, p. 54.

40. McLachlan, *Warrington Academy*, p. 19. Priestley, Wakefield, Walker and Enfield are four of the best known tutors of Warrington who subsequently became involved in abolitionist activity.

41. See in particular her 'Epistle to William Wilberforce, Esq., on the Rejection of the Bill for abolishing the Slave Trade, 1791' and her letter to her brother Dr. John Aikin, February 1788; A. L. Barbauld, *Works* (2 vols. 1825), I, pp. 173–9. II, p. 156; R. Porter, *English Society in the Eighteenth Century* (London 1982), p. 196. Mrs. Barbauld remained a subscriber to the College in the early nineteenth century, long after she had ceased to reside near Manchester. Her brother John Aikin, himself a former Warrington tutor, also subscribed to Manchester College in the York period.

42. Roger Anstey, *The Atlantic Slave Trade and British Abolition, 1760–1810*, (London 1975) p. 283.

43. Davis, pp. 61–2.

44. The helpful list of trustees of Cross Street Chapel in Sir Thomas Baker, *Memorials of a Dissenting Chapel* (London and Manchester 1884) pp. 69–135, has been used for purposes of identification. Several other signatories of 7 February 1786 later became trustees of the chapel.

45. Wellbeloved to Wood, 14 Jan. 1798.

46. The entire connection is discussed in Lester Burney, *Cross Street Chapel, Manchester, and its College* (Manchester 1983).

47. V. A. C. Gatrell, 'Incorporation and the pursuit of liberal hegemony in Manchester 1790–1839', in Derek Fraser (ed), *Municipal Reform and the Industrial City* (Leicester 1982), p. 24.

48. Gatrell, p. 28.

49. Thomas Percival, 'Biographical Memoirs of Thomas Butterworth Bayley Esq.' in Percival, *Works* (4 vols, London 1807) II, pp. 289–305 and McLachlan, 'Cross Street Chapel in the Life of Manchester' in *Essays and Addresses* (Manchester

1950) p. 104, both recognize Bayley's prominent role among the early Manchester abolitionists.

50. Some authorities have regarded Cross Street and Mosley Street Chapel as rivals. Priestley referred to Barnes's jealousy of 'Mr. Hawkes's Unitarian chapel' in a letter to Theophilus Lindsey on 8 October 1789; Priestley, *Works,* I part ii, p. 35: see also John Seed, 'Unitarianism, political economy and the antinomies of liberal culture in Manchester, 1830–50' *Social History*, vol 7 (1982), p. 4. A warning against regarding Mosley Street as a secession from Cross Street because the latter was insufficiently Unitarian, is provided, however, in F. H. Amphlett Micklewright, 'Some Prolegomena to the History of Protestant Dissent in England', *Notes and Queries*, Vol 183 (Sept. 1944), pp. 117–18. Moreover, there was frequent intermarriage between members of the two chapels. One of the earliest patrons of Mosley Street chapel was William Turner, who later became Visitor of Manchester College; cf. Alexander Gordon, *Historical Account of Dob Lane Chapel, Failsworth, and its Schools* (Manchester 1904) p. 42.

51. Gordon, *Dob Lane Chapel*, pp. 44–52.

52. Arnold Thackray, *John Dalton, Critical Assessments of his Life and Science* (Cambridge, Mass. 1972), p. 49.

53. *Ibid.*

54. Cole, *Robert Owen*, p. 78.

55. According to Owen it was Barnes rather than Dalton who became anxious about the nature of these discussions: John Butt (ed) *The Life of Robert Owen, written by himself* (London 1971), pp. 36–38.

56. The way in which Dalton features in the 'Minutes' provides no evidence to justify the strictures of Thackray, *John Dalton*, pp. 49, 176.

57. *Christian Reformer*, N.S. vol xi (1844) p. 1002.

58. *Report*, 1820, p. 4.

59. Derek Orange, 'Rational Dissent and provincial Science: William Turner and the Newcastle Literary and Philosophical Society', in Ian Inkster and Jack Morell (eds.), *Metropolis and Province. Science in British Culture, 1780–1850* (London 1983) p. 221.

60. As a recent historian of the growth of popular anti-slavery has observed, 'Where a Literary and Philosophical Society existed it was commonly strongly represented in the ranks of local abolitionists'; Anstey, *Atlantic Slave Trade*, p. 263. The role of William Turner in this process is well illustrated in Helen M. Nicholson, 'A Brief Account of the Life and Ministry of William Turner of Newcastle upon Tyne, 1761–1859', *Transactions of the Unitarian Historical Society*, Vol. XVIII (April 1983) pp. 22–23, especially p. 27.

61. *Memoirs of the Life of Gilbert Wakefield* (2 vols, London 1804) I p. 269. Wakefield was a former tutor of Warrington Academy.

62. E. M. Hunt, 'The Anti-Slave Trade Agitation in Manchester', *Transactions of the Lancashire and Cheshire Antiquarian Society*, Vol 79 (1977) p. 71 note 24; Gatrell p. 33.

63. A further indication of this interconnection can be seen in the fact that of forty-three members of the Literary and Philosophical Society in 1785, fifteen were trustees or ministers of Cross Street Chapel; Gatrell, pp. 28–9.

64. Anstey, *Atlantic Slave Trade*, ch. 10.

65. 'Memoirs' by Edward Percival in Thomas Percival, *Works*, I, lxxxiv–lxxxv. Further accounts of Thomas Percival's abolitionist activity may be found in Davis, *Manchester College*, pp. 55–6 and Hunt, pp. 50, 55, 58.

66. See the correspondence of Percival printed in *Works*, I, clii–clxii. Like several

prominent abolitionists, including Wilberforce, Percival hoped that the advancement of Necker to the office of director-general of finance in 1788 would promote Anglo-French agreement on abolition.

67. Edward Royle and James Walvin, *English Radicals and Reformers 1760–1848* (Brighton, 1982). Thomas Walker was not directly connected with the College but was a member of the Manchester Literary and Philosophical Society. The yarn merchant Titus Hibbert, subscriber to the College and member of Cross Street Chapel, recorded on 26 Oct. 1787, 'Pd. Mr Delegate Walker & Mr Geo. Barton to defray the charges of an Application to Parliament to abolish the Slave Trade, £2.2.0'. *Household Expenses of Titus Hibbert, 1770–95,* John Rylands University Library of Manchester, English MS. 989, f. 95. Hibbert also belonged to the Society for Constitutional Information.

68. *Manchester Mercury and Harrop's General Advertiser*, 15 Jan 1788. The list was repeated in the same newspaper on 22 Jan, and the issues of 5 Feb, and 12 Feb listed several new subscriptions.

69. The abolitionist committee was set up at a meeting of the 'Society for the Purpose of effecting the Abolition of the Slave Trade' at the Exchange Tavern, Manchester on 27 December 1787. For a list of its 31 members see *Manchester Mercury*, 1 Jan 1788 and for its broadly based nature (it even included the borough reeve and his constables as well as some local Tories), see Hunt, pp. 52–3.

70. The signatories to the Address of 7 February 1786 requesting Barnes and Harrison to accept the responsibilities of managing the College, together with the names of the first committee members, may be found in Appendix I to the *Sermons* preached by Barnes and Harrison at the inauguration of the College in September 1786 (Warrington 1786), pp. 3, 5.

71. *Manchester Mercury*, 13 Nov. 1787. The relevant text is 'And (He) hath made of one blood all nations of men, for to dwell on all the face of the earth'.

72. *Manchester Mercury*, 30 Oct. 1787; Thomas Clarkson, *The History of the Rise, Progress and Accomplishment of the Abolition of the African Slave Trade by the British Parliament* (2 vol: reprint 1968), I, p. 415 ff.

73. *Sermons on various important subjects, by the late Rev. Ralph Harrison; to which is prefixed a Biographical Memoir of the Author* (Manchester 1813). See in particular Sermon V, 'Duties of Masters and Servants', pp. 87–102, which makes the distinction between slavery and contractual forms of labour frequently used by contemporary abolitionists.

74. *Manchester Mercury* 1 and 15 January 1788; William Henry, *A Tribute to the Memory of the late President of the Literary and Philosophical Society of Manchester* [i.e. Thomas Henry] (Manchester 1819) pp. 31–2.

75. *Manchester Mercury* 15 Jan. 1788; Ditchfield, 'Manchester College', p. 84.

76. Lists of College benefactors and annual subscribers in 1786 may be found added to the Appendices in *Sermons* . . . pp. 14–19.

77. Anstey, *Atlantic Slave Trade*, p. 282.

78. Graham Murphy, *William Roscoe. His Early Ideals and Influence* (privately printed 1981), pp. 21–4; *Report, 1817*, p. 1. *Report, 1826*, p. 5; *Monthly Repository* Vol 11 (1816) p. 119.

79. Ditchfield, 'Manchester College', pp. 99, 104; George Walker, *Sermons on Various Subjects* (4 vols 1808), with list of subscribers in Vol III, pp. iii–xii.

80. William Enfield to Gilbert Wakefield, 24 Jan 1790, *Wakefield Memoirs* I, 553–4; Ernest Axon (ed), *Memorials of the Family of Nicholson* (privately printed 1928), pp. 66, 73, 83 ff, 110 ff.

81. Neither Robert Hibbert, a trustee of Cross Street Chapel from 1778 nor his nephew of the same name, the founder of the Hibbert Trust, who were both West

Indian merchants with estates in Jamaica, and defended slavery, were subscribers to Manchester College. See *Dictionary of National Biography*, Baker, *Cross Street Chapel*, pp. 89–90 and Mabel Nembhard, 'Hibberts of Jamaica', *Caribbeana, being Miscellaneous Papers relating to the History, Genealogy, Topography and Antiquities of the British West Indies*, Vol IV (1916) pp. 193–202.

82. Percival, *Works*, I, pp. cxxviii–cxl.

83. Royle and Walvin, *English Radicals and Reformers*, p. 36; *Manchester Mercury* 5 Jan. 1790. A general meeting of the subscribers 'for effecting the Abolition of the African Slave Trade' in Manchester on 4 Jan. 1790 resolved to urge the M.Ps for the County of Lancashire to vote for abolitionist motions in Parliament.

84. Hunt, pp. 55, 67–8.

85. This paragraph is heavily indebted to Hunt, *passim*, and to Anstey, *Atlantic Slave Trade*, pp. 262–3, 266.

86. Percival, Barnes, Thomas Henry and James Potter were members of the Manchester abolition committee in 1792; *Manchester Mercury* 13 March 1792. A list of 95 abolitionist subscribers was printed in the *Manchester Mercury* of 3 April 1792. It includes, among others, Percival, Barnes, James Touchet, William Rigby (Junior), Samuel Jones, James Potter and William Hawkes, each of whom subscribed one guinea.

87. Gatrell, p. 34. William Henry, *Tribute*, pp. 31–2. For the programme of the Manchester Constitutional Society, see Frida Knight, *The Strange Case of Thomas Walker. Ten Years in the Life of a Manchester Radical* (London 1957) pp. 44–45.

88. Quoted in John Pollock, *Wilberforce* (London 1977), p. 87. For other examples of contemporary awareness of the Manchester initiative see the 'Biographical Memoirs' of Thomas Percival, quoted above, p. 16 and Clarkson, I, pp. 415–16, 452. For the verdict of modern research see Hunt, *passim*; Anstey, *Atlantic Slave Trade*, ch. 11, and James Walvin, 'The Public Campaign in England against Slavery 1787–1834' in David Eltis and James Walvin (eds), *The Abolition of the Atlantic Slave Trade. Origins and Effects in Europe, Africa and the Americas* (Univ. of Wisconsin Press, 1981) pp. 64–7.

89. Walvin, 'Public Campaign' p. 66.

90. For a cogent survey of the volume and efficacy of petitioning in the early nineteenth century, see Seymour Drescher, 'Public Opinion and the Destruction of Slavery' in James Walvin (ed) *Slavery and British Society 1776–1846* (London 1982) pp. 22–48.

91. Walvin, 'Public Campaign', p. 65.

92. George Walker, *Essays on Various Subjects, to which is prefixed a Life of the Author* (London, 2 vols 1809); I, clxxxiv. The 'Life' was written by Walker's son.

93. *Manchester Mercury*, 24 Jan. 1792. For other evidence of Walker's abolitionist work see his entry in D.N.B., Anstey, *Atlantic Slave Trade*, pp. 262–3 and Clarkson I, 493 and II, 352. For an example of co-operation between abolitionists in Nottingham and Manchester, see Hunt, p. 55.

94. F. D. Cartwright (ed), *The Life and Correspondence of Major Cartwright* (2 vols, London 1826) II, p. 19.

95. The College Minutes of 14 April 1800 ('Minutes', I, p. 125) record that the Committee agreed to a request from John Cartwright 'for the Rev[d] Mr. Walker to attend in London on the 25th inst. to give evidence in a cause in which Mr. Cartwright is deeply interested'. The 'cause' was a court action brought by Cartwright's younger brother, the inventor Edmund Cartwright, against alleged infringements of his patent of a wool-combing machine, and Walker's aid was sought as an expert witness in his favour; cf. report of 'Cartwright and another v. Amatt and Another', *The Times*, 26 April 1800. Supported by his brother, Edmund

Cartwright ultimately won a rather small award of damages; cf John W. Osborne, *John Cartwright* (Cambridge 1972) pp. 65, 72. In the 1790s Walker was a partner in the Revolution Mill Company of East Retford, Nottinghamshire, one of John Cartwright's more ambitious (though unsuccessful) ventures: W. H. Chaloner and J. D. Marshall, 'Major John Cartwright and the Revolution Mill, East Retford, Nottinghamshire, 1788–1806' in N. B. Harte and K. G. Ponting (eds), *Textile History and Economic History, Essays in Honour of Miss Julia de Lacy Mann* (Manchester 1973) p. 302.

96. The letter of application, and the ministers to whom it was sent may be found in 'Minutes', I, pp. 83–4.

97. Pipe-Wolferstan diary 25 March 1793; 17 March 1796; John Money, *Experience and Identity. Birmingham and the West Midlands 1760–1800* (1967) p. 94. Pipe-Wolferstan first heard of the College from, *inter alia*, the Staffordshire antiquary Charles Chadwick, who was a subscriber to abolition in Manchester in 1788; Ditchfield, 'Manchester College', p. 84; *Manchester Mercury*, 15 Jan. 1788.

98. For Wood's numerous contributions to Manchester College see Charles Wellbeloved, *Memoirs of the Life and Writings of the late Rev. W. Wood, F.L.S.* (London 1809) pp. 94–5 and for his abolitionism see *Monthly Repository* Vol. III (1808), p. 398.

99. *Wakefield Memoirs*, I, 191–7, 302–9; Correspondence between Samuel Kenrick of Bewdley and James Wodrow, Dr. Williams's Library, MSS 24. 157. See especially Kenrick's letters to Wodrow of 13 Feb 1788, 4 Jan, 21 March and 10 April 1792. Samuel Kenrick's great-nephew, John Kenrick, was one of the College's most outstanding tutors in the nineteenth century.

100. Anstey, *Atlantic Slave Trade*, chapter 8.

101. See for instance Davis, pp. 189-91; McLachlan, *Essays and Addresses*, p. 62; Burney, *Cross Street Chapel*, pp. 15–18.

102. *Memoirs of the Life of Mrs. Catherine Cappe*, ed. Mary Cappe (3rd ed. 1826) pp. 322–3. Mrs. Cappe added that because it was disfigured by articles, creeds and emoluments, the ministerial training of the Church of England compared unfavourably with that of Manchester College.

103. *Report, 1828*, p. 4.

104. Seed, 'Manchester College, York', pp. 11–12.

105. D. C. Stange, *British Unitarians Against American Slavery 1833–65* (Fairleigh Dickinson University Press, 1984), pp. 34–5, 221–5.

106. *Ibid*, p. 223.

107. Although much indebted to several sections of Dr. Stange's book the present writer retains several doubts respecting 'evangelical Unitarianism'. They may be summarized as follows: (i) The author himself (p. 222) accepts that some of his 'evangelical Unitarians' did not share the evangelical view of personal redemption, a central concept in the evangelical view of slavery delineated by Professor Anstey. (ii) Some of these 'evangelical Unitarians' were merely exceptions which proved the rule. Philip Carpenter, for instance, became an Anglican, Joseph Hutton was ejected from his chapel because of his Christology and joined the Church of England, while Henry Solly was highly untypical and encountered strong resistance to his views. These figures were far from representative of mid-nineteenth century Unitarianism and shed no light on the years 1786–1833. (iii) In the case of Harriet Martineau it seems highly likely that the materialist influence of Priestley endured longer than that of 'evangelical Unitarianism', if indeed the latter can be said to have existed at all. (iv) of nine leading 'evangelical Unitarian' ministers named by Stange only three (Philip Carpenter, Joseph Hutton and J. R. Beard) studied at Manchester College.

108. Roger Anstey, 'Religion and British Slave Emancipation' in Eltis and Walvin, *The Abolition of the Atlantic Slave Trade*, p. 46.

109. For Wellbeloved's oft-quoted claim that he did 'not teach Unitarianism,—or any *ism*—but *Christianism*', cf. Seed, 'Manchester College, York', pp. 11, 15. See also George William Wood to Wellbeloved, 8 June 1811, Wellbeloved Papers M.C.O.

110. McLachlan, *English Education under the Test Acts*; Seed, 'Manchester College, York' pp. 11, 15; James Drummond and C. B. Upton, *The Life and Letters of James Martineau* (2 vols London 1902), II pp. 255–263. Such teaching is evident in some of the College examination papers of this period; see the 'Political philosophy' paper which is undated but initialled 'G.W.W.' (i.e. George William Wood) and clearly belongs to the early nineteenth century: envelope marked 'Letters re M.N.C. York, etc, early 19C', M.C.O.

111. Davies, pp. 116–18.

112. R. K. Webb, *Harriet Martineau. A Radical Victorian* (London, 1960) p. 88.

113. *Ibid.*

114. Percival, *Works*, I, cxxiv–cxxvi.

115. Thomas W. Davis (ed), *Committees for Repeal of the Test and Corporation Acts. Minutes 1786–90 and 1827–8* (London Record Society 1978) p. 32.

116. G. M. Ditchfield, 'The Campaign in Lancashire and Cheshire for the Repeal of the Test and Corporation Acts, 1787–1790', *Transactions of the Historic Society of Lancashire and Cheshire*, Vol. 126 (1977) p. 132.

117. 'Life' of Walker in *Essays on Various Subjects*, I, clxvii.

118. G. M. Ditchfield, 'The Parliamentary Struggle over the Repeal of the Test and Corporation Acts 1787–1790', *English Historical Review*, Vol. LXXXIX (1974) p. 567; John Pollock, *Wilberforce* (London 1977) p. 154; Wellbeloved, *William Wood*, pp. 60–5.

119. Anstey, *Atlantic Slave Trade*, p. 276.

120. Theophilus Lindsey to John Rowe, 6 March 1792: Lindsey Papers, John Rylands University Library of Manchester.

121. See, for instance, the denunciation of Unitarianism in the *Manchester Mercury*, 22 May 1792, shortly after the rejection of the Unitarian Petition in the House of Commons.

122. Gordon, *Dob Lane Chapel*, pp. 41–2.

123. *Ibid*, 48–50; Knight, *Thomas Walker*, ch. IX.

124. See Alan Booth, 'Popular loyalism and public violence in the north-west of England, 1790–1800', *Social History*, vol. 8 No. 3 (Oct. 1983) pp. 305–6.

125. Letter I 'on Congregational Unitarian Funds' from 'A Friend to the Spread of Truth.' *Monthly Repository* XII (1817) p. 673.

126. Legal toleration of worship was granted by Act of Parliament to English Catholics in 1791 and Scottish Episcopalians in 1792, while at the same time the Unitarian petition for much the same thing was rejected by the House of Commons.

127. McLachlan, *Warrington Academy*, p. 29.

128. Theophilus Browne (tutor in classics and mathematics 1807–9) was a Whig of the Lindsey school who had resigned his Anglican benefice; William Hincks (tutor in mathematics and natural philosophy 1827–39 and himself a York student) went somewhat further and is described as a 'philosophical radical' in Davis, p. 94.

129. Seed, 'Manchester College, York', p. 12; Wellbeloved to William Wood, 15 Oct. 1801, Wellbeloved Papers, M.C.O.

130. James Martineau, *In Memoriam. John Kenrick* (London 1878), pp. 15, 21–2; Kenrick to G. W. Wood, 8 Sept. 1827, Kenrick Papers, M.C.O.
131. John Kenrick to Archibald Kenrick, 13 May 1831; Norah Kenrick (ed), *Chronicles of a Nonconformist Family, The Kenricks of Wynne Hall, Exeter and Birmingham* (Birmingham, 1932) pp. 215–18.
132. Kenrick to G. W. Wood, 2 Dec. 1830, Kenrick Papers, M.C.O.
133. *Report*, 1834, p. 5. See also the essay entitled 'Influence of Toleration upon National Wealth and Prosperity, illustrated from History' (23 June 1819), by Edward Strutt, subsequently M.P. for Derby and Baron Belper; volume of College essays, 1816–19, M.C.O.
134. H. McLachlan, *Essays and Addresses*, p. 207; Kenrick to G. W. Wood, 23 Nov. 1830; William Hincks to G. W. Wood, 18 Nov, 1833, Kenrick Papers, M.C.O.
135. *'Minutes'*, p. 19.
136. Wellbeloved, *Life of William Wood*, p. 131; obituary of G. W. Wood in *Christian Reformer*, N.S. Vol. X (1843) p. 728. This comment on G. W. Wood might be compared with that on Thomas Henry quoted above, p. 199.
137. *Monthly Repository*, Vol. 10 (1815), *passim*; *Report*, 1819 p. 11.
138. Obituary of Pecchio (by John Kenrick) in *Christian Reformer* N.S. Vol II (1835) pp. 590–1.
139. Giuseppe Pecchio, *Semi-Serious Observations of an Italian Exile during his residence in England* (London 1833) pp. 428–9, observed that Unitarians favoured 'a liberal mixed government of King, Lords and Commons, and, without desiring a republic, are for the maximum of liberty compatible with the order and dignity of the government'. His work on the political economists of Italy was favourably noticed in the *Edinburgh Review*, Vol. 50 (Oct. 1829–Jan. 1830) p. 356. Pecchio appears to have left the College (in 1828) because of the financial independence which he attained on marriage.
140. See, for instance, Losh to Brougham, 2 Sept. 1825; Edward Hughes (ed) *The Diaries and Correspondence of James Losh* (2 vols, Surtees Society, Vols. CLXXI and CLXXIV, 1956–9), II, p. 178.
141. *Ibid*, I, p. 15.
142. *Ibid*, II, p. 11.
143. James Walvin, 'Introduction', in James Walvin (ed) *Slavery and British Society*, p. 19.
144. See, for example, E. M. Wilbur, *A History of Unitarianism in Transylvania, England and America* (Boston, U.S.A. 1945), pp. 325–6; H. L. Short, 'Presbyterians under a new name', in C. Gordon Bolam, Jeremy Goring, H. L. Short and Roger Thomas, *The English Presbyterians, from Elizabethan Puritanism to Modern Unitarianism* (London 1968), p. 235.
145. John Tilt Bache to G. W. Wood, 23 July 1815, 'MCY c/29', M.C.O. I owe this reference to Mr. David Wykes. J. T. Bache (d. 1837) was father of Samuel Bache (1804–76) who trained at Manchester College, York and was subsequently minister at the New Meeting, Birmingham, and Visitor of the College. See the entry for Samuel Bache in *D.N.B.*
146. *Report 1836*, pp. 4–5.
147. Seed, 'Manchester College, York', p. 15.
148. Short, 'Presbyterians under a new name', pp. 247–52.
149. Robert Currie, Alan Gilbert and Lee Horsley, *Churches and Churchgoers. Patterns of Church Growth in the British Isles since 1700* (Oxford 1977) pp. 213, 215, 216–18.
150. There were 135 pupils between 1786–98 and 235 in the York period, 1803–40. In addition there were perhaps ten or twelve more (including Stanley Pipe-

Wolferstan) between 1798 and 1803 in the latter part of the first Manchester period, when records of their names were apparently not kept.

151. In 1833 Unitarian congregations presented to Parliament four petitions for slave emancipation, carrying 425 signatures; Stange, *British Unitarians Against American Slavery*, p. 50. Although these low numbers are admittedly ironic in view of the prominence of Unitarians in stimulating earlier abolitionist petitions, the mass of petitions from elsewhere in 1833 is eloquent testimony to the way in which what had been a radical device, at least as far as Anti-Slavery was concerned, had now become an established political practice.

152. John Kenrick to G. W. Wood, 11 April 1834; Kenrick Papers, M.C.O.

153. *Monthly Repository*, XIII (1818) p. 462. In June 1823 Timothy Hawkes also delivered an oration on slavery; *Ibid*, XVIII (1823), p. 416.

154. John Kenrick to G. W. Wood, 'Spring 1833', Kenrick Papers, M.C.O.

155. Stange, *British Unitarians Against American Slavery*, pp. 59–60.

156. The *Roll of Students* . . . indicates that Samuel Smith, who subsequently became a barrister, attended the College between 1811 and 1813. His identification as the son of William Smith M.P. is confirmed by *Monthly Repository* VIII (1813), p. 216 and by Joseph Hunter's account of 'Manchester New College' in 'Collectanea Hunteriana: Memoirs to serve for a History of Protestant Dissenters', British Library Add. Ms. 24 412, f. 13v. William Smith presented to the College a number of copies of the 'Improved Version' of the New Testament which was published by the Unitarian Society in 1808, *Monthly Repository*, Vol VI (1811) p. 440. I owe several of the references in this paragraph to the kindness of Mr. David Wykes.

157. *Reports, 1817–20.*

158. Anstey, 'Religion and British Slave Emancipation', pp. 37–8; K. Charlton, 'James Cropper and Liverpool's contribution to the Anti-Slavery Movement'; *Transactions of the Historic Society of Lancashire and Cheshire*, Vol. 123 (1971) pp. 57–80.

159. *Report, 1817*, which lists 22 subscribers from the Bristol area.

160. Davis, p. 76; entry for Lant Carpenter in D.N.B.

161. *Report, 1820*, p. 14. This was probably either Catherine Wedgwood (1774–1823) or Sarah Elizabeth Wedgwood (1776–1856), both unmarried daughters of Josiah Wedgwood.

162. John Ashton Yates, *Colonial Slavery. Letters to the Right Hon W. Huskisson . . . on the present condition of the slaves and the best means adapted to promote the . . . extinction of slavery in the British colonies* (London 1824).

163. *Reports, 1832–34*; M. Stenton, *Who's Who of British Members of Parliament: A Biographical Dictionary of the House of Commons* (4 vols, Hassocks, 1976–81) Vol I, *passim*. John Seed, 'Unitarianism, political economy and the antinomies of liberal culture in Manchester, 1830–50', *Social History*, Vol 7 (1982) p. 7 note 30, identifies John Marshall M.P. for Leeds 1832–35 as a former pupil of Manchester College. But that John Marshall, second son of John Marshall, M.P. for Yorkshire, is described by Stenton (Vol I, p. 261) as a manufacturer at Leeds in partnership with his father. The John Marshall who attended the College in 1817–19, on the other hand, is listed in the *Alumni of Manchester College* as hailing from London and subsequently becoming a barrister. In a letter of G. W. Wood of 17 Oct. 1817, (M.C.O.) moreover, John Kenrick observed that the father of his pupil John Marshall was a member of Lloyds of London. It thus seems unlikely that the John Marshall who studied at Manchester College was the same John Marshall who entered the House of Commons as M.P. for Leeds in 1832.

164. Hansard, *Parliamentary Debates*, XVIII, 587–8 and 598–9.

165. *Ibid*, XIX, 1219–20.
166. *Ibid*, XX, 220.
167. Izhak Gross, 'The Abolition of Negro Slavery and British Parliamentary Politics, 1832–1833', *Historical Journal*, Vol. 23 (1980), pp. 81–4. On the apprenticeship issue in March and May 1838, M.Ps connected with the College were divided between those (T. Thornley, G. W. Wood) who supported the immediate abolition of apprenticeship and those (M. Philips, E. Strutt, J. A. Yates) who favoured T. F. Buxton's more cautious move for a Select Committee to investigate alleged abuses of the apprenticeship system. See the division lists in *Hansard's Parliamentary Debates*, XLII, 257–61; XLIII, 123–6 and 430–3, and Izhak Gross, 'Parliament and the Abolition of Negro Apprenticeship, 1835–38' *English Historical Review*, XCVI (1981) 560–76.
168. Michael Watts, *The Dissenters. From the Reformation to the French Revolution* (Oxford 1978) p. 479.
169.. R. W. Davis, *Dissent in Politics 1780–1830. The Political Life of William Smith M.P.* (London 1971), chapter 7.
170. Samuel Bradburn, *An Address to the People called Methodists concerning the evils of encouraging the Slave Trade* (Manchester 1792) pp. 13–14.
171. Samuel Kenrick to James Wodrow, 10 April 1792, Kenrick Papers, Dr. Williams's Library. By quoting only the first half of this sentence, Watts, *The Dissenters*, p. 482, misses its essential point.
172. For a local example of Unitarian participation in a 'political mobilization across the whole front of liberal culture' over such issues in Manchester in the 1840s, see Seed, 'Unitarianism', p. 17.
173. Rev. George Armstrong speaking at the 22nd Annual Meeting of the British and Foreign Unitarian Association, 1847; *The Inquirer*, Vol. VI (1847) p. 348. I owe this reference to Stange, *British Unitarians Against American Slavery*, p. 39.
174. As is suggested by Stange, p. 33.
175. Theophilus Lindsey to William Tayleur, 1 March 1788; H. McLachlan, *Letters of Theophilus Lindsey* (Manchester 1920) pp. 92–3.
176. Pecchio, *Semi-Serious Observations*, pp. 411–12.
177. David Brion Davis, *The Problem of Slavery in the Age of Revolution* (Ithaca 1975) pp. 350, 356.
178. Gatrell, 'Incorporation and the pursuit of Liberal hegemony', *passim*.

# 8
# JAMES MARTINEAU: THE DEVELOPMENT OF HIS RELIGIOUS THOUGHT

RALPH WALLER
*Chaplain*
*Westminster College*
*Oxford*

The research for this essay was made possible by a grant from the Central Research Fund of the University of London.

In the late Autumn of 1866 (10th November) Augustus de Morgan packed up his books, vacated his study, and resigned his Chair of Mathematics at University College, London, to which he had been appointed some thirty-eight years previously. His students begged him to allow his photograph to be taken for the library of 'our old College'. He replied, 'Our old College no longer exists'. The College was only a reality for him as long as it adhered to its basic principle of refusing all religious disqualifications.

The cause of de Morgan's discontent was simple; earlier that same year the Rev. James Martineau, the strongest candidate for the Chair of Philosphy of Mind and Logic, had been turned down by the College Council; the recommendation of the Senate had been overturned by a coalition of those who wanted no minister of religion to be appointed and those who wanted only a minister of the Church of England. The opposition to Martineau was largely orchestrated by George Grote who argued that it was:

> inconsistent with the principle of complete religious neutrality proclaimed and adopted by University College to appoint to the chair of mental philosophy and logic a candidate eminent as a minister and preacher of one among the various sects which divided the religious world.[1]

What had upset de Morgan (and the aged Crabb Robinson) was that the religious neutrality of University College meant precisely the opposite of Grote's interpretation: it meant the non-exclusion of scholars and teachers on religious grounds. De Morgan expressed his concern to Martineau:

> I came here on the understanding that a man in office may have any theology provided he sticks to his own subject in his class; if the stipulation is to be that a man shall have no theology, I am just as much disqualified as you; and the College, instead of respecting conscience, snubs conscience; instead of comprehending everybody, excludes all but secularists.[2]

Croom Robertson, who was appointed to the Chair, went on to exert a powerful influence on philosophy in England, becoming the founder and first editor of the philosophical journal *Mind*. Martineau returned to his teaching at Manchester New College, of which institution he was shortly to become the Principal; from there he launched his great assaults on the agnosticism of Herbert Spencer and the materialism of Tyndall. These, together with his books, sermons, and addresses, were to be vital contributions to nineteenth century English Christianity and caused A. M. Fairbairn, the first Principal of Mansfield College, Oxford, to write:

> It is largely owing to him that our age was not swept off its feet by the rising tide of materialistic and pseudo-scientific speculation. The qualities of his rhetoric made him the more efficient an apologist for his theistic ideas, and clothed it in an elegance of form that commended it to the fastidious in literary feeling.[3]

The work which Martineau did within the confines of Manchester New College resulted in Gladstone ranking him as the 'first among living English thinkers.'[4] P. T. Forsyth placed him alongside J. H. Newman and F. D. Maurice as the three outstanding theologians of the nineteenth century.[5] But Martineau, the theologian, cannot be separated from Martineau the man; and in order to appreciate his theology to the full, it is important to see the man at work among his contemporaries.

James Martineau was born in 1805, the seventh child of a middle-class merchant family. The house where he grew up still stands in Magdalen Street, Norwich, and is now a bicycle shop, but with a little imagination it can be pictured as it must have been in the opening years of the nineteenth century, with a steady stream of visitors, and with the intense discussions which took place round the fireside in the evenings; especially on a Sunday when Mr. Madge the Unitarian Minister would call.

The whole family worshipped at the nearby Octagon Chapel and it was on this fellowship that its social and cultural life was centred. The Octagon Chapel was a stimulating place: over the years several famous people had worshipped there, including Sir James Edward Smith, the Botanist; John Taylor, the hymn writer and William Smith, Member of Parliament and the grandfather of Florence Nightingale.

The home, too, had its own invigorating atmosphere. There were eight children, and the older children played their part in the formal education of the younger: Thomas, the eldest, taught Latin; Elizabeth taught French, and Henry writing and arithmetic.[6] All this activity took place with the enthusiastic support of their parents, who knew the importance of discerning encouragement in education. James later said of his father that 'he was always ready to strain every nerve to advance the education of his children.'[7]

Of all the children, Harriet and James were the closest and their impact on each other must have been formative. One of Harriet's earliest memories was of the birth of James, and in her autobiography she recalls how one night when he was one year old, she woke him up, pulled him out of the cot, and set him on a chair at the window: 'I wickedly opened the window and the cool air blew in and yet the maid did not wake. The sky was gorgeous and I talked very religiously to the child.'[8]

At the age of fifteen, James was meeting with Harriet at seven in the morning in order to read Bishop Lowth's *Praelections* in the Latin.[9] This in itself is of some significance, since Lowth had been, in the eighteenth century, one of England's pioneer scholars in Biblical criticism, and had advocated the kind of reasonable approach to the scriptures later adopted by Martineau himself.

It was through the influence of Harriet that James, at the age of fourteen, was sent to Dr. Lant Carpenter's school in Bristol. Although in later life Harriet spoke with scorn about Lant Carpenter ('superficial in his knowledge, scanty in ability, narrow in his conceptions and thoroughly priestly in his temper'),[10] there is no doubt, that at this time in her life, she was full of praise. Martineau recorded in his Biographical Memoranda:

> The need of some change in the course of my education had probably been felt by my father and mother, when my sister Harriet brought home with her the happy fruits of a period of school life at Bristol and spoke with enthusiastic gratitude of the influence over her at Dr. Lant Carpenter's classes and pulpit services.

In addition to her gratitude to Lant Carpenter, Harriet attributed to him her love of David Hartley[11] through whom she derived her strong sense of duty:

> I cannot at this hour look at the portrait of Hartley prefixed to his work, or glance at his strange Scholia—which I could almost repeat, word for word,—without a strong revival of the old mood of earnest desire of self-discipline, and devotion to duty which I derived from them in my youth.[12]

Whether or not James drew his own self-discipline and devotion to duty from Harriet is difficult to ascertain, but these were certainly ideas which they held in common.

James and Harriet shared walking tours which they took together both in the Lake District and Scotland. Like many literary figures of the time, such as Wordsworth, Coleridge, and Scott, they were responsive to the beauty which surrounded them.

> To both of us it was a first free admission into the penetralia of natural beauty; and we walked everywhere with hushed feeling and reverent feet. We were perfectly at one, both in the defects which limited our vision, and in the susceptibilities which quickened it, neither of us caring much for the savage romance of Scottish traditions, and both being intensely alive to the appeal of mountain forms and channeled glens, and the play of light and cloud with the forest, the corrie and the lakeside. And in the fresh morning hours, before fatigue had made us laconic, the flow of eager talk, as is usual with young people, ran over all surfaces—even plunged into all depths—human and divine, with just the right proportion of individual difference to prevailing accordance for the maintenance of healthy sympathy. That journey lifted our early companionship to a higher stage, and established an affection which, though afterwards saddened, on one side at least never really changed.[13]

Here the seeds were sown of Martineau's romanticism, and ever afterwards he tried to create beauty in worship and buildings, writings and poetry, in sermons and hymns.

The influence was not all one-sided. Harriet confessed that James filled a larger space in her life and affections than any other person.[14] It was through the persistent encouragement of James that Harriet made her first attempt at writing,[15] which subsequently appeared under the title of 'Female Writers on Practical Divinity' in the *Monthly Repository*.

The first prolonged break with Harriet came when James was sent to Lant Carpenter's school at Bristol, following four unhappy years at Norwich Grammar School; it was here that he came under the dominant influence of his life.

When Martineau arrived in Bristol Lant Carpenter was at the height of his powers. He had recently been awarded the degree of LL.D. by the University of Glasgow and on two occasions had turned down the offer of a teaching post at Manchester College, York, where he was the Visitor and subsequently Vice-President. He was a man of immense energy, wide interests, and infectious enthusiasm, especially in enterprises which improved the opportunities and conditions of others. He joined whole-heartedly in the Anti-Slavery Campaign and expended an enormous amount of energy in the setting up of the Bristol Literary and Philosophical Institution, as he had previously done in the founding of the Exeter Select Library for the use of young people. He was also developing a growing academic reputation with his authoritative writing. This literary output consisted of some forty two major works and papers on a wide variety of subjects. His interests ranged from the *Geography of the New Testament* and *A Brief View of the Chief Grounds of Dissent from the Church of England* to a re-editing of Dr. Watts' hymns for children and *Systematic Education*.

He carried this wide range of interests with him into his school work; he was a man of the world who read the daily papers to the pupils around the dinner table and kept them in touch with the Parliamentary debates. He encouraged his pupils to start their own debating society and to care for the poor from their own funds. He laid great stress on moral and religious education, and introduced his pupils to contemporary Biblical criticism:

> The critical reading of the Greek New Testament every Monday morning gradually accumulated an amount of theological information, respecting both the text and the interpretation of the sacred writings, rarely placed within the reach of any but divines.[16]

In addition, Martineau (along with Russell Carpenter) never forgot that Lant Carpenter's favourite expression to his pupils was 'Try'.[17]

Exactly what Martineau received from Lant Carpenter is not easy to determine; but some sixty years later in a letter to his old teacher's grandson, Estlin Carpenter, Martineau set down some of his memories. He had, he said, been greatly impressed with the breadth of education that he had obtained, and noted that the public Grammar Schools of the time only provided proficient teaching in Greek and Latin along with a little mythology and history. He remembered with pride that 'we had lessons in science, in history, in geography and in Greek Testament and smaller groups for Classics and Mathematics.'[18] This curriculum widened Martineau's horizons and gave him the foundation which enabled him to cope with the scientific revolution of the nineteenth century. But in addition to the curriculum there seems little doubt that he would have gained something of Lant Carpenter's sense of duty which he in turn had inherited from Hartley:

> Hartley (Carpenter wrote) I deem my spiritual father, for it was from him that I first gained accurate and consistent ideas on the subject of human duty.[19]

Even more important than the subject-matter and the patterns of thought

PLATE III

University Hall, Gordon Square, London

PLATE IV

101

Sermons, Morals,
and Metaphysics.

Ea

1. Hobbes's Creed Examined
2. Mottersheads Sermons
3. Placete de la Conscience
4. Sermons de L. A.
5. Sermons de Pictet
6. Lukins Chief Interest of Man
7. Whole Duty of Man
8. 9. Webbs Sermons 2 vol.
10. Repugnancy of Sin to Reason
11. 12. Sermons des Fetes des Saints 2 vol.
13. 14. Malbranche de la Recherche de la Verite 2 vol.
15. Ironmonii Synopsis Metaphysica
16. Cuffe's differences of the Ages of mans life
17. Charron de la Sagesse
18. Cardanus de Propria Vita
19. The great Law of Nature
20. Herbert de Veritate
21. Grotii Sententia Philos. de Fato.

# Manchester College,
YORK.

TO BE

# SOLD BY AUCTION,

# BY MR. HANDS,

ON FRIDAY NEXT, SEPTEMBER 6TH, 1839,
*On the Premises, Manchester College, Monkgate, York,*
A QUANTITY OF
USEFUL HOUSEHOLD

# Furniture,

Consisting of seven Half-tester Bedsteads with Moreen Hangings; seven Feather Beds, Bolsters, and Pillows; fifteen Deal Dressing Tables; six Chamber Services; twelve Iron Fenders; five sets of Fire Irons; eighteen strong Birch Chairs with Rush Seats, (in sets of six); five Mahogany Arm Chairs; five small Ditto with Leather Seats.

☞ *AUCTION to commence punctually at ONE o'Clock.*

85, Micklegate.

JOSEPH MOXON, PRINTER, YORKSHIREMAN OFFICE, PARLIAMENT-STREET, YORK.

developed at Bristol, was the influence of the man. Lant Carpenter was both a deeply religious man and a profound thinker, and his spirit stayed with Martineau for the rest of his life:

> But the gratitude with which I think of those years is due chiefly to the personal influence of Dr. Carpenter, under which my conscience seemed to wake up and life to assume its proper sanctity.[20]

On leaving Bristol Martineau took up an engineering apprenticeship with a Mr. Fox of Derby. He was a kind and practical man, but he was unable to give Martineau a satisfactory theoretical and mathematical grounding for his mechanical interests. This failure, combined with other influences, changed the direction of his life. These included the death of a cousin, Henry Turner, the minister of High Pavement Church, Nottingham, in whose place Martineau felt he ought to serve; and his courtship of Helen Higginson, the daughter of a Unitarian Minister. Combined with his admiration for Lant Carpenter, these influences channelled his aspirations in the direction of the Ministry, and in 1822 he enrolled at Manchester College, York.

At this time Manchester College had a wide and varied curriculum, being a kind of mini-University for ministers and laymen with divinity as its central study. It is worth remembering that the Theology Honours School at Oxford, and the Theological Tripos at Cambridge did not come into operation until as late as 1870–71, when it was recognised that the teaching of theology at both Universities was poor, and there was no real provision for undergraduate theological education.[21] At Manchester College, on the other hand, the tutors were in close contact with German religious thought. As early as 1818 John Kenrick had laid plans to study in Germany and attend the lectures of Schleiermacher.[22]

After the French Revolution and the Napoleonic Wars there was a tendency for England to become more isolated, although contact with Germany in the early part of the nineteenth century was wider than is sometimes believed: Manchester College, through its tutors and students, helped to preserve one of the several important links with Continental thought.

The staff of Manchester College, Charles Wellbeloved, John Kenrick, and William Turner were all competent men. It was the admirable teaching of Turner which gave fresh impetus to Martineau's mathematical studies and enabled him to attain an ambition of reading Newton's *Principia*.[23] Wellbeloved, the Principal, will long be remembered by the fine tribute Martineau paid him in his Opening of Session address to the College in 1858:

> Well I do remember the respectful wonder with which we saw, as our course advanced, vein after vein of various learning modestly opened out; the pride with which we felt that we had a Lightfoot, a Jeremiah Jones and an Eichhorn all in one, yet no mere theologian after all but scarcely less a naturalist and an archeologist as well . . . Many of us have

> found the notes taken in his lecture room our best Cyclopaedia of divinity during the first years of our active ministry.[24]

The ethos of the College was more important than its curriculum. What Martineau found within the small circle of students was a prevailing spirit of devout enthusiasm which bound them together in strong affection, and subordinated their intellectual work to their higher aspirations.[25] His only complaint on leaving the College was that he had been taught Hebrew without points and the fluxational method of calculus rather than the differential method, both of which he had to re-learn in order to teach his students at Trinity College, Dublin.

In 1827, the illness of Lant Carpenter and his consequent absence from the school resulted in Mrs. Carpenter inviting Martineau to Bristol to take charge of the fourteen pupils. He undertook this post for one year and it provided him with two important opportunities. The first came through the good offices of Dr. J. C. Prichard[26] who introduced Martineau to a private Philosophical Society of about twelve members. He looked back on these evening meetings of the Society as one of the most precious passages of life where he 'heard the ablest local men discuss the newest questions of the time and the greatest questions of all time.'[27] He was for ever grateful to one member of the Society, Samuel Worsley, whose thoughtful suggestions and accurate geological knowledge Martineau greatly admired. Such a Society not only broadened his outlook but also laid the foundations for the part he was later to play in the famous Metaphysical Society, and for his defence of theism against those who propounded a purely mechanical evolutionary theory.

The second opportunity was that of hearing the great Baptist preacher Robert Hall on Thursday evenings at Broadmead Chapel. His style of preaching captivated Martineau:

> Persuasion I never found in his preaching, but the contagious elevation of a powerful mind. He influenced men by not addressing them, yet thinking aloud before them. The more he forgot them, the more did their critical mood die down, and their secret sympathy rise up and go with him, till they saw his vision and prayed his prayer.[28]

There is not only the suggestion here of admiration but also of influence; Martineau subsequently decided to adopt a similar form of preaching himself, and kept to it in spite of later persuasion by F. W. Newman to change and become a more popular preacher.

In the Summer of 1828, after one year in Bristol, he accepted the post of Junior Minister of Eustace Street Presbyterian Meeting House, Dublin, with the Rev. Joseph Hutton, the grandfather of Richard Holt Hutton, as his colleague. At the end of the same year, Martineau married Helen Higginson of Derby and settled down to his teaching and ministerial work with the hope of a long and fruitful stay in Dublin. This was an energetic and strenuous time in his life and accompanied by several difficulties. A passage from his Biographical Memoranda shows that the seeds of the present day problems of Ireland had taken root in his time, and it also reveals the direction of Martineau's own sympathies:

> A signature which I had attached to a petition for Catholic Emancipation brought down an explosion of wrath from a blustering but not very lucid gentleman, who had been credibly informed that ministers should not meddle in politics; but who never the less thought it was our duty to sign on the other side. Indeed the anti-Catholic feeling shown by the principal people in the society startled and shocked me beyond measure . . .
>
> In an endowed school connected with the meeting house, some forty ophans were lodged, educated and qualified for apprenticeships, the vacancies being filled by election in open vestry . . . At one of the elections a boy of very winning appearance, brought by a well-mannered father, (the mother was dead) excited a prevailing interest in the members present: but it was suggested that no enquiry had been made respecting the parents' religion. The man was recalled and questioned. The mother had been a Protestant. "And you" said the Chairman. "I'll not be deceiving your Honour", replied the Father. "The boy may follow his mothers road, but I am bound to be a Catholic". "Be gone this minute" exclaimed the Chairman, with a loud stamp of his foot upon the floor, "how dare you show your face here? We have nothing to do with you and yours". On my trying to remonstrate, when the vestry resumed, he lifted his spectacles and looked at me transformed, as a naturalist would look at a live Dodo . . .

In the event, his ministry lasted under four years, owing to his refusal to accept any part of the Regium Donum, the annual grant bestowed by Parliament on Presbyterian Ministers.

Two useful publications came out of Martineau's Dublin Ministry. In July 1830 he preached a sermon before the Synod of Munster on 'Peace in Division: the Duties of a Christian in an Age of Controversy.' It emerged from his own bitter experiences of religious division in Ireland and was a warning against the dangers of Christian controversy and an attempt to throw some light on the duties of the Christian in such circumstances.[29]

The sermon had three main points. First, he maintained that it was the duty of every Christian to remember all the points of belief he held in common with other Christians. Secondly, he reminded his hearers of the moral innocence of mental error,[30] and advocated that if a person is genuinely mistaken in his opinion he is not eternally banished from God. Thirdly, he asserted that it was the duty of every Christian in an age of controversy openly to state his opinions together with the evidence which satisfied him of their truth.[31] This sermon was his first publication and judging by the *Monthly Repository* of 1830, it was well received in England.

His other literary achievement in Dublin was the publication in 1831 of his first hymn book, *A Collection of Hymns for Christian Worship*. The book contained two hundred and seventy three hymns, five of which were by his sister Harriet. Martineau drew his hymns from a wider spiritual tradition than had many previous compilers of Unitarian or Non-Subscribing Presbyterian hymn books. And although he appears at this stage not to have discovered the Wesley hymns, both Watts and Bishop Heber were well represented. Martineau's hymn book and his published sermon both reveal that for him emotion already had an important place in worship and in Church unity.

In the summer of 1832, the Martineaus left their first home, said farewell to their friends, stood in silence together in the French Churchyard by the little grave of their first-born, and then crossed the sea with a son and a daughter to Liverpool to enter upon the most formative and productive period of James' life.

It was here that he formed a close association with J. H. Thom and Charles Wicksteed of Liverpool, and J. J. Tayler of Manchester. They were aided by Blanco White, the turbulent Spanish Roman Catholic Priest, who became an Anglican and member of Oriel College Senior Common Room at the same time as Pusey, Newman and Hampden, and later became a close friend of Archbishop Whately before being introduced by Thom into the Liverpool Unitarian circle.

The four friends had many things in common. They were all young, and all Unitarian Ministers: Martineau, Tayler and Thom served the same congregations for twenty-five, thirty-three and thirty-eight years respectively.[32] They all had the same earnest desire to reconcile modern learning with the gospel, the same reverence for the person and work of Christ,[33] and they shared a growing desire to move away from rationalism to a more spiritual faith. All of them had travelled abroad and studied in Germany, the other three long before Martineau.

They brought together an interesting variety of educational backgrounds. Thom was born at Newry, on the border between Northern Ireland and the Irish Republic, and was educated in Belfast. Wicksteed was a student at Glasgow University; Tayler, like Martineau, was educated at Manchester College, but also at Glasgow University.

For several years while editing the *Prospective Review* these four met once a month at Tayler's home. They dined, spent the evening together and often stayed over-night. These were memorable occasions for all of them. Martineau undoubtedly felt that Tayler and Thom were the outstanding thinkers of the quartet, while he and Wicksteed 'contributed common sense and some knowledge of affairs'.[34] Tayler disagreed in so far as he saw Martineau as the rising star of Unitarianism.[35]

It is difficult to trace direct influences of any one of the four on the others. But there is no doubt from reading their correspondence and reminiscences that they interacted in a special way to stimulate and promote one another's thoughts. Wicksteed had learnt Italian and French and some German, which had enabled him to read the works of De Wette and Paulus. He had even visited Paulus at Heidelberg and discussed at some length the great man's *Leben Jesu*. He had a great love of the traditions of the Church of England, on which he considered himself something of an expert. Of the four he was perhaps the one who was most involved outside the church: he was deeply concerned in the relief of the poor. He had been the President of the Mechanical and Literary Institute of Leeds and was a farmer for a considerable period of his life. His many writings included articles on history, theology, and literature; and his son said in a memoir that he was 'interested in everything'.[36]

Thom was a more serious and learned man. It is probably owing to him that Martineau's interest in Channing of America was stimulated, for his writings had made an important impact on the young Thom while still at College in Belfast in 1828.[37] It was through Thom that Blanco White was drawn into the Liverpool Unitarian Circle: and it was Blanco White who subsequently influenced Martineau in his movement of thought away from cold rationalism towards a religion of feeling.[38] Moreover, Martineau maintained that Thom's three-year-long absence from Liverpool left him (Martineau) with a feeling of desolation which was a major factor in his accepting an invitation to become the full-time colleague of J. J. Tayler at Manchester New College in 1857.[39]

It was Tayler who had the closest association with Martineau. John James Tayler was a gentle, kind, unassuming man, yet someone with a massive intellect, whom Martineau called 'the English Schleiermacher',[40] (a phrase which was also applied to Martineau himself). Like Martineau, Tayler was a romantic, who fell in love with the Lake District, and spent some time with Wordsworth on one of his early visits there.[41] He epitomized, as Martineau did himself, the Victorian sense of love and loss; the loss of loved ones, the loss of loved places, the loss of childhood.[42]

Tayler's collection of published letters form a little anthology of Victorian intellectual life. They show how he kept in touch with German religious thought, having studied at Bonn and Göttingen as early as 1834. From that year onwards he corresponded with several leading German Professors[43] and met them regularly; they included Ewald,[44] the Old Testament Scholar, who was Eichhorn's favourite pupil, and Neander[45] of Berlin, who had been a student of Schleiermacher.

He also formed a close friendship with Baron Bunsen and studied his works several years before they were made famous by Rowland Williams in *Essays and Reviews* in 1860. Tayler had even consulted Bunsen over the appointment of an Old Testament Tutor for Manchester College. He was familiar with Baur's work at Tubingen, and had a close association with Sir Charles Lyell, the geologist, who had called to consult Tayler on matters of faith and reason while writing his book *The Antiquity of Man*.[46] It was Tayler who in October 1847 encouraged Martineau on his study leave in Germany to take the measure of German philosophy, which he thought had not been done recently by anyone from this country, and could prove to be an outstanding service to the cause of religion.[47]

Tayler's friendship with Martineau was of vital importance to them both. For twenty-nine years they served together on the staff at Manchester College. When Tayler's wife died it was to Martineau he turned for support, and it was Martineau who took the funeral service. In 1859 he wrote to Martineau of their friendship. 'In moral endeavours, in spiritual aspirations—in the final aim of our theology, we are one.'[48]

There is a sense in which they always seemed to be in tandem, sharing similar views on the work and person of Christ,[49] sharing the same view of the resurrection (i.e. of the real person, though not of the body).[50] They both shared the same rejection of Priestley's theology,[51] the same aim in fighting for a broader view of the Church and for Catholic Emancipation; they were alike in deploring sectarianism[52] and in showing a willingness to learn from other Christians, especially the Moravians and the Wesleyans.

Both men benefitted greatly from the other. It seems fitting that at the close of his fine Memorial Address on Tayler, Martineau paid this tribute to his friend: 'No one could look at him and say that the power of Christianity is spent.'[53]

It was during these early years in Liverpool that an important shift in Martineau's thought began to occur, which was to prove decisive for the development of Unitarianism in England. In 1833 he wrote a series of three articles on Priestley for the *Monthly Repository*. It was a work which showed areas of agreement between Priestley and Martineau, but it also revealed that Martineau's thought was moving along different lines. This essay painted a sympathetic portrait of Priestley, showing how in the early years of his ministry, deprived of social intercourse and friendship, he devoted himself to theological and linguistic studies. It includes the distressing picture of Priestley at the end of his time in England as 'the Pastor driven from his flock, the author despoiled of his manuscript, the philosopher hunted for his noble sympathy with his race.'[54] Martineau characterised Priestley as the man of truth:

> Were we to designate Dr. Priestley in one word, that word would be "truth"; it would correctly describe the employment of his intellect, the essential feeling of his heart, the first axiom of his morality, and even the impression of his outward deportment.[55]

There is a note of realism in the article in that it also depicts several of Priestley's short-comings; his lack of memory and imagination, his notion of duty as empowered by conviction rather than by affection, and his inability to admit doubt, for he saw that all his investigations must lead to truth or falsehood. Priestley's lack of picturesque illustrations in his narratives diminished their effectiveness, and he had a tendency to over-simplify difficult and complex truths. On the other hand, Martineau was clearly in sympathy with Priestley's sense of life being lived in accordance with a moral principle, a principle which was not a blind superstitious obedience but an expression of conscience. This was finally worked out by Martineau in *The Seat of Authority in Religion* almost sixty years later. Martineau also followed Priestley's doctrine of Christ at this time,[56] although he had substantially altered it by the time he came to write *Endeavours after a Christian Life* ten years later. The essay discloses a romantic element in Martineau's nature (and lacking in Priestley) which can clearly be seen by Martineau's advocating that a theologian should imagine himself in the original setting of the New Testament to 'mingle with the weeping daughters of Jerusalem, and raise a reverential eye towards the crucified, and listen to the fainting cry of filial tenderness.'[57] It was precisely this approach which F. W. Robertson took from Martineau and used so effectively in his Brighton Sermons. The essay shows that Martineau had a good knowledge of German romantic thought, comparing Priestley to the 'noble school of German critics, whose genius has, in our own day, penetrated the mysteries, and analysed the spirit, of poetry and the arts.'[58]

On two important issues Martineau was beginning to move away from Priestley's position: on the characteristics of Christian worship, and on the necessarian theory. With reference to worship, Martineau gave the impression (as had already been hinted at in the preface to his first hymn book) that he was moving away from the rationalistic worship advocated by Priestley to a worship which included emotion and affection, beauty and poetry, which alone could bridge the gap between God and man.

The second area where Martineau began to indicate a shift in thought was on the necessarian theory: Priestley, following Hartley, had concluded that people simply reacted to sensations from outside themselves. Martineau noted that the same sensations produce different reactions in different people.[59] He accounted for these varying results by concluding that individuals must have differing succeptibilities to external phenomena; for him, this began to undermine the determinist position.

In 1834 Martineau wrote a review of Bentham's *Deontology*; it was a straight-forward critical assessment of Bentham's work which Martineau later considered of insufficient importance to be included in any of his collected writings. In this review he outlined Bentham's theory which differentiated between voluntary and involuntary acts, maintaining that voluntary acts are selected on the basis of happiness.[60] Thus any act which increases happiness is looked upon as virtuous, and any act which brings a balance of misery is to be considered a vice.[61] Martineau held that Bentham's system had much to commend it, but he was highly critical of Bentham for his lack of sympathy with any views contrary to his own (a healthy respect for the opinion of others was something Martineau retained all his life). He went on to criticise Bentham for producing a selfish system which omitted benevolence,[62] and which was concerned only with actions rather than motives. Pleasure and pain, for Martineau, came from feelings and emotions as well as from actions. He gave the example of a fireman who might rush into a burning house to rescue a child in order to enhance his reputation or receive a reward. But an onlooker may do the same purely through a feeling of sympathy for the child. If the onlooker had not responded to that feeling it would have brought him pain; if he responded it would have brought him pleasure.[63]

Martineau disapproved of Bentham's practice of evaluating every human action in terms of personal loss and gain, and for portraying human beings as exclusively motivated by views of the future and thus incapable of being influenced by the impulses and stimuli of the past.[64] He further censured Bentham for dispensing with trial by motive and substituting trial by results. Martineau acknowledged that benevolence crept into Bentham's system in that he encouraged individuals to contribute to the happiness of others as this would in return promote their own happiness.

Against this position Martineau believed that true benevolence was expressed by the words of Jesus, 'If ye do good to them that do good to you, what thanks have ye?' In line with this he firmly held that thousands of kind acts were done every day which were not offered as assets in a deposit bank, but as free gifts. Martineau thus concluded that Bentham's work had a fundamental weakness and as such was not to be highly recommended.

It can be seen that by the mid-1830's Martineau had arrived at the basic position of his ethics; that motives, and not results, were the essential criteria for judging a person's actions. Moreover this review of Bentham's *Deontology* revealed the beginning of Martineau's movement away from Utilitarianism (which he increasingly perceived to be a selfish doctrine), towards a theory of action based on inner feelings and compulsions which sprang from the conscience. The review is of additional interest in that it is an indication of Martineau's continuing adherence to aspects of Hartley's philosophy in that he followed Hartley's distinction between voluntary and automatic actions, his belief that everything had a cause, and his differentiation between the cause and the external effect. Where he eventually parted company with Hartley in 1840 (as Coleridge had done previously) was on the necessarian doctrine against which Martineau asserted the free will and personal responsibility of the individual.

In 1836 Martineau published a remarkable little book under the title *The Rationale of Religious Inquiry* which went into four editions and would have been reprinted on more occasions if he had not prevented it. The book was reissued after Martineau's death with the title *What is Christianity*? This was Martineau's first book and its impact was extensive, especially in America where according to the Harvard Tutor, Joseph Henry Allen, it was responsible for starting the Transcendental Movement in American Free Churches:

> The year 1836 may be taken, as well as any, as the birth-year of the Transcendentalism which had so much to do in shaping the form of liberal opinion we have known since; at least, for its emergence in the field of theology, for it was in that year that 'the first gun of a long battle was discharged, in a review by Mr. George Ripley of Martineau's Rationale of Religious Inquiry'.[65]

As far as English theology was concerned it was an important attempt to examine Christianity philosophically. In the Preface Martineau maintained that religion and philosophy had traditionally occupied different spheres with little or no contact between them, except in the field of natural religion.[66] Martineau published these lectures in the hope of providing an improved philosophical method of investigating Christianity; namely that religious truth must not be contrary to reason.[67] The dominant contention of the book was that some aspects of orthodoxy did not stand up to the test of reason. He rejected the Roman Catholic notion of authority being best vested in the Church, on the ground that such a view debased the value and integrity of the individual human mind.[68]

> It indicates an anti-social contempt for the human mind, a suspicion respecting the stability of the great principles of morals, a disbelief in the progressiveness of higher civilization . . .[69]

He rejected the Protestant idea of the Authority of Scripture because it did not allow the individual to interpret scripture according to his own conscience and insight:

> The sense of scripture then denotes your sense: the notions which it awakens in your mind. The denier of the word of God is the reader, to whom the Bible suggests ideas different from yours. The oppugner of divine authority is the recusant of your interpretation; the rejecter of infallible certainty is the disputer of your constructions; the unbeliever in the essentials is the questioner of your favourite conclusions.[70]

Martineau was not advocating that the Christian faith must lie within the limits of reason, but rather that although it goes beyond what reason can prove, it does not go against reason. He expressed this in the phrase, 'A divine right, therefore, to dictate a perfectly unreasonable faith cannot exist.'[71]

*The Rationale* reveals Martineau's essential approach to the Bible, which was that it should be interpreted as any other book.[72] In this approach he moved away from the traditional Unitarian appeal which was to scripture alone. Previously, as Martineau pointed out, Unitarians had denied the doctrines of the Trinity, the Atonement and everlasting punishment, because they were non-scriptural;[73] but Martineau in *The Rationale* took a new direction in Unitarian theology by denying such doctrines because they were irrational.[74] Moreover, *The Rationale* shows that by 1836 Martineau had a good knowledge of German theology[75] and a high regard for it.[76] It is of interest to note, however, that by the time the third edition of *The Rationale* was published in 1845, his high opinion of German Christianity was beginning to wane:

> The delineation of the spirit of an ideal church I still allow to stand. The hope of its early realisation in Germany, however, it seems impossible longer to entertain.[77]

*The Rationale of Religious Inquiry* was not simply rationalistic and critical. Martineau also argued strongly for a supernatural element in religion, to the extent of denying the name Christian to the anti-supernaturalists;[78] a denial he later retracted under the influence of Blanco White. In *The Rationale* glimpses can also be seen of Martineau's romantic spirit, where he speaks in glowing terms of Wordsworth and Scott,[79] and moreover attributes to the imagination a key function in interpreting the Bible.

> We must go forth to labour in the fields of Galilee, and overhear the peasants talk of the new prophet of Nazareth. . . . The ravine of Kedron, the Mount of Olivet, must be like an evening walk, and the shady rills of Siloam like a noon-day rest; the "Beautiful Gate" must be too familiar to dazzle us with its golden reflection of the dawn; the levelled rock of Moriah our feet must daily climb, and pace the cloister of Solomon in frequent meditation . . .[80]

The factors which led Martineau to the theological position of *The Rationale of Religious Inquiry* are uncertain. He did however say that while asking the question 'What is Christianity?' he was struck by the lack of logical preliminaries for settling such a question.[81] H. D. Roberts, in his history of Liverpool non-conformity maintained that it was the young people of Paradise Street Chapel who through their questioning led Martineau to a serious reconsideration of his views.[82] It is an attractive idea which has been reflected in the experiences of many who have taught able young people. Moreover, Martineau's *Biographical Memoranda* lend some credence to this view, where he recalls of his young people's classes:

> I found them a delightful source of intellectual sympathy, with a succession of thoughtful young persons, and a salutary incentive for myself to preserve my mental stores from rusting and enlarge them by fresh accessions.

It is also true, however, that even before his arrival in Liverpool he had acquired a reputation of being a progressive thinker, whose ideas would have been further stimulated by his reading of German theology and by his collaboration with his three colleagues, Tayler, Thom and Wicksteed.

In the development of Martineau's religious thought there were two movements taking place at this time: one was towards a more critical approach to the scriptures and religious tradition, while the other was towards a religion based on feeling which emphasised worship and devotion to Christ. We find elements of both these movements within *The Rationale*, although the critical element dominates. Martineau never perceived these two movements as being contrary to one another. His acute rational criticism of the Bible and tradition was to remove false conceptions in order to make way for faith and true religion. However it was not until 1840 that he found, in the work of Kant (as Coleridge had done before him) an intellectual structure which harmonised these two movements of thought and enabled him finally to jettison his adherence to the necessarian doctrine.

During the 1830s two men, Blanco White and W. E. Channing, exerted an influence upon Martineau's thought. The importance of Channing in this respect has often been acknowledged, while the role of Blanco White in helping to fashion Martineau's religious thought has not been sufficiently recognised by his biographers.

Joseph Blanco White arrived in Liverpool in January 1835 from Dublin where for some four years he had been the guest of Archbishop Whately. He was immediately attracted to Liverpool Unitarianism and formed a friendship with James Martineau and J. H. Thom, who later became his literary executor. In his Biographical Memoranda, Martineau refers to his close and affectionate association with Blanco White:

> During six years' tenancy of our first house, three children were born to us; two daughters and between them a son; whose name Herbert, recalled to me (among other tender memories) the voice that gave it to him—that of Blanco White. Mr. White had lived at no great distance. He was pleased with the idea of a simple service of dedication at the parents' house; and although withdrawn from all public duty, readily consented, in an expression of private friendship to join our thanksgiving and leave us with his benediction.

Little correspondence between the two men has survived; it may well have been that the proximity of their homes resulted in no great need for letter-writing. One letter, however, written by White to Martineau had an important effect on the development of Martineau's religious thought. On the publication of *The Rationale of Religious Inquiry* in 1836, Blanco White penned Martineau a letter in which he set down important aspects of his own thinking and criticised one of Martineau's assertions; namely that of denying the name 'Christian' to the anti-supernaturalist. In the second edition of *The Rationale,* Martineau published White's letter and in the third edition of 1845 added a Preface which conceded White's point:

> There is however, one opinion maintained in the preface to the second edition, and omitted in this, which would be dangerous to pass without a word. The name Christian is there denied to the class of persons usually called Anti-supernaturalists; and for that denial reasons were given which the Author does not now think to be conclusive in their whole extent.[83]

Blanco White's letter had an impact on Martineau's thought, far greater than his biographers realised. White argued against the idea of Christianity being essentially a priestly religion.

> Christ declared himself against all religion which made salvation, or spiritual safety, dependent on priesthood and its peculiar offices.[84]

Three years later Martineau had taken up the same theme which he vigorously propounded in his lecture 'Christianity without Priest and without Ritual' delivered during the Liverpool Controversy of 1839, which he concluded by saying:

> Christianity, then, I maintain is without Priest, and without Ritual. It altogether coalesces with the prophetic idea of religion, and repudiates the sacerdotal. Christ himself was transcendently the Prophet.[85]

Blanco White, also maintained that 'Christ published the religion of conscience, which though essentially grounded upon the nature of man . . . had been obscured, and almost placed beyond the mental reach of the mass of mankind.'[86] It was an idea which became embedded in Martineau's thought and was later developed and expressed in such a way as to represent his complete break with the determinism of Priestley, and the Utilitarianism of Bentham and Mill. In the last sermon he preached from the pulpit of Paradise Street Chapel, before departing for Germany and returning to the newly-built Hope Street Church, he defined what he was attempting with his congregation:

> To substitute among you the Religion of Consciousness for the religion of customs . . . that precisely in proportion as the affections are pure and deep, the conscience clear and strong, and the imagination familiar with great and beautiful examples, are heavenly realities discerned.[87]

The clear strong conscience had become one of the great pillars of his theism.[88]

There are several parallels which can be drawn between White's theology and that of the later Martineau which strongly indicate that White played an important part in shaping Martineau's subsequent theology. It was White who encouraged Martineau to come to terms with the inner nature and discernment of religious truth. White constantly proclaimed:

> Man must turn to the light within him, aided by its developments in Christ—the highest, the purest, the best guide he knows. He must follow that light; he must sacrifice his selfish will to the duties which conscience points out.[89]

These features of the Inner Light, of conscience, of self-surrender and of Christ being the highest and the best known to man, were all to become intrinsic parts of Martineau's thought. In his last letter to Estlin Carpenter written some sixty years after Blanco White's death he spoke of his great admiration for the Society of Friends, who took their stand on 'the inward "Spirit of God" in the responding Conscience.'[90]

Martineau's debt to White made him no less critical of White's failings. He noted with some sadness that White's successive changes in churchmanship were produced by a series of repulsions for his current beliefs rather than by an attraction to new truth.[91] Moreover Martineau felt that White's lack of 'moral enthusiasm' had deprived him of 'strength, and joy, and faith', in his religion,[92] which were precisely the qualities Martineau found in his other great formative influence of the 1830s, that of the American, William Ellery Channing.

In his article on Channing, published in *Essays, Reviews and Addresses*, Martineau maintained that while White and Channing were at one on the essential issues of theology, they were very different in temperament and outlook.

> Blanco White and Channing were attached friends, and in the memoir of each, the correspondence of the other constitutes one of the chief ornaments. On the most momentous topics of human thought, their opinions for many years concurred; yet how different the whole structure of their mental nature.[93]

Martineau was first introduced to the writings of Channing through

Lant Carpenter who was staying with a Mrs. Cappe of York in 1821 when she received a copy of Dr. Channing's sermon on *The Evidences*:

> Dr. Carpenter read it with delight instead of taking his breakfast, for he had hardly time for both; "Aye," said he, "this will do, this will do indeed."[94]

He promptly took it back to Bristol for use in the Lewins Mead Chapel and in his school where Martineau was a pupil. Some thirty years later when Martineau wrote his appreciation of Channing he noted that Channing produced no great or lasting work of history, philosophy or art, but that his influence was 'wide and deep'.[95] Channing's impact on Martineau was considerable, as can be seen from Martineau's paper delivered to the London gathering, celebrating the centenary of Channing's birth. In that Address, Martineau set down what he considered to be the heart of the American's teaching:

> The single thought of which, from first to last, it was the living expression is this, that MORAL PERFECTION IS THE ESSENCE OF GOD AND THE SUPREME END FOR MAN; in the one, an eternal reality, in the other, a continuous possibility, in both the ground of perpetual spiritual communion . . . not of Morality in the mere social sense, of a rule of conduct between man and man; or in the negative sense of a repressive law, saying of this or that, "Thou shalt not"; but of Moral Excellence in the Divine and Positive sense, of an ever-active sway of best affections, an eternal life of holy will, an infinitude of spiritual beauty and love for the true and good inherent always in the Father of Spirits, and open to the approaches of all his children.[96]

Martineau then outlined the resultant effect of this central idea on both Channing's theology and his ethics. In his theology Channing allowed nothing to be said of God which contradicted his moral nature. In his ethics Channing affirmed that everyone had the capacity to discern right from wrong and the power to pursue the right. These were precisely the points which Martineau took up and enlarged in his article on 'Five Points of the Christian Faith', written in 1841, i.e. 'we have Faith in the Moral Perceptions of Man' and 'we have Faith in the Moral Perfection of God.'[97]

In his important Centenary Lecture, Martineau set out clearly his own development of Channing's thought:

> Thus by the simplest expansion of Channing's Primary Thought, Duty becomes supreme over the personal life; Reverence over the social; Aspiration over the spiritual; and love for the true, the beautiful and the good, over all.[98]

In addition to the view shared by both men that morality was central to Christianity, there were four other areas where the ideas of Channing were sufficiently similar to those of Martineau to suggest that the older man had either influenced the younger, or at least had reinforced his religious thought.

Firstly, Channing and Martineau each held that Christ was central to Christianity and both wrestled against those who advocated that Christ was no longer necessary to their religious thought. In a letter to Miss E.

Peabody written in 1841 Channing mantained that there was a profound ignorance of Christ among those who found Him restrictive or who felt that they had out-grown Him.[99] The following month he wrote to Martineau on the same subject:

> Some among them . . . I fear are loosening their hold on Christ. They are anxious to defend the soul's immediate connection with God. They fear lest Christ be made a barrier between the soul and the Supreme, and are in danger of substituting private inspiration for Christianity.[100]

Channing's stand against those who wished to remove Christ from Christianity, was a position which Martineau took up for English Unitarianism and which was forcefully expressed in his letters to V. D. Davis and Francis Newman, against growing opposition.

Secondly, Channing shared with Martineau a view of Unitarianism as a transitory doctrinal position which described the belief of individuals rather than the creed of a Church. Channing's lack of interest in Unitarianism as a denomination was clearly expressed in a letter to W. Trevilcock written in August 1841.

> I distrust sectarian influences more and more. I am more detached from a denomination, and strive to feel more my connection with the Universal Church, with all good and holy men. I am little of a Unitarian, have little sympathy with the system of Priestley and Belsham, and stand aloof from all but those who strive and pray for clearer light, who look for a purer and more effectual manifestation of Christian truth.[101]

This was a position which Martineau adopted and ably expressed both in his correspondence with Professor Knight of St. Andrews, and in his controversy of 1859 with MacDonald of Chester. Martineau wrote to Knight in 1872 pointing out that there was no such thing as a 'Unitarian Body' or a 'Unitarian Denomination,' for Unitarianism was not a Church but a theology held by people of various ecclesiastical affiliations.[102]

Thirdly, Channing confirmed Martineau's own view that divine goodness was intuitively known and inwardly discerned. In a letter to Martineau dated 1841 he answered Martineau's question of how God's goodness is to be reconciled with man's experience of human affairs.

> It is so long since doubts of the Divine goodness have crossed my mind, that I hardly know how to meet them. This truth came to me as an intuitive one. I meet it everywhere. I can no more question it than I can the supreme worth of beauty or virtue.[103]

A few months earlier, Martineau had written to Mary Carpenter expressing the view that the divinity of a person or a thing is always discerned intuitively.[104] Although Martineau never systematically expounded his belief in intuition, there is no doubt that after his contact with Channing it became an intrinsic part of his theory of knowledge.[105]

Fourthly, Channing played an important role in encouraging Martineau to abandon his belief in philosophical necessity, which had been a key feature of Unitarian doctrine since the time of Priestley. As early as 1831 Channing was writing to an English Unitarian, Lucy Aikin, expressing his opposition to Priestley's doctrine of philosophical necessity:

> Now Priestley's system of materialism, of necessity, and of the derivation of all our moral sentiments from sensations variously modified by associations, does seem to strike a blow at our most intimate and strongest moral convictions, whilst it robs our nature of all its grandeur.[106]

Miss Aikin's reply showed that Channing had raised doubts in her mind as to the compatibility of the Scriptures and individual moral decision with the doctrine of necessity.

By 1839 Martineau's own doubts about philosophical necessity, which he had suppressed for some years, were surfacing; so much so that in his lecture on 'Moral Evil' delivered during the Liverpool Controversy of that year, he launched his first tentative attack against the doctrine. On reading this paper Channing wrote to Martineau expressing his full support and encouragement in this movement of thought:

> The part of your discourse which gave me the sincerest delight, and for which I would especially thank you, is that in which you protest against the doctrine of philosophical necessity. Nothing for a long time has given me so much pleasure. I have felt that that doctrine, with its natural connections, was a millstone round the neck of Unitarianism in England.[107]

Some years later, when making notes on the correspondence he had received, Martineau recorded with some pride that his treatment of the doctrine of necessity had been greeted by Channing with 'unqualified satisfaction.'[108]

In 1839 Martineau had been thrown into the Liverpool Controversy when the evangelical Anglican priest of Christ Church, the Revd. Fielding Ould, sent out invitations to the Unitarians of Liverpool to hear a series of thirteen lectures, where the errors of their faith were to be exposed. Three Unitarian ministers, Martineau, Thom and Giles of Toxteth Park, accepted the invitations, sat in what Martineau called the 'condemned pew' to hear the lectures, and each week gave an address in reply. Reading the lectures and mass of correspondence over a century later, it appears that the Unitarians, and especially Martineau, who gave five of the replies, out-thought their opponents by their carefully prepared philosophical and theological arguments. It is not surprising that three orthodox Christians, Samuel Bulley, Isaac Cook and Charles Rawlins, announced their conversion to the Unitarian viewpoint.[109]

In 1840 Martineau's religious thought underwent a dramatic change. His dissatisfaction with necessarian philosophy was brought to a head by his appointment to the staff of Manchester New College, where the need to prepare and deliver lectures compelled him to harmonise the different movements of thought which had been developing in his mind since his arrival in Liverpool. He recorded in his Biographical Memoranda:

> I resumed the systematic study of philosophic literature, and thought out anew the problems which I had to treat. The change of view was very

> inconvenient to me. Almost everything I had written became worthless in my eyes: courses of lectures elaborately prepared for repeated use were laid upon the shelf for ever; the familiar text books could no longer be used in that capacity in my private classes: and every subject had to be melted down again in my own mind and be recast in other moulds. For all this there was ample compensation, in the sense of inward deliverance which I seemed to gain from artificial systems into natural speech. It was an escape from a logical cage into the open air.

It was in the philosophy of Kant that Martineau found the intellectual framework which enabled him to achieve this. Abandoning his discipleship to Priestley and Hartley, Martineau compiled a lecture scheme which combined the critical reason of Kant with English empirical philosophy. Although he subsequently modified this approach by drawing on a wider variety of ideas, notably those of Plato, Aristotle and the Scottish Philosophers, he never gave up his adherence to some of the major insights of Kant's teaching.

The influence of Kant on Martineau's work can be traced from this time onwards in his sermons, articles, essays and books. In *The Study of Religion* for example, there are some sixty references to Kant, several of which are elaborate treatments of Kant's major ideas, such as his views on free will. Further evidence of Kant's influence on Martineau is found in *Types of Ethical Theory* where Martineau explains that he omitted to expound Kant's theory of ethics because it was too similar to his own:

> It is scarcely less a surprise to myself than it can be to my readers, that no pages in this book have been reserved for Kant. The reason, paradoxical as it may seem, is found, not in any slight of his ethical theory, but in an approximate adoption of it.[110]

His sabbatical leave in Germany during 1848–49 served to reinforce the impact of Kant upon his thinking. He recalled how he had used the time to study the works of Hegel and Plato, and that the former, although a valuable discipline in itself, gave him no new insights, 'but rather threw me back upon the position of Kant.'[111]

The immediate influence of Kant's thought on Martineau in 1840 can be traced in an article entitled *Five Points of Christian Faith* (1841), which contains several striking resemblances to ideas propounded by Kant in his *Critique of Practical Reason*, *Religion Within the Limits of Reason Alone* and *Lectures on Philosophical Theology*. These involve the concepts of duty; of God being the highest goodness and intelligence that can be conceived by man; and belief in immortality.

There were also other points of similarity between the thought of Martineau and that of Kant. Both held that the teleological argument deserved to be treated with respect and could be an important confirmation of belief in God, which had been independently gained. But Martineau, like Kant, considered that the teleological argument on its own was not competent to establish anything more than an infinitely intellectual being.[112] His major criticism of the argument was its inability to verify the 'warmer attributes' of God. Martineau also shared with Kant the view that the doctrines of the Church must be carefully scrutinised and the distinction drawn between what was essential and what was inessential in doctrine.

Martineau not only borrowed from Kant, but he also developed and added to Kant's ideas. He was, however, very selective in his use of Kantian material and on several major points he disagreed with Kant's conclusions. The most fundamental difference between the two men concerned the doctrine of God, His existence, and whether He could be personally known.

Kant never wished to ascribe personality to God, except in his little known work *Opus Posthumum* which was published shortly before his death in 1803. His major treatise on moral philosophy and theology *The Critique of Practical Reason* portrays God simply as a 'postulate' to give life meaning and render a reward in the next life to a person who acts according to his conscience in this life. Martineau interpreted Kant's system as representing God as a possible fiction of the imagination. In 1841 he wrote:

> At the opposite role to this doctrine, which makes the perception of "Reason" a part of the activity of God, lies the system of Kant and Fichte, which represents God as an ideal formation, it may therefore be a fiction—arising from the activity of the "Reason" . . .[113]

Martineau moreover maintained that Kant's teaching, along with that of many leading philosophers, portrayed a God who was essentially unknowable:

> Certainly it is that, except in the incomplete cases of Locke and Berkeley, the result of all these researches into the ultimate laws of thought is to banish into the unknown the essential object of Christian belief . . .[114]

Over and against this teaching Martineau asserted that God 'is' a reality who 'is' at work in His world,[115] and that he could be known personally by the individual as 'a Mind directly accessible to all other minds.'[116]

Martineau also departed from the teaching of Kant on three important topics: Christ, the Church, and the devotional life. Kant portrayed Christ simply as a moral example of the best and highest that man could attain; a kind of archetypal man representing the individual's moral duty.[117] Martineau wished to go much further than this and place Christ at the centre of his theism as the one who reveals the very nature of God and the nature of man. In 1841 he wrote:

> We conceive that Jesus of Nazareth lived and died, not to persuade the Father, not to appease the Father, not to make a sanguinary purchase from the Father, but simply to "show us the Father", to leave upon the human heart a new, deep vivid impression of what God is in himself, and of what he designs for his creature man;[118]

Kant held that unity between the churches could be achieved if the different communions would translate their doctrines into moral precepts, where the common ground of unity would be found.[119] Over and against this emphasis Martineau came to the belief that doctrines constantly change and develop within the Christian Church. (Changes in doctrinal emphasis had been a characteristic of the Octagon Church of Norwich where Martineau had grown up). He viewed doctrine as something which was transitory and therefore he looked for a basis of unity in an aspect of religion which he considered to be more permanent; and this he located in what he called, 'the conscious sameness of spiritual relations.'[120] By this term, Martineau meant the communion or 'fellowship' which united Christians across the credal divisions and down through the centuries.

The devotional life was a key point of divergence between the two thinkers. Kant could only find a place in his system of thought for prayer and meditation in so far as it was helpful to the individual's moral stance, and in strengthening and encouraging his sense of duty:

> Praying thought of as an inner formal service of God and hence as a means of grace, is a superstitious illusion . . .[121]

For Martineau, with his belief in a personal God who touched the life of the individual, devotion was central to the Christian Faith. In the Preface to his most famous hymn book, *Hymns for the Christian Church and Home* he defended the place of devotion in the life of the Christian and vigorously attacked the utilitarian approach to worship which he saw simply as a means to heighten a person's awareness of moral conduct and sense of duty.

> Worship is an attitude which our nature assumes, not for a purpose, but from an emotion . . . In opposition to this natural idea of worship stands the Utilitarian, which considers it an "instrumental act"; whether, according to the sacerdotal view, its instrumentality is thought to be mystically efficacious with God; or according to the rationalistic, intelligibly beneficial to man . . . But the churches which begin to justify their outward devotion by appeal to this consideration have already lost their inward devoutness; and the individual who, with this notion of self-operation, speaks a prayer, performs an act of disciplinary prudence, not of Christian piety, and takes the air of heaven for the sake of exercise, rather than in love of the light and quest of the immensity of God.[122]

Kant made a significant impact on Martineau's thought, both positively in terms of influence and negatively because the reading of Kant's work forced Martineau to crystallise his own thought on the issues where he did not agree with the German scholar. In later life Martineau came to look back upon 1840 as the great watershed in his thinking. It has been suggested that his mode of thought was not fixed until his return from Germany in 1849,[123] but the evidence does not seem to support such a conclusion, though Martineau acknowledged the value of his sabbatical leave in Germany. It afforded him freedom for quiet philosophical reflection away from his pastoral duties and teaching responsibilities, as well as the opportunity to familiarise himself with the writing of Plato and Aristotle which widened his spectrum of thought. His basic patterns of thinking were already shaped with his break from necessarian philosophy, as can be seen from his two most popular works produced in the early 1840s, *Hymns for the Christian Church and Home* and *Endeavours after the Christian Life*, which contained the kernel of his thinking found in later writings, although greatly enlarged and developed. Martineau emerged from his study of Kant and his 1840 critics with a deep awareness of human experience, and with the conviction that human beliefs and actions could be accounted for by other factors than simply that of reason. It was this belief that brought Martineau into a close affinity with the religious thought of Samuel Taylor Coleridge.

Coleridge and Martineau never met: but in view of Coleridge's influence on the development of theology in the nineteenth century, it is not surprising to discover that his shadow is cast over much of Martineau's religious thought.

Coleridge and Martineau had several things in common. They both aspired to become Unitarian Ministers; they both abandoned their discipleship to Hartley and the necessarian philosophical position; they both came under the powerful influence of Kant; they both studied in Germany and were indebted to German religious thought. A. Michael Ramsey, when writing of F. D. Maurice, maintained that:

> The importance of Coleridge becomes apparent if we ask what reading could be recommended to a layman in the eighteen-thirties who was looking for some indication of the reasonableness of Christian belief and found the older method of 'evidences' for an external and authoritative revelation no longer satisfying,[124]

A careful comparison of Martineau's writings with those of Coleridge, especially *Aids to Reflection* and *Confessions of an Inquiring Spirit*, not only reveals a close relationship of ideas, but also in some cases a striking resemblance of terminology.

Their approaches to the Bible show this affinity of thought. In 1825, when referring to the Bible, Coleridge said, 'I take up this work with the purpose to read it for the first time as I should read any other work.'[125] This sentiment found an echo in the work of Martineau, who some sixteen years later when discussing how the Bible should be interpreted, wrote: 'that in interpreting these Scriptures, we follow the same rules which we should apply to any other books . . .'[126]

Similarly, Martineau followed Coleridge in his theory of morals. One of the important questions for ethics in the Victorian era was whether the motives of the moral agent, or the actions performed by the moral agent were central to the theory of morals. On this question Martineau, like Coleridge, affirmed the former to be more important, against Whetwell and Sidgwick who held the opposite view. Sidgwick's obsession with Martineau was probably due to the fact that Martineau offered the only serious philosophical attempt in Britain since Coleridge, to assert the pre-eminence of motive over action in morality.[127]

The resemblance of thought between the two men was not just limited to doctrinal issues, but also extended to general observations. Coleridge, for example, had asserted that almost all errors could be attributed to 'truths misunderstood . . . half truths taken as the whole.'[128] This was an idea which Martineau used to great effect in his own sermons.[129] He began his sermon on 'Great Principles and Small Duties', with words remarkably similar to those of Coleridge, 'Every fiction that has ever laid strong hold on human belief is a mistaken image of some great truth.'[130]

Both Coleridge and Martineau sought to bring into harmony religion and philosophy;[131] they both advocated the fearless pursuit of truth,[132] and they both saw Christianity not simply as the revelation of a Book or a Church but as the crowning perfection of all intelligence.

If Martineau had not acknowledged his debt to Coleridge, the affinity of their ideas could have been accounted for simply by the fact that they were both caught up in the spirit of the age and were moving along parallel lines of thought. In 1856, however, Martineau wrote to one of his former pupils, Susanna Winkworth, expressing his appreciation of her translation of Tauler, and implying that Coleridge was one of his 'sacred guides'.

> I see at once that the book will be, for the rest of my life, one of my sacred guides, and will stand, after my Bible, with Plato, and Leighton, and the Theologia Germanica, and Coleridge and Tennyson, and the German and Wesley Hymns. A strange jumble you will say, of heterogeneous springs of thought. Yet all, I think, assuaging to the same thirst.[133]

The most direct evidence of Martineau's debt to Coleridge can be found in an important paper he wrote entitled 'Personal Influences on Present Theology' (1856). It was to this article that David Pym referred in *The Religious Thought of Samuel Taylor Coleridge*, when he noted that Martineau along with five other mid-Victorian theologians had published tributes to Coleridge[134] which helped at the time to arouse interest in Coleridge's theological ideas.

Martineau's article is of importance because instead of giving a general treatment of Coleridge's theology, he highlighted his central theological position with which he was in total agreement:

> The great strength of this school lies, we think, in its faithful interpretation of what is at once deepest and highest in the religious consciousness of men; and its recognition, in this consciousness of a living Divine person, instead of mere abstractions without authority, or the dreams of unreliable imagination.[135]

It must be admitted that the extent to which Martineau owed the origin of many of his ideas to Coleridge is difficult to assess. The two certainly held many notions in common and Coleridge's modes of thought were reflected in Martineau's writings. It is also worthy of note that Martineau helped to attract attention to Coleridge as a religious thinker, in addition to his standing as a poet. Martineau's tribute to Coleridge as one of the three great personal influences on mid-Victorian theology reinforces the belief that Coleridge's impact on Martineau was considerable. At the very least Coleridge served as a buttress to reinforce concepts which enabled Martineau more confidently to meet the challenge of Spencer, Tyndall and Sidgwick.

It was while on the staff of Manchester College that he formed a lifelong friendship with Francis Newman, the gifted brother of John Henry

Newman. A bundle of letters written from Newman to Martineau survives in Manchester College Library and presents us with a splendid insight into their close friendship. They deal with Victorian life in general, as well as presenting Martineau with penetrating and searching questions about his theology and especially his devotion to Christ.

During his remaining seventeen years in Liverpool he wrote some fifty-five major articles, contributed to several nineteenth century journals, as well as producing his outstanding collection of sermons, *Endeavours after the Christian Life*. This was probably his most popular and influential work and by 1892 it had gone into nine editions. Martineau was ministering continuously to his congregation, apart from a period of eighteen months in 1847–8 when he studied in Germany. He had the Church rebuilt while he was away, replacing the old octagonal shape with a fine Gothic structure, which he felt was more in tune with the spirit of the age. It had elaborate carvings, stained-glass windows, choir pews and a high altar. The last two were never used, but were there to create the right atmosphere.

In 1853 Manchester College moved to London, but by then the railways had arrived, bringing London within six hours of Liverpool; Martineau was able to keep his post at the College, travelling up to London two days a fortnight to lecture and still having time to carry out his ministerial duties in Liverpool.

In 1857 he joined the full-time staff of the College, which since the departure of Francis Newman as Professor of Classics had changed character, in that it no longer tried to supply a complete system of University education but had become more of a theological school in association with University College, London. He remained in London for the rest of his working life, first as Professor and later as Principal of Manchester College. On his retirement he published his major works: *Types of Ethical Theory*, *A Study of Religion*, *A Study of Spinoza*, and *The Seat of Authority in Religion*. These were in part the results of his three year cycle of lectures.

Martineau was too broadminded to be a disciple of any school. He was eclectic in his nature and gathered ideas from every source which appealed to his own intellect and emotional character. Thus his philosophical theology was shaped more by his personality and the movements of the age than by a particular school of thought. He, in himself, was a record of nineteenth-century theology; born only three years after the death of Kant and living on into the twentieth century, he engaged or commented on almost every theological personality or movement of the age, as a glance at his four volumes of collected *Essays, Reviews and Addresses* reveals.

An indication of his importance to nineteenth century religious thought can be ascertained from the fact that he was highly regarded by his contemporaries or near-contemporaries. Tennyson considered him to be the most brilliant mind of the Metaphysical Society,[136] which included among its members, Dean Stanley, Cardinal Manning,

W. G. Ward, Thomas Huxley and R. H. Hutton. Gladstone and P. T. Forsyth, as we have already seen, rated him highly among the intellectuals of the day.

He also deserves a place in the history of English religious thought because of his influence upon others. He was a churchman who was able to cross the denominational boundaries, and through his writings and friendships, exerted a powerful influence on broad-churchmen such as Bishop Colenso and F. W. Robertson.

It was Martineau's *Endeavours after the Christian Life* which caused John Colenso, as a young and earnest student at Cambridge to write home enthusiastically to his fiancée about James Martineau, 'I have never seen a book—I think I may say—so full of brilliant and truthful passages as this little work . . .'[137] This influence was clearly revealed some twenty-five years later when Colenso wrote his *Natal Sermons* which showed a considerable reliance upon Martineau's published sermons.[138] Moreover it is of interest to note that when Colenso became depressed with his situation in South Africa; unable to support his clergy or pay for the upkeep of his churches, Martineau tried to secure a teaching post for him at Manchester New College.[139] The move, however, was blocked by the College Council.

F. W. Robertson of Brighton was the most famous Anglican preacher of the Victorian era, and his sermons were still studied by Anglican Ordinands in the 1920s. According to his biographer, Robertson 'read James Martineau's books with pleasure and profit. The influence of "The Endeavours after the Christian Life" can be traced through many of his sermons.'[140] In an interesting article written in 1903, John Hoatson studied the impact of Martineau's sermons on Robertson and concluded that: 'Examination reveals traces of the influence of thirty-seven out of forty-three sermons in Endeavours upon at least sixty two of the one hundred and twenty five published sermons of Robertson.'[141]

There were also those who were attracted to Unitarianism because of him; the two best known being Stopford Brooke and L. P. Jacks. The prominent place Brooke ascribed to Martineau can be perceived from the famous question he once put to Dean Stanley when discussing the widening comprehension of the Church of England: 'Will it broaden sufficiently to enable James Martineau to be made Archbishop of Canterbury?'[142] The appeal of Martineau for the younger man extended over many years, and as early as 1857 when Brooke was only twenty-five his diary reveals that he was reading Martineau's works.[143] Moreover, when Brooke left the Church of England, the aged Martineau joined his London congregation at Bedford Chapel.

In Liverpool Martineau formed a class for young ladies, several of whom became prominent in later life. The most famous of these were Mary Carpenter, Catherine and Susanna Winkworth and Anna Swanwick, who was to become the President of Bedford College, London and was associated with the founding of Girton College, Cambridge and Somerville College, Oxford. Her biographer wrote:

> The teaching of James Martineau at that time appears to have acted as a wonderful stimulus to her mental development, revealing vistas undreamt of in her narrow course of reading . . . She felt grateful all her life for his assistance and guidance in her youth, and the friendship thus begun, continued during a period of sixty-five years.[144]

There were others who came under Martineau's influence. R. H. Hutton, editor of the *Spectator*, was one of his students and a life-long friend. Joseph Hertz, who later became the Chief Rabbi of Great Britain, came under his influence and wrote a Doctoral Thesis in 1894 on Martineau's ethics. Baron von Hügel went out of his way to meet Martineau, and the story that Martineau told him was taken up and used by Alec Vidler in his retirement sermon, preached in King's College Chapel, Cambridge.[145]

Martineau's more direct contribution to English religious thought is accurately assessed in the writings of Hugh Walker, sometime Professor of English at St. David's College, Lampeter, who in 1910 said of him:

> At an earlier time Martineau the Unitarian would have been anathema to the orthodox; but while the rank and file were still absorbed in Gorham controversies and Jerusalem bishoprics, the more intelligent saw that the main battle was raging round the central positions, and were glad to welcome an ally who would help to hold these . . . No one probably did more effective work than he in opposition to materialism, altruism, positivism, and all the schemes of thought which seemed to threaten the very existence of Christianity; and therefore many, even of those who found all the truth within the limits of the Thirty-nine Articles or the Westminister Confession, learnt to look upon him as the champion of a cause which was theirs as well as his.[146]

It was a sentiment which echoed the words of Stopford Brooke, preached at Martineau's funeral service and which was due to be repeated several times in the decades that followed, by A. M. Fairbairn, Principal of Mansfield College, Oxford;[147] by S. C. Carpenter in the 1930s; and more recently by Owen Chadwick in *The Victorian Church*.[148]

Martineau disliked controversy and often felt himself badly equipped for it; but he was drawn into controversy, and even seemed to attract it and create it. His importance for nineteenth-century Christian thought can be seen more in his sermons and controversies than in his later systematic writings. Of the many controversies in which he engaged three stand out as being of major importance: they were his controversy with Spencer on Agnosticism, with Tyndall on Materialism, and with Sidgwick on Ethics, the last of which has already been fully discussed by J. B. Schneewind in *Sidgwick's Ethics and Victorian Moral Philosophy*.

Herbert Spencer was the most famous philosopher of the nineteenth century to develop the evolutionary theory. He held that evolution proceeded from the simple to the complex, and that progress was not an accident or the work of a great Architect, but simply a necessity. He recognised the existence of what he called the 'Unknowable', and maintained that by definition nothing could be known about it. D. C.

Somervell held that Spencer was read widely by the intellectual general public of the day, but was not studied in the Universities, where he was despised.[149] An indication of the seriousness with which Spencer was taken, and the strength of the opposition he aroused, can be seen from his 'Replies to Criticisms' of his *First Principles*, where he attempts to deal with the adverse criticism from Principal Caird, Dr. Mansel, Dr. Hodgson, Professor Max Müller, Mr. Henry Sidgwick and James Martineau whom he saw as an 'able metaphysician' and one of his most effective critics.[150]

In 1862 Herbert Spencer published his *First Principles*, which was the opening section of his colossal five part work on *Synthetic Philosophy*. In October of the same year Martineau printed an article in the *National Review* under the title, 'Science, Nescience and Faith' which was chiefly a criticism of Spencer's work. This essay provided one of the best apologies of the nineteenth century for the theistic position. It is a masterly paper in which the author used a wide variety of methods in pursuit of his argument: irony, detailed analysis, *reductio ad absurdum* and rhetoric; each one being appropriately chosen to fit the situation.

Martineau argued that the theist, the atheist and the pantheist all agreed that the problem of whether there is a Supreme Being behind the world is worthy of serious consideration, and that all three embark on such an investigation in the belief that a result is possible. 'Without the assumption that knowledge is possible, the very attitude of the quest is impossible.'[151] Martineau attacked Spencer on the grounds that the positivist and theistic positions are both understandable, but that Spencer's intermediate position that there was a first cause which cannot be known is the least tenable of all possibilities:

> We can understand the Positivist with whom laws are ultimate, and who turns causation out of the doors into metaphysical night. We can understand the Theist, who says that, on whatever ground you know the First Cause to exist, on the same ground you know that Cause to be a free Mind. But we cannot understand the intermediate position which allows a field to Ontology, but condemns it to perpetual barrenness.[152]

Martineau criticised Spencer for maintaining that to affirm anything about the Infinite was to introduce boundaries and to close doors on other possibilities. According to Martineau, Spencer was asking, 'How can the Infinite be the object of thought, for to think is to predicate, and to predicate is to limit, thus the Infinite becomes the finite and is consequently destroyed.'[153] Martineau affirmed that to remain consistent in this process, no predicate not even that of existence could be attributed to the Infinite. Martineau held that to maintain the Infinite exists but is totally unknowable is a contradiction in terms. He thus summed up his argument:

> The denial for all minds, of any possible knowledge of God, is tantamount to the denial, for him, of real being . . . Mr. Spencer must, it strikes us, concede either more to ontology or less; either fall back on the maxim, "All we know is phenomena"; or go forward from his assurance,

> that the Infinite Cause, is to admit some possible apprehension of what it is.[154]

Behind Martineau's criticism lay a deep feeling that if Spencer's philosophical system was not refuted it could undermine the basis of Christian worship. At the end of his article Martineau pointed out that Spencer's approach denied any communication between the Divine and the human in terms of thought or conscience or affection and left no possibility of communication of the living God with living souls.[155] Although Martineau acknowledged that Spencer had preserved the mystery of religion (which he, Martineau, had so vigorously contended for in the Liverpool Controversy) Martineau also maintained that a religion could not be constituted out of mystery alone.[156]

In the Spring of 1872 Martineau published a lecture entitled *The Place of Mind in Nature and Intuition in Man*, which was in part an attack on Spencer's account of evolution. In his *Synthetic Systems of Philosophy*, Spencer had attempted to give an account of evolution which dispensed with an Infinite Intelligence and Will.

This debate was of less importance than that on *Science, Nescience and Faith* for it revealed little of the shape of Martineau's philosophical theology. On balance Spencer possibly got the better of the scientific arguments, but he seems to have made few inroads into Martineau's basic assumption that behind the evolutionary process, 'Mind is first and rules for ever.'[157] At the centre of this controversy was Martineau's argument that theism was compatible with evolution and Spencer's reply that theism was not necessary to evolution.

Three years after Martineau's death Spencer wrote his Autobiography and proclaimed himself the victor, maintaining that 'The refutation of his argument was an easy task.'[158] However some who were able to take a more distant view of the confrontation and who wrote from a less biased position tended to award the honours to Martineau. S. C. Carpenter, for example, when writing his *Church and People, 1789–1889*, said of Martineau, 'He met Spencer and Tyndall on their own ground, and showed that the Monism of one and the Materialism of the other failed to cover all the facts.'[159] The German Philosopher, Otto Pfleiderer also commends Martineau's 'forcible criticism' of Spencer's work.[160] Although Martineau did not respond to either of Spencer's replies, when he came to write *A Study of Religion* and *Types of Ethical Theory* he again took issue with Spencer.

Drummond and Upton wildly overstated their case when they referred to Martineau's controversy with the agnostics, including Spencer:

> All these impressive papers prove, I think conclusively, that the phenomena of nature owe their origin to spiritual activity, and that the right clue to the meaning of all causality is found in our consciousness of volitional effort.[161]

Martineau did not defeat Spencer in the sense of proving that Spencer was wrong, or that he, Martineau, held the only tenable view. What he did so successfully was to show that neither the agnostic case, nor the case for unaided evolution were proven, for both contained many unexplained elements; and moreover he demonstrated that there were many factors which pointed towards a theistic conclusion.

During the last thirty years, modern scholarship has tended to under-emphasise the conflict between religion and science in the ninteenth century. This is in no small part due to the fact that much recent research has been focused on the debate between Huxley and Wilberforce, and has questioned the importance of that controversy:

> It is now of course widely acknowledged that as a symbol, the Oxford confrontation is totally misleading, indeed, the so-called conflict of religion and science has largely disappeared under the searching microscope of the historial revisionists.[162]

The true situation is more complex: the major battle of this conflict was not centred on Huxley and Wilberforce, but on Martineau and Tyndall, in whose writings a crucial debate concerning religion and science was taking place. Martineau's campaign was largely defensive and concentrated on two fundamental issues. He argued against matter being self-sufficient, able to create and construct out of its own necessity and thus removing the need for God; and he vigorously opposed religion relinquishing to science the intellectual sphere and thus being confined to the emotional realm of man's nature.

Martineau's controversy with Professor John Tyndall over materialism brought him to the forefront of English theology and philosophy in the 1870s and earned him the reputation of being 'a champion of theism'.[163] There were several reasons for this in addition to the content and strength of Martineau's argumentation. The eminence of John Tyndall both as a respected scientist and as a famous mountaineer ensured for his critic, Martineau, a wide publicity. Moreover Martineau's two papers in the dispute were not lost in some obscure theological journal, but were printed in the *Contemporary Review* and thus captured a broad readership in England and America.[164]

Tyndall's own remarks suggest that Martineau's essays were read by many prominent figures in public life: 'my attention had been directed by several estimable, and indeed eminent, persons, to an essay by the Rev. James Martineau, as demanding serious consideration at my hands.'[165] Tyndall's theory of materialism was attacked by the Press, especially the Religious Press[166] and several leading Churchmen of the day, including the Bishop of Manchester and Cardinal Cullen. But his biographers maintain that the 'most able and temperate antagonist was James Martineau.'[167] The general interest that the controversy aroused can be gauged from the two articles contributed to the *Spectator* by R. H. Hutton, both of which criticise Tyndall and praised Martineau's work.[168]

The debate between the two men commenced with Tyndall's Presidential Address to the British Association meeting in Belfast on 19th August, 1874. This speech which was reported in *The Times* of the following day and subsequently produced as a separate booklet, brought forth an immediate response from Martineau in his address at the Opening of Session of Manchester New College, in October 1874. This was enlarged and published the same month, in the *Contemporary Review* under the title, 'Religion as Effected by Modern Materialism'. The following year in November 1875, the *Fortnightly Review* carried Tyndall's rejoinder to Martineau, entitled, 'The Rev. James Martineau and the Belfast Address'. The final blow in this confrontation was struck by Martineau with his article, 'Modern Materialism: its Attitude Towards Theology', which appeared in the April edition of the *Contemporary Review* for 1876 and which drew no further reply from Tyndall.

Martineau's paper, 'Religion as Affected by Modern Materialism', was a clear statement of his thinking on this topic, and is of historical importance as it was the most effective defence of theism offered in the face of Tyndall's attack. Early in his paper, when outlining the principles upon which the students at Manchester College were being trained, Martineau set out his own theological position so that his comments on Tyndall's *Belfast Address* could be seen clearly in relief against it. He held that:

> The Universe which includes us and folds us round is the life-dwelling of an Eternal Mind that the World of our abode is the scene of a Moral Government incipient but not yet complete and that the upper zones of Human Affection, above the clouds of self and passion, take us into the sphere of a Divine Communion.[169]

Martineau's general comment on Tyndall's *Belfast Address* was that it contained many true aspects of scientific investigation which were unfortunately linked together by a questionable philosophy.[170] He attacked Tyndall's formula for ending the conflict between religion and science, which limited religion to the emotional part of man's nature and assigned the intellect to science. Martineau asserted:

> No partnership between the physicist and the theologian can be formed on these terms, of assigning the intellect to one and the feelings to the other.[171]

Martineau's own solution to the problem was to reintroduce the distinction he made in his argument with Spencer, which was that of Religion asking the 'Whence' of all phenomena while science asked the 'How'. He qualified this by maintaining that science observed what is happening in the clusters of phenomena while religion asserted that behind those clusters there is a Divine Mind at work.[172]

Martineau maintained that Tyndall's teaching of 'a known materialism and a created God' presented a combination which was rejected both by reason and reverence. He made the counter-claim that the atomic hypothesis was 'a thing not known but created, while God is not created but known.'[173] Martineau concluded his paper by restating his conviction that the conflict between religion and science would not be ended by ascribing reason to one and imagination to the other, in order to keep them from quarrelling, but by recognising:

> A Duality in the function of Reason itself, according as it deals with

phenomena or their ground, with law or with causality, with material consecution or with moral alternatives.[174]

An indication of the impact of Martineau's contribution to this controversy can be found in the life of Charles Hargrove who in the 1870s was moving his churchmanship from being a Jesuit to a Unitarian. From his writings it appears that he followed closely Martineau's debate with Tyndall and was profoundly influenced by Martineau's argument; perhaps it is no mere coincidence that he became a Unitarian shortly after Martineau published his second paper of the dispute. In a lecture on Shakespeare, Hargrove acknowledged his debt to Martineau and extensively quoted from Martineau's first paper of the controversy:

> To me, indeed, it seems that the assumption laid down as the basis of all theological training by the greatest religious teacher of our age, and approved by the greatest living teacher of science, would not unwillingly have been subscribed by Shakespeare also. First, that the universe which includes us is the dwelling of an Eternal Mind. Second, that the world of our abode is the scene of a moral government not yet complete. Third, that the upper zones of human affection, above the clouds of self and passion, take us into the sphere of divine communion. Into this overarching scene it is that growing thought and enthusiasm have expanded to catch their light and fire. And Professor Tyndal(l) adds: "Alpine summits must kindle above the mountaineer who reads these stirring words; I see their beauty and feel their life."[175]

It is not difficult to see why R. H. Hutton designated Martineau as the 'chief' critic of Tyndall's *Belfast Address*; for although Martineau was writing before Rutherford had split the atom and Einstein and others had shown that matter and energy were interchangeable, his argument still retains much of its cogency even today.

As stated at the beginning of this chapter, in 1866 Martineau failed to be appointed to the Chair of Philosophy of Mind and Logic at University College, London. This was probably the greatest personal disappointment of his life, but if the stature of a man is judged more by how he deals with failure rather than with success, then it is here that we see the largeness and grace of Martineau's spirit. In the years that remained he continued to teach at Manchester College, encouraging his students, being involved in the affairs of the wider church, and seeking to promote a deeper understanding between Christians of different denominations.

James Martineau died in the early days of January 1900. His death was followed by a proliferation of newspaper articles, essays, and editorials in the Denominational and National Press, as well as in the Philosophical and Religious Journals of the day. Five biographies were written about him between 1900 and 1907, although as far as I am aware none went into a second edition; for interest in Martineau died much more quickly than his biographers could have anticipated. Little has been published on him since 1909, with the exception of Alfred Hall's extracts of his works published in 1950 and Dr. Short's splendid chapter in *The English Presbyterians* (1968); a few prayers and short articles in several general theological and philosophical works, the best being Geoffrey Rowell's chapter in *Hell and the Victorians* (1974), and J. B. Schneewind's *Sidgwick's Ethics and Victorian Moral Philosophy* (1977). In 1959 Henry Emerson Fosdick included a series of Martineau's Prayers in a book entitled *Public Prayers* but neglected to attribute them to Martineau. It would be difficult to escape the impression that Martineau's influence on the twentieth century has been negligible.

This may be due in part to the collapse of nineteenth century romanticism in the harsh realities of the First World War, where so many lost their faith and their lives in the fields of Flanders and the mud of the Somme. Subsequently, the rise of Biblical Theology in the 1930s, with Karl Barth in Germany and Edwyn Hoskyns in this country, would have discouraged interest in Martineau, with his radical criticism of the Bible, and his view of biblical inspiration.

But the spirit of the present age may once again be conducive to Martineau's thought: his stress on feelings, and on conscience, and on a reasoned approach to the scriptures has much to say to our time. Moreover, the renewed interest in Schleiermacher also augurs well for one once called the 'English Schleiermacher', and holds open the possibility that he may attract renewed interst as P. T. Forsyth did in the 1960s.

## NOTES

1. *Dictionary of National Biography*, Eds., Leslie Stephen & Sidney Lee (London, 1890), XXIII, 29.
2. James Martineau, *'Biographical Memoranda'*, Manchester College, Library, Oxford.
3. H. McLachlan, *The Unitarian Movement in the Religious Life of England*, (London, 1934), p. 250.
4. J. Estlin Carpenter, *James Martineau* (London, 1905), p. 5.
5. P. T. Forsyth, 'Dr. Martineau', *The London Quarterly Review*, Vol. 93 (1900), p. 217.
6. Harriet Martineau, *Autobiography* (London, 1877); Virago Edition (London, 1983), 2 vols. p. 53.
7. James Martineau, *'Biographical Memoranda'*.
8. Harriet Martineau, *Autobiography*, p. 17.
9. Ibid. p. 101.
10. Ibid. p. 95.
11. Ibid. p. 104.
12. Ibid. p. 105.
13. James Martineau, *'Biographical Memoranda'*.
14. Harriet Martineau, *Autobiography*, p. 99.
15. Ibid. p. 118.
16. Russell Lant Carpenter, *Memoirs of the Life of the Rev. Lant Carpenter L.L.D.* (London, 1842), p. 352.
17. Ibid. p. 15.
18. Letter from James Martineau to J. Estlin Carpenter, dated December 20th, 1878, Manchester College Library, Oxford.

19. Russell Lant Carpenter, *Memoirs of Lant Carpenter*, p. 89. It is worth noting that during the Liverpool Controversy of 1839 Martineau turned to Lant Carpenter's *An Examination of the Charges made against Unitarians and Unitarianism by the Rt. Rev. Dr Magee* for help in this doctrinal dispute. Not only did he quote Lant Carpenter as an authority on that occasion, but a comparison of Martineau's five lectures in the Controversy, with Carpenter's work reveals several points of influence, especially in dealing with the whole question of the Improved Version of the Bible.

20. James Martineau, *'Biographical Memoranda'*.

21. V. H. H. Green, *The Universities* (Hamandsworth, 1969), p. 264.

22. J. H. Thom, ed., *Letters of John James Tayler*, 2 vols. (London, 1872), I, 24.

23. James Martineau, *'Biographical Memoranda'*.

24. James Martineau, *Essays, Reviews and Addresses* 4 vols. (London, 1890–91), IV, 54.

25. James Martineau, *'Biographical Memoranda'*.

26. Dr. James Cowles Prichard M.D., F.B.S., M.R.I.A. was author of *Researches into the Physical History of Mankind*; a member of the National Institute of France; a member of the Royal Academy of Medicine of Paris, and Hon. Fellow of King's and Queen's College of Physicians in Ireland.

27. James Martineau, *'Biographical Memoranda'*.

28. Ibid.

29. James Martineau, *Studies of Christianity* (London, 1858), p. 480.

30. Ibid. p. 483.

31. Ibid. p. 488.

32. James Martineau, *Essays, Reviews and Addresses*, I, 385. P. T. Philips ed., *View from the Victorian Pulpit* (Toronto, 1978), p. 212. J. H. Thom, *A Spiritual Faith* (London, 1895), p. xxv.

33. J. H. Thom Ed., *Letters of J. J. Tayler*, I, 307, II, 151. J. H. Thom, *A Spiritual Faith* (London, 1895), p. xi. P. H. Wicksteed, *Memorials of C. Wicksteed* (London, 1886), p. 216.

34. J. H. Thom, *A Spiritual Faith*, pp. xix, xx.

35. J. H. Thom, ed., *Letters of J. J. Tayler*, II, 59.

36. P. H. Wicksteed, *Memorials of the Rev. C. Wicksteed*, p. 34.

37. J. H. Thom, *A Spiritual Faith*, p. xii.

38. J. Martineau, *The Rationale of Religious Inquiry*, Fourth Edition (London, 1853), p. 110.

39. J. H. Thom, *A Spiritual Faith*, p. xxiv.

40. J. Martineau, *Essays, Reviews and Addresses*, I, 392.

41. J. H. Thom, *Letters of J. J. Tayler*, I.

42. See J. Martineau, *Endeavours After the Christian Life*, Ninth Edition (London, 1892), p. 227. J. H. Thom, *Letters of J. J. Tayler*, II, 47. J. R. Watson, *Everyman's Book of Victorian Verse* (London, 1982), p. xiv.

43. J. H. Thom, *Letters of J. J. Tayler*, I. 117.

44. Ewald was born in 1803 at Göttingen, where at the age of 24 he was appointed Professor of Oriental Languages. He later became the first Professor of Philology at Tübingen, before joining the department of Theology at Tübingen. In 1848 he returned to his chair at Göttingen, but eighteen years later he was compulsorily retired when he refused to take the oath of allegiance to the King of Prussia. For a time he represented Hanover in the German Reichstag. He quarrelled with Strauss and wrote his own *Life of Jesus*; his field of expertise was

not in the New Testament, but in his Oriental and Old Testament researches. He died in 1875.

45. W. A. Neander was born in 1789 at Göttingen, and was appointed to a professorship in Berlin in 1813, from where he exercised a beneficent influence. His best known works were *History of the Propagation and Administration of the Christian Church by the Apostles* (1832) and his *Life of Jesus* (1836) which at the time was hailed as a great achievement. In the Strauss Controversy of 1835 he came over as a magnanimous and dignified representative of theological science; and although censuring Strauss's work, he asked the Prussian Government not to suppress it. Albert Schweitzer speaks highly of him in *The Quest of the Historical Jesus*.

46. J. H. Thom, *Letters of J. J. Tayler*, II, 191, 223.

47. Ibid. I, 257.

48. Ibid. II, 126.

49. Ibid. II, 142.

50. Ibid. II, 180.

51. Ibid. II, 27.

52. Ibid. I, 272.

53. J. Martineau, *Essays, Reviews and Addresses*, I, 395.

54. Ibid. I, 33.

55. Ibid. I, 36.

56. Ibid. I, 15.

57. Ibid. I, 25.

58. Ibid. I, 15.

59. Ibid. I, 40.

60. James Martineau, 'Review of Bentham's Deontology', *Monthly Repository* (1834), p. 613.

61. Ibid. p. 613.

62. Ibid. p. 618.

63. Ibid. p. 618.

64. Ibid. p. 621.

65. Joseph Henry Allen, *Our Liberal Movement in Theology* (Boston, 1883), p. 23.

66. James Martineau, *The Rationale of Religious Inquiry* (London, 1836), p. iii & p. iv.

67. Ibid. p. v.

68. Ibid. p. 36.

69. Ibid. p. 36.

70. Ibid. p. 44.

71. James Martineau, *The Rationale of Religious Inquiry*, Third Edition (London, 1845), p. 26.

72. James Martineau, *The Rationale of Religious Inquiry*, p. 62.

73. Ibid. p. 64.

74. Ibid. p. 64.

75. Ibid. p. 70.

76. Ibid. p. 73.

77. James Martineau, *The Rationale of Religious Inquiry*, Third Edition, p. 73.

78. James Martineau, *The Rationale of Religious Inquiry*, p. 72.

79. Ibid. p. 88.

80. Ibid. p. 59.

81. Ibid. p. iii.

82. H. D. Roberts, *Hope Street Church Liverpool, and the Allied Non-Conformity* (Liverpool, 1909), p. 393.
83. James Martineau, *The Rationale of Religious Inquiry*, Fourth Edition, p. vii.
84. James Martineau, *The Rationale of Religious Inquiry*, Third Edition, p. 111.
85. James Martineau, 'Without Priest and Without Ritual', in *Unitarianism Defended* (Liverpool, 1839), p. 38.
86. James Martineau, *The Rationale of Religious Inquiry*, Third Edition, pp. 110–111.
87. James Martineau, *Essays, Reviews and Addresses*, IV, 426.
88. Alfred Caldecott, *The Philosophy of Religion in England and America* (London, 1901), p. 343.
89. Joseph Blanco White, *Observations on Heresy and Orthodoxy* (London, 1877), p. xxxi.
90. Letter from James Martineau to Estlin Carpenter, July 18th 1898, Manchester College Library, Oxford.
91. James Martineau, *Essays, Reviews and Addresses*, I, 147.
92. Ibid. I, 147.
93. Ibid. I, 146.
94. Russell Lant Carpenter, *Memoirs of Lant Carpenter*, p. 260.
95. James Martineau, *Essays, Reviews and Addresses*, I, 144.
96. James Martineau, 'The London Meeting', in *The Channing Centenary 1880* (London, 1880), p. 36.
97. James Martineau, *Studies of Christianity*, pp. 179, 184.
98. James Martineau, *Channing Centenary*, p. 38.
99. W. H. Channing, *The Life of William Ellery Channing D.D.* (Boston, 1880), p. 454.
100. Ibid. p. 454.
101. Ibid. p. 427.
102. William A. Knight, *Inter Amicos. Letters between James Martineau and William Knight 1869–72* (London, 1901), pp. 79–80.
103. W. H. Channing, *The Life of William Ellery Channing*, D.D., p. 454.
104. Letter from Mary Carpenter to James Martineau dated February, 1841, Manchester College Library, Oxford.
105. Alfred Caldecott, *The Philosophy of Religion in England and America*, pp. 348–352. G. O. Mculloch, 'The Theism of James Martineau' (unpublished doctoral dissertation, University of Edinburgh, 1933).
106. Anna Letitia Le Breton, *Correspondence of William Ellery Channing and Lucy Aikin from 1826–1842* (London, 1874), p. 81.
107. W. H. Channing, *The Life of William Ellery Channing D.D.*, p. 447.
108. See Martineau's notes on his correspondence in Manchester College Library, Oxford.
109. H. D. Roberts, *Hope Street Church Liverpool*, p. 404.
110. James Martineau, *Types of Ethical Theory*, 2 vols (London, 1889), II, 566.
111. James Martineau, 'Biographical Memoranda'.
112. James Martineau, *National Duties and other Sermons and Addresses*, p. 231.
113. James Martineau, *Studies of Christianity*, p. 190.
114. James Martineau, *A Study of Religion*, 2 vols (London, 1900), I, 36.
115. James Martineau, *Endeavours after the Christian Life* (London, 1892), p. 304.
116. James Martineau, *National Duties and other Sermons and Addresses*, p. 233.

117. Immanuel Kant, *Religion within the Limits of Reason Alone*, p. 54.
118. James Martineau, *Studies of Christianity*, p. 193.
119. Immanuel Kant, *Religion within the Limits of Reason Alone*, pp. 132–6.
120. James Martineau, *Essays, Reviews and Addresses*, II, 405.
121. Immanuel Kant, *Religion within the Limits of Reason Alone*, pp. 182–183.
122. James Martineau, *Hymns of the Christian Church and Home* (London, 1840), pp. v–vi.
123. Rudolf Metz, *A Hundred Years of British Philosophy* (London, 1938), p. 209.
124. A. Michael Ramsey, *F. D. Maurice and the Conflicts of Modern Theology* (Cambridge, 1951).
125. Samuel Taylor Coleridge, *Aids to Reflection*, Bohn's Edition (London, 1913), p. 294.
126. James Martineau, *Studies of Christianity*, p. 199.
127. J. B. Schneewind, *Sidgwick's Ethics and Moral Philosophy* (Oxford, 1977), p. 247.
128. J. S. Mill, *Mill on Bentham and Coleridge* (London, 1959), p. 161. (Quoted from Literary Remains III, 145).
129. T. Sadler, ed., *Diary, Reminiscences and Correspondence of Henry Crabb Robinson*, 3 vols (London, 1869), III, 230.
130. James Martineau, *Endeavours after the Christian Life*, p. 23.
131. J. S. Mill, *Mill on Bentham and Coleridge*, p. 161. James Martineau, *Rationale of Religious Inquiry*, p. iv.
132. J. S. Mill, *Mill on Bentham and Coleridge*, p. 163. James Martineau, *Studies of Christianity*, p. 488.
133. Margaret J. Shaen, *Memorials of Two Sisters: Susanna and Catherine Winkworth* (London, 1908), p. 164.

   It is probable that Martineau's interest in Bishop Robert Leighton was chiefly due to his attempts to bring about church unity in Scotland.
134. David Pym, *The Religious Thought of Samuel Taylor Coleridge* (Gerrards Cross, 1978), p. 10.
135. James Martineau, *Essays, Reviews and Addresses*, I, 263.
136. A. H. Craufurd, *Recollections of James Martineau* (Edinburgh, 1903), p. 3.
137. George W. Cox, *The Life of John William Colenso D.D.* 2 vols. (London, 1888), I, 39.
138. Jeff Guy, *The Heretic: A Study of the Life of John William Colenso* (Johannesburg & Pietermaritzburg, 1983), p. 162.
139. Ibid. p. 246.
140. Stopford Brooke, *Life and Letters of the Rev. F. W. Robertson (London, 1872)*, p. 418.
141. John Hoatson, 'James Martineau and Frederic Robertson: A Study of Influence, *Expositor*, 8 (1903), p. 204.
142. L. P. Jacks, *Life and Letters of Stopford Brooke*, 2 vols (London, 1917), I, p. 324.
143. Ibid. I, 78, 119.
144. Mary L. Bruce, *Anna Swanwick* (London, 1903), p. 22.
145. Alec Vidler, *Scenes from Clerical Life* (London, 1977), p. 169.
146. Hugh Walker, *The Literature of the Victoran Era* (Cambridge, 1910), pp. 195–6.
147. H. McLachlan, *The Unitarian Movement in the Religious Life of England*, p. 250.
148. Owen Chadwick, *The Victorian Church*, 2 vols. (London, 1966 & 1970), I, 398.

149. D. C. Sommervell, *English Thought in the Nineteenth Century* (London, 1929), p. 137.
150. Herbert Spencer, *Essays: Scientific, Political, and Speculative*, Third Edition (London and Edinburgh, 1878), pp. 290–1.
151. James Martineau, *Essays, Reviews and Addresses*, III, 194.
152. Ibid. III, 212.
153. Ibid. III, 199.
154. Ibid. III, 200.
155. Ibid. III, 217.
156. Ibid. III, 217.
157. Ibid, IV, 586.
158. Herbert Spencer, *Autobiography*, 2 vols. (London, 1904), II, 246.
159. S. C. Carpenter, *Church and People, 1789–1889* (London, 1933), p. 476.
160. Otto Pfleiderer, *The Development of Theology in Germany since Kant, and its progress in Great Britain since 1825* (London & New York, 1909), pp. 339–40.
161. James Drummond and C. B. Upton, *The Life and Letters of James Martineau*, 2 vols. (London, 1902), II, 360.
162. Sheridan Gilley and Ann Loades, 'Thomas Henry Huxley: The War between Science and Religion', *The Journal of Religion*, vol. 61, No. 3 (1981), p. 285.
163. A. S. Eve and C. H. Creasey, *Life and Work of John Tyndall* (London, 1945), p. 188.
164. John Tyndall, *Fragments of Science*, Sixth Edition, 2 vols. (London, 1879), II, 237.
165. Ibid. II, 226.
166. Ibid. II, 204.
167. A. S. Eve and C. H. Creasey, *Life and Works of John Tyndall*, p. 188.
168. R. H. Hutton, 'Mr. Martineau on Materialism' and 'Professor Tyndall on Materialism' in *Aspects of Religions and Scientific Thought* (London, 1899), pp. 71–79 and 80–88.
169. James Martineau, *Essays, Reviews and Addresses*, IV, 167–8.
170. Ibid. IV, 167.
171. Ibid. IV, 168.
172. Ibid. IV, 172.
173. Ibid. IV, 194.
174. Ibid. IV, 194.
175. L. P. Jacks, *From Authority to Freedom: The Spiritual Pilgrimage of Charles Hargrove* (London, 1920), pp. 277–8.

9

# THE LIFE AND WORK OF J. ESTLIN CARPENTER

ARTHUR J. LONG
*Principal of the Unitarian College*
*Manchester*
*Honorary Lecturer in Faculty of Theology*
*University of Manchester*

*Introduction*

In the year 1927, the Public Orator of Oxford University lamented the passing of one whom he described, in sonorous Latin phrases, as a 'learned, gentle and most Christian soul, mourned by Manchester College and by Theology.'[1] He was referring to Joseph Estlin Carpenter, perhaps the most eminent of all the scholars associated with the College during the last hundred years.

Curiously enough, outside the Unitarian community, his name is now little remembered, and even within Unitarian circles, he no longer enjoys the fame of earlier times. But it would be difficult to exaggerate his importance in the history of Manchester College or his pre-eminence in the world of scholarship in his own day.

In 1875, after a comparatively brief period in the Unitarian ministry, Carpenter returned to Manchester New College, London, where he had been a student, to become Professor of Ecclesiastical History, Comparative Religion and Hebrew, and he was to remain very closely involved in the work of the College from that time onwards. He moved with it to Oxford in 1889, served as Principal from 1906 to 1915, and was the President from 1920 to 1925. Throughout the whole of his career, he remained deeply committed to the cause of ministerial training, taking a close personal interest in his students, not only while they were under his care, but also throughout their subsequent ministries. This was, in a way, part of his wider concern for the life and welfare of the Unitarian movement to which he remained profoundly attached and which he served unstintingly in many practical ways. But what makes Estlin Carpenter a particularly remarkable figure is the extent to which, despite his commitment to Manchester College and the Unitarian denomination, he also managed to secure for himself a unique place in the world of academic scholarship. Here he came to be recognised as one of the leading authorities in two quite separate fields, for not only was he one of the great pioneers in the realm of Higher Criticism, with an unrivalled knowledge of both the Old and New Testaments, but he also became one of the supreme Comparative Religionists of his day, an acknowledged expert in the field of Buddhism in general and the Pali Scriptures in particular.

But there was never anything of the dessicated academic about Estlin Carpenter. Perhaps there is a sense in which he deserves to be remembered primarily, not as a scholar, but as a striking modern 'saint'—a man of deep piety and self-effacing humility, who was endowed with lively spiritual insight and a great genius for human friendship.

In this essay in his honour which I offer as a contribution to the Manchester College Bicentenary Volume, I have endeavoured to give a brief sketch of his life and achievements, together with an assessment of his significance, both as scholar and saint. For the biographical details, I am much indebted to the memorial volume edited by C. H. Herford and published in 1929.[2] I have also had the privilege of consulting the Estlin Carpenter papers in the library of Manchester College, and am particularly grateful to Miss Jane Deacon of Manchester for allowing me to make use of the thesis on Carpenter which she submitted to Lancaster University in 1977.[3]

## *An Outline of the Life of Estlin Carpenter*

The religious faith of Estlin Carpenter was catholic and comprehensive. His sympathetic attitude to the religions of the East went hand in hand with a deep appreciation of the essential insights of Christianity, and he was always a devoted disciple of Jesus of Nazareth. But he was also a very emphatic Unitarian. Unlike some of his brethren in the faith, he had no inhibitions about the use of that name, and throughout his life he was always closely involved in Unitarian affairs. So it comes as no surprise to discover that he had an impressive Unitarian pedigree. His grandfather was the famous Dr. Lant Carpenter, Unitarian minister and schoolmaster, pastor of Lewins Mead Meeting House, Bristol, supporter of Catholic Emancipation and social reform, founder and director of that select boarding school, which included James Martineau among its pupils.[4]

Perhaps the most famous of Lant Carpenter's four children was his daughter Mary, pioneer worker in the field of ragged schools, juvenile delinquency and reformatories, and an early feminist, whose activities extended beyond this country to India, which she visited on several occasions. There was always a particularly close affinity between Mary Carpenter and her nephew, Estlin. His later interest in India is said to have been partly due to her influence, and after her death, he wrote her biography. Her brother, Estlin's father, was Lant Carpenter's eldest son, William Benjamin Carpenter. The two other sons, Russell and Philip, followed their father into the Unitarian ministry, but William's career led him into the world of medicine and natural science. He became famous as a noted physiologist and zoologist, and he is described in the DNB as 'one of the last examples of an almost universal naturalist'. William Carpenter always remained a committed Unitarian, and later in life was a prominent member of the Rosslyn Hill congregation in Hampstead. His pronounced Unitarianism is said to have twice prevented his election to the chair of physiology at Edinburgh, but he held a number of distinguished appointments in the medical world, and was at one time Principal of University Hall in London, later to become the home of Manchester New College and in 1856 he was appointed Registrar of London University.

His eldest son, Joseph Estlin Carpenter, was born on October 5th 1844. In later life, he was always known as J. Estlin Carpenter rather than Joseph. One is perhaps entitled to suspect that there may be some significance in the fact that Estlin was the surname of Lant Carpenter's family doctor, who had been instrumental in persuading William to take up a medical career. By a curious circumstance, Estlin was born during the short period when his father found himself in uncongenial surroundings as tutor to the children of Lord Lovelace at Ripley in Surrey. 'I feel the loss of public worship,' he wrote to his brother in December 1844, two months after Estlin's birth, 'more than any other kind of inconvenience. I have a most pecular attachment to Lewin's Mead, and to the worship as there conducted.'[5]

But the family was soon able to move to happier surroundings in London, and Estlin grew up in a home dominated by scientific zeal and rational religious faith, presided over by a cultured academic, whose multifarious commitments meant that his children often saw very little of him. Significantly, two of the family's most treasured possessions were an organ (always whimsically known as 'Dagon') and a microscope. A regime of strict temperance, firmly based on William Carpenter's physiological knowledge, was the rule of the house, and Estlin remained a confirmed abstainer throughout his whole life. The family were committed members of the Rosslyn Hill Unitarian congregation at Hampstead, where William served for some time as organist and choirmaster.

After a period at University College School, having decided to follow his uncles into the Unitarian ministry, Estlin moved on to University College London and then to Manchester New College, where his intellectual ability and dedication, his personal charm, and a ready willingness to help others, made a very favourable impression on his contemporaries. Among his fellow-students was another of Manchester College's very distinguished sons, that very remarkable polymath Philip Henry Wicksteed, who became Carpenter's lifelong friend and companion.

Carpenter began his theological studies at a time when the impact of Darwin's *Origin of Species* was first beginning to make itself felt. 1864, when he was nearly 20, was the year of the famous encounter between 'Soapy Sam' (Bishop Wilberforce) and 'Darwin's Bulldog' (Thomas Huxley)—one of the great landmarks in the struggle between religion and science. But thanks to his family background, Carpenter had been taught to see no conflict at all between religion and science. It is most unlikely, therefore, that he experienced any of the doubts and tensions which beset the many pious souls who were appalled by Darwin's 'gospel of dirt' and his denial of Holy Writ. It is true that William Carpenter appears to have retained a belief in the possibility of miracles, but he was quite happy to accept the Darwinian hypothesis, provided it could be enlarged to include a place for some Divine Purpose. It is clearly not without significance that Estlin's entire religious philosophy, particularly as manifested in his maturity, was completely dominated by evolutionary concepts.

In his later life, like most Unitarians, Estlin Carpenter must have seemed the very embodiment of the religion of healthy-mindedness and a supreme example of the 'once-born' soul—as delineated in William James's *Varieties of Religious Experience*. So it comes as something of a surprise to discover that during his student days, he had gone through a period of spiritual aridity which was only finally resolved by what, in other religious traditions, would have been described as a conversion experience. 'There is a valley in Wales,' he wrote to his wife, soon after their marriage, 'which has associations with my religious thoughts and feelings of an altogether peculiar kind. It was there that my real religious life began.'[6] It was not until many years later that he described the experience in detail in a letter to a friend—who had apparently deprecated a religion based on 'feeling'. The passage has often been quoted and it occasionally appears in religious anthologies.[7] But it seems especially appropriate to reproduce it here.

> 'I was in a condition of religious apathy for a long time when I was at MNC. I had no intellectual doubts: I do not think I am able to enter into them: that means perhaps that I had not departed widely from the philosophy in which I was trained. But though I had no doubts, I had no religion. I had no sense of personal relationship with God. I thought I ought to leave the College, for services were a weariness to me. I never wished particularly to pray. I hoped that if I went for a time to work in some way among the poor and ignorant, my religion might in some way be renewed in me. It was brought about but not in that way. Dr. Martineau persuaded me to wait in the College, and one summer I went to stay with Wicksteed at his father's house in North Wales. Shall I tell you what happened to me? Well, I shall not see you smile, and I have no secrets from you. You know how to respect confidences. I went out one afternoon for a walk alone. I was in the empty unthinking state in which one saunters along country lanes, simply yielding oneself to the casual sights and sounds which give a town-bred lad with country yearnings such intense delight. Suddenly I became conscious of the presence of some one else. I cannot describe it, but I felt that I had as direct a perception of the being of God all around me as I have of you when we are together. It was no longer a matter of inference, it was an immediate act of spiritual (or whatever adjective you like to employ) apprehension. It came unsought, absolutely unexpectedly. I remember the wonderful transfiguration of the far-off woods and hills as they seemed to blend in the infinite being with which I was thus brought into relation. The experience did not last long. But it sufficed to change all my feeling. I had not found God because I had never looked for him. But he had found me . . . I could now not only believe in him with my mind, but love him with my heart . . . This event has never happened to me again. . . . It is not necessary. The sense of a direct relation to God then generated in my soul has become a part of my habitual thought and feeling. You will see why I am a believer (after my fashion, not Paul's or Calvin's) in election.'[8]

It can hardly be doubted that this experience was to remain the continuing inspiration for Carpenter's whole life. He may indeed have been in many respects, the epitome of the tradition of Rational Dissent—but that tradition has never been, despite the allegation of some of its critics, merely a matter of unfeeling intellectualism.

When his College career was completed, he spent an extended holiday in Switzerland which enabled him to indulge in what were afterwards to remain two of his favourite relaxations—rowing and climbing. It also gave him an opportunity to perfect his knowledge of German, an ability which was later to become a considerable factor in his rise to fame in the academic world, not least in the field of Old Testament criticism. Then in the autumn of the same year (1866) he returned to Bristol, the city which had been his father's home, where he became minister of the newly-opened Oakfield Road Church, Clifton. His revered teacher, James Martineau, presided over the induction and the other eminent Unitarian ministers present included his uncle Russell Carpenter and John James Tayler and Thomas Sadler. His distinguished aunt, Mary Carpenter, was also there. She soon returned to her work in India, but before leaving, advised her nephew to remain true to the family tradition of social commitment. This he endeavoured to do to the best of his ability, but he also displayed from the start a special interest in the intellectual approach to religion, and he supplemented his ministry with frequent academic lectures on a variety of topics.

In 1869, he accepted an invitation to the famous Mill Hill congregation in Leeds where Joseph Priestley had ministered in the 18th century. This was an appointment of much prestige and responsibility, Mill Hill Chapel being one of the foremost examples of the typical prosperous middle-class industrial Unitarian Churches of the period. Carpenter, with his southern breeding and intellectual background (he was at that time engaged on translating Ewald's *History of Israel*) was, perhaps, in some ways a rather unlikely candidate. But he soon proved himself a highly acceptable minister, able to relate easily not only to the formidable Lupton clan[9] and their prosperous fellow-worshippers who then dominated the congregation, but also to the more humble members. The spiritual quality of his prayers and preaching commended itself especially to his people, and helped to make his advanced theological views more readily acceptable. Someone is said to have observed that one of Carpenter's Sunday morning services was 'sufficient for a month'—a comment which present-day ministers would find somewhat ambivalent. But even Northern Unitarians at this period looked for an intellectual and well-educated ministry, and Carpenter was still able to supplement his Sunday services with regular academic lectures on many different subjects, not only in Leeds itself but also in neighbouring towns. He also involved himself, as a Unitarian minister was expected to do, in social activity, and he showed particular concern for Sunday School work and the training of Sunday School teachers and social workers. He also took an active part in local Unitarian affairs. 'The root of it all,' says C. H. Herford 'was the vision of an infinite divine Presence encompassing and penetrating Nature and Man, working everywhere for good, supporting all man's efforts, and accessible to him whenever and wherever he opens himself to its sway. This was for him the "Fountain of Life".'[10]

One of the highlights of his time at Leeds was the sermon entitled 'The influence of science on the religious imagination' which he preached in 1873 to mark the meeting of the British Association in Bradford and which he subsequently published. Another incident of some note was the visit which he made, in company with George Buckton (later to become his father-in-law) to Charles Voysey, a radical Anglican clergyman, afterwards ejected from the Church of England. This necessitated a five-mile winter walk from Boston Spa to Healaugh near Tadcaster. As Carpenter related to his uncle in a letter, they were received most cordially and offered whisky '—which, of course, the teetotal Carpenter "declined with thanks" '. In the same letter, Carpenter regrets, in a typical reflection of his own brand of comprehensive ecumenism, that some Unitarians had already been 'pestering' Voysey to join their ranks.[11]

Carpenter's stay at Mill Hill Chapel, however, was a short one, thanks to a rather unexpected circumstance; for after three years, he began to be increasingly troubled by a speech defect which greatly hampered his preaching and lecturing. His congregation, with a generosity indicative of the warm esteem in which they held him, made him take a long holiday, first in Switzerland, and then in Egypt and Palestine. An assistant minister was also appointed. But all to no avail. Carpenter's future in the ministry seemed very uncertain. But in February 1875, the situation was resolved when he availed himself of the opportunity of a switch to an academic career. He accepted an invitation to become Professor of Ecclesiastical History, Comparative Religion, and Hebrew, at Manchester College, London where James Martineau was now Principal. His speech defect was not in fact finally eradicated until some nine years later in 1884.[12] This episode remains an interesting instance of the kind of ailment, probably psychosomatic in origin, which seems to have afflicted a number of eminent Victorians.

Carpenter's ministry at Leeds was formally concluded, with much sorrow on both sides, in June 1875. He told his aunt in a letter that his last days in Leeds had been lightened by a 'certain gladness in the evidences of regard which were so abundantly bestowed upon me. But,' he continued with typical modesty, 'looking back over the past six years . . . I see only too clearly many things imperfectly, some unwisely done. But I do not altogether throw away these results of experience, for they will guide me in my work hereafter, and I shall at any rate be able to warn my students sometimes against the mistakes which are only too vivid in my memory.'[13]

So Carpenter returned to Manchester College in London, after an absence of only nine years, and he was to spend the whole of the rest of his life in the academic sphere, in London first of all, and then in Oxford. It is important to note that at the time of his appointment, he had no particular eminence in the disciplines which he was called upon to teach. Indeed, it might not be inappropriate to enquire how it was that he came to receive the invitation. But with typical zeal and dedication, Carpenter at once set to work to remedy the situation, taking particular care, to begin with, to improve his knowledge of Hebrew and Semitics, and he soon came to be recognised, even beyond Unitarian circles, as a leading authority on Biblical Criticism in general and on the Old Testament in particular. But he also now became increasingly committed to Comparative Religion. In collaboration with Dr. T. Rhys Davids, the foremost Buddhist scholar of the time, he entered on a systematic study of the

Buddhist scriptures in the original Pali, a language which he learnt with the help of Rhys Davids.

The new environment in which he found himself proved to be extremely congenial. It gave him an opportunity, in particular, to renew his friendship with Philip Wicksteed, who at this time was minister of the Little Portland Street Chapel, and just beginning his remarkable career as an extra-mural lecturer on a surprisingly diverse range of topics. Carpenter's early days in London also brought an agreeable change in his personal circumstances when he became engaged to the second daughter of one of his closest friends, George Buckton. Buckton had become his friend in Leeds and they remained on terms of close friendship after his move to London, despite the difference in their ages. Estlin Carpenter and Alice Buckton were married at Mill Hill Chapel in 1878 and though the marriage was childless, it was a particularly close and happy union. He and Alice had many interests in common, not least a love of the open air, mountain scenery and foreign travel. Throughout the whole of Carpenter's subsequent career, Alice remained his loving companion and helpmeet.

From this point onwards, one cannot fail to be impressed by the incredible 'busy-ness' of Carpenter's life. He was clearly a man of fantastic methodical industry whose disciplined and well-ordered time-table enabled him to pursue simultaneously an immense variety of interests and obligations, and still find plenty of space for leisure-time pursuits and physical exercise. Constantly reading and studying to improve his own knowledge and abilities, he now also began to produce a steady stream of books—including *The Life of Mary Carpenter* (a biography of his aunt), *Nature and Man* (a collection, with an introductory memoir, of some of the scientific and philosophical essays by his father, William Benjamin Carpenter), and *The First Three Gospels, The Historical Jesus and the Theological Christ*, and *Life in Palestine when Jesus Lived.* The latter volume, first published in 1884, was particularly successful. It was subsequently reissued many times and was still in print until quite recently.

Even at this stage, Carpenter still found time for social service and he was for some years the very active secretary of the London Domestic Mission Society, a pioneer Unitarian organisation for work among the poor, which had counterparts in some of the other industrial conurbations of the day, and owed its original inspiration to the work of the American Unitarian, Dr. Joseph Tuckerman of Boston.

But his main concern, of course, was the work of the College and the training of students for the ministry, along with his colleagues James Martineau, Charles Upton and James Drummond. Several generations of students were later to bear eloquent testimony to Carpenter's brilliant and informative lectures, and to the spiritual influence of his personality. His interest in his pupils was never confined to the classroom. They all received regular invitations to share the hospitality of Leathes House, his home in Hampstead, and he sometimes arranged excursions to cathedral cities and other places of interest. To some of his contemporaries who knew him less well, Carpenter seemed a somewhat austere figure, but to those who came under his care he always extended a very warm and intimate personal friendship, which continued throughout the years, even when College days had long since ended. The memorable Sunday evenings at Leathes House, with music and poetry readings, were later supplemented by even more memorable summer holidays at Leathes Cottage, the country home which the Carpenters acquired at Borrowdale in the Lake District. Here, parties of students, former students and other friends were able to enjoy generous hospitality, stimulating conversation and vigorous mountain walks. There were also opportunities, at least as far as Carpenter himself was concerned, for regular study. Guests coming down to breakfast were sometimes surprised to find that their host had already been at work for two hours on his Pali texts. He also made a point of taking lessons from his students, if they had some special ability, and he learned Italian in this way from L. P. Jacks.

Meanwhile, back at the College in London, a far-reaching change was being contemplated. After much heart-searching and not a little controversy, Manchester College had decided to move once again, this time to Oxford. The once familiar initials 'MNC' were about to change to the now even more familiar 'MCO'. To some, this seemed a foolhardy enterprise indeed. What possible place could there be, it was asked, for the radical tradition of Warrington in the notorious 'home of lost causes', the very embodiment of establishment obscurantism? Martineau, though no longer Principal, had advised against the move. But Carpenter, on the whole, was in favour of it. There was, after all, another side to Oxford. Benjamin Jowett, Broad Church protagonist and close friend of Martineau, was still Master of Balliol, and the new philosophy of T. H. Green, despite his own premature death nine years earlier, was gaining ground. What is more, the new discipline of Comparative Religion had already secured a niche in the University, thanks to the pioneering activities of Max Müller, who has been described as being 'among the most learned and popular figures in post-Tractarian Oxford'[14], and who was later to become one of Estlin Carpenter's closest friends. The anthropologist E. B. Tylor, already one of Carpenter's oldest associates, was by this time Director of the Oxford Museum. Nor was this all. With the advent of Mansfield College, presided over by A. M. Fairbairn, another friend and admirer of Martineau, liberal Non-Conformity had already secured a place in Oxford—and by an interesting co-incidence, Manchester College was later to make its permanent home at the other end of the road to which Mansfield College had given its name.

So when Manchester College finally moved to Oxford in 1889, taking Carpenter with it, he himself was by no means averse to the change, and it was above all with the College in Oxford and with Oxford University, that he was to remain particularly associated for the rest of his life. As one who had always been a great admirer of the old English Cathedrals, he later came to take a particular delight in the handsome Neo-Gothic premises which the College eventually built. He certainly came to be regarded as being in many respects the supreme embodiment of the new ethos of the College, and his own increasing eminence in the academic world did much to secure its acceptance in Oxford. To begin with, he retained his original professorship at the College and his main concern continued to be the work of ministerial training. But in 1899, for what were described as 'personal reasons' and in circumstances which are still not entirely clear, he resigned, retaining only the Case Lectureship in Comparative Religion. It seems likely that this decision to reduce his responsibilities was prompted by a desire to devote himself more thoroughly to academic pursuits, and the period which followed saw the publication of two of his major works, the *Oxford Hexateuch* (which he produced in collaboration with G. Harford Battersby) and *James Martineau*, a comprehensive biography of his former teacher. It was at this time that he gained an international reputation as a leading authority in the field of both Biblical Studies and Comparative Religion. In 1901, he acted as President at a meeting of the International Council for Liberal Religious Thinkers, held in London. Two years later, a meeting of the same Council at Amsterdam invited him to give an address, which later became the basis of his book on *The Place of Christianity among the Religions of the World*, and on two separate occasions, he was invited to lecture at Harvard.

But the break in his full involvement in the work of Manchester College was only temporary. In 1906, he was invited to become Principal in succession to James Drummond, and he accepted. He was in all respects the most obvious choice, particularly in view of the fact that his own personal interest in the College and his intimate friendship with the students had continued unabated. From this time onwards, he seems to have succeeded in retaining a total commitment to the College without any reduction in his outside activities. In 1908, when the Third Congress of Religion met in Oxford, he acted as joint-secretary along with the distinguished anthropologist and Oxford scholar L. F. Farnell—and this marked the beginning of what was to become another close personal friendship as well as academic collaboration. He was also twice responsible for an Oxford Summer School in Theology, and the eminent speakers which he invited included Archbishop Nathan Söderblom of Sweden and Dean Inge of St. Paul's.

In 1913, he published a manual on Comparative Religion in the Home University series, and in 1914, the University honoured him with the appointment of Wilde Lecturer in Comparative Religion. He was by this time widely recognised as a leading authority in this field, with an unrivalled knowledge of the religions of the East. He had also established close and friendly contacts with the leaders of liberal religious movements in India and Japan. He retired from the Principalship of Manchester College in 1915 on reaching the age of 70, but he retained the Wilde Lectureship at the University until 1924. From 1920 to 1925 he held the honorary office of President of the College. After his retirement, he remained active in the field of scholarship, and his later publications included *Buddhism and Christianity, Theism in Medieval India*, and *The Johannine Writings*.

Throughout his time at Oxford, despite his commitment to the College and his multifarious academic pursuits, Carpenter continued to retain a close interest and a practical involvement in the affairs of the Unitarian denomination. In this respect, it could be said that he departed to some extent from the College ethos, which, particularly during its earlier Oxford phase, had firmly maintained the non-sectarian tradition of James Martineau. (Even today, those who get married in the College Chapel will discover from their certificates that they have been joined together 'according to the rites and ceremonies of those who do not wish to be designated'.) But Carpenter never shrank from proclaiming his Unitarian commitment, and his practical involvement increased after his retirement. During his retirement years especially he was a vigorous campaigner, often at some personal cost, on behalf of both the Sustentation Fund for the increase of ministerial stipends, and the Ministers' Pension and Insurance Fund.

A continuing concern for social service also characterised his Oxford years. In 1911, he was invited to inaugurate the School for Social Science and Training for Social Work at Liverpool University, and he used the occasion to give an address on the place of social awareness in university education. Side by side with his continuing personal commitment to abstinence from alcohol, he retained a keen awareness of the social evils of drink, and in 1916, he accepted the Presidency of the National Unitarian Temperance Association. His increasing concern for the promotion of greater understanding between men and women of diverse faiths gave him, especially in the latter part of his life, a special concern for the cause of international peace. In 1912, he addressed the National Peace Conference at Westminster and like many of his contemporaries he showed a confidence and optimism which were to be rudely shattered by the horrors of the First World War. In 1916 he edited a not altogether successful symposium entitled *Ethical and Religious Problems of the War*, and in the post-war years, he was an ardent supporter of the League of Nations.

Throughout most of his life Estlin Carpenter was blessed with a robust constitution which enabled him to enjoy frequent physical exercise and adventurous foreign travel, both of which activities remained his chief leisure-time interest. But in his final years he was beset by debilitating illness which necessitated several operations and he had to endure some personal tragedies, though his devoted wife survived him. Nothing could shake his simple personal faith and among the many friends who continued to be a source of great consolation, the closest to him at the end was his life-long companion, Philip Wicksteed, but the latter predeceased Carpenter by three months. The deep warmth of the relationship of these two stalwart embodiments of the MCO tradition is strikingly underlined in the moving and erudite dedication which Wicksteed added to his *magnum opus, The Reactions between Dogma and Philosophy,* first published in 1920 and re-issued in 1926:

JOSEPH OESTLIN CARPENTER
AMICE CONSTANTISSIME
DILECTISSIME
TU MIHI PRIMITIAS INGENII TUI
DEDICASTI JUVENIS
TIBI POST OCTO LUSTRA
MEMBRA HAEC LIBRI DISIECTA
SENEX RETULI
MAJORA VIRIBUS MEIS
TU SEMPER DE ME SPERABAS
MINORA HEU QUANTI SPE TUA
BENIGNE TAMEN ACCIPIAS

This astonishing Latin epigram (for which it was naturally assumed no translation was necessary) is an eloquent testimony not only to a great friendship, but also to the classical learning of the two men and the high standards of scholarship taken for granted in an earlier generation. In English it would have read somewhat as follows:

To Joseph Estlin Carpenter
Most dear and constant friend
as a young man you dedicated to me
the first fruits of your genius.
Now I, as an old man, have offered back to you
after forty years these fragments of a book.
You always used to expect more of me
than I was capable of.
May you nevertheless graciously accept
what is so much less, alas, than you hoped for.

Estlin Carpenter died at Oxford on June 2nd 1927, full of years and honour. Both Manchester College and Theology generally mourned the passing of a 'learned, gentle and most Christian soul'. The Oxford Orator could hardly have chosen a more appropriate epitaph.

### *Estlin Carpenter in Perspective—An Attempted Assessment*

At the present day, Carpenter's name is little known. References to him are rarely if ever encountered in the field of academic endeavour. Perhaps this should not surprise us. 'The moving finger writes, and having writ, moves on.' Fitzgerald's words apply to the world of scholarship no less than to anything else. In the sixty years which have elapsed since Carpenter's death, much water has flowed under the bridges. In both of the spheres in which he excelled, many of the theories which he presented and expounded with such cogent clarity, are now accepted as commonplaces. Perhaps this in itself merely serves to underline his importance. His role was primarily that of a pioneer. He was undoubtedly among the noble band of those who toiled unceasingly to convince their contemporaries that the canons of critical analysis and objective judgment had to be applied even in the realm of religion and theology, and his own more recent eclipse is, in a sense, a measure of the success which he achieved.

No doubt other reasons could be found for his current lapse into comparative obscurity. It has to be acknowledged, for example, that his contribution to both biblical studies and comparative religion reflects an emphatically evolutionary approach which is no longer as fashionable as it once was. But whatever his present reputation, it can hardly be denied that Carpenter was a man of quite immense learning, who in his own day was universally acknowledged as a scholar of impressive authority. This is reflected above all in the many friendly contacts which he enjoyed with his eminent contemporaries. Carpenter was obviously a great letter-writer who enjoyed correspondence. This was an aspect of his genius for friendship, a facet of his personal character already mentioned and to which we shall return in due course. He was also a meticulous and methodical individual who seems to have carefully preserved all the letters he ever received, both personal and professional. In the catalogue of correspondence in the Carpenter Papers at MCO, there are, on the one hand, messages of greeting from the humble and obscure. But there are also many letters from the famous names of the past—among them T. H. Huxley, Frederic Harrison, J. H. Moulton, B. H. Streeter, F. C. Coneybeare, Frances Power Cobbe, F. Max Müller, T. R. Glover, A. S. Peake, Gilbert Murray, W. R. Sorley, Jean Reville, Paul Sabatier, Rendel Harris, George Adam Smith, J. G. Frazer, R. R. Marrett, S. R. Driver, L. R. Farnell, Rudolf Euken, Edward Carpenter, F. C. Burkitt, Flinders Petrie, Otto Pfleiderer and Nathan Söderblom. It is true that some of these are merely brief formal acknowledgements or replies to invitations or queries. But others indicate a close and long-standing friendship or collaboration and include a frequent ready acknowledgement of Carpenter's scholarship. A good instance of the latter is a brief note from Max Müller: 'Could you, without much trouble, tell me what is the latest date that can safely be assigned to Exodus 3.14?'[15]

Unfortunately and tantalisingly the Carpenter correspondence at Manchester College includes very few letters from Carpenter himself and one is usually left to infer the nature and content of his contribution from the reply which he received. There is a longer letter from A. S. Peake, dated 'Mat 28th (sic—presumably March or May) 1924', which illustrates the high reputation which Carpenter enjoyed among his contemporaries. Though, so far as we know, Carpenter's letter prompting this one has not survived, and the nature of the point at issue remains a matter of speculation, it does seem likely that Peake's letter concerns a comment which Carpenter had made on Peake's book *The Messiah and the Son of Man*. Peake mentions 'the difficulty of dealing at all adequately with the questions you raise, and the new suggestions you make'. The problem itself, he continues, 'is one that has pressed upon me for a long time. I may have been wrong in leaving it out, but I deliberately limited the scope, partly because I wanted to deal simply with the analysis of Jesus' own self-consciousness . . . Presumably I was too rigorous in my anxiety not to go beyond purely historical investigation. I realise that you may justly feel that the historical question cannot be adequately discussed without raising the problem you mention. Anyhow my treatment has had the advantage that it has brought me your very stimulating and suggestive letter, which gets added value from your Comparative Religion studies. I don't feel I am entitled to express an opinion on the points where your special knowledge gives you so exceptional a claim to be heard.'[16]

Carpenter was convinced that Jesus had *not* identified himself with the apocalyptic Son of Man. Peake took the more traditional view.[17] Whether or not this was the matter at issue, what is clear is Peake's deference to Carpenter's scholarship and insight.

But it is perhaps another letter from a less eminent scholar, A. J. Edmunds, which underlines most clearly the respect in which Carpenter was held and his position of special authority in the two quite separate fields of Biblical Studies and Pali Buddhism. One is able to infer from the letters, and from some other items of correspondence in the MCO Collection, that Carpenter had expressed critical opinions of a book which Edmunds had published in 1911 called *Buddhist Texts Quoted as Scripture by the Gospel of John*. In his letter to Carpenter, Edmunds writes:

> I maintain that a scholar can only be judged by his peers. Indeed, it is not too much to say with Shelley: 'He must be judged by a jury empaneled from the selectest of the wise of many generations.' (Only the reputation of a scholar is necessarily shorter-lived than a poet's). Now, I have often said to my friends: 'There are hundreds of scholars who know more about the New Testament than I do, and scores who know more about the Pali Texts; but I know of only one man on earth who is equally well acquainted with the two, and that man is Estlin Carpenter.
>
> So you see your criticism means more to me than anyone else's. Even Anesaki is not so well qualified as you. Of course he knows more Buddhism, but I doubt if he knows the Gospels as we do, I mean from the analytical point of view, in which every section is seen as a point on a map.'[18]

There is also a rather delightful post-script to this particular piece of correspondence. A later letter from Edmunds contains the following:

> Your lovely letter makes amends for the taunt which the late Morris Jastrow directed against me as a result of reading your remarks. . . . I am only anxious now to forget my hurt egoism and realise what a fine old Christian gentleman you are.[19]

Carpenter's reputation in his own day was partly the consequence of his activities as an organiser of, or contributor to, many congresses and summer schools. But his books and regular articles in learned journals were also much admired and respected. Reference has already been made, in the biographical section of this essay, to most of Carpenter's major publications. His work on both the Old and New Testaments is admirably summarised by A. S. Peake in his contribution to the Herford Memorial Volume (section iv—p. 133) in which he stresses in particular the value of Carpenter's more popular books—such as *The Bible in the 19th Century* (1903) and *The First Three Gospels* (1890—with several subsequent editions) both of which played a significant part in securing a wider acceptance of Biblical criticism. Carpenter's most important work in the Old Testament field, of which Peake speaks at some length, was his contribution to what came to be known as *The Oxford Hexateuch*. This monumental study of the first six books of the Bible was a committee production, prepared under the joint editorship of Carpenter and G. Harford Battersby. After nearly ten years of work, it finally appeared in 1900 under the impressive title of '*The Hexateuch according to the Revised Version, arranged in its Constituent Document by members of the Society of Historical Theology, Oxford*'. Carpenter himself was in fact the one who bore the main responsibility for the enterprise. Most of the lengthy introduction was written by him, and in 1902, Volume I was reprinted separately under the title: *The Composition of the Hexateuch—An Introduction by J. Estlin Carpenter with an Appendix by George Harford.* As Peake rightly observes:

> The whole work was a great credit to English scholarship and it left other works on the subject far behind. Since it built the whole fabric up from the foundations, it was eminently suited to the beginner; since it completed the structure to its minutest details, it was no less suited to the advanced student.[20]

It probably did more than anything else to secure the acceptance among discriminating British students of what came to be known as the Graf-Wellhausen hypothesis, with its now familiar source symbols, J, E, D and P.[21] So, as Peake himself notes, when he came to prepare what was afterwards to become his enormously successful popular one-volume Bible Commentary, Carpenter was the obvious choice for an introductory article on the Pentateuch.[22] Carpenter's 12-page essay in *Peake's Commentary*, which is in effect a summary of his contribution to the *Oxford Hexateuch* is still one of the best introductory statements of the JEDP theory. It is, of course, quite true, as even Peake was able to point out as early as 1929 (the date of the Herford Memorial Volume) that Old Testament scholarship has made further progress since 1900, the date of the *Oxford Hexateuch*, and that the work of such specialists as Kennett and Hölscher have brought new theories about the nature, content and dating of Pentateuch sources. It is also true that it is now considered unlikely that the Book of Joshua was ever linked with the Pentateuch. But even today, many of the basic features of the Graf-Wellhausen hypothesis still hold good, and to this extent, Carpenter's introduction has not been entirely superseded. Moreover, whatever new theories may eventually emerge, Carpenter will always hold a secure place in the history of Old Testament criticism.

The same is true also in the New Testament field and this again is adequately dealt with by Peake, who commends Carpenter's popular works and the part which he played in familiarising Bible students with the now accepted conclusions of Synoptic Criticism. He also gives favourable mention to Carpenter's manual on *Life in Palestine*—and notes in passing a significant and often overlooked fact, namely that Carpenter was amongst those who, at an early date, stressed the importance of the eschatological approach usually associated with the names Weiss and Schweitzer. On a somewhat different plane, Peake also points out the interesting gap in Carpenter's New Testament studies—an almost complete neglect of the work of St. Paul. But he deals at some length with what he believed to be one of Carpenter's most important works, *The Johannine Writings*. Here again, though one has to acknowledge that much has happened in this field since 1927, it can still be argued that Carpenter's book has much to commend it as a clear and detailed statement of the generally accepted conclusions of Johannine criticism, namely that the Fourth Gospel was almost certainly not written by either the Apostle John, or by the author of the Apocalypse.

On the matter of Carpenter's contribution to the other field in which he excelled, Comparative Religion, this also is excellently summarised in Herford's book by L. R. Farnell (section v—p. 162). Farnell rightly stresses the advantages provided by Carpenter's Unitarian background and 'the strength and breadth of his religious sympathies and imagination'. His own Christian belief, he says was 'less formal, less incisively dogmatic than that proclaimed by most of the Christian churches or sects; he was not therefore debarred from appreciating with genial sympathy whatever there was of noble or spiritually impressive in the messages or utterances of non-Christian theology'.[23] Later in his contribution, Farnell also suggests that it was his study of Comparative Religion and eastern mythology which enabled Carpenter to commend objective impartiality in any approach to the New Testament. 'Much of the strength of traditional orthodoxy,' he says, 'has rested on the widespread belief that its dogmas and legends are wholly unique.' But comparative study shows this to be erroneous. So when 'our credulity refuses to believe a miraculous story when told of the Buddha, the doubt is likely to arise whether we must believe the same story or the same type of story when told of Christ'.[24] This observation suggests that Estlin Carpenter could still make a not insignificant contribution to the current debate on the necessity, even for Christianity, of myth and symbolism.

It would probably still be agreed that one of Carpenter's most significant achievements in the field of Comparative Religion was the work which he undertook, in collaboration with Rhys Davids, for the Pali Text Society, a task which occupied him for nearly thirty years. It was not until 1911 that the third and final volume of the *Digha-Nikaya*, for which Carpenter alone was responsible, was completed. It was his initial study of the Pali texts which gave him an ever-increasing interest in Indian religion, and he eventually became one of the leading authorities on both Pali and Sanskrit literature. An article for *The Inquirer*, later reprinted separately, which he called *A Century of Comparative Religion—1810 to 1910*, amply illustrates his grasp of the subject, and, as we have already noted in 1913 he published a manual for the Home University Library, entitled simply *Comparative Religion*. The latter was perhaps one of his less successful publications and it was, from the first, subjected to some criticism. But it is still not without value as a short introductory handbook on the subject—and the extent to which it reflects the now out-moded evolutionary approach is in itself of some interest. It is on the 'great idea' of evolution, he says,

> that the whole study of the history of religion is now firmly established. At the foundation of all endeavours to classify the multitudinous facts which it embraces, lies the conviction that whatever may be the occasional instances of degeneration or decline, the general movement of human things advances from the cruder and less complex to the more refined and developed.[25]

Today, we are all less confident about this kind of affirmation, and there will always be those who find any proclamation of the essential unity of all religions misleadingly superficial. But others will feel that the comprehensive catholicity of Carpenter's vision is by no means irrelevant to the present age. 'The old classifications,' he says, 'based on the idea that religions consisted of a body of doctrines which must be true or false, reached by natural reflection or imparted by supernatural relevation, disappear before wider views. Theologies may be many, but religion is one.'[26]

Carpenter's two main later works on the field of Comparative Religion were *Theism in Medieval India* (1921) and *Buddhism and Christianity* (1923). The latter book was translated into both Hungarian and Japanese. Farnell describes *Theism in Medieval India*, a book of over 500 pages, as 'a monument of learning and of philosophic and religious insight, written in lucid and attractive style',[27] and he notes that its scope is far wider than its title indicates. *Buddhism and Christianity* he calls 'an original contribution to the history and philosophy of religion' and a treatise which shows that he had attained 'to that which was the goal of his studies, the discovery and penetration of a new spiritual realm of rich endowment for the religious imagination'.[28] Some would no doubt question whether these works really merit such extravagant praise. Maybe one has to remember that Farnell was speaking, with some feeling, of a recently departed and obviously much-loved colleague. But his words once again underline the high reputation of which Carpenter enjoyed among his contemporaries, and in some ways it is indeed rather curious that his reputation has not stood the test of time. This is, perhaps, particularly the case if one is thinking primarily of the Comparative Religion field—for two reasons.

In the first place, it can surely be argued that in spite of his pre-eminence in his own way in the Biblical sphere, his most significant contribution to the world of scholarship is to be found in what he did for Comparative Religion, the department of religious studies in which, in a sense, his main interest always lay. After all, when in 1899 he temporarily gave up most of his teaching responsibilities at MCO, he still retained the Case Lectureship in Comparative Religion, and the only actual University appointment which he ever held at Oxford was the Wilde Lectureship in

Comparative Religion, a post which he retained after he retired from the principalship of Manchester College.

Then, in the second place, it can be argued, as Farnell had noted, that Carpenter's Unitarian ethos enabled him to approach non-Christian faiths with an objective impartiality which makes him, in some respects, a harbinger of an attitude increasingly commended, even among committed Christians, in our present-day multi-faith world. It is interesting to note that, in his own day even some of Carpenter's Unitarian colleagues found his comprehensive catholicity a little suspect. In 1898, speculating on Carpenter's forthcoming resignation, James Martineau had written to his son Russell:

> If the study of Pali and the Buddhistic doctrines interest him more than the content of the Hebrew, Greek or Latin thought or things human and divine, it is well, both for him and the College that he should release himself from the limits inherent in his share of our training for the Christian ministry. But to seek to escape from these limits . . . by graduating in the school of Buddha appears to me to be a retrogression from articulate to matriculate speech.[29]

He went on to suggest that there was no time in the College course for what he called 'a mere excursus from the indispensable practical needs of the devout life and earnest duty in our England as it now is'.

In actual fact, of course, Carpenter himself always retained a deep personal commitment to the Christian tradition, which makes Martineau's rather caustic comment somewhat ironic. It could indeed be argued that one of the reasons why he no longer holds the place he once did in comparative studies is that he now seems somewhat less objective than he did to some of his contemporaries. Even in his own day, there were those who saw only too well where his sympathies lay. When he wrote some articles for *The Inquirer* on the place of Christianity among the religions of the world, he received the following comment:

> I like your definite statement of our relation to Jesus. . . . It is greatly needed and I am so glad you show so clearly that whatever other religions may have to teach or affirm, still she (Christianity) is our mother and we cannot help loving her above all mothers.[30]

This probably goes some way to explain why Estlin Carpenter is no longer regarded as an authoritative figure in the world of Comparative Religion. But in spite of changing times and changing attitudes, it can still be justly claimed that he made a notable contribution to the development of modern religious studies, particularly in what is now more often called the History of Religions, and the Carpenter Library of Comparative Religion at Manchester College, originally formed from his personal library, one of the most important collections of its kind anywhere in the world, is still perhaps the most significant memorial to his life and work.

In view of his immense reputation in his own day, it is not surprising that many honours were conferred upon him during his life-time. Oxford made him an honorary MA in 1901, an honorary Doctor of Literature in

1903, and eventually, in 1923, a Doctor of Divinity—a unique distinction for a Unitarian. By then, Glasgow, Jena and Geneva had bestowed similar honours upon him. The Vice-Chancellor at Oxford when he received his DD was his old friend and colleague Dr. Farnell, who was prevented from being present at the ceremony, but he wrote to Carpenter immediately as follows: 'I have been meaning to write a word to you . . . to tell you how sorry I was that I could not preside over the Degrees last Saturday, so as to have the pleasure of welcoming you to the Doctorate. As an old friend who deeply appreciates the splendid work you have done, I very much wished to be there. But I felt it incumbent upon me to attend the memorial service at Magdalen in honour of Dr. Bradley.'[31]

Carpenter's academic eminence during his life-time made him an object of particular veneration in the Unitarian movement, and what endeared him particularly to his co-religionists was his very practical involvement in the affairs of the denomination. As we have already noted, in spite of his very busy academic life, from his earliest years right up until his death, he always remained a very active committed Unitarian. He preached the annual sermon of the British and Foreign Unitarian Association on two occasions, and in 1895, he gave the Essex Hall Lecture (on *The Relation of Jesus to His Age and Our Own*). Reference has already been made to his zealous campaigning, in his declining years, on behalf of the Sustentation and Pension Funds. The denomination was also proud to be able to make use of his very considerable intellectual abilities. He contributed to a number of specifically Unitarian publications, and at one time, he gave regular courses of academic lectures on behalf of the British and Foreign Unitarian Association in various different parts of the country. The present Unitarian Congregation in Cambridge where he is especially remembered, owes its origin to such a venture.

But for any final assessment of the abiding significance of Estlin Carpenter, one perhaps has to turn aside altogether from the academic sphere. It will be remembered that at the time of his death, the Oxford Orator, while acknowledging his learning, also described him as a 'gentle and most Christian soul'. These were indeed the qualities which always made the greatest impression on his contemporaries, and, as was suggested at the outset of this essay, Carpenter deserves to be remembered not only as a remarkable and very assiduous scholar, but also as one who can be described in all seriousness as something of a saint. It is highly significant that A. S. Peake ends his learned and discriminating contribution to the Herford Memorial Volume on what he describes as 'a more personal note'. He goes on to speak of Carpenter's striking qualities as a lecturer, mentioning in particular his 'gracious courtesy' and 'the ease and mastery with which he seized and enforced the significant points as only a scholar and thinker of great range could have done. No difference of theological opinion,' he says, 'chilled the warmth of his appreciation or compromised the fairness of his tribute.' But he also stresses how impressed he had been when he once heard Carpenter preach, and how beautiful it had been 'to see the simplicity and tenderness' with which he had spoken to the parents at a baptismal service which had followed the sermon. 'Many knew him,' he says, 'more intimately than I did, but I knew him well enough to recognise the loftiness and nobility of his character.'[32]

There were perhaps two complementary aspects to the endearing and charismatic spirituality of Estlin Carpenter. On the one hand, there was his deep personal faith, manifested in sincere humility and gentle serenity. On the other, there was the tender loving concern which he extended to all those with whom he came into contact. Although, as we have seen, he always maintained a firm allegiance to a tradition which, in the opinion of some, cannot be regarded as truly Christian, there is a sense in which the Oxford Orator was absolutely right when he described Carpenter as 'a most Christian soul'. Despite the rationalistic assumptions of his religious background, his familiarity with the intricacies of Eastern philosophy and his sympathetic awareness of the truths of many faiths, his own personal religion sprang from a profound yet simple awareness of the love of God revealed in Jesus Christ, and this was something which lay at the very heart of his being and determined his whole outlook.

Throughout his life, even when most immersed in scholarship, this personal faith always remained the central focus of all his activities. His immediate successor as Principal, L. P. Jacks, once said that of all places on earth, the Chapel at Manchester College was the one dearest to him.[33] All his fellow-worshippers were always particularly impressed by the warmth and spirituality of his prayers. A short selection of the latter, made by his friend and admirer, V. D. Davies, and published by the Lindsey Press shortly after his death, still constitutes a moving testimony to strength and reality of Carpenter's personal faith, so clearly characterised by a profound sense of gratitude for the loving kindness of God. It is reflected also in the one or two fine hymns which he composed—especially that for an anniversary occasion: 'Eternal God whose changeless will encircles all our changing years.' His was a broad and catholic faith, marked by a true humility, a complete absence of sectarian arrogance, and an absolute trust in a Divine Love able to transcend all the heart-aches and mysteries of our human lot. It was a faith summed up in the homely lines of J. G. Whittier, which can still be found pasted in one of his note-books:

> I see the wrong that round me lies,
>   I feel the guilt within,
> I hear, with groan and travail-cries,
>   The world confess its sin;
> Yet, in the maddening maze of things,
>   And tossed by storm and flood,
> To one fixed stake my spirit clings:
>   I know that God is good.[34]

It will be remembered that it was as a student in a valley in Wales that

Estlin Carpenter first became aware of the graciousness of God. Throughout his life, he was not disobedient to the heavenly vision.

'Grace abounding to the chief of sinners' is not a phrase normally associated with the liberal tradition, but for Carpenter, the graciousness of God always seemed entirely unmerited, and something, therefore, which imposed upon him tremendous obligations. So his was essentially an outgoing faith, and not something just for private enjoyment. From first to last, he strove to extend to others that experience of loving kindness which he had found in his own life. This was the source of his life-long concern for social service. But it is also the clue to that remarkable genius for friendship which repeatedly broke through a personal shyness which some were initially inclined to interpret as detachment or aloofness. There is a very real sense in which Carpenter's whole career, in all its aspects, has to be thought of in terms of ministry or even the cure of souls. This was above all true of his years as a teacher. To all his students, especially those who had experienced trial or difficulties or who had come as strangers from overseas, he always extended a loving concern. This is particularly stressed in the personal reminiscences which J. H. Weatherall, a former pupil and later among his successors as Principal, contributed to the Herford Memorial Volume,[35]—and, as we have already noted, Carpenter's friendships, once established, were never broken. 'The intimacies of College days,' says Weatherall, 'were sustained and extended in the after years. I don't suppose he ever lost sight of an old student of his. He remembered them spontaneously, sending one of his beautifully written and conceived letters upon the occasion of a wedding, the birth of a child, a change of ministry, a publication, a bereavement. Or he would send an author's copy of one of his books with a friendly greeting to make the gift still more kind.'[36] Weatherall also mentions that his students would always recall 'that they never heard from him a discourteous, impatient, or mean word, and never a censorious judgement'.

In the Carpenter Papers at MCO, there are many expressions of deep appreciation for the message of condolence which he seems to have made a particular point of sending to all his many acquaintances, both obscure and famous, on occasions of bereavement. He clearly had a remarkable ability for saying a fitting word at such times. The extent to which he was amongst those who are able to find 'the soul of goodness in things evil' is also reflected in the language of his prayers, which repeatedly stress an abiding faith in an eternal Loving Purpose transcending all the sorrows of mortality.[37]

Would it be too fanciful to conclude this assessment of the significance of Estlin Carpenter with the suggestion that one can perhaps find in his gentle saintliness a possible explanation of the striking contrast between his former eminence and his current obscurity? The posthumous decline in his reputation would have been, for Carpenter himself, a matter of no consequence whatever, for he was a man of great humility who never entertained an inflated opinion of his capabilities. But it is a little surprising that one who at one time meant so much to so many should now be so little remembered. Throughout this essay, it has been the contention that he is indeed worthy of a place of some importance amongst the names of those who have made a notable contribution to the advancement of religious knowledge. But it may very well be the case that it was primarily because of the deep personal impression which he made upon his contemporaries, his gentle spirituality, his loving concern for others, the complete absence from his make-up of that arrogance and tetchiness which so often accompany academic brilliance, that he was held in such high regard. Now that the direct influence of his personality has gone, he seems, inevitably, a somewhat lesser figure, one who did indeed make a considerable contribution to scholarship, but who can hardly be regarded as a theological giant.

But to those who belong to the same tradition as he did and who share his basic presuppositions, he still retains a touch of greatness—and most of us will still feel, with John Drinkwater:

> When the high heart we magnify,
> And the sure vision celebrate,
> And worship greatness passing by,
> Ourselves are great.[38]

Estlin Carpenter remains one of the finest examples of the essence of the MCO tradition, a reflection of all that is best in the precious inheritance which we have received from the school of Rational Dissent. To some, this is still thought of as a tradition somewhat lacking in spirituality and characterised by a cold and austere piety, constantly on guard against the excesses of an unseemly enthusiasm. Estlin Carpenter is the supreme refutation of that assumption.

In the closing pages of *Buddhism and Christianity*, he gives as his own testimony what he describes as 'the last utterance of Ernst Troeltsch' (surely another much-neglected liberal scholar):

> In our earthly experience, the divine Life is not One but Many. But to discover the One in the Many is the special task of Love.[39]

Here we see reflected what Alexander Gordon, another eminent representative of the Manchester College Oxford tradition and a distinguished Principal of 'the other place', the Unitarian College, Manchester, was once pleased to call 'the Catholicity of the Old Dissent'.[40] But it is perhaps the final stanza of a little known hymn by Ebenezer Sherman Oakley, at one time much beloved among Unitarian congregations, which best sums up the life and work of Estlin Carpenter, scholar and saint:

> Save us, Lord, from seeking
> Earth's unhallowed goals;
> May our life-long passion
> Be the love of souls
> Let us live and labour,
> Father in thy sight,
> Through the grace of Jesus,
> By the Spirit's might.[41]

## NOTES

1. *'Animam mitem christianissimam plorat collegium Mancuniense, plorat Theologia.'* See Joseph Estlin Carpenter—*A Memorial Volume,* edited C. H. Herford, p. 90.
2. Ibid. Subsequently referred to in these notes as *Herford.*
3. *Joseph Estlin Carpenter—An Intellectual Biography* by Jane Anne Deacon—submitted for the degree of Master of Arts in the Department of Religious Studies in the University of Lancaster, December 1977. (Subsequently referred to as *J. A. Deacon*).
4. The school at Bristol is described in R. L. Carpenter, *Memoirs of the Life of the Rev. Lant Carpenter,* pp. 340–352, 1842. J. Drummond & C. B. Upton, *Life and Letters of James Martineau* pp. 18–22.
5. *Herford*—p. 2.
6. Ibid.—p. 8.
7. See for example *A Lectionary of Christian Prose,* ed. A. C. Bouquet, p. 196.
8. *Herford*—pp. 9–10.
9. Obituary notices in 'The Inquirer' give details of this family: see Johnston *'Index of Obituaries in Dissenting Periodicals'* (MSS. the Library, Manchester College, Oxford).
10. *Herford*—p. 30.
11. Ibid.—p. 34.
12. The cure was apparently effected by a book on voice production, *Voice, Song, and Speech* by Lennox Browne and Emil Rehnke. See note on p. 35 of *Herford.*
13. *Herford*—p. 37.
14. *Oxford Dictionary of the Christian Church* (2nd Edition)—article on F. Max Müller, p. 896.
15. Letter, April 8th 1892—quoted *J. A. Deacon,* p. 69.
16. Carpenter Papers at MCO.
17. See A. S. Peake in *Herford,* pp. 139–40.
18. Carpenter Papers at MCO.
19. Ibid.
20. A. S. Peake in *Herford,* pp. 147–8.
21. For further developments in scholarship in this field see *Cambridge History of the Bible,* 1962–1970.
22. A. S. Peake in *Herford.*
23. L. R. Farnell in *Herford,* p. 162.
24. Ibid.—pp. 169–70.
25. J. E. Carpenter, *Comparative Religion,* p. 33.
26. Ibid.—p. 34.
27. L. R. Farnell in *Herford,* p. 173.
28. Ibid.—pp. 176–7.
29. MCO Collection—quoted *J. A. Deacon,* p. 37.
30. Quoted *J. A. Deacon,* p. 59.
31. Carpenter Papers at MCO.
32. A. S. Peake in *Herford,* pp. 160–61.
33. *The Inquirer,* Jan. 25th 1927—quoted *J. A. Deacon,* p. 69.
34. See notebook among the MSS in the Carpenter Papers, MCO—mentioned in Note 11 to Chapter 8 in *J. A. Deacon.* The lines also form part of a Unitarian hymn—see *Hymns of Worship,* p. 421, and *Hymns of Worship Revised,* No. 382.

35. *Herford*, Section II, p. 93ff.
36. Ibid.—pp. 115–16.
37. See for example, No. XX on p. 60 of *Prayers* by J. E. Carpenter, ed. V. D. Davis.
38. These lines appear in Drinkwater's play *Abraham Lincoln*.
39. *Buddhism and Christianity*, p. 307.
40. See the essay on Philip Dodderidge, No. VII in *Addresses Biographical and Historical* by Alexander Gordon, p. 185.
41. Hymn No. 353 in *Hymns of Worship*: 'In life's earnest morning'.

# 10
# RATIONALITY, ECONOMIC MAN AND ALTRUISM

## in Philip H. Wicksteed's *Common Sense of Political Economy*

IAN STEEDMAN
*Professor, Faculty of Economics and Social Studies*
*University of Manchester*

I should like to thank the Leverhulme Trust and the Italian Consiglio Nazionale delle Ricerche (NATO Visiting Professorship Scheme) for financial support and the Facoltà di Scienze Politiche, Catania, for generous hospitality.

## PHILIP HENRY WICKSTEED (1844–1927)

Wicksteed was born in October 1844 in Leeds, where his father, Charles Wicksteed, was a Unitarian minister. He died, at the age of 83, in March 1927, at Childrey in Berkshire. He attended Ruthin Grammar School in North Wales and then University College School, London, before studying at University College London (1861–1864) and at Manchester New College (1864–1867) in Gordon Square nearby. He received his master's degree with a gold medal for classics, in 1867. Wicksteed then became a Unitarian minister, first at Taunton in Somerset (1867–1869), then at Dukinfield, east of Manchester (1870–1874), and finally at Little Portland Street Chapel, London (1874–1897). He left the ministry in 1897 and thereafter earned his living by writing and lecturing. From 1887 to 1918 Wicksteed was a most active University Extension Lecturer, lecturing on Wordsworth, Dante, Greek tragedy, Aristotle and Aquinas—and economics. He never held a university post.

The great breadth of Wicksteed's intellectual activity was far from being confined to his Extension lecturing. He had a considerable linguistic talent; whilst a Minister in Dukinfield, for example, he learned Dutch for the express purpose of translating into English Oort and Hooykaas's *Bible for Young People* (six volumes, 1873–1879). And he completed a translation, with F. M. Cornford, of Aristotle's *Physics* only days before his death. Yet it was as a translator, expounder and interpreter of Dante that he became most widely known; his work as a Dante scholar, which extended over more than forty years, included translations of and commentaries on the *Vita Nuova*, the *Convivio, De Monarchia* and the *Divina Commedia*. Combined with his theological and philosophical interests, this study of Dante led Wicksteed to Aquinas and thus to the writing of his *Dante and Aquinas* (1913) and his *Reactions between Dogma and Philosophy, illustrated from the Works of S. Thomas Aquinas* (1920). That a study of Aquinas' thought by a former Unitarian minister could be reviewed favourably in the *Blackfriars Review* is perhaps an indication of the catholicity of Wicksteed's interests and capacities. Nor did those interests extend only to the past; for example, Wicksteed publicly defended the poetry and drama of Ibsen at a time when Ibsen's work was the object of considerable hostility in England. And Wicksteed's numerous contributions to the *Inquirer*, the Unitarian newspaper, over a span of some fifty years, relate not only to theological and literary matters but also to many economic and political issues.

While he had earlier been influenced by the thought of Comte and of Ruskin, Wicksteed's first direct contact with political economy took the form of reading Henry George's *Progress and Poverty*, of corresponding with George in 1882 and 1883 and of being a co-founder, in 1883, of the Land Reform Union, which supported George's lecture tour of England and Scotland in 1883–1885. (He continued to support some form of land nationalisation long after this time.) It was probably late in 1882 that

Wicksteed began to study the work of Jevons and thus to become 'Jevons's only disciple'. By early 1884, however, he was playing an active role in promulgating Jevonian theory in the Economic Circle, which met until 1888 or 1889. Wicksteed became a close friend of George Bernard Shaw and of Graham Wallas, and was well-informed about Fabian and other aspects of the 'social movements' of the 1880s and 1890s, but was generally an acute and sympathetic observer of, rather than a direct participant in those movements. He was, however, a founding member, in 1891, of the Labour Church movement and continued to give that movement strong support even after other early supporters had withdrawn their active sympathy.

'Before Wicksteed wrote, it was still possible for intelligent men to give countenance to the belief that the whole structure of Economics depends upon the assumption of a world of economic men, each actuated by egocentric or hedonistic motives. For anyone who has read the *Common Sense*, the expression of such a view is no longer consistent with intellectual honesty. Wicksteed shattered this misconception once and for all.'

LIONEL ROBBINS
*October 1932*

Philip Henry Wicksteed (1844–1927) was a man of catholic interests and wideranging activity; a student of Comte's sociology, a Unitarian minister, a Dante scholar, a defender of Henry George's views on land nationalisation and of Ibsen's drama, a tireless University Extension lecturer, a translator of Aristotle and a leading supporter of the Labour Church. (See Herford's biography, 1931). He was also a forceful advocate of the Jevonian, or marginal, economics who pursued to its limits the economic implications of the theory of rational choice. His work might therefore provide a useful point of entry for a consideration of the relations between rational choice theory, as understood in economics, and a perhaps broader conception of the individual in society, who might (or might not) have altruistic purposes, social and ethical ideals, and a complex set of social relationships. The purpose of this paper is not at all ambitious but is simply to draw attention to certain strands of Wicksteed's thought, as presented in his major work in economics, and thereby to provoke reflection on the relations between rationality and altruism. With but few exceptions, our discussion will centre on Wicksteed's *Common Sense of Political Economy, Including a Study of the Human Basis of Economic Law*, of 1910. (Unless otherwise indicated, all page references will refer to the Robbins edition of 1933.)

## I. CHOICE BETWEEN ALTERNATIVES

### *The Relative Scale*

On the opening page of the *Common Sense* Wicksteed writes that 'In the ordinary course of our lives we constantly consider how our time, our energy, or our money shall be spent' (p. 1). This simple statement —which Wicksteed would doubtless have been happy to describe as obvious—already contains within it two central themes of Wicksteed's book. The first is that we are for ever making choices, whether minor or momentous; the second is that choices directly concerned with the spending of money are just one kind of choice amongst many. The importance, to Wicksteed, of this second theme will be considered in subsequent sections but we begin by considering Wicksteed's treatment of choice itself. Even here, however, the second theme already intrudes, for he is emphatic that 'the general principles which regulate our conduct in business are identical with those which regulate our deliberations, our selections between alternatives, and our decisions, in all other branches of life . . . We must regard industrial and commercial life, not as a separate and detached region of activity, but as an organic part of our whole personal and social life' (p. 3). The standpoint which enables Wicksteed to emphasise what different types of activity have in common is that 'Selection between alternatives . . . is the most generalised form under which we can contemplate the ordinary acts of administration of resources, whether in the market place, the home, or elsewhere' (p. 28), for 'selection between alternatives' is involved in all choosing and deciding, whether or not the issue at hand would normally be described as an economic one. For Wicksteed, 'the laws which they [Economics and the economic life] exhibit and obey are not peculiar to themselves, but are the laws of life in its widest extent' (p. 160).

The single principle 'laid down by Jevons' which 'is not exclusively applicable to industrial or commercial affairs, but runs as a universal and vital force through the administration of all our resources' (p. 3), is that of diminishing marginal significance. This principle, the application of which Wicksteed is far from restricting to economic goods and services, enables Wicksteed to argue that, in equilibrium, the most heterogeneous items can be regarded 'as substitutes for each other' (pp. 6–7), on the margin; 'a man's "scale of preferences" or "relative scale", then' (p. 36), can thus be aligned, at the margin, with the relative terms on which alternative items are available. While Wicksteed's earlier *Alphabet of Economic Science*, of 1888, contained such phrases as 'marginal utility' (p. 78) and 'the differential coefficient of the total utility' (p. 79) the argument of the *Common Sense* is conducted throughout in terms of the scale of preference, diminishing marginal significance and equivalence at the margin. (C.f. Robbins, p. xix; *all* the references to Final Utility, Utility, and Variation of Utility in the index to Robbins's edition of the *Common Sense* are to works other than the main text itself.)

*Some more detailed considerations*

(a) Wicksteed does not suppose that an individual's 'scale of preferences' is always transitive. (Wicksteed uses the term 'consistent'.) Thus he writes, 'if I would choose A rather than B and would choose B rather than C, it does not follow (as it ought to do) that *a fortiori* I should choose A rather than C' (p. 33; c.f. p. 122). Yet, as is implicit in the parenthesis '(as it ought to do)', he considers that 'The man of alert intelligence and sound judgement will reduce [such inconsistencies] to a minimum' (p. 34). On the other hand, Wicksteed emphatically asserts the completeness of the scale of preferences; 'Any alternatives, however constituted, which could conceivably be offered to the man would find him either decisively preferring one to the other or unable to decide between them; that is to say, every conceivable alternative stands either above or below any other that you may select, or on a level with it' (pp. 122–3).

(b) Wicksteed does not assume that one's scale of preferences is always present to the conscious mind. On the contrary, he asks 'why we are so seldom conscious of this ever-present fact of selection between alternatives, particularly in our money purchases' (p. 34). His answer is that 'our scale of preferences often asserts itself automatically. Life would be impossible if we were always in the state of mind professed by the lady who said she liked "to get up every morning feeling that everything was an open question" . . . if we are moderately wise we pretty generally act without reflection in the manner which reflection would have indicated' (pp. 35–6). It is perhaps of some interest that immediately before raising the above question about 'unconscious choice', Wicksteed writes in a way which evokes rather strongly the 'revealed preference' approach. (He does not, of course, use this term.) Thus he writes that, 'A man's . . . successive acts of choice, whether purchases or other selections, are constantly revealing fragments of it [his actual scale of preferences], as he determines that at this price he will take this instead of that, and on these terms he will select this alternative and reject the other' (p. 34). This striking passage is perhaps an exception to the general orientation of the *Common Sense* but should be recalled later in the light of Wicksteed's insistence that the theorist should consider either all motives *or none* (see below).

(c) Since reference was made above to diminishing marginal significance and equivalence, through substitution, at the margin, it should be noted that, in relation to purchased commodities, Wicksteed is particularly careful *not* to assert that, in equilibrium, the ratio of marginal significances is equal to the corresponding price ratio, for every pair of commodities. Such an equality, he explains very clearly, holds only when both commodities are actually possessed (in positive quantities).

### *The Objects of Choice*

As will be discussed in greater detail in a later section, Wicksteed was strenuously opposed to the idea that the economic theorist need attend only to the way in which marketable commodities enter an individual's scale of preferences; in his view, account must be taken of *all* the agent's objects of choice. Wicksteed seems to have been very fond of specific examples—his *Alphabet* of 1888 has only one index, an index of examples—and it will be appropriate here to follow him in this respect. Early in the *Common Sense*, Wicksteed's heroine is the housewife who administers resources both in the market place, where she allocates money, and within the household, where she allocates time, effort, attention and physical goods to the needs of the members of the household—the cat and the dog not being forgotten. Even within this simple example Wicksteed indicates at once that the objects of choice can be complex. When Materfamilias is deciding whether to purchase chicken or cod to be served at a small dinner party for her neighbours, she has to balance the money saved by choosing cod against the somewhat smaller respect thus shown to her guests; and 'If the entertaining housekeeper suspects that one or more of her guests will know the price of cod and chickens as well as she does, a complication is introduced, for cod will be still less of a compliment at 6d. than at 10d. a pound' (pp. 21–2). Moreover, a 'father and mother may have ambitions with respect to the education or accomplishments of their children [and such] parents may be willing to incur the twofold reproach of being mean and being stuck up, by entertaining their guests less sumptuously than custom demands, and at the same time getting French or violin lessons for their children' (p. 22). And if 'the members of a family have been deeply affected by the news of an Indian famine' (p. 23) then 'our housekeeper's purchases of chickens may certainly be effected not only by the price of cod, or by the price of French or music lessons . . . but also by the fact there there is a famine in India and that machinery by which she and her family can help to alleviate it has been brought to her door' (p. 24). It is entirely typical of Wicksteed's method of argument that through a simple, homely example he should quickly arrive at the general point that the objects of choice can include social standing, respect shown to others, concern for one's children and concern for distant suffering.

Equally typical is his keen awareness that careful administration of resources and balancing of margins is itself costly in terms of time, effort, attention and spontaneity, all of which have their own value. With respect to 'a housekeeper who lives in the country, but deals with one of the great London Stores, and who is making out her list' (p. 81), for example, Wicksteed writes: 'And the yet further question of how much thought and time it is worth while to give, in the hope of making yet further reductions, is meanwhile settling itself under the pressure, high one day and low another, of the competing claims of other duties and pleasures, the resentment or irritation of weariness, or the sudden protest of a raised consciousness that she is in danger of bartering life for halfpennyworths of rice and sugar' (p. 82). (Many related observations are made at pp. 13, 20–1, 36, 77–80, 119, 121–2, 412, 431.) Indeed Wicksteed suggests that, 'Perhaps we oftener complain of having wasted time than of having wasted money. We are bitterly conscious of having spent "more time than it was worth" on this or that trifle' (p. 92). The objects of choice, then, include not only social respect, etc. but also freedom from excessive calculations and from 'bartering life for halfpennyworths of rice and sugar'; and allocation of one's time is no less important than that of one's money.

It is tempting to suppose that the 'housekeeper who lives in the country' was Mrs. Emily Wicksteed, for in 1901 the Wicksteeds had moved from London to Childrey in Berkshire. Indeed the choice between town and country provided Wicksteed with an example which he used repeatedly, in the *Alphabet* of 1888 (pp. 52–3), in the *Common Sense*, of 1910, and in his 'Scope and Method of Political Economy', of 1914. In the *Common Sense* he formulated this example as follows: 'If we are considering . . . whether to live in the country or in the town, such different things as friendship and fresh air or fresh eggs may come into competition and comparison with each other. Shall I "bury myself in the country", where I shall see little of my dearest friends, but may hope for fresh eggs for breakfast, and fresh air all the day? Or shall I stay where I am, and continue to enjoy the society of my friends?' (p. 32). The point of this example, for Wicksteed, is that the most heterogeneous satisfactions are in fact weighed against one another (and that the final decision will depend on estimates of the extent to which a move to the country, say, will reduce contact with friends in the town). That heterogeneity, indeed, can extend well beyond 'personal pleasures' in any normal sense of the term: 'we shall find the clue to the conduct of men in their commercial relations, not in the first instance amongst those characteristics wherein our pursuit of industrial objects differs from our pursuit of pleasure or of learning, or our efforts for some political and social ideal, but rather amongst those underlying principles of conduct and selection wherein they all resemble each other' (p. 3). For Wicksteed, the principles of choice, of selection amongst alternatives, are the same in all fields of activity and the most diverse objects of choice can in fact be compared.

It has already been implied that the items entering an individual's scale of preferences need not all be exchangeable commodities but this point must now be emphasised and extended. 'One man might be willing to sacrifice a title if he could get rid of a constitutional tendency to neuralgic headaches, and another man might be willing to contract such a tendency if it would secure him the title; but though there is a diversity in the tastes of these two men, and each possesses what he relatively undervalues, no exchange can take place' (p. 132). Objects of choice may not be exchangeable. More importantly, perhaps, exchangeable items are never themselves ultimately desired objects of choice, according to Wicksteed. 'Into this circle of exchange enter a vast number of the things which I desire, and the command of which I believe will affect my well-being . . . these things, of which money gives us command, are, strictly speaking, never the ultimate objects of deliberate desire at all . . . That is to say, there is no ultimate object of desire which itself enters into the circle of exchange and can be directly drawn thence . . . as soon as we deliberately desire possession of any external object, it is because of the experiences or the mental states and habits which it is expected to produce or to avert . . . no single thing that we ultimately desire is in the circle of exchange or can be directly drawn from it' (pp. 152–3). What then are the ultimately desired objects of choice? Wicksteed does not attempt to provide an exhaustive list—perhaps wisely—but does offer as examples freedom from weariness and from hunger (p. 146), the presence of health, happiness and domestic affection (p. 146), the enjoyment of music (p. 402), the opportunity to study (p. 403) and, somewhat more generally, 'a sense of heightened vitality and enjoyment of life, or relief from pain, or assuagement of anxiety, or sense of power' (p. 360). Perhaps he would also have been ready to include the pursuit of social ideals? Be that as it may, Wicksteed is insistent that the ultimately desired objects of choice never enter the circle of exchange directly and, conversely, that commodities are never themselves the ultimately desired objects. (C.f. Wicksteed's statement in his 'Scope and Method' paper of 1914, that, 'The ends, which are always subjective experiences of some kind, whether of the senses or the will or the emotions, are not in any direct way exchangeable' (p. 777).) If there is a 'scale of preferences' over commodities, then, it is at most a derivative scale, descending from the scale of preferences over ultimately desired experiences, etc.

*

As a Unitarian minister from 1867 to 1897, Wicksteed was the direct employee of his congregation; he was thus well aware that 'the teachings and the ministrations of religion' do in a sense 'come into the circle of exchange and can therefore be commanded by money' (p. 163). (C.f. 'A man may be paid for . . . conducting ceremonies or rites which are believed favourably to affect our relations with the spiritual world, or delivering exhortations which will be conducive to our inward harmony. All these services, then, are in the circle of exchange' (p. 317).) In so far as this is so, then, Wicksteed must hold, in order to be consistent, that 'the teachings and the ministrations of religion' are not ultimately desired objects. He does, however, in the same passage, refer to 'spiritual enjoyment and edification' as being included amongst exchangeable things and it is perhaps difficult to see how this can fail to contradict his insistence that ultimately desired objects never enter the circle of exchange. Perhaps Wicksteed should rather have written that the activity of a minister of religion can enter the circle of exchange—and does so in Unitarian and in some other churches—but that teachings, spiritual enjoyment and edification never do so, in any *direct* way?

The distinction between ultimately desired objects of choice and what may provide them is also of importance with respect to the clear understanding of declining marginal significance: 'in speaking of declining [marginal] significance we are never dealing with the ultimately desired experiences themselves, but always with something that we value as likely to produce such experiences . . . we saw that, other things being equal, [a man] would value a fifth concert per week less than a fourth. We did not say that a fifth "unit of enjoyment of music" would be less valuable to him than a fourth . . . Indeed it would obviously be nonsense to say that equally desired experiences have a declining significance, for if their significance declines they are not equally desired' (pp. 402–3).

## *Some Complications*

It is not to be expected that a writer as thorough and as thoughtful as Wicksteed could be satisfied with any suggestion that selection between alternatives is always both simple and rationally executed. Apart from noting some minor difficulties in the constant equating of marginal significances (p. 96ff), he argues that 'A great part of our conduct is impulsive and a great part unreflecting; and when we reflect our choice is often irrational' (p. 28). (The concluding phrase in this passage is, of course, ambiguous; I take it to mean 'when we reflect *ex post*, our past choice is often seen to have been irrational'.) Wicksteed's argument is that we may indeed shrink from performing some unpleasant action, even if rational consideration would show that, in the light of our own preferences, the benefit resulting from the performance of the action would more than 'repay' the unpleasantness of the action; yet if the 'price' of not performing it becomes high enough, the action will be undertaken—the irrational aversion will be overcome (pp. 30–1). 'Our irrational shrinkings then, as well as our rational preferences, "have their price". And as irrational aversion or dread does not supersede the principle of price, so neither does irrational attraction or fancy . . . the man who has "fallen in love" with a house, a horse, a book, or a scheme of business or pleasure . . . will nevertheless be daunted when [the price] rises beyond a certain point' (p. 31). (See also pp. 114, 118; it is to be noted that Wicksteed sometimes uses 'price' in a metaphorical sense.) As a specific example of 'irrationality', it is suggested that 'even the diseased estimates of the miser will not escape the general law' (p. 299), for if the 'price' of further accumulation becomes too high—i.e. consumption becomes too small —the miser's rate of saving will be checked. Wicksteed also presents a somewhat similar analysis of the effects of habit, conventional behaviour and tradition. Thus he writes that, 'Habit or impulse perpetually determines our selection between alternatives without any reflection on our part at all; and the terms on which alternatives are offered us may change within wide limits without affecting us. But if they are altered beyond a certain point the habit will be broken or the unconscious impulse checked, and we shall enter a stage of conscious choice. The power of habit or impulse to resist the intrusion of deliberate choice is quantitatively defined, and may be overcome on certain terms' (pp. 28–9; see also pp. 114–19). There is, moreover, a positive aspect to custom and habit, related to the need not to devote excessive time, effort and attention to reflection and calculation; customary and habitual behaviour contribute 'to the saving of much fretting upon the higher strings of motive and efforts of will' (p. 119).

## II. ECONOMIC MAN, MOTIVES AND ECONOMIC RELATIONS

Shortly before he began to write the *Common Sense* (see Robbins, p. xviii), Wicksteed reviewed Pareto's *Manuale di Economia Politica*, in the *Economic Journal* of December 1906. Referring to 'Pareto's own principle' that the marginal significance of any object of desire depends on the quantities of all the objects of desire which are possessed, Wicksteed writes that, 'when this principle is driven through to its legitimate conclusion, we shall understand the impossibility of drawing a line between economic and non-economic phenomena' (p. 816). Thus when he observes that Pareto's 'opening chapter is designed to emphasise not the connection so much as the difference between the methods of sociology generally and of economics . . . Pareto, therefore, is by no means inclined to obliterate the boundaries of economic science' (p. 817), Wicksteed's tone is firmly critical. It was no coincidence that the review of Pareto's *Manuale* should have contained a passing reference to Comte, for Wicksteed had earlier studied Comte's writings with attention and, although never 'a Positivist', had been impressed by Comte's work. It is indeed striking that Wicksteed chose to place on the very title page of the *Common Sense* the following quotation from Comte: 'L'analyse économique proprement dite ne me semble pas devoir finalement être conçue ni cultivée, soit dogmatiquement, soit historiquement, à part de l'ensemble de l'analyse sociologique, soit statique, soit dynamique.' It is thus not to be expected that Wicksteed should be greatly enamoured of the concept of 'the economic man'.

In his Introduction to the *Common Sense* Wicksteed announces that, 'I shall try to show that it is time frankly and decisively to abandon all attempts to rule out this or that "motive" from the consideration of the Economist, or indeed to attempt to establish any distinction whatever between the ultimate motives by which a man is actuated in business and those by which he is actuated in his domestic or public life . . . this does away at a stroke with the hypothetically simplified psychology of the Economic Man which figured so largely in the older books of Political Economy, and which recent writers take so much trouble to evade or qualify' (p. 4). While the whole text of the *Common Sense* could reasonably be said to constitute Wicksteed's attempt to show the inappropriateness of the economic man concept, it is in Chapter V, 'Business and the Economic Nexus', that he addresses these issues most directly. 'But when we pass . . . to the phrase "the economic motive" . . . we are in the presence of one of the most dangerous and indeed disastrous confusions that obstruct the progress of Economics. Many writers have thought that the Economist, as such, must not only limit his consideration to certain actions and conditions which concern exchangeable and mainly material things, but must also shut out of consideration all *motives* that are not "economic". And the economic motive is generally defined as the "desire to possess wealth". The widest definition of wealth, in this connection, would make it include all exchangeable things, but nothing else. Now since we have already seen that no ultimate object of desire can ever be the direct subject of exchange at all, we perceive at once that to regard the "economic" man (as he is often called) as actuated solely by the desire to possess wealth is to think of him as only desiring to collect tools and never desiring to do or to make anything with them' (p. 163). It is thus quite arbitrary to suppose that one can usefully argue in terms of an 'economic man' actuated by a single 'motive', or even by a limited set of particular 'motives'. 'The truth is that the relative intensity of another man's desire to possess any exchangeable thing, regarded as a fact, apart from his reasons, undoubtedly helps to fix the terms on which possession of that thing is offered to me. If I regard it in this light all considerations of motive are irrelevant . . . If, on the other hand, I look at the matter from his point of view and am interested to know how he comes to want this thing, I must be prepared to recognise all motives that are actually at work . . . We may either ignore motives altogether, or may recognise all motives that are at work . . . but in no case may we pick and choose between the motives we will and and motives we will not recognise as affecting economic conditions' (pp. 164–5). For Wicksteed, then, 'economic man' and his limited 'motives' must be abandoned, either in favour of a purely external or behavioural approach, or in favour of a consideration of the 'whole' individual. In practice, Wicksteed nearly always adopts the latter stance.

(It is perhaps worthwhile to turn aside briefly to indicate that Wicksteed was not attacking a straw (economic) man. In his *Unsettled Questions*, of 1844, J. S. Mill described *homo economicus* as 'a being who invariably does that by which he may obtain the greatest amount of necessaries, conveniences, and luxuries, with the smallest quantity of labour and physical self-denial with which they can be obtained in the existing state of knowledge' (1877, p. 14). And Bagehot observed that 'Political Economy deals not with the entire real man as we know him in fact, but with a simpler, imaginary man—a man answering to a pure definition from which all impairing and conflicting elements have been fined away' (1880, p. 74).

If all motives are to be considered, and if the principles guiding economic activity are simply the principles guiding all human activity, what defines the particular object of study of the Economist? For Wicksteed, the answer lies in the concept of *'economic relations'*; 'economic investigation is concerned [with] the things a man can give to or do for another independently of any personal and individualised sympathy with him or with his motives or reasons' (pp. 4–5). No man can meet his needs unaided, or 'simply by enlisting the co-operation directly inspired by sympathy with him or with his purposes. But by direct and indirect processes of exchange, by the social alchemy of which money is the symbol, the things I have and the things I can are transmuted into the things I want and the things I would . . . and all this independently of any interest in these desires of mine, or any knowledge of them, on the part of very many of the persons who assist me to accomplish them . . . Why, then, do they co-operate with me at all? Not primarily, or not solely, because they are interested in my purposes, but because they have certain purposes of their own . . . A vast range, therefore, of our relations with others enters into a system of mutual adjustment by which we further each other's purposes simply as an indirect way of furthering our own. All such relations may be fitly called "economic" ' (p. 166). When persons A and B stand in an economic relation, they may well be furthering each other's purposes but A enters the relation with no thought or intention of promoting B's ends and B, likewise, is motivated by no desire to further the purposes of A; however rich and complex may be the motivations of A and of B, the economic relation between them is an impersonal one.

(Wicksteed's description of economic relations—'social alchemy', 'further each other's purposes'—may seem to verge on a description of 'economic harmony'. It should therefore be noted explicitly that Wicksteed was no apologist for market capitalism and, indeed, had harsh words to say about 'the seductive picture of "economic harmony"' (p. 184); see pp. 184–6, 190, 210, 302–3, 333, 355–7, 395–8, 659, 667, 696, 822.)

## III. NON-TUISM, ALTRUISM AND ETHICS

It might seem at first glance that the economic relation, as defined by Wicksteed, is an inherently egoistic one, a relation in which persons A and B each act from purely selfish motives. Wicksteed, however, expressly devotes pp. 170–183 of the *Common Sense* to arguing 'That the economic relation is entered into at the prompting of the whole range of human purposes and impulses, and rests in no exclusive or specific way on an egoistic or self-regarding basis' (p. 169). He begins by returning to the example of the housewife and suggests that 'It would be transparently absurd to say that she is only thinking of herself in the market place, and thinking chiefly of others in the home; or that her motives are entirely egoistic when she is buying the potatoes, and preponderatingly or exclusively altruistic when she is helping them. And as it will be generally admitted that she conducts her marketing in the main on business principles, it follows that the difference between what we are to consider a business transaction and what we are not so to consider is not determined by the selfishness or unselfishness, the egoism or the altruism, of the inspiring motive' (p. 170). Wicksteed's point here is certainly not that, while the housewife is not selfish, the 'household' must be regarded as acting selfishly in its economic relations with others. He thus considers next the example of a 'group of men who unite to propagate a set of religious doctrines or to call attention to a social or national wrong, or to secure a sanitary or dietary reform, or to preach any gospel or advertise any fad' (p. 171). 'It would be ridiculous to say that the enthusiasts who give the printer an order for ten thousand copies of their most effective tract are actuated by purely "egoistic" motives, and if we choose to imagine the case that the printer, on his side, in getting weary of his trade, but keeps on in order to be able to make handsome subsidies to a certain "cause" in which he in his turn is interested, it would be equally ridiculous to say that his motives were "egoistic". Yet the relation on both sides might be purely economic. Each might enter upon it altogether in furtherance of his own purposes, and in no degree from sympathy in the other's' (p. 172). More generally, then, 'What makes it an economic transaction is that I am not considering you except as a link in the chain, or considering your desires except as the means by which I may gratify those of some one else—not necessarily myself. The economic relation does not exclude from my mind every one but me, it potentially includes every one but you' (p. 174). To stress this point Wicksteed introduced the term 'non-tuism', which serves to focus our attention upon the fact that, in an economic relation, A's lack of concern for the purposes of B (and vice-versa), by no means entails that A acts from selfish motives. 'The specific characteristic of an economic relation is not its "egoism" but its "non-tuism"' (p. 180).

It follows from the above clarification of the nature of the economic relation that, 'The proposal to exclude "benevolent" or "altruistic" motives from consideration in the study of Economics is . . . wholly irrelevant and beside the mark' (p. 179). The members of a Society acting for a 'cause', the above-mentioned printer, the trustees of an estate (p. 175) and the 'administrators of a charitable fund' (p. 176), all enter into economic relations for non-selfish reasons. Nor is the point to be restricted to 'special cases' since, as has already been noted, Wicksteed is insistent that all motives (if any at all) must be considered in relation to each economic agent. 'If I am in control of a stock of timber (however I come to be so) which I desire to transmute into the maximum of literature or art or missionary activity, or political propaganda, or knowledge of mathematics, or silk and satin garments, or anything else that cannot be made of wood, I shall sell it at the highest price I can get' (p. 375). (Further on altruism, see pp. 4, 164, 168.)

Wicksteed offers no explicit discussion of the familiar suggestion that *every* action is necessarily self-interested ('I am pursuing *my* concern that others should be able to . . .') but we have already seen that he describes as 'ridiculous' the claim that the enthusiasts for a cause, or their printer who handsomely subsidises some other cause, are activated by purely 'egoistic motives'. In the earlier *Alphabet of Economic Science* he had considered the following case: 'we may suppose that Sarah Bernhardt is charging three hundred guineas as her fee for reciting at an evening party, and that the three hundred guineas would provide a week's holiday in the country for six hundred London children. A benevolent and fashionable gentleman is in doubt which of these two methods of spending the sum in question he shall adopt, and after much internal debate makes his selection. What do we learn from his decision? We learn whether *his* desire to give his friends the treat of hearing the recitation or to give the children the benefit of country air is the greater' (p. 85). After noting that the desires of the friends and of the children do not enter the matter at all, in any direct manner, Wicksteed appends a footnote: 'It is interesting to note that there are considerable manufactures of things the direct desire for which seldom or never asserts itself at all. There are immense masses of tracts and Bibles produced, for instance, which are paid for by persons who do not desire to use them but to give them away to other persons whose desire for them is not in any way an effective factor in the proceeding. And there are numbers of expensive things made expressly to be bought for "presents", and which no sane person is ever expected to buy for himself' (p. 86, n*). (Page 85 bears the heading 'Vicarious Demand'.) In the *Common Sense*, Wicksteed considers the case of charitable appeals, as an example of declining marginal significance. If I give one guinea towards the relief of famine in India, 'I can hardly believe that a second guinea would relieve suffering perceptibly less intense than that relieved by the first . . . Why do I not pay a second guinea and a third, and so on? The answer is twofold. In the first place, in the majority of cases it is not really the famine in India but my own conscience that I am appeasing, and my own conscience becomes perceptibly less clamorous after the first guinea has been paid . . . The point is that the demand I am meeting is, as a matter of fact, perceptibly reduced by what I have done to meet it' (p. 413). (And even if I consider the need in India, rather than my own conscience, as I give guinea after guinea the marginal significances of *other* purposes will increase until they equal the—almost constant-—marginal significance of guineas given for famine relief.)

Wicksteed's claim, then, seems to be that each agent selects from amongst the many possible objectives available to that agent in the light of (or as expressed by?) that agent's scale of preferences and that those objectives may (or may not) be 'non-egoistic' in that they may (or may not) have, as their primary concern, the interest(s) of others. It is, necessarily, the agent who makes the agent's choices but the interests pursued may or may not be those of the agent. That the division will not always be clearcut is illustrated by Wicksteed's discussion of compulsory education. 'On what grounds', he writes, 'may we suppose that the individual citizen came to consider the education of every child his concern? It may be that he felt he would be relieved from personal risk or some detriment by the general enforcement of education. If it were merely argued that a community is safer and more comfortable to live in if its children are schooled, the appeal would be to each citizen's personal interest. But, if the argument were that a child who has been schooled is more likely to live a worthy and satisfactory life himself, then the person who decrees taxes for educational purposes is actuated by a desire for the well-being of the children, and that well-being becomes one of his own direct interests and purposes' (p. 663). While Wicksteed does not say so himself, it is clear that the 'egoistic' and 'altruistic' reasons for supporting compulsory education could perfectly well coexist amongst the motives and purposes of a single agent. (For further references to children and to posterity, see pp. 22 (cited above), 110, 334, 375, 484, 699–70; further on 'mixed motives', see below.)

### *Some special points*

(a) In discussing the altruism of Materfamilias within the household, Wicksteed implies that this should not involve 'a stupid appetite for martyrdom . . . Self-sacrifice would be no less fatal than self-assertion, and altruism and egoism are alike lost in the communal sense of which she is the organ. If she has occasionally to rebuke the egoism and appeal to the altruism of the little barbarians around her, it is because their communal sense is underdeveloped; and she is well aware of the danger of turning them from barbarians into prigs if she develops altruism when it is the communal sense that needs development' (p. 178). It seems—but is not made fully explicit—that, for Wicksteed, there is a 'communal sense' when there is no 'conscious distinction between what I do for my own sake and what I do for the sake of others' or, in other words, when it is not appropriate to speak of altruism, or of egoism, or of non-tuism (p. 179).

(b) In a manner which foreshadows some of the ideas of Frank H. Knight (who refers to Wicksteed several times in his *Risk, Uncertainty and Profit* of 1921), Wicksteed also suggests that the categories of egoism and altruism may not apply to the businessman engaged in making a bargain: 'He wants to make a good bargain or do a good piece of business, and he is directly thinking of nothing else . . . He is not thinking either of missions to the heathen or of famine funds, or of his pew rent, or of his political association. But neither is he thinking of his wife and family, nor yet of himself and the champagne suppers he may enjoy with his bachelor friends . . . He is exactly in the position of a man who is playing a game of chess or cricket. He is considering nothing except his game . . . At the moment the categories of egoism and altruism are irrelevant' (pp. 180–81). On the other hand, Wicksteed sometimes suggests that the businessman will not always pursue a rigidly non-tuistic approach to his dealings but will refrain from taking what he regards as an 'unfair advantage', so that an element of altruism may intrude even in business transactions (pp. 197, 226, 388).

(c) Wicksteed devotes a complete section of his Chapter V, 'Business and the Economic Nexus', to a discussion of mixed motivations. The housewife at the market may favour one stall-keeper rather than another because he 'goes to the same place of worship that she does . . . or because his wife has just been confined, or because she knows he has recently had bad luck' (p. 193). Moreover, relations which are at first purely economic may themselves engender, on the part of the employee, a direct interest in the well-being of the employer. Wicksteed cites as possible examples 'the doctor, the lawyer, and, most of all, the minister of religion' (p. 195); 'the employed person, whether a doctor or a factory hand, is called upon for specific services which may breed devotion to his work and to those for whom he does it' (p. 196). In such cases the employee may cease to regard the employment relation in a purely non-tuistic manner. More generally, 'in choosing his business or profession a man is not necessarily or even probably moved by merely economic forces' (p. 198) but is also influenced by the (un-)pleasantness of the work itself and by the (un-)desirability of such work's being done at all (pp. 198–201). (See also Wicksteed's discussion of whether, under 'collectivism', it will be possible to find 'competent men' who will work, for no wages, 'with the primary object of serving the community' (pp. 678–9).)

*Remarks on Ethics*

The *Common Sense* is not, of course, a treatise on ethics but, in the light of Wicksteed's insistence on the unity of the principles of choice, it is not surprising that it should contain a number of remarks on the relations between ethics and Wicksteed's principles of selection between alternatives and of diminishing marginal significances. Indeed, in introducing Book III of the *Common Sense*, Wicksteed observes that, 'In the course of our examination of any one of [certain social policy] questions we shall find abundant illustration of that interdependence of economic, social and moral questions which has been so often insisted upon in the body of this work' (pp. 627–8). We shall not consider here Wicksteed's discussions of these policy issues or, of course, his remarks on altruism, etc. which have already been referred to; rather we shall draw attention, very briefly, to some of Wicksteed's more general observations.

In his 'Scope and Method' paper, of 1914, Wicksteed is rather more forthright about his view of the relations between ethics and economic analysis, than he is in the *Common Sense* (perhaps because the paper was necessarily brief) but his view is unchanged. He writes: 'the inner core of our life problems and the gratification of all our ultimate desires . . . obey the same all-permeating law. Virtue, wisdom, sagacity, prudence, success, imply different schemes of values, but they all submit to the law formulated by Aristotle with reference to virtue, and analysed by modern writers with reference to business, for they all consist in combining factors χατ ὀϱθὸν λόγον, *in the right proportion,* as fixed by that distribution of resources which establishes the equilibrium of their differential significances in securing the object contemplated' (p. 776); and 'if we really understand and accept the principle of differential significances we shall realise . . . that Aristotle's system of ethics and our reconstructed system of economics are twin applications of one identical principle or law' (p. 779). These statements are, of course, from Wicksteed's standpoint, but special formulations of his principle that the laws of economic conduct are simply the laws of life.

Wicksteed is not implying that economic and ethical issues are, at root, of equal standing. On the contrary, he insists in 'Scope and Method' that 'our economic investigations . . . derive their whole significance from their social and vital bearings . . . this ultimate significance is determined by ethical considerations [and] the sanity of men's desires matters more than the abundance of their means of accomplishing them' (p. 783). This point is made even more vividly in the *Common Sense*: 'The man who can make his fellows desire more worthily and wisely is doubtless performing a higher task than the one who enables them more amply to satisfy whatever desires they have. The prophet and the poet may regenerate the world without the economist, but the economist cannot regenerate it without them. Yet he, too, has his place. He may help to guide if he cannot inspire. If he can give no strength he may save strength from being wasted. It is his misery that he cannot glorify the purposes to which he ministers, but it is his triumph that he can be glorified by them. He works in faith, for he knows that his work is barren unless others greater than he are working too, but he believes that wherever they are he can serve them. If he can give sight to some blind reforming Samson he too has served' (pp. 123–4). The principles of economic, ethical—and other —choices may be the same but economic considerations are always of derivative, not primary importance.

It is also to be noted that Wicksteed's 'unification' of the principles of choice in different fields of conduct is not rooted in a hedonistic calculus. Pages 423–34 of the *Common Sense* are indeed devoted 'to the discovery of interesting relations between a hedonistic calculus and current moral judgements' (p. 401) but Wicksteed immediately insists that, 'Nothing that has been said in this chapter must be taken as committing the author to a hedonistic theory of ethics. Suppose a man deliberately desires to cultivate impulses, and to train himself to a sense of values which he does not expect to give him the maximum of personal happiness. Suppose there are things that he really does care for more than his own happiness . . . the general principles on which our investigations are based, while throwing light on the hedonistic calculus, do not suppose a hedonistic theory, but are equally applicable to any other' (p. 434–5). (These remarks perhaps throw light on Wicksteed's opinion, cited above, that it would be 'ridiculous' to describe as 'egoistic' the motives of the supporters of a 'cause', when they order tracts to be printed.)

If Wicksteed's theory of human conduct is not hedonistic, it is, of course, very firmly centred on the notion of equating marginal significances (when the 'quantity possessed' is positive). He is therefore led to consider the following challenges to his theory: 'But it is sometimes asked, "Is not the case different when questions of duty are concerned? Does not duty always remain paramount, however much of your powers and resources you have already devoted to its demands? And are not the claims of compassion always superior to those of selfishness, however much you may have indulged the former and starved the latter? Is it possible for a well-regulated mind to bring about a marginal coincidence of value between the means of satisfying desires which are on essentially different ethical levels? Can such qualitative distinctions be reduced to questions of quantity?" ' (p. 403). Wicksteed discusses the compassion/selfishness question via the Indian famine example, which has already been considered above. As to the claims of 'duty', Wicksteed is somewhat dismissive, arguing that, 'we shall generally find, on analysing any dilemma, that the dictum "Duty before all things" is only maintained by giving the name of "duty" to whatever, under the circumstances, properly comes first; and that our determination on this point is influenced both by the terms on which the alternatives are offered to us and by the extent to which we have already paid tribute to the one or the other claim. The label can only be attached after the conclusion is reached, and cannot indicate any short cut by which to reach it' (p. 409). He takes far more seriously, however, the case of 'the martyr who has borne the rack [and] is ready to be burnt to death sooner than depart a hair's breadth from the formula of his confession' (p. 404) and that of the man for whom there are 'certain things which he would not do for any amount of money, however large' (p. 405). How are these forms of conduct to be interpreted in terms of the equating of marginal significances? Wicksteed's central argument in this regard is that, when 'one of the main issues of life' (p. 407) is at stake, other considerations may well sink below the *minimum sensibile*. Thus 'it is perfectly possible for the extremest pressure that can be brought to bear upon either [the martyr or the "incorruptible"] to be quite negligible, so that it would no more be recognised as a reason (even an inadequate one) for doing the abominable thing than fear of staining my cuffs would be recognised as a reason against helping a wounded child' (p. 408). Since Wicksteed insists that, other things being equal, an increase in, say, the bribe offered to the incorruptible will not even incline him towards acceptance, let alone lead him to accept it (pp. 405–6), it is perhaps not clear that Wicksteed's concept of the *minimum sensibile* is really doing any more than provide a polite reconciliation between his equality of marginal satisfactions and the presence of a *lexicographic priority* of honour over money, or of keeping the faith over escaping torture. A lexical ordering is, of course, perfectly consistent with Wicksteed's general concept of selection amongst alternatives but is incompatible with his emphasis on diminishing marginal significance. More generally, how could Wicksteed defend his insistence that ethical considerations have priority over others *without* allowing for at least some element of lexical ordering of alternatives?

## IV. CONCLUSION

In Wicksteed's view, then, there simply is no problem of the form, 'How can altruism be reconciled with rational economic behaviour?' No ultimately desired objects of choice are directly exchangeable and the general principles of choice, of selection amongst alternatives 'in the right proportion', are the same for all aspects of conduct. Consequently there is no line between economic and non-economic 'motives' and the economist should both abandon 'economic man' and admit *all* motives—including altruistic, benevolent and 'ideal' motives—in economic analysis (if any motives at all are to be considered). The heterogeneity of objects of choice constitutes no difficulty since, according to Wicksteed, everything can be rendered equivalent at the margin of choice. If there is a useful distinction to be drawn between economics and the study of other human relationships it is to be found in the concepts of an 'economic relation' and, correspondingly, of 'non-tuism'; this distinction has nothing to do with egoism and would, indeed, be important in a world in which altruistic motivations predominated.

It is perhaps not entirely clear how Wicksteed viewed the role of consciousness in the selection of alternatives, according to the relative scale of preferences. Nor is it clear that *all* of his examples and arguments are fully compatible with the principle of equating diminishing marginal significances; in certain cases, it has been suggested, Wicksteed was in effect allowing some elements of lexical ordering in the scale of preferences. Neither of these doubts, however, even if fully justified, affects Wicksteed's claim that altruistic conduct, when it occurs, is fully consistent with rational economic conduct.

## REFERENCES

W. Bagehot (1880), *Economic Studies*, ed. R. H. Hutton, London, Longmans, Green & Co.

C. H. Herford (1931), *Philip Henry Wicksteed, His Life and Work*, London, Dent and Sons.

F. H. Knight (1921), *Risk, Uncertainty and Profit*, Boston, Mass., Houghton Mifflin.

J. S. Mill (1877), *Essays on Some Unsettled Questions of Political Economy*, London, Longmans, Green & Co.

L. Robbins (1932), Editorial Introduction to Wicksteed (1933)

P. H. Wicksteed (1888), *The Alphabet of Economic Science*, London, Macmillan.

P. H. Wicksteed (1906), 'Review of Professor V. Pareto's *Manuale di Economia Politica*', *Economic Journal*, XVI, pp. 553–7.

P. H. Wicksteed (1914), 'The Scope and Method of Political Economy in the Light of the "Marginal" Theory of Value and Distribution', *Economic Journal*, XXIV, pp. 1–23 (as reprinted in Wicksteed, 1933). This paper was a revised version of Wicksteed's 1913 Presidential Address to Section F of the British Association.

P. H. Wicksteed (1933), *The Common Sense of Political Economy*, Robbins edition, London, Routledge and Kegan Paul Ltd.

# LIST OF OFFICERS OF MANCHESTER COLLEGE

The first three names on the list are of the Divinity Tutors who were not yet designated Prinicipal

## PRINCIPALS

| | |
|---|---|
| Thomas Barnes | 1786–1798 |
| George Walker | 1798–1803 |
| Charles Wellbeloved | 1803–1840 |
| Robert Wallace | 1840–1846 |
| John Kenrick | 1846–1850 |
| George Vance Smith | 1850–1853 |
| John James Tayler | 1853–1869 |
| James Martineau | 1869–1885 |
| James Drummond | 1885–1906 |
| Joseph Estlin Carpenter | 1906–1915 |
| Lawrence Pearsall Jacks | 1915–1931 |
| John Henry Weatherall | 1931–1938 |
| Robert Nicol Cross | 1938–1949 |
| Herbert John McLachlan *(Acting)* | 1949–1951 |
| Sydney Spencer | 1951–1956 |
| Lancelot Austin Garrard | 1956–1965 |
| Harry Lismer Short | 1965–1974 |
| Bruce Findlow | 1974–1985 |
| Anthony John Cross | 1985– |

## SECRETARIES

| | |
|---|---|
| George Duckworth | 1786–1806 |
| Thomas Henry Robinson | 1811–1821 |
| Rev. John Gooch Robberds | 1814–1822 |
| Samuel Dukinfield Darbishire | 1821–1836 |
| | 1840–1852 |
| Rev. John James Tayler | 1822–1835 |
| | 1836–1840 |
| William Rayner Wood | 1835–1839 |
| Rev. James Martineau | 1839–1840 |

| | |
|---|---|
| Rev. William Gaskell | 1840–1846 |
| Rev. Robert Brook Aspland | 1846–1857 |
| Robert Worthington | 1852–1855 |
| Robert Dukinfield Darbishire | 1855–1892 |
| Rev. Charles Beard | 1857–1879 |
| Rev. Henry Enfield Dowson | 1880–1903 |
| Arthur Henry Worthington | 1893–1917 |
| Rev. Henry Gow | 1903–1922 |
| Philip Milner Oliver | 1917– |
| Rev. Valentine David Davis | 1922–1930 |
| P. M. Oliver<br>Rev. W. H. Drummond | 1930–1932 |
| P. M. Oliver<br>Rev. C. M. Wright | 1932–1946 |
| P. M. Oliver<br>Rev. E. G. Lee | 1946–1950 |
| P. M. Oliver<br>Rev. E. Shirvell Price | 1950–1954 |
| Rev. E. Shirvell Price<br>Sir Felix Brunner | 1954–1963 |
| Rev. E. Shirvell Price<br>Mrs. Amy Howarth | 1963–1981 |
| Rev. B. Golland | 1981– |

NOTE In the interval between the first two Secretaries, the Treasurer appears to have acted in that capacity.

## TREASURERS

| | |
|---|---|
| Josiah Birch | 1786 |
| James Touchet | 1786–1798 |
| Samuel Jones | 1798–1803 |
| Ottiwell Wood | 1803–1808 |
| George William Wood | 1808–1843 |
| William Rayner Wood | 1844–1852 |
| Samuel Dukinfield Darbishire | 1852–1854 |
| Robert Needham Philips | 1854–1860 |
| Thomas Ashton | 1860–1873 |
| David Ainsworth | 1874–1891 |
| Charles William Jones | 1892–1908 |
| Grosvenor Talbot | 1908–1919 |
| Henry Philips Greg | 1919–1930 |
| Stephen Grosvenor Lee | 1930–1941 |
| A. Wynn Kenrick | 1941–1963 |
| Sir Felix Brunner | 1963–1973 |
| Geoffrey Head | 1973– |

## PRESIDENTS

| | |
|---|---|
| Thomas Percival | 1793–1800 |
| Samuel Shore, Jun. | 1808–1813 |
| Samuel Shore | 1813–1815 |
| Benjamin Gaskell | 1815–1817 |
| Joseph Strutt | 1817–1826 |
| Samuel Shore, Jun. | 1826–1829 |
| Daniel Gaskell | 1829–1834 |
| Robert Philips | 1834–1837 |
| G. B. Strutt | 1837–1840 |
| Sir Benjamin Heywood | 1840–1842 |
| Mark Philips | 1842–1846 |
| Thomas William Tottie | 1846–1848 |
| Robert Philips | 1848–1853 |
| James Heywood | 1853–1858 |
| John Pemberton Heywood | 1858–1860 |
| Thomas Ainsworth | 1860–1863 |
| Samuel Dukinfield Darbishire | 1863–1867 |
| Samuel Robinson | 1867–1871 |
| Mark Philips | 1871–1874 |
| Timothy Kenrick | 1874–1876 |
| Samuel Sharpe | 1876–1878 |
| Edward Enfield | 1878–1880 |
| Joseph Lupton | 1881–1886 |
| Rev. James Martineau | 1886–1888 |
| Henry Russell Greg | 1888–1894 |
| George Holt | 1894–1896 |
| David Ainsworth | 1896–1900 |
| William Colfox | 1900–1904 |
| Rev. Samuel Alfred Steinthal | 1904–1907 |
| Rt. Hon. William Kenrick | 1907–1909 |
| Rt. Hon. Lord Airedale | 1909–1911 |
| Rt. Hon. Sir John T. Brunner | 1911–1917 |
| Rev. Henry Enfield Dowson | 1917–1920 |
| Rev. Joseph Estlin Carpenter | 1920–1925 |
| Hugh Reynolds Rathbone | 1925–1928 |
| Sir John F. L. Brunner | 1928–1929 |
| Arthur Henry Worthington | 1929–1932 |
| W. Byng Kenrick | 1932–1936 |
| Rev. Henry Gow | 1936–April 1937 |
| (W. Byng Kenrick vice-president) | 1937–1939 |
| Rev. W. H. Drummond | 1939–1942 |
| N. Bishop Harman | 1942–1945 |
| Rev. Alfred Hall | 1945–1949 |
| Professor F. J. M. Stratton | 1949–1951 |
| Rev. R. F. Rattray | 1951–1954 |
| Sir Charles Odgers | 1954–1955 |
| Allan C. Bentley | 1955–1958 |

| | |
|---|---|
| Sir Alister Hardy | 1958–1980 |
| Rev. Lancelot A. Garrard | 1980– |

## CHAIRMEN OF COMMITTEE

| | |
|---|---|
| Thomas Robinson | 1817–1832 |
| Benjamin Heywood | 1832–1834 |
| John Touchet | 1834–1836 |
| T. B. W. Sanderson | 1836–1837 |
| John Touchet | 1837–1838 |
| Isaac Harrop | 1838–1840 |
| J. Aspinall Turner | 1840–1852 |
| Robert Needham Philips | 1852–1853 |
| William Gaskell | 1853–1884 |
| S. Alfred Steinthal | 1884–1889 |
| J. Edwin Odgers | 1889–1891 |
| Harry Rawson | 1891–1897 |
| S. Alfred Steinthal | 1897–1903 |
| H. Enfield Dowson | 1903–1917 |
| Arthur H. Worthington | 1918–1929 |
| C. Sydney Jones | 1929–1941 |
| Stephen Lee | 1941–1952 |
| F. J. M. Stratton | 1952–1953 |
| Allan C. Bentley | 1953–1972 |
| George C. Morrison | 1972– |

## HONORARY FELLOWS

James Luther Adams (U.S.A.)
Annie Margaret Barr
Sir Adrian Boult
Sir Felix Brunner
Josef Ferencz (Bishop, Hungary)
Lancelot Austin Garrard
Herbert Gimson
Fritz H. Heineman
Miloslav Kanak (Czechoslovakia)
Lajos Kovacs (Bishop, Romania)
Herbert John McLachlan
Ralph H. Mottram
Eric Shirvell Price
Dudley Eric Richards
Harold W. Spicer
Dorothy Tarrant
Malcom Read Sutherland (U.S.A.)

# Index